Pleistocene vertebrates in the British Isles

Pleistocene vertebrates in the British Isles

A. J. Stuart *University of Cambridge*

Longman *London and New York*

Longman Group Limited
Longman House
Burnt Mill, Harlow, Essex, UK

*Published in the United States of America
by Longman Inc., New York*

First published 1982

British Library Cataloguing in Publication Data

Stuart, A.J.
    Pleistocene vertebrates in the British Isles.
    1. Vertebrates, Fossil   2. Paleontology –
    Great Britain
    I. Title
    569' .0941   QE841

    ISBN 0-582-30069-X

Library of Congress Cataloging in Publication Data

Stuart, A. J., 1945–
    Pleistocene vertebrates in the British Isles.

    Bibliography: p.
    Includes index.
    1. Vertebrates, Fossil.   2. Paleontology –
Pleistocene.   3. Paleontology – Great Britain.
I. Title.
QE841.S77   566' .0941   81-8389
ISBN 0-582-30069-X   AACR2

Printed in Great Britain by William Clowes (Beccles) Ltd
Beccles and London

To Jackie

Contents

Preface

Within the most recent division of geological time, the Pleistocene or Quaternary period, the British Isles were at various times the home of such exotic beasts as: mammoth and other extinct elephants, extinct rhinos, hippopotamus, several extinct giant deer, lion and spotted hyaena, together with many other species of mammals and birds either extinct or no longer native to Western Europe.

Throughout the two million years or so of the Pleistocene, considerable climatic fluctuations, over periods of several thousands of years, were accompanied by spectacular shifts in the geographical distributions of plants and animals, superimposed on longer-term patterns of evolution and extinction. The synthesis of information from the wide variety of disciplines involved with Pleistocene research is resulting in an increasingly better understanding of the environmental changes which occurred in the British Isles during this time. The study of fossil vertebrates contributes significantly to this synthesis, and in turn the complex history of the vertebrate fauna can be related to detailed patterns of environmental change.

In writing this book I have aimed to present an up-to-date account of the results of research on the non-marine Pleistocene vertebrates of the British Isles in the context of Pleistocene studies as a whole. Accordingly the book includes a review of the stratigraphy, chronology, environments and palaeobotany of the Pleistocene of the British Isles. The taxonomy of the most important vertebrates is discussed with illustrations of their appearance in life, and also of fossil material as an aid to identification.

A large part of the book is concerned with reconstructing the faunal history of the period, and there are also chapters on taphonomy and palaeoecology – the latter including comparisons with modern animals. The Pleistocene history of man in Britain and his interaction with the rest of the vertebrate fauna is considered, and the final chapter is concerned with the still young but fast-growing field of evolutionary studies on Pleistocene vertebrates.

Acknowledgements

I wish to express my gratitude to the many colleagues who have not only given help and advice in the writing of this book, but also contributed to my research projects, field work and related activities over the last thirteen years. In particular I take the opportunity of thanking Dr F. M. Broadhurst for his many kindnesses when I was his research student at the University of Manchester, Dr K. A. Joysey and Prof. R. G. West for their continuing support and interest since I have been in Cambridge, and Mr A. P. Currant and Dr A. J. Sutcliffe for much helpful discussion. The financial support of an NERC Research Fellowship, and Research Grants (via Dr Joysey), is also gratefully acknowledged.

I have also especially benefited from discussion with Mr Michael Bishop, Dr P. L. Gibbard, Dr A. R. Hall, Dr H. D. Kahlke, Dr A. Lister, Dr D. F. Mayhew, Mr J. Rackham, Dr C. Stringer and Dr C. Turner. In addition, thanks are due to the following: Dr P. J. Andrews, Dr E. N. Arnold, Mr M. J. Ashby, Dr H. J. B. Birks, Dr Martin Bishop, Dr D. Bramwell, Dr P. Callow, Mrs J. Cook, Dr P. Coxon, Mrs K. Scott, Mr M. Dorling, Dr C. L. Forbes, Dr A. E. Friday, Mr J. S. Hallam, Mr P. Lawrance, Mr J. Lightwing, Mr R. Long,

Mr B. McWilliams, Mr R. A. D. Markham, Mr C. M. Newton, Mr R. D. Norman, Dr E. M. Northcote, Mr P. J. Osborne, Mrs S. Peglar, Prof. F. W. Shotton, Prof. R. Singer, Dr D. W. Yalden and Mr J. J. Wymer.

I am grateful to the following for providing photographs used in the book: Mr I. Bryant (Fig. 8.4), Mr B. Conway (Figs. 5.35, 7.7), Dr C. L. Forbes and the Sedgwick Museum of Geology (Fig. 7.10), Dr K. A. Joysey (Fig. 8.3), Mr J. Lightwing (Fig. 3.49), Dr J. O'Connor and the National Museum of Ireland (Fig. 8.9), Prof. R. Singer (Fig. 3.13) and Dr A. J. Sutcliffe (Fig. 7.13).

Finally my deepest thanks go to my wife Jackie for her constant encouragement and interest.

A. J. Stuart
Cambridge
January 1981

Acknowledgements

We are grateful to the following for permission to reproduce copyright material:

The Trustees of the British Museum (Natural History) for our figs. 3.28, 3.36, 3.41, 3.51, 3.60, 3.61, and 3.69; Norwich Castle Museum for our figs. 3.27, a, b, 3.34, 3.39, 3.42, 3.53, a, b, 3.55, 3.63, 5.37, a, b, and 5.38; Sedgwick Museum of Geology, Cambridge for our figs. 3.33, a, b, c, 3.48, a, b, c, d, 3.54, b, and 7.10; A. Barlow, supplied by Sedgwick Museum for our fig. 3.54, a; University Museum of Zoology, Cambridge for our figs. 3.70, 3.71, a, b, and 4.1; National Museum of Ireland for our fig. 8.9; B. Conway for our fig. 5.35 and 7.7; A. J. Sutcliffe for our figs. 4.2 and 7.13, a, b, c; Iain Bryant for our fig. 8.4; P. Coxon for our fig. 6.2; K. A. Joysey for our fig. 8.3, a, b; J. Hallam for our figs. 8.6 and 8.7; Professor R. Singer for our fig. 3.13; J. Lightwing for our fig. 3.49; Department of Earth Sciences, Birmingham for our fig. 3.50; A.J. Stuart for our figs. 3.5, a, b, 6.3, 6.4, 7.3, a, b, c, 7.4, 7.5, 7.9 and 7.14.

Blackwell Scientific Publications Ltd. for our fig. 2.13 from fig. 3, p. 292, 'Studies in the postglacial history of British vegetation,' *Journal of Ecology*, 39, by H. Godwin and P. A. Tallantire (1951); Oxford University Press for our fig. 2.1 from fig. 19.3 *British Quaternary Studies: Recent Advances* by F. W. Shotton (1977); *The New Phytologist* for our figs. 2.8, 2.9 and 2.11 from figs. 3.9, and 14 from 'Pleistocene forest history in East Anglia' by R. G. West (1980); *The Royal Society's Philosophical Transactions B* for our fig. 2.3 from fig. 2, p. 236 from 'Early and Middle Devensian flora and vegetation' 280 by R. G. West, (1977): our fig. 2.4 from fig. 2, p. 321, 'Fossil coleopteran assemblages', 280 by G. R. Coope (1977); our fig. 2.10 from fig. 15 'The Middle Pleistocene deposits at Marks Tey', 257 by C. Turner (1970): our fig. 2.12 from fig. 5, p. 233 'The history of the mammal fauna' by A. J. Stuart (1976) and our fig. 5.33 from fig. 7, p. 95 'The vertebrate fauna . . .'. by A. J. Stuart (1980).

1 Introduction

The Pleistocene or Quaternary (see Ch. 2 for discussion of terminology) was a period of marked climatic fluctuations which culminated, during cold phases, in the repeated glaciation of large areas of North America and Eurasia. These fluctuations resulted in global sea-level changes and continual shifts in the distributions of plants and animals. It is against this background that we view the evolution and origin of our modern vertebrate faunas and the biological and cultural evolution of man.

This book is concerned essentially with the British Isles, on the western fringes of the Eurasian Continent, and a small part of the earth's land surface. This area is, however, exceptionally rich in fossiliferous Pleistocene deposits which are the subject of continuing intensive research. Moreover the geographical situation of the British Isles is well suited for recording climatic and biotic changes because the combination of a northerly latitude and proximity to the North Atlantic maximizes the contrast in the floras and faunas between cold and temperate phases.

Finds of Pleistocene fossil vertebrate material, especially of large mammals, from gravel pits, excavations for buildings, coastal exposures and caves and fissures are frequently made in most parts of the British Isles, especially in the Midlands and southern England. Much of this material is collected casually and many a mammoth tooth may adorn a mantelpiece or find its way to a school or private fossil collection. Such finds, however, are generally of little scientific value without accompanying stratigraphical data. Nevertheless the role of the serious amateur in acquiring and preserving some of the best and most complete Pleistocene vertebrate collections is of the greatest importance. The majority of fossils in the major museum collections were in the past obtained from private hands, for example the British Museum collections from the Cromer Forest-bed Formation were largely purchased from A. C. Savin, a local amateur, who ac-

quired the fossils by patient searching over many years from the late nineteenth to the first half of the present century.

Many of these old finds can be related to modern stratigraphy, either because they were adequately documented at the time, or because they come from localities where there is only a single fossiliferous horizon. Modern collecting is done wherever possible in close collaboration with specialists in other Pleistocene (Quaternary) disciplines, so that fossil vertebrate records can be precisely related to stratigraphy, and contemporaneous environmental conditions deduced from sediments, and plant and invertebrate fossils.

Occasional finds of the fossil bones and teeth of Pleistocene large mammals have no doubt been made in the British Isles throughout historical times. Serious studies, however date back to the beginning of the nineteenth century, including notably the, at the time, sensational results of the investigations of Dean William Buckland at Kirkdale Cave, North Yorkshire. Buckland (1822) concluded, correctly, that the assemblage of mammalian bones and teeth in the cave, which included many extinct and non-British animals, had been accumulated by spotted hyaenas *Crocuta crocuta* (see Ch. 7) (Boylan 1967b, 1972). The period when these beasts inhabited the British Isles was conjectured to pre-date the Biblical Flood. Later Buckland came to embrace the 'glacial theory', which postulated that ice had covered large areas of land in the Northern hemisphere in comparatively recent geological time and convincingly explained many of the geological phenomena formerly attributed to the Flood.

Also in the first half of the nineteenth century Sir Richard Owen published a number of papers on Pleistocene mammals, and his well-known book on British fossil mammals and birds (Owen 1846) includes descriptions of many Pleistocene forms. Falconer (Murchison 1868) also made a major contribution to nineteenth century studies. In the later part of the nineteenth, and the beginning of the present century, following after the general acceptance of the glacial theory, considerable advances were made, principally due to the researches of E. T. Newton and W. B. Dawkins. Newton published detailed accounts of the faunas of the Lower Pleistocene and Cromer Forest-bed Formation (Newton 1882a, 1891) as well as many papers on later Pleistocene assemblages. Dawkins published a number of papers mainly on Upper Pleistocene sites, and was largely responsible for the earlier Palaeontographical Society Monographs on British Pleistocene mammals (Dawkins & Sanford 1866–72; Dawkins in Dawkins & Reynolds 1872–1939). Important workers in the first few decades of the present century include S. H. Reynolds and especially M. A. C. Hinton, who laid the founda-

tions for the modern studies of Pleistocene voles and lemmings (e.g. Hinton 1926).

The last twenty years or so have seen an accelerating revival of interest in the Pleistocene vertebrates of the British Isles, stimulated by the impresssive advances in our understanding of stratigraphy, floras, invertebrate faunas and the many other aspects of Pleistocene research. It will be apparent from reading this book that there is enormous scope for research on the many aspects of Pleistocene vertebrates, even within our present framework of knowledge. Continuing advances in research into the Pleistocene period, especially in correlation and dating methods, hold out still more exciting prospects for future work on the complex history of the vertebrate fauna of the British Isles and Europe.

2 The Pleistocene of the British Isles

The term 'Pleistocene', is used here to refer to the period of geological time, from approximately two million years ago up to and including the present day. This usage follows the original meaning of Lyell, who coined the term 'Pleistocene' in 1839, as advocated by West (1977a). 'Pleistocene', as a division of Caenozoic time, is preferred here to the synonymous 'Quaternary', because the latter term implies a fundamental distinction from the preceding Tertiary period, which appears to be unjustified.

Elsewhere the term 'Holocene' is commonly applied to the period from 10 000 radiocarbon years B.P. to the present day, while 'Pleistocene' is used in a rather more restricted sense for the period prior to this date. Since the boundary between the Last Cold Stage and the postglacial is similar to that of previous cold stage–interglacial boundaries, such a distinction seems unwarranted.

The definition of the lower boundary of the Pleistocene with the Pliocene period depends on the criteria adopted. These may include clear evidence of climatic deterioration in the stratigraphical succession of a chosen area, or the boundary between particular geomagnetic epochs. In the British Isles the Plio–Pleistocene boundary has been conventionally placed at the base of the Pre-Ludhamian (Waltonian) Stage, and above the Coralline Crag. Comparison with the Netherlands sequence suggests, however, that the boundary might more appropriately be placed within or above the Red Crag, so that the Pre-Ludhamian would then fall within the Pliocene (West 1977a, Ch. 12). It is here provisionally retained as the first stage of the Pleistocene.

The following account of the Pleistocene of the British Isles is necessarily only an outline, with particular relevance to the interpretation of the vertebrates, and the reader is referred to much more comprehensive accounts given elsewhere, especially West (1977a), Shotton (1977a) and Mitchell *et al*. (1973). Descriptions of the Pleistocene sequences and details of many sections in most regions of the British Isles were published in a series of guidebooks for the 1977 INQUA excursions (Bowen 1977).

Sediments and stratigraphy

The importance of collecting vertebrate fossils from horizons of known stratigraphical position cannot be emphasized too strongly. In the absence of stratigraphical context few such fossils are of much scientific value.

An ideal situation is one in which vertebrate remains occur in relatively simple sequences of lacustrine or fluviatile sediments containing primary pollen plus hopefully other fossils, such as plant macrofossils, molluscs and beetles. Vertebrate remains from sediment also containing pollen, preferably also with plant macrofossils, can in most cases be assigned a relative age, often to a considerable degree of accuracy (pollen assemblage zone or subzone). Moreover, such vertebrate records can be related to contemporary plant communities, as interpreted from the palaeobotanical evidence, a matter of great importance in reconstructing the ecology of Pleistocene vertebrates.

Absolute dating methods are clearly also of great value, but so far only radiocarbon dating is of sufficient reliability for our purposes, and its useful range unfortunately does not extend much beyond 60 000 years B.P.

Sediments and depositional environments

The Pleistocene period in Britain is represented by

Table 2.1. Main depositional environments and sediments represented in the Pleistocene of the British Isles.

Major depositional environments	Principal sediment types
1. Non-marine	
Cave	Cave earths, breccias
Glacial	Tills, outwash gravels, sands, silts
Periglacial	Loess, coversands, solifluction deposits
Bog	Peats
Lacustrine	Silts, clays, marls, organic muds
Fluviatile	Gravels, sands, silts, clays, organic muds
2. Transitional	
Deltaic } Estuarine }	Gravels, sands, silts, clays
3. Marine	
Littoral Infralittoral } Sublittoral }	Gravels, sands, silts, clays

a wide range of sediments laid down in a variety of depositional environments (Table 2.1) (West 1977a). The latter can usually be deduced from the size and shape of the sediment body, sedimentary structures (e.g. cross-bedding, laminations), composition and texture of the sediments and from their fossil content (e.g. marine versus non-marine mollusc shells). Pleistocene vertebrate remains in primary context are known mainly from fluviatile, lacustrine and cave deposits, but also occur in transitional and marine sediments in association with marine vertebrates (Ch. 3).

Stratigraphical interpretations

The stratigraphical sequence for the British Pleistocene has largely been built up from very many observations of field relationship of deposits (lithostratigraphy – recording sections, borehole data and geological mapping) combined with correlation of strata by their fossil content, especially pollen (biostratigraphy).

The lithostratigraphical units of the marine Lower Pleistocene can often be traced laterally for some distance. A sequence of alternating temperate and cool stages have been recognized on their fossil content of pollen, foraminifers and marine molluscs, which enable correlations to be made between sites.

With the Middle and Upper Pleistocene, stratigraphical interpretation is largely a matter of iden-

tifying fossiliferous interglacial or interstadial sediments separating largely unfossiliferous sequences of tills and other glacial deposits, solifluction deposits or horizons with evidence of permafrost. Correlation of interglacial deposits by pollen spectra utilizes the differences in vegetational history between each of the interglacial stages as discussed later in this chapter. Radiocarbon dating is an important stratigraphical tool for sorting out the events of the Middle and Late Devensian since there exists no continuous biostratigraphical record for this cold stage in Britain. The accuracy of absolute dating techniques for earlier periods of the Pleistocene is such that it is not possible to correlate deposits and events within most of the Anglian and Wolstonian cold stages, except in a very crude way. The early and late glacial parts of these stages are, however, represented in the pollen record, in continuity with the interglacial sequences.

Till sheets can be correlated from one region to another within the British Isles on lithological characters, including erratic pebble content and heavy mineral suite, and by stone-orientation directions. It is possible, however, that successive ice sheets could pick up the same rock materials when passing over the same areas, so that lithological similarity in two tills is not necessarily proof of contemporaneity. Lithological characters combined with evidence of current-flow directions and heights of deposits within terrace sequences are used to correlate river or glacial outwash sands and gravels. As in the case of interpreting till sequences, these are best com-

	N.W.			S.E. ‖ N.		S.
	CHESHIRE – SHROPSHIRE RIVER SEVERN	LEICESTERSHIRE WARWICKSHIRE RIVER AVON	OXFORD ‖	HOLDERNESS LINCOLNSHIRE	NORFOLK – SUFFOLK	ESSEX LOWER THAMES
Devensian	Wolverhampton Moraine — Irish Sea Till — Chelford — Four Ashes	Terrace Gravels 1 to 5	Terrace Gravels ‖	Withernsea (purple) Till — Skipsea (drab) Till — Marsh Till — Hunstanton Till	Sands, Gravels Marine Silts Loess	Terraces, Loess, Head
Ipswichian			‖	Sewerby — –<5m raised beach — – ?	Ipswich, Wretton Wortwell Morston	Aveley & Ilford Terraces
Wolstonian	Triassic Tills — Ridgeacre Till — Thrussington Till	Oadby (Chalky) Tills — Wolston Sand — Bosworth Clays — Lake Harrison — Baginton-Lillington Gravels	Moreton Moraine ‖	Basement Till	Sands, Gravels & ? Loess	Head & Coombe Rock
Hoxnian		Quinton & Nechells	‖	Kirmington	Hoxne – Marks Tey – Clacton	Boyne Hill and Swanscombe Terraces
Anglian	Nurseries	Bubbenhall Clay Plateau Drift	‖	Wragby (chalky) Till Lowestoft (chalky) Till Corton Sands — Cromer Till		Hornchurch Lobe
Cromerian			‖	Cromer Forest – bed Formation		

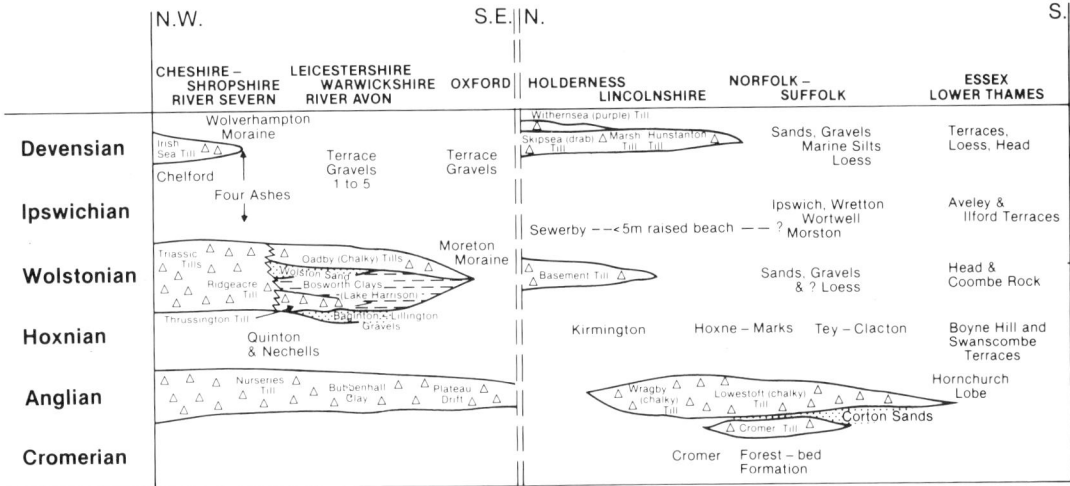

Fig. 2.1. Correlation diagram (schematic) for the Middle and Upper Pleistocene of the Midlands (left) and eastern England (right). (After Shotton *et al.* 1977)

bined with biostratigraphical evidence if fossiliferous deposits can be found.

Examples of interpretation and correlation of Pleistocene deposits are given in Fig. 2.1.

The Pleistocene succession is divided into a series of standard stratigraphical stages, each of which is fundamentally climatically controlled but expressed in terms of both lithostratigraphy (sediments) and biostratigraphy (fossils) (Table 2.2). Radiocarbon chronology is, however used as the basic stratigraphical framework for the last 50 000 years or so.

An interglacial defined in palaeobotanical terms, in the sense in which it is used in this book, is a period with a climatic optimum at least as warm as the Flandrian (postglacial) climatic optimum, allowing the development of temperate deciduous forest in north-west Europe. Interstadials are lesser temperate periods where the climatic amelioration was either too short or not warm enough to permit the growth of temperate forests, and are accompanied by the development of boreal forest only. It is important to note that the distinction between 'interglacial' and 'interstadial' is not fundamental, but merely one of degree. Moreover, it is obvious that the episodes of climatic amelioration which they represent will be expressed differently according to geographical location, and interstadials registered by boreal forest in northern Europe may be represented by temperate forest of more interglacial type further south. The duration of the previous cold phase, distance of a particular locality from temper-

ate-plant refugia, and barriers to plant migration are all important in determining the response of vegetation to climatic change (West 1980b).

The cold stages are characterized by both lithostratigraphical and biostratigraphical evidence for cold climate. The boundary between interglacial and cold stages is placed where the vegetation changes from an open subarctic park landscape to a wooded landscape with temperate trees and vice versa (West 1977a).

Each stage is defined on a standard succession of deposits at a type site, taking its name from the locality or geographical region. Other deposits within the region, which can be correlated with those at the type site by pollen spectra, or sometimes by other palaeontological evidence, can also be referred to by the appropriate stage name. Local sequences are thus built up with local stage names which are only subsequently correlated with local sequences from other areas. This system is intended to avoid the past pitfalls of extrapolating stages, lacking proper definition, from one region to another on the basis of correlations subsequently shown to be false. In particular the unwise application of Penck and Brückner's Alpine stages (Günz, Mindel, Riss, Würm), which were proposed in the first decade of this century, to much wider geographical areas has resulted in a confusion which has not entirely disappeared even today.

In recent years much interest has been shown in the continuous sedimentary record obtained from deep-sea cores. Oxygen isotope ($^{18}O : ^{16}O$) ratios

Table 2.2. British Pleistocene stages and principal deposits. (Based on Mitchell *et al.* 1973; West 1977a; Funnell, Norton & West 1979)

		Gaps in succession	Years B.P. (base)	Climate	Crags	Cromer Forest-bed Formation	Marine deposits	Freshwater deposits	Cave and fissure deposits
Upper	Flandrian		10 000	t			+	+	+
	Devensian		c. 110 000	c,p,g			(+)	+	+
	Ipswichian			t			+	+	+
	Wolstonian			c,p,g				+	(+)
Middle	Hoxnian			t			+	+	
	Anglian			c,p,g				+	
	Cromerian		?c. 350 000	t			+	+	+[1]
	Beestonian	•••		c,p,?g			+	+	
Lower	Pastonian	•••		t			+	+	
	Pre-Pastonian	•		c,?p			+		
	Bramertonian			t			+		
	Baventian			c	NC		+		
	Antian	•		t			+		+[2]
	Thurnian			c			+		
	Ludhamian	•	?c. 2 000 000	t			+		
	Waltonian			c	RC		+		
	(Pre-Ludhamian)								
	[PLIOCENE]				(CC)		(+)		

t : temperate
c : cold
p : evidence for permafrost
g : glacial deposits known
NC : Norwich Crag
RC : Red Crag
CC : Coralline Crag

1. Westbury deposit, exact stratigraphical position uncertain
2. Dove Holes deposit, stratigraphical position uncertain

from the $CaCO_3$ of foraminiferan shells show variations with time, interpreted as due to global ice volume changes plus sea temperature changes (e.g. Shackleton & Opdyke 1973; Shackleton 1977a, 1977b). The curves obtained from many parts of the world match remarkably well, and the sequences have been calibrated by palaeomagnetic stratigraphy. Correlations with the terrestrial sequence seem premature, however, except probably stages 1–5, the most recent of the stages recognized in the deep sea sequence, which appear to represent

the period including the last Interglacial (equated with substage 5e) to the present day.

The British Pleistocene succession

Many workers involved in various ways with Pleistocene studies are currently dissatisfied with what has been accepted as the standard stratigraphical sequence for the British Isles, published by the Geological Society of London (Mitchell *et al.* 1973).

Table 2.3. Probable correlations of British, Irish and Continental (Netherlands, Germany) Pleistocene stages.

Britain	Ireland	Netherlands, Germany
Flandrian	Littletonian	Flandrian (or Holocene)
Devensian	Midlandian	Weichselian
Ipswichian	(not formally named)	Eemian
Wolstonian	Munsterian	Saalian
Hoxnian	Gortian	Holsteinian
Anglian	–	Elsterian
Cromerian	–	[Voigtstedtian of Voigtstedt, East Germany – Erd 1965]
(Earlier correlations uncertain)		

The Geological Society sequence is based essentially on a piecing together of lithostratigraphical and pollen biostratigraphical evidence, utilizing radiocarbon dating for the last 50 000 years of so. It was in fact never intended to constitute the rigid last word on the subject, but very properly does adhere to strict criteria for defining stages.

Criticism of the accepted British Isles sequence stems mainly from the observation that there are considerably more low ^{18}O peaks in the deep-sea record (see above), for the period since the Brunhes–Matuyama palaeomagnetic boundary, than there are interglacial periods recognized in the British terrestrial Middle and Upper Pleistocene. At present, however, there exists no means of direct correlation between the deep-sea and terrestrial records (except for the very youngest portions within the range of radiocarbon dating), so that we have no way of determining exactly how the processes producing ^{18}O fluctuations in deep-sea cores would be expressed in terrestrial sequences. Moreover the Lower Pleistocene succession in Britain is undoubtedly very incomplete and it is also probable that several stages of the early Middle Pleistocene, ante-dating the Cromerian, but post-dating the Brunhes–Matuyama boundary, are not represented – or have not yet been found in the British Isles.

The possibility that further Middle and Upper Pleistocene interglacial stages, and hence also intervening cold stages, are missing from the British sequence, or have yet to be discovered, should certainly be always borne in mind. If deposits of such a stage should come to light, the new stage should then be formally described, defined, named from its type locality, and the standard sequence modified to accommodate it. Far more disturbing, however, is the suggestion that deposits in reality representing more than one interglacial are being confused, and that each new site discovered is being uncomfortably pigeonholed into the conventional sequence. Since the stratigraphical framework for the British Pleistocene relies heavily on the correlation of interglacial deposits by their pollen spectra, a brief explanation of the basis of pollen biostratigraphy is now given.

Intensive research on the vegetational history of the Flandrian in Britain and Europe, calibrated by radiocarbon, have shown how pollen spectra change both with time and over extensive geographical areas on one time plane. In the case of earlier Middle and Upper Pleistocene interglacial periods, the pollen profiles from various British sites fall into quite distinct groups, within which there is a striking consistency both in terms of the presence and relative abundance of the main taxa present, and significantly also in the patterns of the pollen curves – especially in the order of appearance and expansion of the tree taxa (see Figs. 2.9, 2.10, 2.11, 2.13, Table 2.5). These patterns reflect such factors as the locations of refugia during the preceding cold stage and detailed climatic changes, combined with migration rates, competition, and evolutionary changes in the ecological tolerances of the tree species. It is therefore highly improbable that these factors could have been repeated exactly in different interglacial cycles, and give rise to identical pollen sequences.

The currently recognized stages of the British Pleistocene are given in Table 2.2. Possible correlations with Continental stages are given in Table 2.3.

Lower Pleistocene

Lower Pleistocene deposits, almost entirely confined to East Anglia, comprise clays, silts and shelly sands and gravels – the 'Crags'. The entire sequence is marine, mostly deposited inshore, with the exception of minor freshwater horizons in the Pre-Pastonian and Pastonian. The stages of the Lower Pleistocene are based largely on pollen analysis of a borehole through the Crag at Ludham, Norfolk (West 1961), which were supported by studies on the Foraminifera (Funnell 1961). Further evidence comes from another borehole at Stradbroke, Suffolk (Beck *et al.* 1972), and from several surface exposures in particular Easton Bavents, Suffolk (Funnell & West 1962), Bramerton, Norfolk (Funnell, Norton & West 1979) and the Norfolk coast (West 1980a). Both pollen and Foraminifera indicate alternating periods of cool and temperate climate. The Lower Pleistocene temperate stages are especially characterized by the presence of *Tsuga*, the hemlock spruce, which is, however scarce in the Pastonian. The flora is discussed in more detail below. Much information on local environmental conditions has been obtained from studies on the marine mollusc faunas (e.g. Norton 1967, 1977).

The Lower Pleistocene sequence as shown in Table 2.2 is undoubtedly incomplete and a number of stratigraphical hiatuses are present. Many more climatic stages have been recognized on the other side of the southern North Sea, in the Netherlands, where the sequence is very much thicker (e.g. Zagwijn 1975).

Beestonian and Cromerian

The Cromer Forest-bed Formation (CF-bF), a series of freshwater, estuarine and marine deposits, occurs at intervals along the coast of Norfolk and again in a small part of the north Suffolk coast. The CF-bF has been thoroughly studied over a period of years by Professor R. G. West (West 1980a) using pollen analyses, and is now known to represent several climatic stages (Table 2.2). The marked differences between the vertebrate faunas of the Pastonian and Cromerian, combined with evidence of a widespread unconformity, suggest a stratigraphical hiatus, possibly representing a considerable time gap, within the CF-bF. On vertebrate faunal grounds the Pre-Pastonian and Pastonian stages are best included in the Lower Pleistocene.

The type section for the Cromerian stage is in the cliff at West Runton, Norfolk (see Fig. 7.2) where freshwater organic muds with abundant plant, in-

vertebrate and vertebrate fossils are overlain by estuarine sands and silts. The pollen diagram reveals a complete interglacial vegetational cycle. Other Cromerian deposits, which can be correlated with West Runton, occur extensively in the CF-bF sections, mostly in the cliffs, whereas the Pastonian and older deposits are generally found in the foreshore or beneath the modern beach. The preceding Beestonian cold stage is represented by both marine gravels and freshwater gravels, sands and marls. Ice wedge casts penetrating older deposits but sealed by the Cromerian deposits prove the existence of permafrost at some time during the Beestonian stage. The marls have yielded a 'cold' fossil flora (West 1980a). At Sugworth, Berkshire, organic sands and silts from a river channel in the Kimmeridge Clay have yielded an abundant flora and fauna indicating a Cromerian age (Briggs, Gilbertson *et al.* 1975; Shotton *et al.* 1980). The deposit appears to postdate part of the local 'Plateau Drift', thought to be a till, thus providing evidence of a pre-Cromerian, perhaps Beestonian, glaciation, which if correct is the earliest known in the British Isles (Shotton *et al.* 1980).

A series of deposits filling a former cave in Carboniferous Limestone at Westbury-sub-Mendip, Somerset, have yielded abundant fossil vertebrate remains (Bishop 1974). Since at present the only reliable evidence of their age is from the fauna, it is difficult to assess accurately the stratigraphical position of the deposits, although a date at the end of, or rather later than, the Cromerian seems certain. The question is considered more fully in Chapter 7.

Anglian

The CF-bF is everywhere overlain by glacial deposits, both till and outwash gravels of the Anglian glaciation, and the type site of this stage is at Corton, Suffolk. During the Anglian, ice sheets extended as far south as north London, and glacial deposits are also known from the Vale of St Albans and the Midlands (Fig. 2.2). At least two major periods of ice advance are recorded by tills separated by non-glacial sediments. Ice wedge casts occur below the till penetrating the CF-bF. Fossiliferous deposits of Anglian age are extremely rare, other than those representing the very beginning of the stage (Arctic Freshwater Bed of the CF-bF sections), overlying fossiliferous Cromerian deposits, or the very end of the stage underlying fossiliferous Hoxnian deposits. Non-glacial deposits of Anglian age with plant fossils are known from Lowestoft,

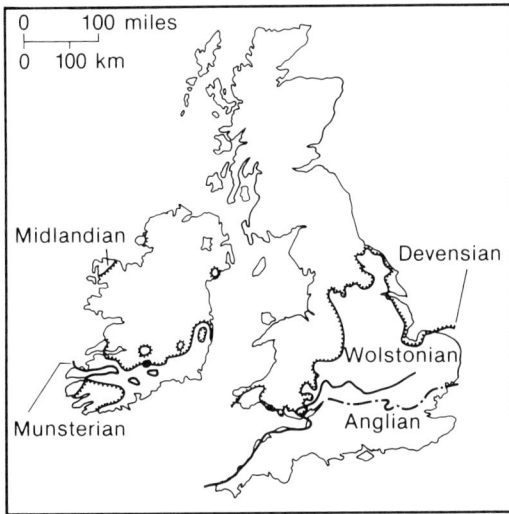

Fig. 2.2. Limits of the main ice advances in the British Isles. (Adapted from West 1977a) NB. during the Munsterian Stage all of Ireland was glaciated except for a few nunataks in the south.

Suffolk, and two vertebrate faunas, from the Wallingford Fan Gravels and from the Homersfield Terrace gravels, Norfolk, may correlate with this stage (Ch. 8). The Wallingford Fan Gravels, a complex deposit of fluviatile gravels and sands disturbed by solifluction, may relate altitudinally to the Lynch Hill Terrace of the Thames of Anglian age, but could perhaps belong to the Wolstonian Stage. The Homersfield Terrace sands and gravels occur above the Broome Terrace which is biostratigraphically dated to the Wolstonian stage (Coxon 1979). The presence of till (chalky boulder clay) within the higher terrace probably indicates an Anglian age.

Hoxnian
The Hoxnian interglacial stage is represented by a number of lacustrine deposits in East Anglia, e.g. the type site Hoxne, Suffolk (West 1956), and Marks Tey, Essex (Turner 1970), the Midlands and in Ireland (Gortian stage). Fluviatile deposits are known from Clacton, Essex, and Swanscombe and Ingress Vale, Kent. The last two sites have not yielded unequivocal primary pollen but can be satisfactorily assigned to the Hoxnian on a variety of other grounds, especially the molluscan and vertebrate faunas (Kerney 1971; Sutcliffe 1964). Marine deposits are known from Clacton and from the Nar Valley, Norfolk. The Marks Tey lake de-

posit records the vegetational history of the entire Interglacial at one site (see Fig. 2.10)

Wolstonian
The Wolstonian cold stage takes its name from the type area of Wolston, Warwickshire, where a sequence of fluviatile, outwash and glacial deposits occur. These deposits overlie interglacial deposits at Nechells and Quinton, in the Birmingham area, which have produced pollen spectra of Hoxnian age. Several ice advances attributed to the Wolstonian are recorded in the Midlands region. A number of river terrace gravels are also of this age. A pre-Ipswichian till attributed to the Wolstonian (Basement Till) occurs in east Yorkshire and Lincolnshire, but the existence of Wolstonian till in East Anglia is uncertain and controversial. The till of south-west England is thought to be of Wolstonian age (Fig. 2.2) and the older Munsterian till of Ireland is usually also correlated with this stage. Many river terrace gravels in East Anglia and the Thames Valley with a 'cold' flora or fauna, and stratigraphically pre-dating Ipswichian deposits, are correlated with the Wolstonian.

A channel at Brandon, Warwickshire, has yielded a flora of interstadial type and a temperate fish fauna (Ch. 8).

The Glutton and Bear Strata from Tornewton Cave, Devon (Sutcliffe & Zeuner 1962) underlie a horizon of probable Ipswichian age, and have yielded remains of arctic mammals implying a Wolstonian age. Unfortunately, however, the deposits are clearly mixed and faunal material from a temperate horizon is also represented (Ch. 8).

Ipswichian
Ipswichian interglacial deposits with pollen are widespread within river terrace sequences in central, southern and eastern England. At no site is the entire Interglacial represented, although most of the interglacial vegetational sequence was recorded in a recently discovered lacustrine deposit at Wing, Rutland (Hall 1980). Only the first half of the stage occurs at the type site of Bobbitshole, Ipswich.

It has been suggested, however, by Sutcliffe (e.g. Sutcliffe & Kowalski 1976) that two distinct interglacials are represented by these deposits. The arguments are based essentially on the interpretation of the relationships of the fossiliferous deposits at Ilford and Aveley to those of Trafalgar Square in the Lower Thames Valley. The question is discussed by Stuart (1976a). The pollen sequences from these sites are closely similar, indicating that they date from the same interglacial (Franks 1960; West *et al.* 1964; West 1969).

On the assumption that *Hippopotamus amphibius*, in a post-Anglian context, is diagnostic of the Ipswichian (Ch. 9), many lacustrine, fluviatile and cave deposits, lacking palaeobotanical data, can be assigned to this stage. The faunas from these sites are all closely similar to zone Ip II faunas from the pollen-dated sites (Ch. 7).

Marine or estuarine Ipswichian deposits have been discovered recently in the southern Fenland and there are raised beaches at a number of localities in southern and eastern England, as far north as Sewerby, east Yorkshire.

Devensian
Radiocarbon chronology is available for about half of the Devensian stage and the Devensian is subdivided on this basis into Early (pre-50 000 years B.P. and largely beyond the range of radiocarbon), Middle (50 000 to 26 000 years B.P.), and Late

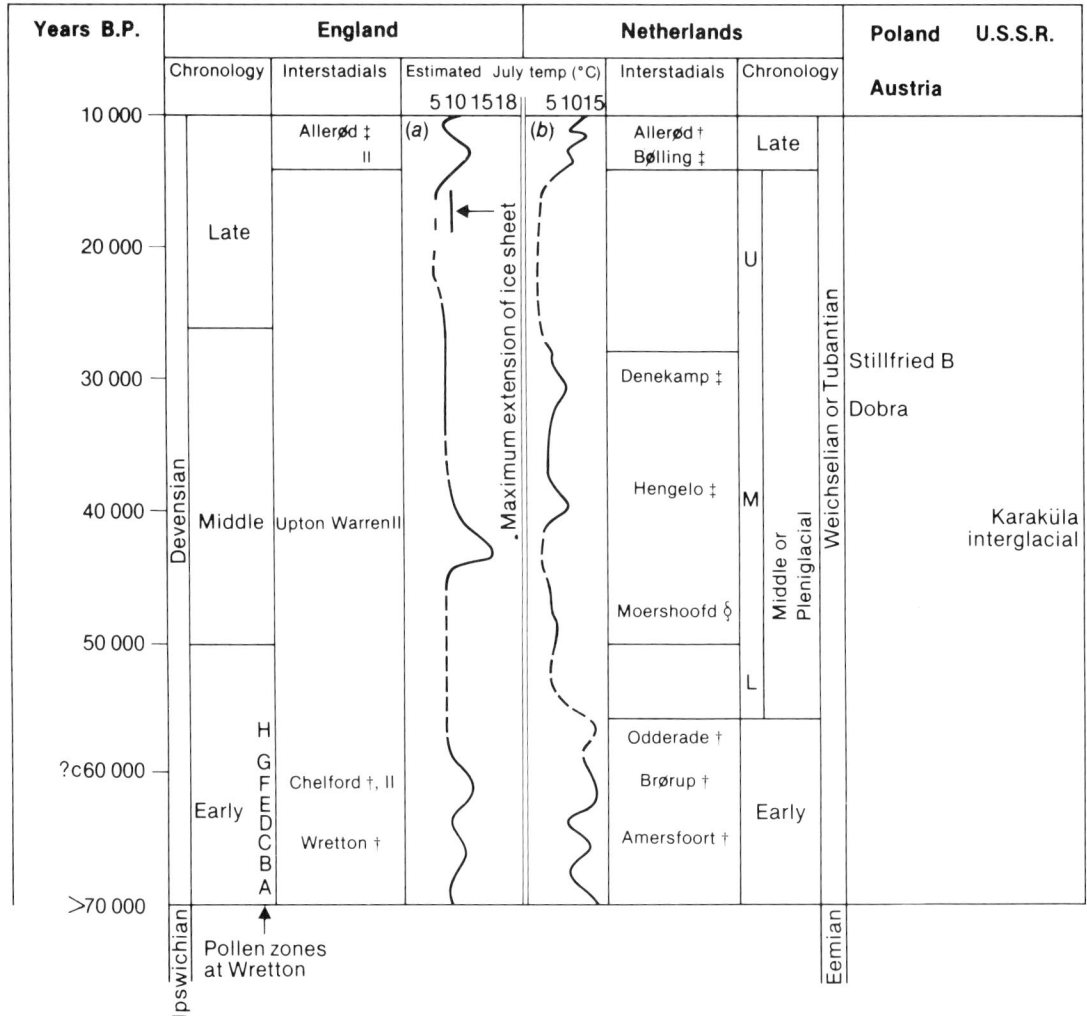

Fig. 2.3 A classification of the Devensian. (After West 1977b.) Correlation with the Netherlands and some central and eastern European sites are shown. The figure shows the positions of interstadials and the basis for the definition of each: †, pollen-based interstadial, woodland; ‡, pollen-based interstadial, shrub-tundra; §, pollen based interstadial, tundra; ‖, beetle-based interstadial. (a) curve based on beetles back to Chelford Interstadial, and below this on palaeobotany; (b) curve based on palaeobotany.

(26 000 to 10 000 years B.P.) substages (Fig. 2.3). A review of Devensian chronology and stratigraphical succession is given by Shotton (1977b).

The type site for the Devensian is at Four Ashes, Staffordshire, where deposits covering most of the stage were recorded (Morgan 1973).

Tills and outwash deposits of Devensian age occur over much of Ireland, Scotland, Wales and northern England extending to the Cheshire Plain in the west, and down the east coast as far as northwest Norfolk (Fig. 2.2). The main ice advance is generally thought to have occurred late in the stage (Late Devensian), between about 18 000 and 15 000 years B.P. Minor readvances occurred in pollen zone III (see Fig. 2.5), between 10 300 and 10 800 years B.P.

Extensive non-glacial sediments of Middle and Early Devensian age are not surprisingly confined to the area south of the Devensian till limit. Most of these deposits are sands and gravels, sometimes yielding large-mammal remains, with occasional silty and organic horizons containing plant fossils, datable by radiocarbon, together with beetles and other invertebrates and sometimes also vertebrates.

Early Devensian deposits, recognized by the inclusion of horizons, with pollen spectra characteristic of the Chelford interstadial, are known from Chelford itself, in Cheshire (Simpson & West 1958), and Beetley (Phillips 1976), Coston and Wretton (West *et al.* 1974), all in Norfolk. Such deposits are close to, or perhaps beyond, the limit of reliable radiocarbon dating. Chelford is dated to 60 800 ± 1500 years B.P. but is probably older. This interstadial is probably the correlative of the Brørup interstadial of Denmark and others with similar pollen spectra described from the Netherlands and Germany (Fig. 2.3).

Further evidence for the Early Devensian sequence comes from Wretton, where the pollen spectra indicate three herb biozones separated by two woodland interstadials, the younger of which is equated with Chelford (West *et al.* 1974; West 1977b) and the older is perhaps the equivalent of the Continental Amersfoort interstadial. The younger interstadial horizon, however, yielded a beetle fauna suggesting very cold conditions (Coope, in West *et al.* 1974; Coope 1977). This contradiction has not yet been resolved.

Minor interstadials are known from the Pleniglacial part of the Netherlands sequence but do not register in British deposits of the same age, from which only rather uniform herb-dominated

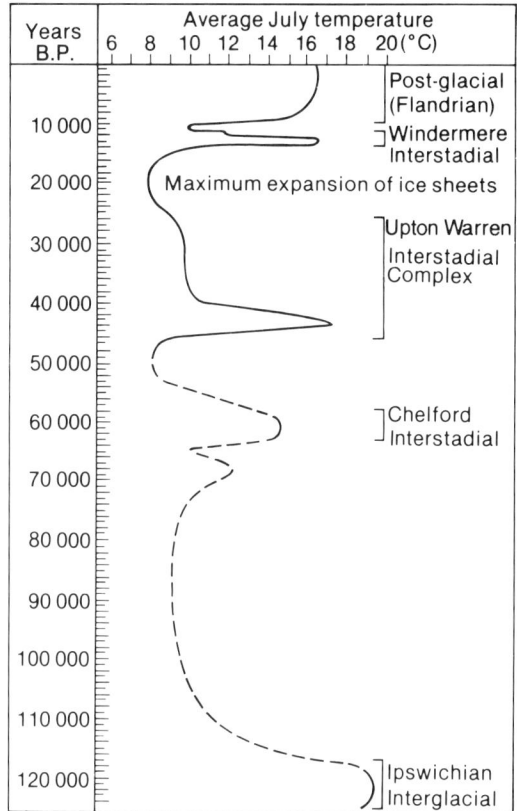

Fig. 2.4. Temperature curve for the Devensian (and Flandrian) based on interpretation of fossil beetle faunas. (After Coope 1977.) Note the very high values attributed to the peak of the Upton Warren Interstadial and also to the Windermere Interstadial. The date given for the Chelford Interstadial should be regarded as a minimum.

pollen spectra are known. The inferred climatic changes for the Middle Devensian in Britain are based on the interpretation of radiocarbon-dated beetle faunas (see Coope *et al.* 1971; Coope 1977, and Fig. 2.4). Important fossiliferous sites include Upton Warren and Fladbury, Worcestershire, Isleworth, Middlesex, and Tattershall Castle and Kirkby-on-Bain (Tattershall Thorpe), Lincolnshire (Coope *et al.* 1961; Coope 1962; Coope & Angus 1975; Girling 1974).

Few floras or beetle faunas are known from the first half of the Late Devensian, and there is a general impression of deterioration of climate, prior to the main extension of ice sheets.

The subdivisions of Late Devensian time based on radiocarbon chronology and palaeobotany are

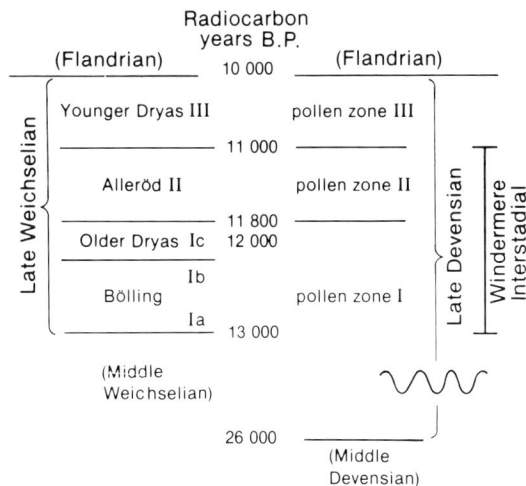

Fig. 2.5. Subdivisions of the Late Devensian and Late Weichselian based on radiocarbon chronology and palaeobotany. (Modified from Pennington 1977.) Duration of the Windermere Interstadial according to palaeobotanical evidence. (After Coope & Pennington 1977.)

shown in Fig. 2.5. The amelioration of climate after about 15 000 years B.P. was interrupted by a relatively short and sharp cold spell, zone III or the 'Younger Dryas', between about 11 000 and 10 000 years B.P. The preceding warming, designated the Windermere interstadial in Britain, is taken as from about 13 000 to 11 000 years B.P. on palaeobotanical evidence, but is considered to have begun some 1 500 years or so earlier on beetle evidence (Pennington 1977; Coope & Pennington 1977).

In addition to glacial and fluviatile deposits, the Late Devensian is represented by fine-grained lacustrine sediments, organic in the late horizons, sometimes containing large mammal remains, e.g. the zone II deposits at Ballybetagh and many other Irish localities (Jessen & Farrington 1938; Watts 1977).

Cave deposits of Devensian age are common in many parts of the British Isles but have seldom been dated with any accuracy. Radiocarbon dates on bone collagen from well-stratified samples are the most promising line of approach, but few sites have been carefully excavated and systematically recorded. Several horizons can be assigned fairly confidently on the evidence of faunas and radiocarbon dates, to the end of the Late Devensian, while others belong to the Middle Devensian including

Castlepook Cave, Ireland, and Picken's Hole (Layer 3), Somerset (Ch. 8). Early Devensian faunas are difficult to recognize in cave sequences, as they are beyond the range of radiocarbon dating.

Flandrian
The beginning of the Flandrian is taken for convenience at 10 000 radiocarbon years B.P. Flandrian deposits occur over the whole of the British Isles, and include river sediments, lake muds and marls, fen peats, blanket peats, tufas and archaeological deposits. Marine clays and silts occur in numerous coastal situations and in estuaries.

Continuous pollen records, often with radiocarbon dates, have been described from many sites and Flandrian vegetational history is the object of much intensive research (Godwin 1975).

Vertebrate remains, however mostly come from river deposits, which on the whole have been little investigated palaeobotanically, and from archaeological sites.

Chronology

The subject of chronology of the British Pleistocene, and Pleistocene sequences in general, has been discussed at length by West (1977a).

Relative dating methods

Relative dating is simply a matter of working out the sequence of events by establishing the stratigraphical succession, whereas absolute dating methods seek to establish the dates of such events in years.

The classic and still most important method of relative dating is by fossils, especially in the case of the British Pleistocene by pollen. The sequences of pollen assemblage zones indicate detailed differences in vegetational history between different interglacials. Radiocarbon calibration of Flandrian pollen zones suggests that interglacial pollen zones are almost synchronous within restricted areas and broadly equivalent over larger distances, e.g. across western Europe, at similar latitudes. The Flandrian pollen-zone boundaries, however, tend to lag in time with increase in latitude and altitude. Other fossils of importance for biostratigraphy include Foraminifera, molluscs, beetles, and mammals (Ch. 9).

Palaeomagnetic chronology uses the pattern of normal and reversed polarity of the earth's magnetic field which has changed several times during the course of the Pleistocene. The direction of this field is imprinted upon certain magnetic minerals in both igneous rocks at the time of cooling, and certain fine-grained sedimentary rocks at the time of deposition. There are no known igneous rocks in the British Pleistocene, but measurements of remnant magnetism have been successfully made at a few Lower and Middle Pleistocene sites representing the Pre-Ludhamian, Baventian, Pastonian, Cromerian, Anglian and Hoxnian stages (Montfrans 1971). All of these deposits show normal polarity, but in view of the fact that stages are missing from the British Lower Pleistocene succession it is difficult to correlate these deposits with the standard palaeomagnetic sequence. Such correlations need to be done in conjunction with other methods of dating unless long sequences are available.

More detailed studies on variations in declination, inclination and magnetic intensity have been made on both Flandrian and Hoxnian lacustrine deposits. The potential of both palaeomagnetic dating methods is considerable, because the changes are on a global scale.

Absolute dating methods

Absolute dating techniques include dendrochronology (tree ring dating), varve chronology, and a number of geochemical methods.

The first of these methods, although extremely accurate, is only possible back to about 7 000 years B.P., but provides valuable evidence of detailed climatic changes and calibration of radiocarbon chronology.

Varved, or annually layered, sediments associated with ice retreat are not widespread in the British Pleistocene and cannot be used as the basis of a varve chronology as is available for the Late Weichselian and Flandrian of Fennoscandia.

Laminated lacustrine sediments of Hoxnian age, with alternate light and dark layers, interpreted as annual pairs, have been investigated at Marks Tey, Essex, giving an estimate of *c.* 20 000 years for the entire Hoxnian interglacial (Turner 1970). This method provides a floating chronology in that it

gives the duration of a particular event, but not when it occurred.

Radiocarbon is the most widely applied and accurate of geochemical dating methods. It relies on the fact that all living organisms contain the radioactive isotope ^{14}C in equilibrium with that in CO_2 in the atmosphere, freshwater and the sea. On the death of the organism, ^{14}C no longer enters or leaves the system, but the percentage gradually decreases due to radioactive decay. Determination of the age of a carbon sample involves measuring its remanant radioactivity since the decay proceeds at a known rate, with a half-life conventionally taken as 55 680 years. In practice it is possible to date samples as old as 30 000–40 000 years, and as far back as 64 000 years with isotopic enrichment. Errors due to contamination, however, become grossly exaggerated in such very old samples. The method is therefore essentially restricted to the Flandrian period and approximately the second half of the Devensian.

Sources of error include contamination of samples by more recent carbon, and conversely incorporation of very old carbon from dissolved limestones during photosynthesis by aquatic plants ('hard water error'). It now appears certain that the percentage of ^{14}C in CO_2 in the atmosphere has varied through time so that there is some deviation of radiocarbon years from astronomical years. Attempts are being made to make precise calibrations between the two, in particular by comparing tree-ring and radiocarbon dates on the same wood samples.

Potassium–argon dating, which utilizes the radioactive decay of isotope ^{40}K to ^{40}Ar, covers the Lower and Middle Pleistocene and back into the Tertiary but is otherwise at present much less satisfactory than radiocarbon. Firstly, it is only possible with volcanic rocks, so that the method is not directly applicable to the British Pleistocene, and further, there are a number of sources of error which lead to much larger percentage errors than with radiocarbon.

Further methods utilize the decay of particular uranium isotopes and their products. Provisional uranium dating of bones by Szabo and Collins (1975) suggests ages of 245 000 $^{+35\,000}_{-25\,000}$ years B.P. (Clacton) and more than 272 000 years B.P. (Swanscombe) for the Hoxnian interglacial, and 125 000 $\pm$ 20 000 years B.P. (Stutton) and 174 000 $\pm$ 30 000 years B.P. (Brundon) for the Ipswichian interglacial. Uranium series dating of stalagmite from caves is proving valuable in assessing the ages of cave vertebrate faunas beyond the range of radiocarbon (Gascoyne, 1981).

Other geochemical dating methods include amino-acid racemization, thermoluminescene, and fission-track dating, the last applicable only to igneous rocks. The first method can be used on bones and shells, but has the disadvantage of being temperature dependent. These methods have considerable potential, but need much further work.

Chronology of the British Pleistocene

The outline chronology included in Table 2.2 is based on radiocarbon dating of Flandrian and Weichselian (Devensian) deposits in Britain and north-west Europe back to about 60 000 years B.P. The date of c. 110 000 years B.P. for the beginning of the Devensian assumes a correlation with the marine record. The Middle and Lower Pleistocene dates are based on potassium—argon dates for possible correlative volcanic rocks elsewhere in Europe, and are only very approximate. A reliable absolute dating method for the Pleistocene before about 60 000 years B.P. is badly needed.

It has become increasingly apparent in recent years, from several lines of evidence, that the interglacials of the Middle and Upper Pleistocene of north-west Europe represent relatively short periods of time compared with the cold stages. In other words, the later part of the Pleistocene was characterized by predominantly cold climates punctuated by geologically brief temperate phases.

The duration of interglacials has been estimated from counts of presumed annually laminated lake sediments in Germany and England. Estimates are 9 000–11 000 years for the Eemian (Ipswichian), 16 000–17 000 years for the Holsteinian (Hoxnian) and c. 20 000 years for the Hoxnian (see above) (Turner 1975a). These compare with 10 000 years elapsed so far for the Flandrian period based on radiocarbon and other chronologies. On the other hand, radiocarbon dating indicates a duration of at least 60 000 years for the Devensian cold stage.

A continuous pollen record from lacustrine deposits covering much of the Pleistocene from Macedonia (Wijmstra 1969) shows a series of climatic fluctuations recorded broadly as alternations between Mediterranean woodland and *Artemisia* steppe. It shows a number of warm periods comparable

with the postglacial in both intensity and duration as estimated crudely by sediment thickness. In addition to these probable interglacial periods are a number of less marked warm periods which would perhaps register as interstadials in north-west Europe. The same general picture is given by the pollen profile from Grande Pile, eastern France (Woillard 1978, 1979), which appears to represent the time from just before the Eemian (Ipswichian) interglacial to the present day. A series of radiocarbon dates at the Macedonian site indicate a remarkably uniform rate of sedimentation, which can be extrapolated to give estimates of roughly 15 000 years for the duration of the Last Interglacial (Eemian/Ipswichian), and about 72 000 years for the duration of the Last Cold Stage (Devensian/Weichselian). The latter is taken as including two rather less pronounced warm periods immediately following the Eemian, probably equivalent to the Early Weichselian/Devensian interstadials of north-west Europe.

The oxygen isotope records from deep-sea cores also show a series of high ^{16}O peaks which may represent interglacials in the terrestrial sequence (see above). If this is so then again interglacial durations of the order of 10 000–15 000 years are indicated.

Climatic changes

Fluctuations in climate are the outstanding characteristic of the Pleistocene, and it is the elucidation of these changes which constitutes one of the major aims of Pleistocene research. The causes of the changes remain uncertain (see e.g. West 1977a).

Evidence for climatic changes

A large number of climatic parameters can be distinguished, of which temperature, especially the mean values for the warmest and coldest months, rainfall, snowfall and hours of sunshine, are all important for living organisms. Studies of sediments and fossils can give much general, and some specific, data on Pleistocene climatic conditions, especially temperature.

The presence of ice sheets in the British Isles at various times in the Pleistocene clearly argues for considerably lower temperatures than at the present day, but does not give any detailed information. Ice wedge casts, common in many exposures, on the other hand are thought to indicate past annual mean temperatures in the range $-6\,°C$ to $-8\,°C$ or below. Loess (wind-blown silts) is thought to indicate a continental dry climate.

The studies of fluctuations in past temperature and global ice volumes based on $^{16}O : {}^{18}O$ ratios in biogenic carbonate from deep-sea cores (e.g. Shackleton & Opdyke 1973; Shackleton 1977a, b) are clearly of great importance to the understanding of Pleistocene climatic changes in the British Isles, as elsewhere, but their relevance to the terrestrial record will remain uncertain until such time as definite correlations can be made.

Comparison of present and Pleistocene distributions of animals and plants can give valuable information on past climates. There are, however, some inherent difficulties in this approach. Firstly, the present distributions of organisms may be imperfectly known, and there are many factors other than climate which control these distributions. Moreover, it is necessary to assume that the ecology of organisms used for climatic interpretation has not altered significantly over the years. This may be partly overcome if the fossil assemblage indicates a consistent picture of the climate, but there are further problems in that many Pleistocene assemblages exhibit mixtures of nowadays geographically separate taxa, reflecting Pleistocene climatic conditions with no exact equivalents at the present day.

The presence of mixed oak forest at a site in Britain indicates a climate at least as warm as, and with similar precipitation to, the present day. Its absence, however, may not be due to climatic factors, but may merely indicate that not enough time had elapsed for the immigration of these forest trees, i.e. the climate and flora are not in equilibrium. The presence of *Ilex* (holly) and *Hedera* (ivy), whose climatic tolerances have been well-studied, imply mean temperatures of the coldest month not below $-1.5\,°C$ (since these genera are frost-sensitive). Several plant taxa, e.g. *Trapa natans* (water chestnut), recorded from interglacials in Britain, now occur only well south of the British Isles, implying warmer climates in the past.

Temperature is claimed to be the main factor controlling the past and present distributions of many species of *Coleoptera* (beetles) especially Carabidae, except when a species is tied to a particular food plant (e.g. Coope 1977). Temperatures have

thereby been directly deduced from various, mostly Devensian, Coleopteran assemblages, as their speed of migration is thought to be much faster than the plants, certainly than trees.

With regard to vertebrates, it is difficult to assess the role of climatic parameters in directly influencing the distributions of mammals, but the cold-blooded fishes, amphibians and reptiles are clearly much influenced by temperature.

Foraminifera and non-marine Mollusca also provide much information on past temperatures.

Climatic changes in the Pleistocene of Britain

A general impression is gained from the Pleistocene sequence of both Britain and elsewhere of climatic fluctuations with the cold phases increasing in intensity in the Middle and Upper Pleistocene. Ice wedge casts show that mean annual temperatures reached to $-6\,°C$ or below during the coldest phases of each cold stage from the Beestonian to the Devensian.

Detailed temperature curves for the Devensian cold stage have been deduced from both plant and beetle evidence (Figs. 2.3 and 2.4). The bettle faunas of about 42 000 years B.P. are interpreted by Coope (1977) as revealing a very rapid and intense amelioration of climate (Upton Warren Interstadial) which was responded to by the beetles but not the flora. The timing of the Late Devensian amelioration (Windermere Interstadial) is also considered, on the evidence of beetle faunas, to have differed from that of the traditional Allerød (zone II) interstadial based on palaeobotanical evidence, and modern investigations of the floras give some support to the beetle-based climatic curve, which indicates the peak of warming in the 'pre-Allerød' zone I.

The interpretation of beetle evidence conflicts with the interpretation based on pollen for the existence of the Chelford woodland interstadial at Wretton, Norfolk. There is, however, good agreement between floras and beetle faunas in the case of the interstadial deposits at Chelford, Cheshire (Simpson & West 1958; Coope 1959), several Mid- and Late Devensian sites, and from the few interglacial samples from which the beetle faunas have been investigated.

The presence of mixed oak forests in the middle (zones II and III) of interglacials implies temperate climates at least as warm as today. There is palaeobotanical evidence from each of the interglacials, including the Flandrian, that, at the optimum, mean summer temperatures exceeded those of the present day by at least 2 or 3 °C (Phillips 1974; West 1977a). This conclusion is supported by the occurrence of non-marine molluscs now with distributions well to the south of the British Isles (e.g. *Corbicula fluminalis*, *Belgrandia marginata*) (Sparks 1964) and southern beetles (e.g. a Mediterranean dung beetle *Onthophagus opacicollis*) (Coope 1974). Further evidence comes from finds of the thermophilous European pond tortoise *Emys orbicularis* (Ch. 5).

The abundance of pollen of *Alnus*, *Hedera* and *Ilex* in Hoxnian deposits may indicate a more oceanic climate than prevailed during other interglacials, and this is supported by the occurrence of *Ilex* much further east than now in deposits of the correlative Holsteinian interglacial on the Continent. On the other hand, the Ipswichian shows evidence of a more continental climate. Phillips (1974) considered that the climate changed from a rather Mediterranean aspect (warm summers and mild winters) in zone Ip II to one of more continental type (warm summers and cold winters, perhaps drier) in zone III, continuing in zone IV. The persistence of *Corbicula* and *Emys* in zone IV indicates that summer temperatures remained high until late in the Ipswichian stage. Many taxa of plants and animals are recorded well north of their present ranges from the correlative Eemian interglacial on the Continent.

The Flandrian climatic optimum, based on plants, molluscs and *Emys* occurred about 7 000 to 5 000 years B.P. (zone VIIa/Fl IId) when annual mean temperatures are thought to have been about 2 °C above those of the present day. At this time a number of now southern plants and animals occurred as far north as southern Scandinavia.

Studies of Foraminifera, coccoliths and Radiolaria from deep-sea cores taken in the North Atlantic indicate that there have been dramatic changes in ocean circulation in this region with time (Fig. 2.6). During interglacials the climate of the British Isles is and was subject to the benevolent influence of the Gulf Stream Drift and the boundary between warm and polar waters, the 'polar front', is pushed far north of the British Isles. On the other hand, during cold stages the polar front was depressed at times as far south as Spain, holding the British Isles in an icy grip. These results have very

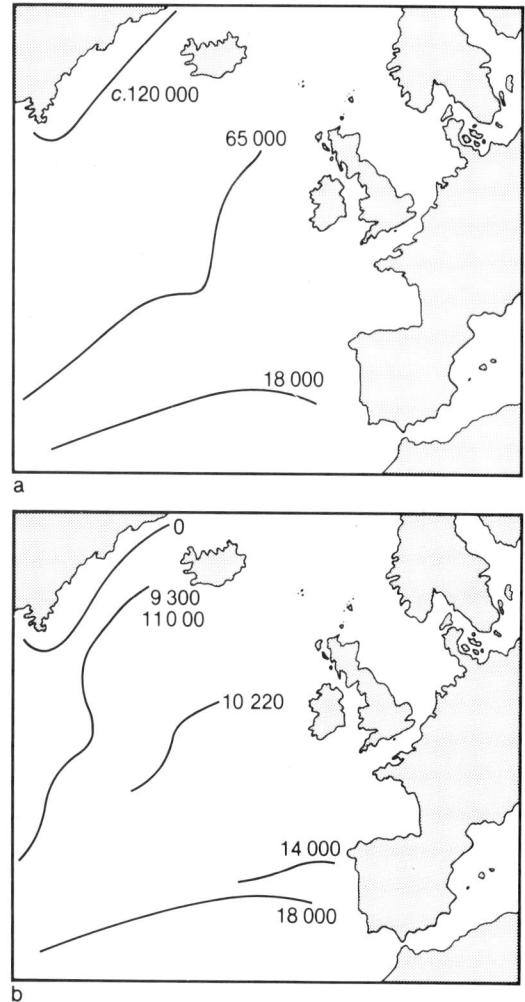

Fig. 2.6. Polar front positions in the North Atlantic from the Last Interglacial to the present day, based on analyses of Foraminifera from deep-sea cores. (Adapted from Ruddiman *et al.* 1977.) Numbers show dates in years B.P. (a) cooling of North Atlantic from the Last Interglacial to the coldest part of the Last Cold Stage; (b) overall warming from 18 000 years B.P. to present day. Note reversal of trend, indicated by polar front position at 10 220 years B.P. (zone L-De III, 'Younger Dryas').

interesting implications in that they suggest why there are such marked contrasts between the inferred climates of cold and interglacial stages in Britain and north-west Europe, and why for example forests occurred in the Middle Weichselian of Poland, when the climate was apparently too cold for tree growth in Britain (West 1977b).

Land/sea-level changes and palaeogeography

The subject of land/sea-level changes in the British Pleistocene has been discussed by West (1972, 1977a). Former sea levels are best directly assessed from measurements on heights of dated marine deposits rather than from heights of river terrace deposits which may be misleading. Transgression (freshwater to brackish or marine) and regression (brackish or marine to freshwater) contacts are especially valuable for recording changes in environmental conditions at a particular locality and height.

There are considerable difficulties in attempting to distinguish world sea-level (eustatic) changes from local changes in the level of the land due to tectonic movements, or isostatic adjustments in response to the weight of ice sheets or accumulating sediments.

Lower Pleistocene

The problems of distinguishing the two components of land/sea-level changes are particularly evident with the Lower Pleistocene of East Anglia where marine sediments ('Crags'), deposited in shallow water in a subsiding basin now extend down to -49 m O.D. These deposits continue across the North Sea into Belgium and the Netherlands where they are much thicker. On the other hand, deposits of possible Red Crag age on the North Downs at about $190-200$ m O.D. suggest that early Lower Pleistocene sea levels were high and that the Straits of Dover area was submerged. It is thought, however, that a tectonic rise of a chalk ridge in south-east England in later crag times closed the Straits of Dover so that Britain remained connected to the Continent, despite vicissitudes of sea level, until the Upper Pleistocene (King 1977).

Interglacials

Interglacial sea levels have been estimated from heights of marine and brackish sediments dated by pollen, but again differential isostatic and tectonic movements have certainly occurred. The biogeographically significant question of connection to or isolation from the Continent is clearly to a large ex-

tent dependent on sea level, but also on the local topography in the southern North Sea and eastern English Channel area.

There is evidence from each interglacial of brackish or marine transgression in the second half of the stage or sometimes within pollen zone II (West 1972).

In east Norfolk, Cromerian estuarine deposits extend up to 7 m O.D., with a freshwater/estuarine contact at about O.D. Hoxnian marine clays occur up to 20 m O.D. in north-west Norfolk and there is a freshwater/marine contact at about O.D. in south-east England. Again in the Ipswichian, a freshwater/marine contact is known at about O.D. in south-east England and beach gravels in the same area occur up to 12 m O.D. There is evidence, from both floral and faunal comparisons with the Continent, that the Straits of Dover were open during some part of the Ipswichian interglacial, but not during earlier interglacials. Additional evidence comes from the existence of raised beaches of probable Ipswichian age on either side of the Channel and the presence of a marine molluscan fauna of southern affinities in the Eemian (Ipswichian) of the Netherlands (for discussion see Stuart 1976a).

The pattern of sea-level changes during the Flandrian are the subject of much research, and controversy. It is probable, however, that sea levels rose from about -40 m O.D. at the beginning of the stage (10 000 years B.P.) and had reached to within a few metres of present level by 5 000 years B.P. Freshwater peats ('moorlog') occur widely over the southern North Sea area. Pollen analyses have demonstrated that they represent zones IV, V and the very beginning of VIa (Fl Ia to IIa) and imply that the area was not covered by sea, separating Britain from the Continent, until at least a time within zone VI (Godwin 1943, 1975) i.e. about 8 500 years B.P.

The question of former connections between Britain and Ireland is more difficult. A drop in sea level of at least 60 m would be necessary at the present day to connect the two islands via south-west Scotland and northern Ireland (Fig. 2.7), which is far lower than would be expected anywhere within an interglacial stage. This does not, however, take into account the possibility that, for example, morainic ridges across the Irish sea may have been subsequently depressed by isostatic movements or eroded away by the sea (Mitchell 1960, 1976). It nevertheless seems probable that the Flandrian sea-

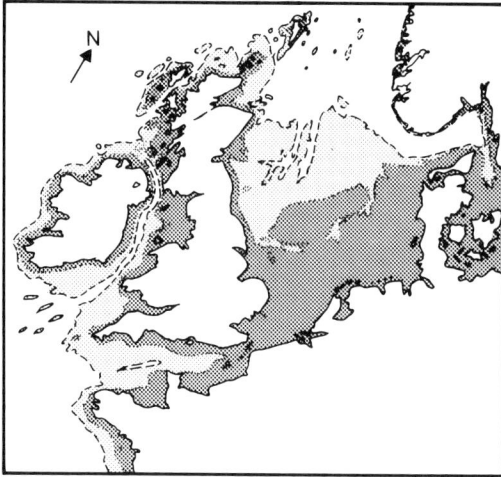

Fig. 2.7. 50 m and 100 m submarine contours around the British Isles. The 100 m contour gives a general impression of the maximum area exposed by fall in sea level during the Devensian (Weichselian) cold stage. In the Flandrian, extensive areas of the southern North Sea were still dry land as late as *c.* 8 500 years B.P.

level rise would have isolated Ireland very quickly indeed, probably before 9 500 years B.P., and that similar situations probably prevailed in earlier interglacials.

Cold stages

During cold stages the maximum eustatic fall in sea level, due to the incorporation of large quantities of water in the world's accumulating ice sheets, is thought to have been about 100 m or so. This drop would have broadly connected Britain to the Continent and Ireland to Britain via a narrow isthmus (Fig. 2.7), but there may perhaps have been additional connections across the Irish Sea from Wales (Mitchell 1960, 1976).

It is not known to what extent sea levels may have varied with climatic fluctuations within these stages.

Vegetational history

In studying fossil vertebrates it is clearly desirable to know as much as possible about the contempor-

aneous vegetational conditions, which can be deduced from fossil pollen and macroscopic plant remains.

Pollen and spores are incorporated in accumulating sediments in enormous numbers. They originate mostly from fall-out (pollen rain) from the atmosphere and represent both regional and local plant communities. They have extremely resistant coats (exine) and survive many chemical processes but are rapidly destroyed by oxidation.

Samples for pollen analyses, usually each of a few cubic centimetres, are taken at intervals (e.g. 5 or 10 cm) through the sediment profile. Preparation involves chemically removing both inorganic and organic sediment and leaving the pollen unscathed. The pollen and spore grains are identified and counted, and a pollen diagram constructed usually on a percentage basis (West 1977a).

Changing pollen percentages reflect regional and local climatic, edaphic (soil) and biotic changes. Plant macro-fossil, e.g. fruits and seeds, can provide much information on the plants growing close to or at the depositional site, and enable a valuable distinction to be made between the regional and local pollen rain.

Studies of modern pollen rain from a variety of vegetational types is proving invaluable in better understanding the past vegetation represented by fossil pollen. Pollen from lake deposits gives a much better representation of regional vegetation as the pollen fall-out is from a wide area, whereas on the other hand pollen from river deposits shows a much greater component of locally derived pollen.

Reviews of the Pleistocene history of the British flora are given by Godwin (1975, 1977) and West (1970). Interglacial and interstadial forest vegetation is discussed at length by West (1980b), and the method of correlation of deposits by pollen spectra, and pollen zonation, are described by West (1970).

Lower Pleistocene floras

The pollen spectra from the Lower Pleistocene crag sequence of East Anglia indicate periods of cool climate with oceanic heath alternating with periods of temperate climate with mixed coniferous and deciduous forest (West 1977a, 1980b) (Fig. 2.8). There are, however, difficulties in interpreting the vegetational types represented, as not enough is known at present concerning deposition of pollen in marine environments. The tree *Tsuga* (hemlock

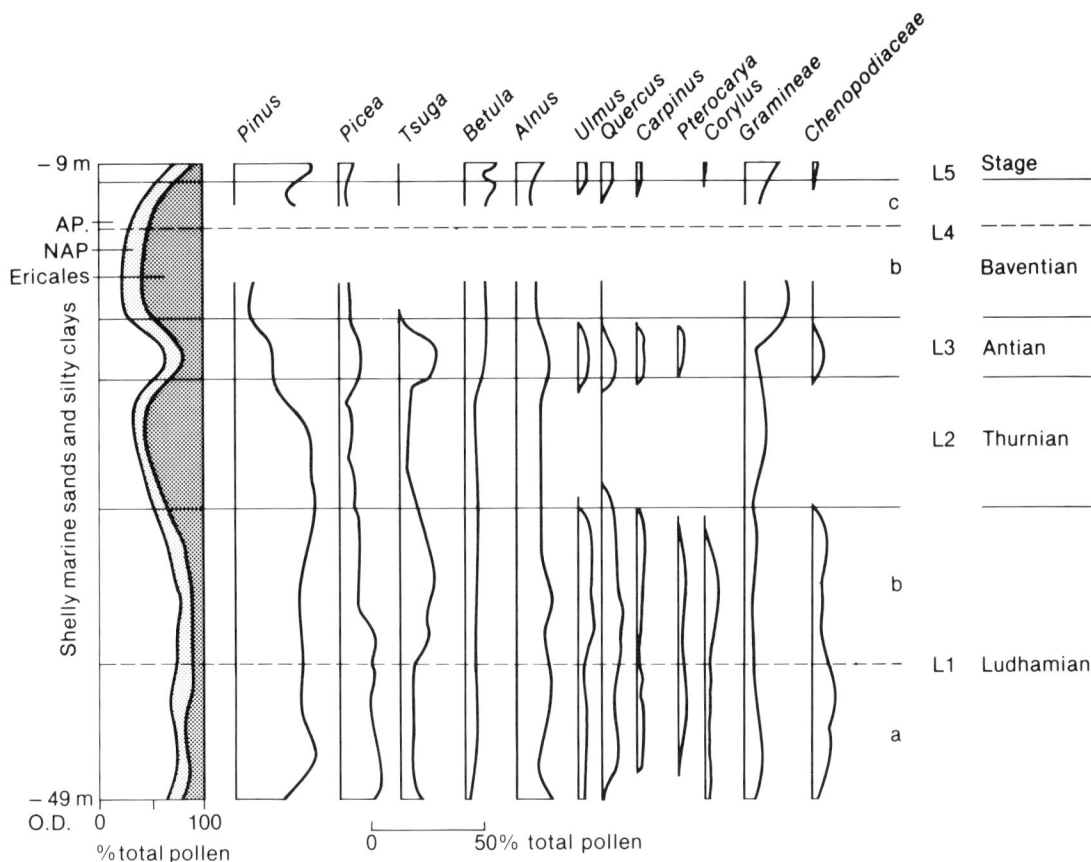

Fig. 2.8 Schematic pollen diagram through the crag at Ludham, Norfolk, covering several Lower Pleistocene stages. (After West 1980a.)

spruce), now extinct in Europe, but still living in eastern Asia and North America, is characteristic of these Lower Pleistocene temperate stages, although present in only small amounts in the Pastonian. The pollen sequence for the Pastonian can be divided into four pollen assemblage zones as for the interglacial stages (see below).

Interglacial floras

The interglacial stages of the Middle and Upper Pleistocene are characterized by the presence of mixed oak forest (West 1980b), indicating that climatic amelioration proceeded at least as far as in the Flandrian (postglacial). It is convenient to treat the Flandrian stage also as an interglacial, since its natural vegetational development so far is generally similar to that of other interglacial stages.

The pollen diagrams for each interglacial record a broadly similar pattern of vegetational development, and can each be divided into four major zones (pollen assemblage biozones) (Turner & West 1968; West, 1977a). These vegetational changes are thought to be related to a sequence of climatic and edaphic changes. The climate is ameliorating at the beginning of the stage and deteriorating at the end. Edaphic changes, on the other hand, proceed from fresh solifluced or glacially deposited sediments weathered into brown earths at the first half of the interglacial, becoming progressively podzolized as nutrients are leached out, in the second half. The vegetational sequence is shown in Table 2.4.

The vegetational history of each stage differs in detail, so that it is possible to assign a fossiliferous deposit to a particular interglacial on the basis of its pollen spectra. Zone characters for the interglacial stages are given in Table 2.5.

Table 2.4. General scheme of vegetational changes through an interglacial stage. (After Turner & West 1968.) (Youngest at top.)

Vegetational aspect	Zone	Important pollen types	Vegetation
[Early glacial]		[Herb]	[Herb-dominated]
Post-temperate	IV	*Pinus, Betula* (higher herb)	Coniferous forest (more open)
Late-temperate	III	M.O.F. genera + *Carpinus* (*Abies*)	Mixed oak forest with tree taxa not prominent in zone II
Early-temperate	II	M.O.F. genera	Mixed oak forest
Pre-temperate	I	*Betula, Pinus*	Coniferous forest
[Late-glacial]		[Herb]	[Herb-dominated]

Table 2.5. Zone characters of interglacial stages (the frequency references are to pollen percentages). (Modified from West 1970.)

Cromerian		Hoxnian		Ipswichian		Flandrian	
[e Ang]		[e Wo]		[e De]			
Cr IV	*Pinus, Picea, Betula, Alnus,* Ericales	Ho IV	*Pinus, Betula* N.A.P. higher	Ip IV	*Pinus*, N. A.P. higher		—
Cr III	M.O.F., *Abies, Carpinus*	Ho III	M.O.F., *Abies, Carpinus*	Ip III	*Carpinus*	Fl III[1]	Deforestation, low *Ulmus*, (*Fagus, Carpinus*)
Cr II	M.O.F., high *Ulmus*, low *Corylus*	Ho II	M.O.F., *Taxus, Corylus*	Ip II	M.O.F., *Pinus, Acer*, high *Corylus*	Fl II	M.O.F.
Cr I	*Pinus, Betula*	Ho I	*Betula, Pinus*	Ip I	*Betula, Pinus*	Fl I	*Betula, Pinus,*
[l Be]		[l Ang (*Hippophaë*)]		[l Wo]		[l De]	

l late	Fl Flandrian	Ho Hoxnian	M.O.F. mixed oak forest
m middle	De Devensian	Ang Anglian	N.A.P. non-arboreal pollen
e early	Ip Ipswichian	Cr Cromerian	
	Wo Wolstonian	Be Beestonian	

1. NB. The pollen spectra for zone Fl III reflect vegetation much affected by human activities.

Cromerian pollen spectra and macroscopic plant fossils are known from estuarine and freshwater deposits of the CF-bF on the Norfolk and Suffolk coast (West 1980a) (Fig. 2.9), and from only one site outside East Anglia, at Sugworth, Berkshire, where only subzone Cr IIIb was represented (Gibbard & Pettit 1978).

The Hoxnian is relatively well represented in England, mostly in East Anglia and the Midlands, by a number of lake deposits giving long pollen sequences (Fig. 2.10) and macroscopic plant fossils. Pollen spectra from the Irish Gortian, probably the equivalent of the Hoxnian, include a number of genera indicative of a highly oceanic climate, and this is also seen, although less strongly, in the English diagrams. Pollen spectra are also known from fluviatile deposits at Clacton, Essex, and from marine deposits at Clacton and from the Nar Valley, Norfolk.

Several of the Hoxnian pollen diagrams from East Anglia show a short period of deforestation near the end of zone Ho II marked by sharp increases in non-tree pollen, whereas otherwise the herb pollen values are very low. This high 'non-tree

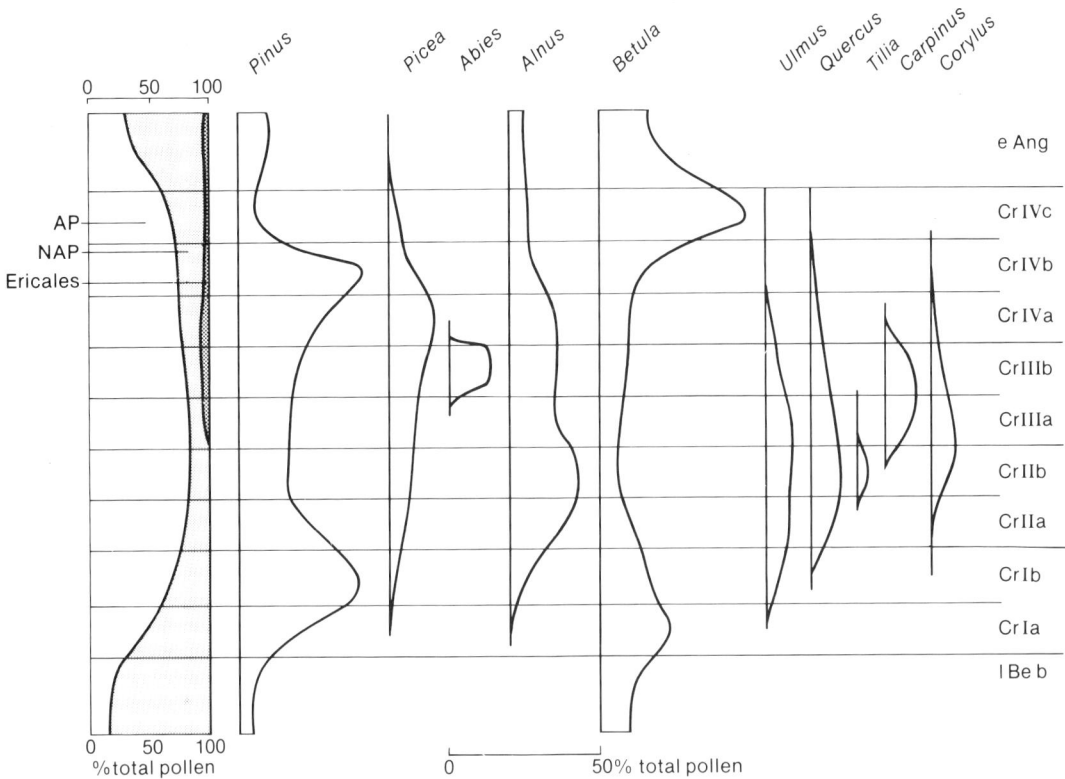

Fig. 2.9. Schematic pollen diagram for the Cromerian Interglacial. (After West 1980a) Cr Ia–Cr IVc, Cromerian pollen zones and subzones; 1 Be, late Beestonian Cold Stage; e Ang, early Anglian Cold Stage.

pollen phase' may record destruction of the forest by fire (West 1956; Turner 1970) (see Ch. 10).

Ipswichian pollen spectra and macroscopic plant fossils are mostly known from fluviatile deposits, from a number of sites in south and east England. None of these sites has yielded a diagram covering the entire interglacial, although there is ample data on which to base a composite diagram (Fig. 2.11). Recently, however, a lake deposit yielding a pollen diagram spanning much of the Ipswichian has been described from Wing, Rutland (Hall 1980). A very interesting feature of nearly all Ipswichian diagrams is the marked increase in herb pollen percentages as early as zone Ip III, suggesting regional thinning of the forest. The herb pollen percentages from sub-zone Ip IIb spectra are also, however, highly variable, up to over 90 per cent total pollen at Barrington, Cambridgeshire (Fig. 2.12). Bearing in mind that the local component is important in the pollen rain at these river valley sites, it is probable that at

some sites the floodplains were extensively deforested, and that these local areas of herb-dominated vegetation were maintained and partly initiated by the browsing, grazing, trampling and tree-felling activities of large herbivorous mammals (Phillips 1976; Turner 1975b; Gibbard & Stuart 1975; Stuart 1976a). Turner has also pointed out that modern *Hippopotamus amphibius* graze on land, but defecate in the water, thus potentially leading to a vast over-representation of herb pollen in the sediment. This phenomenon may partly account for the very high herb pollen levels at Barrington, but the presence of rather extensive treeless vegetation is also suggested by the mammalian fauna (Ch. 7).

The presence of certain plant taxa, especially aquatics, indicates warmer summers than in the Flandrian, and a climate of more continental or Mediterranean aspect. A beetle fauna from the type site Bobbitshole, Ipswich, also confirms this impression (Coope 1974). The success of hornbeam

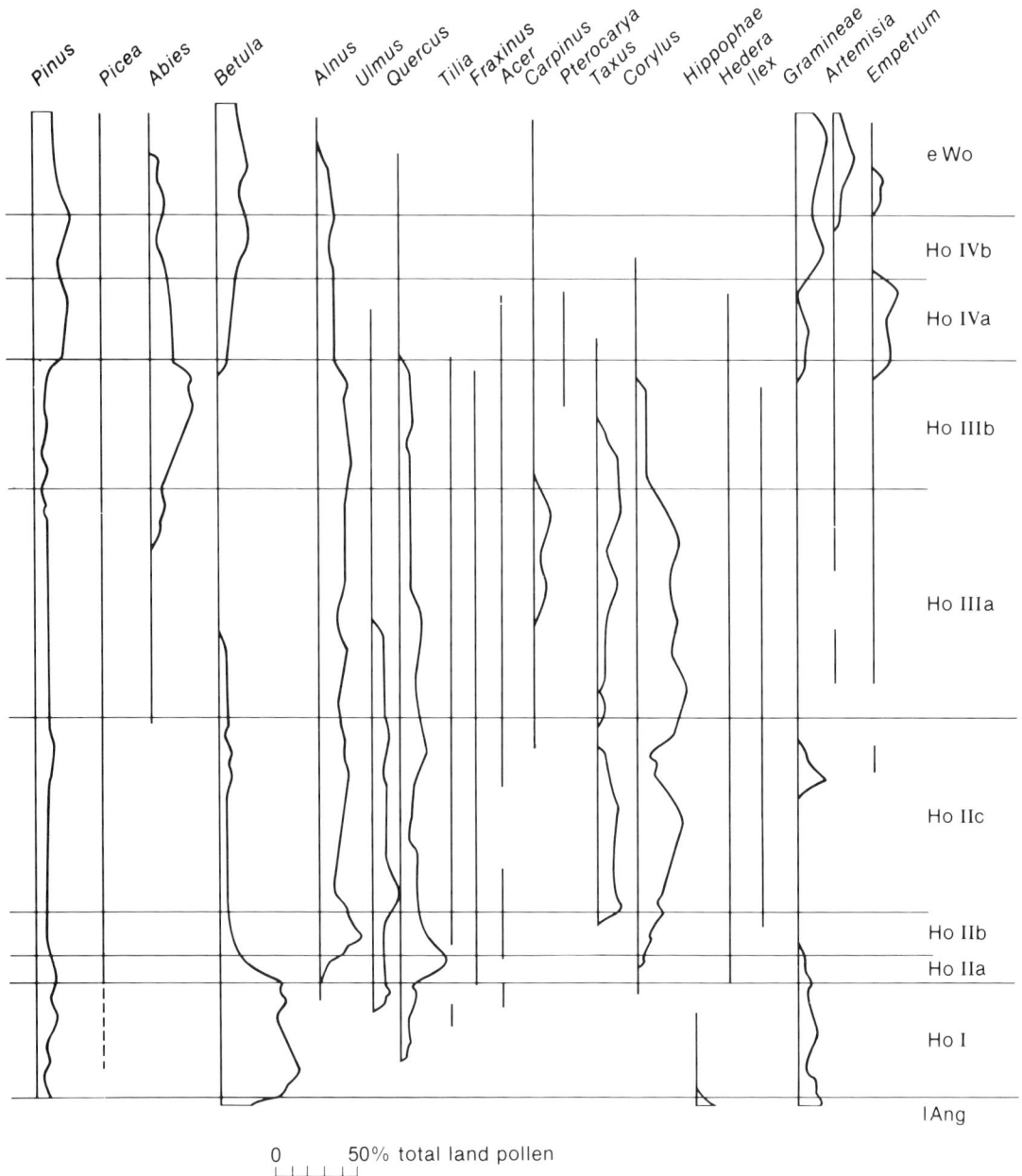

Fig. 2.10. Pollen diagram of the Hoxnian Interglacial at Marks Tey, Essex. (After Turner 1970) Ho I–Ho IVb, Hoxnian pollen zones and subzones; 1 Ang, late Anglian Cold Stage; e Wo, early Wolstonian Cold Stage.

Carpinus in zone Ip III may indicate increasing continentality in the second half of the stage (Phillips 1974).

Numerous Flandrian sites have been studied in most parts of the British Isles (Godwin 1975; Birks 1977). The majority of investigations, however, have been in lake or peat bog sites, very rarely in river deposits, and from upland areas, although there are many diagrams from the Fenland and Breckland of East Anglia. A Breckland pollen dia-

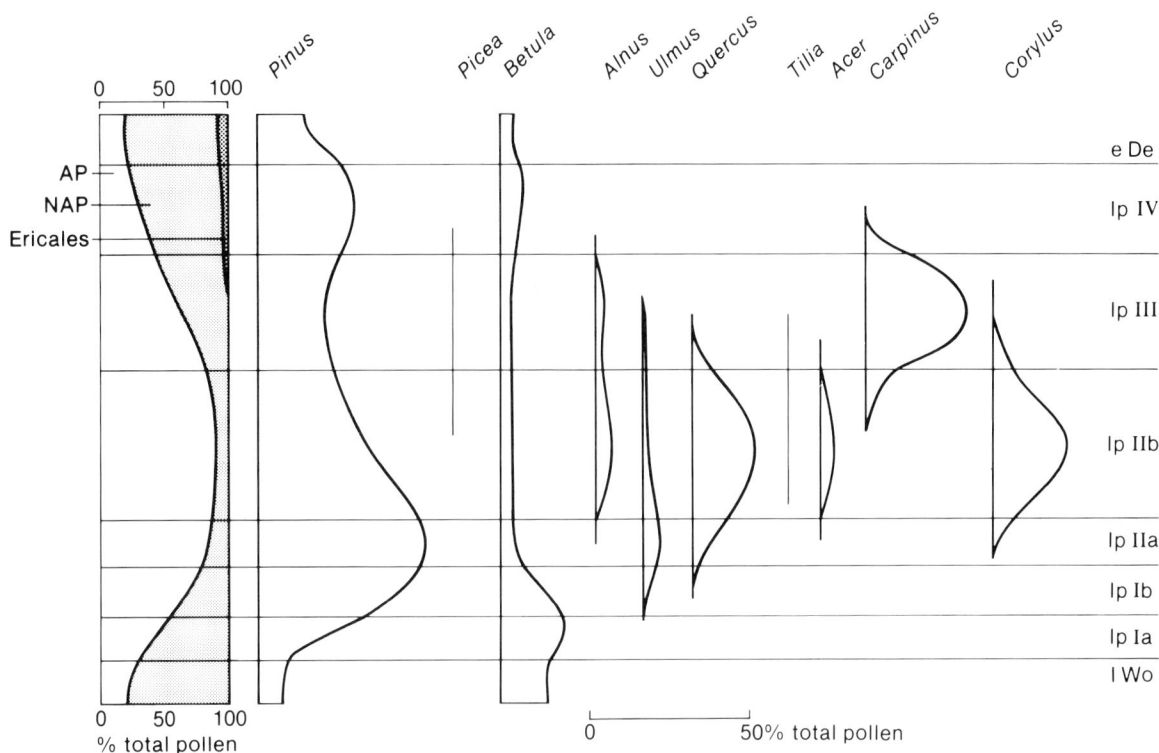

Fig. 2.11. Schematic pollen diagram for the Ipswichian Interglacial. (After West 1980a) Ip Ia–Ip IV, Ipswichian pollen zones and subzones; 1 Wo, late Wolstonian Cold Stage; e De, early Devensian Cold Stage.

gram showing conventional Flandrian zonation and probable equivalents in the Turner and West scheme is reproduced in Fig. 2.13. The natural vegetational development was drastically altered after about 5 000 years B.P., when Neolithic farmers first started clearing the forests and planting crops. The Flandrian pollen zones have been calibrated by radiocarbon and the zone boundaries shown to be mostly diachronous over the British Isles especially from north to south (Smith & Pilcher 1973). They vary far less, however, within smaller regions at similar altitudes, which suggests that pollen zones for earlier interglacials may be almost synchronous within southern England, for example.

The Flandrian vegetational cycle is of course incomplete, and at the present day we appear to be in the late-temperate zone (Fl III) (West 1980b).

Cold stage floras

Fossil floras have been described from each of the Middle and Upper Pleistocene cold stages although only the Devensian floras are at all well known (West 1977a, 1977b). Herb-dominated floras from the middle part of the stage are known from the Beestonian (Norfolk Coast) (West 1980a), Anglian (Corton Beds – Lowestoft) (West & Wilson 1968), Wolstonian (Summertown – Radley Terrace) (Duigan, 1955), and Brandon, Warwickshire (Kelly, 1968) and from many Devensian localities. Early Devensian floras from Wretton, Norfolk, are also of similar composition. They all show large quantities of sedge and grass pollen and a variety of other herbs. Small amounts of tree or shrub pollen, especially willow *Salix*, birch *Betula* (mostly dwarf birch, *B. nana*, type), juniper *Juniperus* and pine *Pinus*, are usually also present. The vegetation appears to have been almost entirely herbaceous with a variety of grasses, sedges and other herbs, and a scarcity of trees. Plants of a wide variety of ecological and plant geographical categories are represented, including arctic-alpines, halophytes and even some southern taxa. A steppe-like aspect is suggested by commonly high frequencies of mugwort *Artemisia*. The flora clearly, however, has no

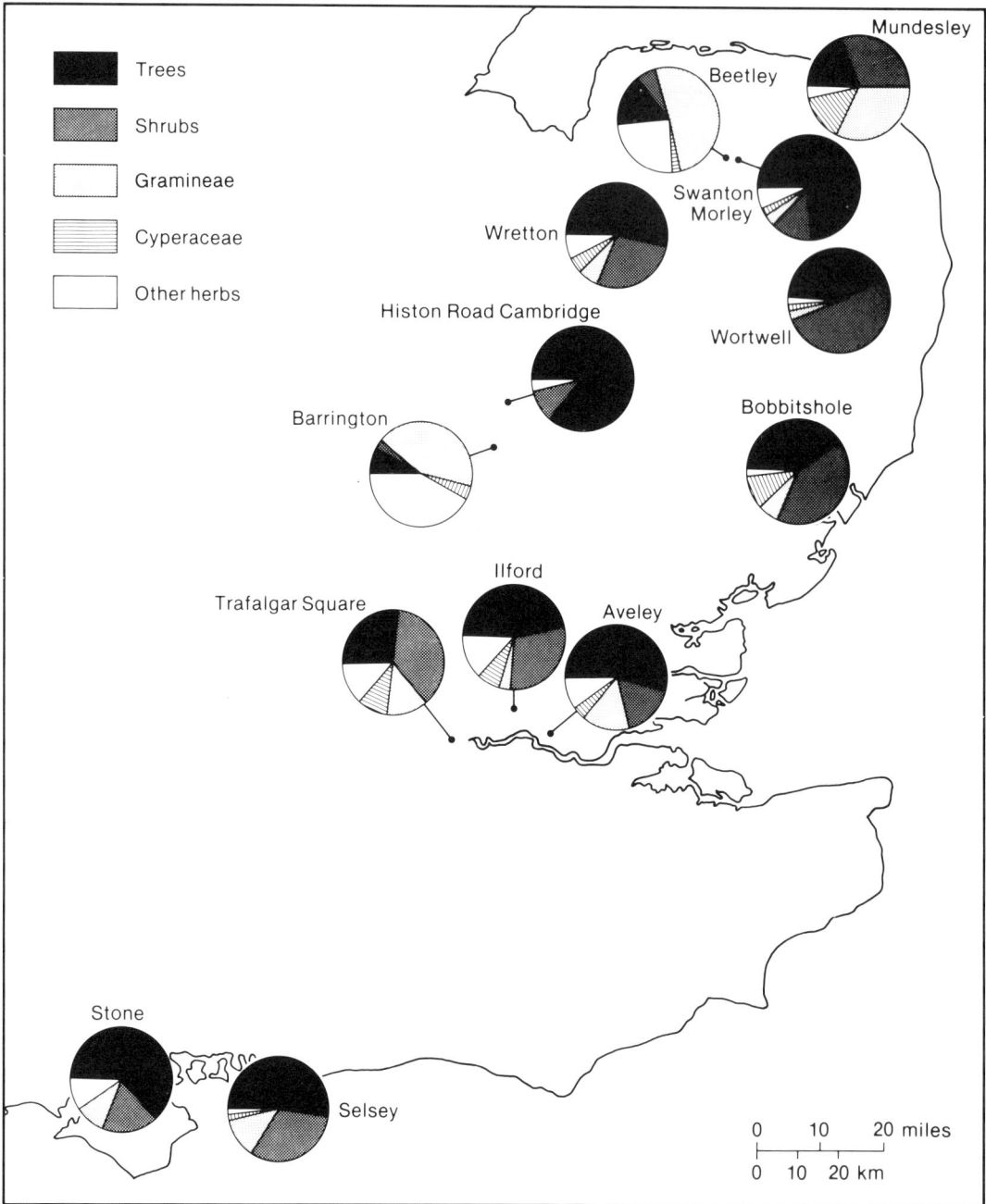

Fig. 2.12. Variation in land pollen percentages (schematic) in deposits of Ipswichian subzone Ip IIb at sites in southern England. (After Stuart 1976a.)

precise modern equivalent, but shares some of the characteristics of both modern steppe and tundra. West (1977b) has suggested that such floras result from the influence of the cool north Atlantic pro-

ducing severe long winters and short sharp summers, promoting herb vegetation but severely restricting tree growth.

The flora of the 'late-glacials', immediately pre-

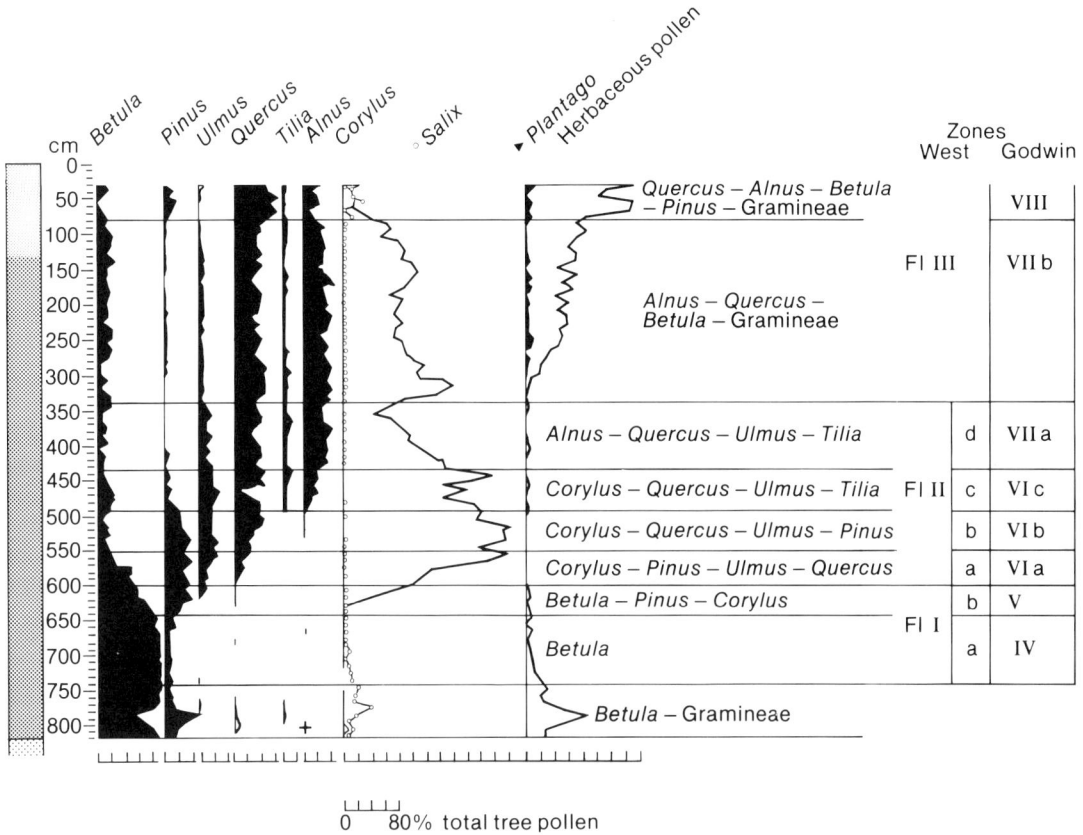

Fig. 2.13. Pollen diagram of the Flandrian at Hockham, Norfolk. (After Godwin & Tallantire 1951; Flandrian pollen zones added after West 1980b)

ceding interglacial sequences, are similar to those described above, but may show higher percentages of *Betula* and shrub pollen. Fluctuations of climate and vegetation within the sequence are known from the Anglian and Devensian 'late glacials'. The Late Devensian shows a marked amelioration of climate, the Windermere Interstadial, between 13 000 and 10 800 years B.P. Tree birch *Betula* shows a marked increase in this interstadial, indicating birch woodland, and juniper *Juniperus* was also widespread. In the south and east, pine *Pinus* woods may have been present. The interstadial was followed by a return to herb-dominated vegetational conditions (Pennington 1977).

Interstadial floras recording the development of woodland are also known from the Wolstonian (Brandon, Warwickshire) where birches were the only trees present (Kelly 1968), and from the Early Devensian of Chelford, Cheshire (Simpson & West 1958) (radiocarbon dated to about 60 800 years B.P.), and a few other sites, where *Betula–Pinus–Picea* forest, of a type now found in northern Finland, was present. In addition to this Chelford interstadial, an earlier period with coniferous woodland was recognized at Wretton, Norfolk (West *et al.* 1974); West 1977b; West 1980b).

3 Taxonomy and identification

In contrast to the practice when dealing with Tertiary and older fossil vertebrates, where the specialist works mainly with genera, in Pleistocene, as in living animals, the species is the basic taxonomic unit. Exactly what constitutes a species, even in present-day animals, is much debated. Nevertheless a useful working definition of the species is an interbreeding population which in the wild is genetically distinct from other populations; this distinction being maintained by behavioural or physiological factors, preventing interbreeding with other populations. The genetic differences may be expressed also as morphological differences. Generally in practice the taxonomist working with modern material defines species on morphological characters. The palaeontologist also defines species on morphological characters but is restricted to working with the hard parts of animals only. The latter limitation, however, is not very serious in the case of vertebrates since their skeletons yield so much information. In particular mammalian teeth are extensively used for taxonomic purposes in modern as well as fossil animals.

The fossil record for many Pleistocene mammals is sufficiently good to present problems in attempting to distinguish temporal species within continuous lineages, as well as on any one time plane. In older parts of the geological record, stratigraphical breaks often provide convenient temporal taxonomic boundaries. In the Pleistocene the species boundaries in a continuous lineage are best arbitrarily separated on stratigraphical grounds, as advocated by Joysey (1972).

If they are to have biological meaning, fossil species should be recognized on comparable morphological criteria to those used by zoologists working with living animals; a view emphasized for Pleistocene vertebrates, in that many of the species occurring as fossils are still extant.

Unfortunately, many Pleistocene vertebrate (mainly mammalian) species have been in the past, and continue to be, described on a purely typological basis, not taking into account the range of variation that occurs within modern species. Moreover, fossil species are frequently described on the basis of material scarcely different, or indistinguishable from that of living species.

Excessive 'splitting' of species has resulted in a confusing welter of names in the literature, especially discouraging to anyone new to the study of Pleistocene vertebrates. To err on the side of 'lumping' species together at least has the virtue that the simplified taxonomy is much easier to grasp.

According to the international rules of zoological nomenclature the valid name for a species, living or fossil, is the one first published, beginning with those in the tenth edition of Linnaeus' *Systema Naturae* of 1758. There are always disagreements, however, concerning the valid names of particular species, since in the case of older literature opinions differ as to what constitutes a publication, and it may not be clear to which material or animal an author was referring. Such questions can be submitted to the International Commission for Zoological Nomenclature for ruling.

Nowadays biometrical techniques are extensively used as an aid to both taxonomy and identification. When presenting biometrical data it is very important to state unambiguously exactly where each measurement was taken, preferably with an explanatory diagram. Brachyodont mammalian teeth are ideal for biometrical purposes because they cease to grow once formed. Hypsodont and continuously growing teeth, however, can also yield useful results. Mammalian bones substantially cease growing after the fusion of epiphyses, but some age-related morphological changes take place, especially some increase in width in mandibles and long bones in many taxa. The bones of birds also cease growing in adult animals. The bones of lower vertebrates continue to grow throughout life, and the size of an individual is a function of environmental conditions as well as age.

Single variables can be readily represented in histograms, and are especially useful for depicting changes with time (see Ch. 11).

Bivariate plots (scatter diagrams), in which any two sets of measured variables are plotted against one another on x and y axes, are a simple but very useful method of analysing biometrical data. Material of closely related taxa in a single fossil assemblage may plot separately because of differences in absolute size, and/or proportions, i.e. the populations lie on different allometric axes. It is necessary to plot all combinations of the measured variables since differences may be evident in certain plots and absent in others. There is commonly a strong correlation between certain morphological characters and size, when these are matched up, and this may allow all, or nearly all, specimens to be assigned to a particular taxon, even though the scatters overlap (Fig. 3.1). Sometimes, however no clear separation can be obtained, although it is clear from the high variance that more than one taxon is present, and here the use of multivariate techniques may be appropriate. Multivariate techniques, capable of coping simultaneously with several variables, necessitate the use of a computer, and can also be used to give much more sophisticated comparisons between samples than can be achieved by bivariate methods, but for most purposes the latter are usually adequate.

A complication, although of considerable interest in itself, is the occurrence of sexual dimorphism in

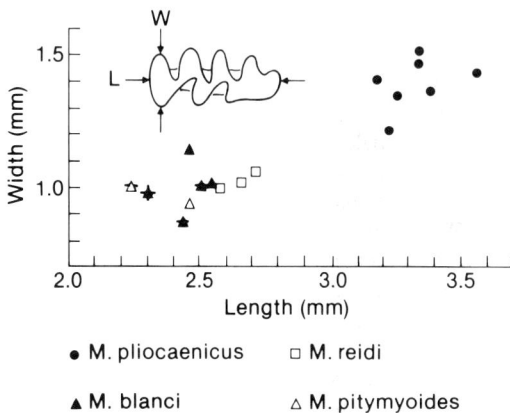

Fig. 3.2. Scatter diagram showing sexual dimorphism in metatarsals of the extinct bison *Bison priscus* (Middle Devensian, Isleworth, Middlesex).

size in many vertebrates including among birds: swans (Northcote 1980a) and in mammals: moles (Talpidae); bears (Ursidae); mustelids (Mustelidae); bovids (Bovidae); and deer (Cervidae), in which the males are larger (Kurtén 1969) (Fig. 3.2).

The figures and descriptions in this chapter are intended to give an impression of both the nature of the available material and of the characters useful in taxonomy and identification. Particular attention has been given to the Insectivora and Rodentia, since illustrations of these are not conveniently available elsewhere. For the identification of most fossil vertebrate material reference collections of both recent and fossil material, used in conjunction with relevant literature, are essential.

Accompanying the descriptions of fossil material in this chapter are sketch representations of many of the animals (mostly mammals) in life. The sketch restorations of extinct taxa are of course somewhat tentative except where there is evidence from exceptionally preserved soft tissue and/or artistic representation (cave art).

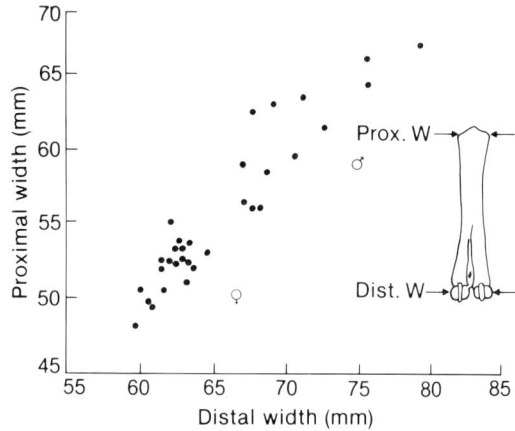

● M. pliocaenicus   □ M. reidi

▲ M. blanci   △ M. pitymyoides

Fig. 3.1. Scatter diagram of length vs width of the M_1 in an assemblage of Lower Pleistocene vole molars (Pastonian, West Runton, Norfolk).

Fishes: Class Osteichthyes

Freshwater fishes are abundant as fossils in British Pleistocene deposits, but have so far received little

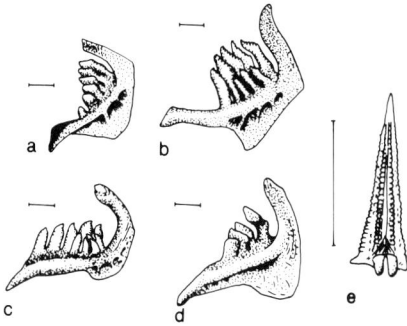

Fig. 3.3. Examples of freshwater fish material. (a–d) pharyngeal bones with teeth of modern cyprinid fishes. (Based on Spillman 1961) (a) roach *Rutilus rutilus*; (b) rudd *Scardinius erythropthalmus*; (c) barble *Barbus barbus*; (d) tench *Tinca tinca*; (e) dorsal spine of three-spined stickleback *Gasterosteus aculeatus* (Cromerian, West Runton, Norfolk). (Scales = 1 cm.)

attention. All of the taxa recorded still occur in Britain at the present day, but exotic fishes may well be discovered by serious study of available material.

Generic or specific identifications can often be made on the basis of vertebrae, scales or other skeletal elements. For example the vertebrae of the common eel *Anguilla anguilla* are characteristically laterally flattened, and the dorsal spines of the three-spined stickleback *Gasterosteus aculeatus* are highly distinctive (Fig. 3.3). The pointed teeth of pike *Esox lucius* are also fairly characteristic, and the jaw bones more so (Newton, 1882a).

The various species of Cyprinidae, the most abundant family of freshwater fishes in Europe, can be distinguished by their pharyngeal teeth. In many cases isolated teeth are sufficient but especially useful are entire pharyngeal bones (Fig. 3.3).

Pleistocene fishes have been described from many Continental localities, for example Voigtstedt, Thüringia, East Germany (Deckert & Karrer 1965).

Amphibians: Class Amphibia

Bones of frogs and toads are common fossils in small-vertebrate assemblages but no serious mod-

ern work has been done on Pleistocene Amphibia from the British Isles.

The considerable diversity in morphology of many modern European amphibian bones, especially the pelvic bone, posterior vertebra and some of the skull bones, allows identification of fossil material to generic and often specific level. Böhme (1977) has published excellent figures of several bones from a number of modern European frog and toad species. Detailed descriptions of fossil material from the Continent have been given for example by Młynarski and Ullrich (1975).

Reptiles: Class Reptilia

Reptiles are mostly rather rare fossils in the British Pleistocene. The finds of European pond tortoise *Emys orbicularis* (Fig. 3.4) have been reviewed recently by Stuart (1979), but otherwise no modern work has been done on this group.

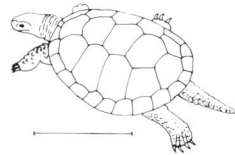

Fig. 3.4. European pond tortoise *Emys orbicularis*. (Scale = 10 cm.)

The bones, especially those of the shell, of *E. orbicularis*, the only non-marine chelonian represented in the Pleistocene of northern Europe, are unlikely to be confused with those of other animals (Fig. 3.5). Snake vertebrae, probably in the main attributable to grass snake *Natrix natrix*, occur in most small-vertebrate assemblages of interglacial age. With care, specific identification of snakes is probably possible on vertebrae and other skeletal elements. Material of lizards *Lacerta* spp., and slow-worm *Anguis fragilis* have also been reported from British Pleistocene deposits. Several species of snakes and lizards now exotic to the British fauna, would be expected to have occurred in England during interglacials, and reliable identifications of any of these as fossils would be of considerable interest.

(a) ⊢———⊣

(b) ⊢————————⊣

Fig. 3.5. European pond tortoise *Emys orbicularis*. (a) carapace (Flandrian, East Wretham, near Thetford, Norfolk); (b) part of plastron (Ipswichian, Swanton Morley, Norfolk). (Scales = 2 cm.)

Birds: Class Aves

Fossil bird bones are usually easy to recognize as such because of their light hollow structure and dis-

tinctive morphology of most of the bones. Bird skeletons are much less variable in size and morphology than those of mammals and the identification of bird bones to species usually relies on subtle differences. The problems are aggravated by the large number of bird species that could have been present at any one time in the past, bearing in mind the richness in species of the modern European avian fauna.

Reference collections of modern skeletal material are essential, and ideally one would need several individuals of each modern species to adequately represent intraspecific variation. Similarly it would be best if the record of any species from a locality were based on the identification of more than one skeletal element. Unfortunately, the rarity of bird bones at most sites means that many published species records are each based on a single bone fragment.

Newton (e.g. 1882a, 1883, 1891) described and figured many fossil bird bones. Recent studies of British Pleistocene birds have been made principally by Fraser and King (1954), Bramwell (e.g. 1960, 1964, 1977), Harrison (1978), 1979a, 1979b), Harrison and Cowles (1977), Harrison and Walker (1977) and Northcote (1980b, 1981). Detailed descriptions of birds from Continental sites have been

Fig. 3.6. Examples of birds, now extinct or with restricted distributions in the British Isles, recorded as fossils from Pleistocene deposits. (a) Dalmatian pelican *Pelecanus crispus*; (b) sarus crane *Grus antigone*; (c) common crane *Grus grus*; (d) great auk *Pinguinus impennis*; (e) eagle owl *Bubo bubo*; (f) ptarmigan *Lagopus mutus*. (Scale = 10 cm.)

given by a number of authors, e.g. Mourer Chauviré (1975a, 1975b), Jánossy (e.g. 1965). Most of the birds recorded from the Pleistocene of the British Isles are native species at the present day, although many of the fossil occurrences are well outside the modern distributions. In addition a few species now exotic to the British fauna are recorded (Fig. 3.6), and Harrison has claimed several extinct species based on fragmentary fossil material (see Chs. 7, 8).

Mammals: Class Mammalia

Mammals are by far the best represented and the most intensively studied of Pleistocene vertebrates, but nevertheless most mammal groups are badly in need of detailed modern study. Published works on particular orders and families are cited in the following pages in their appropriate sections. Descriptions,

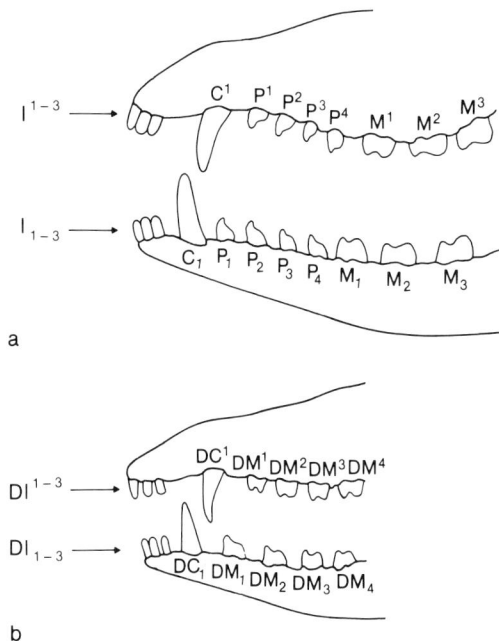

a

b

Fig. 3.7. The dentition (left side view) in a generalized placental mammal, showing nomenclature. A, permanent adult teeth; B, deciduous ('milk') teeth. I, incisor; C, canine; P, premolar; M, molar; DI, deciduous incisor; DC, deciduous canine; DM, deciduous 'molar' (premolar).

including figures, of vertebrate fossils from the Cromer Forest-bed Formation and the Lower Pleistocene were given by Newton (1882a, 1891).

Mammals show a great diversity in both morphology and size, a fact which facilitates identification of their skeletal remains. The presence of a permanent and complex dentition in most taxa is also of considerable value in taxonomy and identification. Their fossil record is sufficiently good for microevolutionary changes at generic and specific levels to be followed, for many lineages (Ch. 11).

The nomenclature used for mammalian teeth is illustrated in Fig. 3.7. In nearly all species of Pleistocene and living mammals the dentition is variously reduced from the generalized ancestral condition, but the same nomenclature applies; for example, if the first premolar (P_1) is absent the remaining premolars are numbered P_2, P_3, P_4.

Useful aids to identifying fossil mammal bones and teeth include Miller (1912), Schmid (1972) and Sissons and Grossman (1968). There is unfortunately, however, no substitute for comparative reference collections of modern and preferably also fossil material.

Insectivores: Order Insectivora

Hedgehogs: Family Erinacaeidae (Genus: Erinaceus) (Fig. 3.8)
Fossil hedgehogs are extremely rare in European Pleistocene deposits. A single M^1 is known from the Cromerian of West Runton. Sparse finds of early Flandrian age appear to be indistinguishable from *E. europaeus*.

Shrews: Family Soricidae (Genera: Sorex; Neomys; Beremendia; Crocidura) (Fig. 3.8)
Shrews are, next to voles, the most common small mammals in the British Pleistocene, and nearly all finds are referable to one of the several known species of *Sorex*.

The mandible is the part of the skeleton most often found in fossil form. That of *Neomys*, the water shrew, has a characteristically sturdy ascending ramus, slender articulation and smooth incisor (Fig. 3.9e). The extinct *Beremendia* is similar except that it is far larger than any other European shrew. Three molars constitute the only British material found to date (Fig. 3.9F). The *Neomys* from the Cromerian has been distinguished as an extinct species *N. newtoni* Hinton, on the grounds

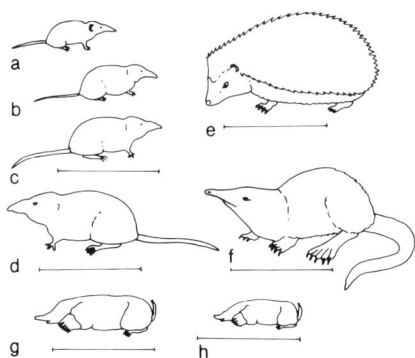

Fig. 3.8. British Pleistocene insectivores. (a) lesser white-toothed shrew *Crocidura suaveolens*; (b) common shrew *Sorex araneus*; (c) extinct shrew *Sorex savini* (sketch restoration); (d) extinct shrew *Beremendia fissidens* (sketch restoration); (e) hedgehog *Erinaceus europaeus*; (f) Russian desman *Desmana moschata*; (g) common mole *Talpa europaea*; (h) extinct mole *Talpa minor* (sketch restoration). (Scale = 10 cm.)

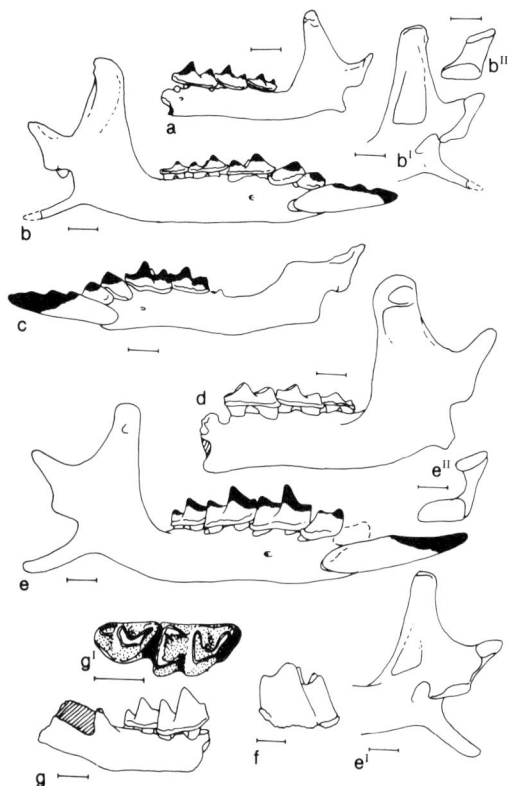

Fig. 3.9. Mandibles and teeth of British Pleistocene shrews. (a) *Sorex minutus*, partial left mandible (Ipswichian, Swanton Morley, Norfolk); (b) *Sorex araneus* right mandible; (b′) internal view of ascending ramus; (b″) posterior view of condyles (Ipswichian, Swanton Morley); (c) *Sorex runtonensis*, left mandible (Cromerian, West Runton, Norfolk); (d) *Sorex savini*, partial left mandible (Cromerian, West Runton); (e) *Neomys fodiens*, right mandible; (e′) internal view ascending ramus; (e″) condyles (recent, England); (f) *Beremendia* cf. *fissidens*, left molar (M_1 or M_2) (Cromerian, Sugworth, near Oxford); (g) *Crocidura* cf. *suaveolens*, partial right mandible, (g′) crown view of M_2 and M_3 (Ipswichian, Aveley, Essex). (Scales = 1 mm.)

of its smaller size and shape of mandibular articulation (Hinton 1911), from the living *N. fodiens*. Another fossil species described by Hinton as *N. browni* from Grays, Essex, may also be valid, but its stratigraphical position is uncertain.

The mandible in *Crocidura* spp., the white-toothed shrews, is readily distinguishable by such features as the reduced talonid on M_3, the large size of the teeth in proportion to the jaw and, as the name suggests, the absence of the striking pigmentation (red in fresh material; black or brown in many fossils) on the tooth cusps in most other shrew genera. Caution is needed, however, in using this last character, because the tooth staining is not always preserved in fossils. A large species of *Crocidura*, probably either *C. russula* or *C. leucodon* is recorded from the 'Vivian Vault' (possibly of Ipswichian age) of Tornewton Cave, Devon (Rzebik 1968) and a small species, almost certainly the lesser white-toothed shrew *C. suaveolens*, from the Ipswichian at Aveley, Essex (Fig. 3.9g).

The various species of *Sorex* can be distinguished on the basis of such characters as overall size, relative sizes of teeth and the position of the mental foramen in relation to the molars (Fig. 3.9).

Moles and desmans: Family Talpidae (Genera: Desmana; Talpa) (Fig. 3.8)
The Middle Pleistocene desmans from Britain (Schreuder 1940) are very similar to, and probably conspecific with, the living Russian desman *Desmana moschata*. They are not at all closely related to the other extant species *Galemys pyrenaica* Geoffroy, which now occurs much closer to Britain in northern Iberia and the Pyrenees.

In *D. moschata*, the skeleton is broadly mole-like, but very robust for such a small animal and most of the bones have unusual and distinctive shapes, and are therefore easily recognized. For example, the

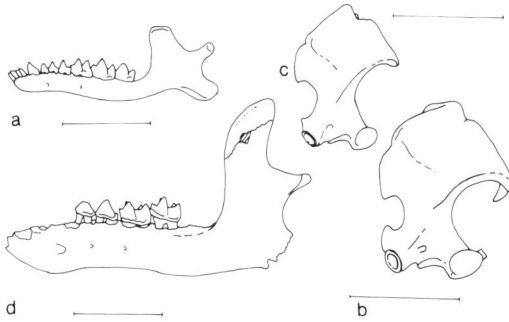

Fig. 3.10. British Pleistocene mole (a–c) and desman (d) material. (a) *Talpa europaea* left mandible (recent, Wales); (b) *T. europaea* humerus (recent, England); (c) *Talpa minor* humerus (Cromerian, Ostend, Norfolk); (d) *Desmana moschata* incomplete left mandible (Cromerian, West Runton, Norfolk). (Scales = 1 cm.)

caudal vertebrae are hexagonal in cross-section and are flanked by H-shaped chevron bones. The cheek teeth are again reminiscent of *Talpa*, although considerably larger (Fig. 3.10) but the incisors are highly modified – those on the premaxilla being reduced to one large canine-like tooth on either side.

A single P^4 from the Pastonian crag of West Runton, Norfolk, is referable to another as yet unnamed species of desman found in the Tiglian stage Tc 5 of Tegelen, the Netherlands (Freudenthal *et al.* 1976).

Moles of the genus *Talpa* are represented in the British Pleistocene by two species differing markedly in size: the extinct small *T. minor*, perhaps conspecific with one of the small present day species, and the much larger living common mole *T. europaea*. There is also a considerable degree of sexual dimorphism in size in both species, which can cause problems in identification of fossil material.

The bones of *Talpa* are highly distinctive, especially the figure-of-eight-shaped humerus (Fig. 3.10).

Bats: Order Chiroptera

Insectivorous bats: Suborder Microchiroptera
At present there are thirteen species of bat that actually breed in the British Isles, plus two more that occur as vagrants from the Continent. Because of their rarity as fossils in the British Pleistocene, however, they are not discussed in detail here. Dis-

tinction of genera and species can be made using dental characters (e.g. Brink 1967; Miller 1912), or the humerus (Felten *et al.* 1973).

Primates Order Primates

Hominids: Family Hominidae (Genus Homo)
All of the late Pleistocene hominid finds from Britain are attributable to modern man *Homo sapiens* (Mollison 1977). Neanderthal man may have been present at certain periods in the Upper Pleistocene, as he was on the Continent, but there are no British finds, apart from some fragmentary material from La Cotte de St Brelade, Jersey, attributed to the early part of the Last Cold Stage.

Earlier finds are represented solely by the famous skull from Swanscombe, Kent, of Hoxnian interglacial age. This material, comprising both parietals and the occipital, is generally similar to the much more complete female skull from Steinheim, southwest Germany, which probably dates from the same interglacial stage (Fig. 3.11). The only significant difference is that the Swanscombe skull fragments are much thicker and larger than the corresponding Steinheim bones, which suggests that the former is of a male.

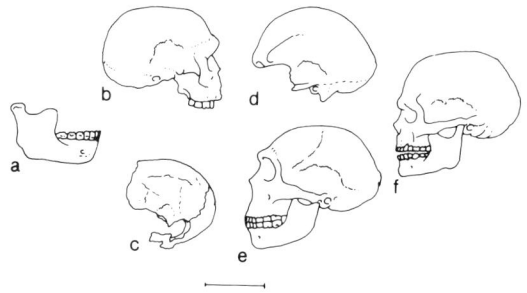

Fig. 3.11. Representative hominid fossils from the Pleistocene of Europe. All can be treated as variants of *Homo sapiens*. (a) mandible from Mauer, Heidelbergh, West Germany (probably Cromerian); (b) female skull from Steinheim, West Germany (Holsteinian); (c) partial male skull from Swanscombe, Kent (Hoxnian = Holsteinian); (e) partial skull of Neanderthal type from Ehringsdorf, Weimar East Germany (Eemian = Ipswichian); (e) skull of late Neanderthal type, France (early part of Last Cold Stage = Devensian); (f) skull of Cro-Magnon type, France (late part of Last Cold Stage). (Adapted from various sources) (Scale = 10 cm.)

Both skulls are thought to represent an early form of *H. sapiens* and show features which anticipate those of the Neanderthals (Stringer 1974). The Steinheim/Swanscombe man could be a very ancient ancestor of both Neanderthals and modern man. The people of the time in western Europe appear to have been larger than the earlier *H. erectus*, robustly built, with large brow ridges and relatively large jaws. Their brains were probably slightly smaller than those of modern man. The postcranial skeleton is unknown. Representative hominid skulls and mandibles from the Pleistocene of Europe are illustrated in Fig. 3.11.

Old World monkeys: Family Cercopithecidae (Genus Macaca) (Fig. 3.12)
The few finds of monkey from Britain are probably all attributable to the modern barbary ape *Macaca sylvana*. The postcranial bones are fairly easy to recognize as belonging to monkey, since they resemble human bones in miniature. The teeth are also generally similar to those of man (Fig. 3.13) although the canines in male *Macaca* are very large with deep grooves.

Lagomorphs: Order Lagomorpha

Pikas: Family Ochotonidae (Genus: Ochotona) (Fig. 3.12)

Fig. 3.12. British Pleistocene primate (a) and lagomorphs (b–d). (a) macaque *Macaca sylvana*; (b) rabbit *Oryctolagus cuniculus*; (c) mountain hare *Lepus timidus*; (d) steppe pika *Ochotona pusilla*. (Scales = 50 cm.)

In the British Pleistocene, pikas appear to be represented solely by the living species *Ochotona pusilla*. Pikas differ from other lagomorphs in their small size, and much shorter ears and hind legs. The cheek teeth, form of the mandible (Fig. 3.14), fenestration of the maxilla, presence of grooves on the upper incisors, and other skull characters, are as in all lagomorphs.

Hares and rabbits: Family Leporidae (Genera: Hypolagus, Oryctolagus, Lepus) (Fig. 3.12).
Considering their prominence in the present-day fauna of Europe, leporids are surprisingly rare in Pleistocene deposits. The record of the extinct *Hypolagus brachygnathus*, from the Norwich Crag of Bramerton, Norfolk, is based on a single P$_3$ (Mayhew 1975). It is distinguished from *Lepus* in

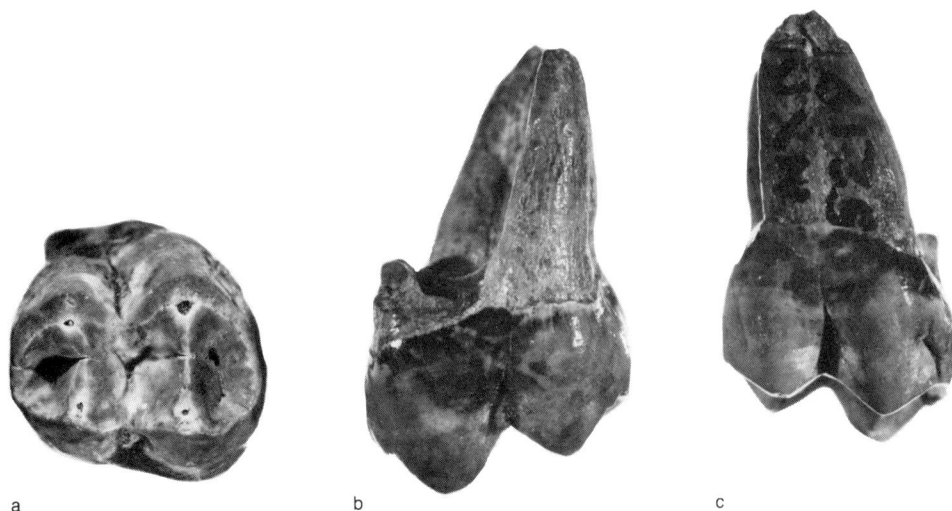

Fig. 3.13. Macaca cf. sylvana, macaque. Left M^2 (a) occlusal; (b) buccal; (c) lingual views. (Hoxnian, Hoxne, Suffolk). (After Singer *et al.* 1981) (Scale = 2 cm.)

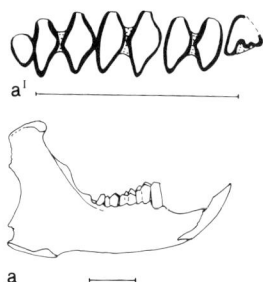

Fig. 3.14. (a) right mandible of steppe pika *Ochotona pusilla*; (a'), crown view of cheek teeth (Late? Devensian, Merlin's Cave, Wye Valley, Herefordshire). (Scale = 5 mm.)

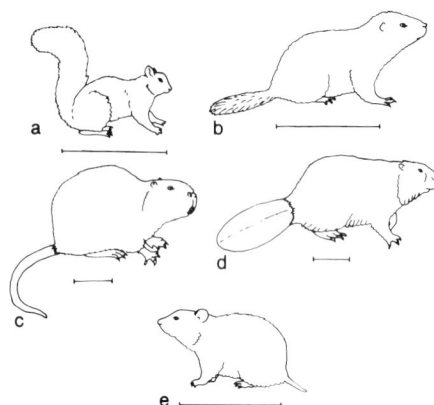

Fig. 3.15. British Pleistocene squirrels, beavers, and hamster. (a) red squirrel *Sciurus vulgaris*; (b) ground squirrel or suslik *Spermophilus* sp.; (c) extinct beaver *Trogontherium cuvieri* (sketch restoration); (d) beaver *Castor fiber*; (e) common hamster *Cricetus cricetus*. (Scales = 20 cm.)

that the median enamel fold only penetrates halfway across the tooth, whereas it extends to the lingual side in *Lepus*.

Mayhew (1975) has demonstrated that the rabbit *Oryctolagus cuniculus* is represented both in the Hoxnian Swanscombe deposits, and in early Flandrian sediments at Thatcham, Berkshire. Fossil remains of *Oryctolagus* are best distinguished from those of *Lepus* by biometrical techniques – the calcaneum being especially useful.

Of the two species of hare *Lepus timidus* and *L. capensis* occurring in Britain at the present day, only the former has been definitely recorded as a fossil (Mayhew 1975).

Rodents: Order Rodentia

Squirrels: Family Sciuridae (Genera: Sciurus; Spermophilus) (Fig. 3.15)

In the British Pleistocene Sciuridae are represented by rare arboreal squirrels (*Sciurus*) and more common ground squirrels, or susliks (*Spermophilus*).

Sciurus whitei is known in Britain from the type specimen a single fourth upper premolar from zone Cr III of the Cromerian (Hinton 1914). A humerus from Ostend, Norfolk, probably from zone Cr IV of the Cromerian (Newton 1882a), is also referable to *Sciurus*. The living British species *Sciurus vulgaris* is unknown as a fossil except for a few poorly stratified cave records.

Two species of *Spermophilus* (Fig. 3.16) with distinct dentitions are clearly represented by British material. The first, referred to the extinct *S. (Urocitellus) primigenius* Kormos by Sutcliffe and Kowalski (1976), but probably to be equated with a

Fig. 3.16. Upper cheek teeth of suslik *Spermophilus* cf. *undulatus* (Ipswichian, Crayford, Kent). (Scale = 1 mm.)

living Siberian species *S. undulatus* (Mayhew, 1975), is recorded from the early Anglian (Newton 1882b) and from Crayford, Kent – the latter probably of late Ipswichian age. The second species, again referred to an extinct species – *S. superciliosus* (Kaup) by Sutcliffe and Kowalski – but probably conspecific with the living *S. major* (Mayhew, 1975) is known from several Devensian localities. Unfortunately the taxonomy of living *Spermophilus* is still confused (although for a recent account see Corbet 1978) and it is not surprising that there are difficulties in sorting out fossil material.

Beavers: Family Castoridae (Genera: Castor; Trogontherium) (Fig. 3.15)

The two Pleistocene beavers, the living *Castor fiber* and the extinct *Trogontherium cuvieri*, can easily be distinguished on the basis of a number of characters in both dentition, skull and postcranial skeleton. In particular, the cheek-tooth pattern is quite different and those of *Trogontherium* lack cement (Fig. 3.17).

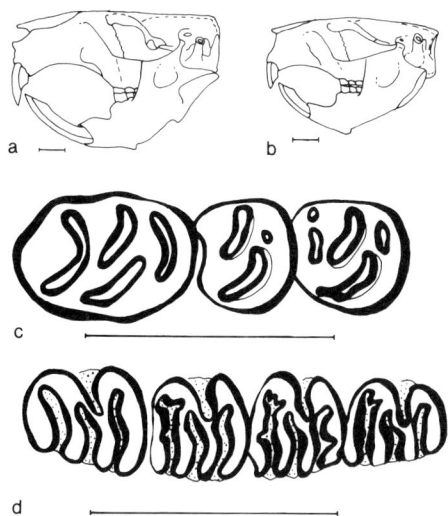

Fig. 3.17. (a) reconstruction of skull of extinct beaver *Trogontherium cuvieri*; (b) skull of beaver *Castor fiber*; (c) *T. cuvieri* crown view, lower left cheek teeth (P_4–M_2); (d) *C. fiber* crown view, lower right cheek teeth (P_4–M_3) (both Cromerian, West Runton, Norfolk). (a, b based on Mayhew 1978). (Scales = 2 cm.)

The incisors are disproportionately large in *Trogontherium*, they have a rounded anterior cross-section and the enamel is finely wrinkled. In *Castor* the smaller incisors have a flat face and the enamel is smooth.

Mayhew (1978) has shown that all *Trogontherium* remains from the Pleistocene of Western Europe belong to a single species, *T. cuvieri*. A small species, *T. minus*, is known from the Red Crag Nodule Bed (Pliocene) of Suffolk.

The areas for muscle attachment on the skull show that the jaw muscles in *Trogontherium* functioned rather differently to those of *Castor*. In *Trogontherium* the absence of the strong lateral processes on the tail vertebrae seen in *Castor*, indicate that the tail was not dorso-ventrally flattened as in the latter animal (Mayhew 1978).

Hamsters: Family Cricetidae (Genera: Cricetus; Allocricetus) (Fig. 3.15)
Hamsters are rare fossils in the British Pleistocene. As in mice the cheek teeth are low-crowned, but unlike mice the cusps are not paired but arranged alternately (Fig. 3.18).

Two species are known; the larger *Cricetus cricetus* (common hamster) is known from the

Fig. 3.18. Common hamster *Cricetus cricetus*, right upper molars (Cromerian, West Runton, Norfolk). (Scale = 2 mm.)

Cromerian (Newton 1909) and from the Glutton Stratum of Tornewton Cave, while the smaller referred to cf. *Allocricetus bursae*, an extinct species, by Sutcliffe and Kowalski (1976) is known from the Glutton Stratum of Tornewton Cave. It seems very likely that *A. bursae* will prove to be conspecific with one of the living small hamsters of the Palaearctic steppe.

Voles and lemmings: Family Cricetidae (Genera: Clethrionomys; Mimomys; Pliomys; Arvicola; Microtus; Pitymys; Lagurus; Lemmus; Dicrostonyx) (Fig. 3.19)
The voles and lemmings are today the most successful group of rodents throughout the Palaearctic region, and are among the most common, but not the most conspicuous, fossil mammals in British and European Pleistocene deposits. A review of

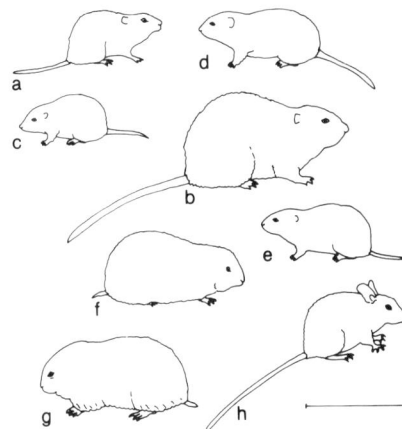

Fig. 3.19. British Pleistocene voles, lemmings and mouse. (a) bank vole *Clethrionomys glareolus*; (b) water vole *Arvicola terrestris*; (c) pine vole *Pitymys* sp.; (d) northern vole *Microtus oeconomus*; (e) field vole *Microtus agrestis*; (f) Norway lemming *Lemmus lemmus*; (g) arctic lemming *Dicrostonyx torquatus*; (h) wood mouse *Apodemus sylvaticus*. (Scale = 5 cm.)

British fossil species was given by Hinton (1926). This work is still very useful although the taxonomy rarely agrees with modern ideas. An up-to-date review, although lacking detailed descriptions of characters, is given by Sutcliffe and Kowalski (1976).

Voles and lemmings are all small, predominantly herbivorous mammals with high or very high crowned cheek teeth, wherein the cusps of the ancestral brachyodont cricetid have become elongated prisms, comprising a hard enamel rim surrounding a dentine core, which wear to produce a pattern of alternating triangles. In advanced species additional strength is provided by packing the valleys with crown cementum.

As in most mammals, the primitive condition was to form roots on the cheek teeth after completion of the crown, as is the situation in the living voles genus *Clethrionomys* and in the fossil genera *Mimomys* and *Pliomys*. An outstanding feature of microtines as a whole is parallel evolutionary trends towards increased hypsodonty. This was achieved, independently in different evolutionary lines, by retarding the timing of root formation in the cheek teeth until progressively later in the lifetime of the individual, until a point was reached where the teeth ceased to root altogether and the crowns became permanently growing. Since such teeth are continuously renewed, they are much better suited to dealing with grasses which are a widely available but highly abrasive food.

Experimental work by Koenigswald and Golenishev (1979) has shown that the non-rooted molars of small voles and lemmings (*Microtus, Dicrostonyx, Lagurus*) grow at the spectacular rates of 0.4–0.9 mm per week so that the entire tooth is replaced in 6–12 weeks. Therefore each animal uses 20–45 mm of tooth per year, and consumes between 4 and 13 crown heights in its short lifespan of about 12–18 months. By contrast, the rooted teeth of *Clethrionomys glareolus* grow (roots) by only 0.05 mm per week and the original crown height suffices for the lifetime of an individual.

When dealing with permanently growing vole cheek teeth it should therefore be borne in mind that the morphology and dimensions of a fossil specimen may depend to some extent on the age of the individual.

In most evolutionary lines this transition from rooted to permanently growing cheek teeth occurred within the lower Pleistocene as shown by finds from the Continent, but not recorded by British

material. In the water voles of the *Mimomys–Arvicola* lineage, however, the transition appears to have taken place within the Cromerian interglacial in Britain, and this and subsequent evolutionary changes can be followed therefore in considerable detail (Ch. 11).

The cheek teeth of the various genera of Pleistocene voles and lemmings can be readily distinguished on the basis of crown patterns, the presence or absence of roots (applicable to adult teeth only) and the presence or absence of crown cementum (Fig. 3.20).

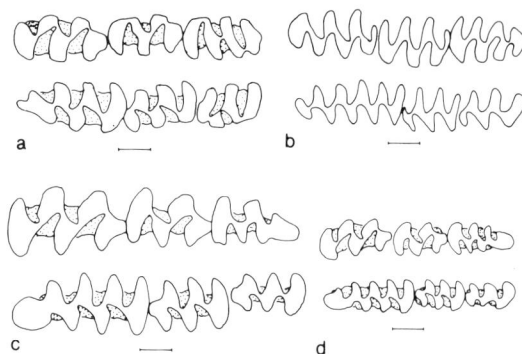

Fig. 3.20. Outline crown molar patterns in lemmings and voles. Right upper molars above; left lower molars below; anterior to left. (a) *Lemmus lemmus* (recent Norway); (b) *Dicrostonyx torquatus* (Devensian, Angel Road, Edmonton, North London); (c) *Arvicola terrestris* (recent, Shropshire); (d) *Microtus oeconomus* (recent, Norway).

Identification of species within a genus, however, is usually a matter for the specialist and is indeed often a matter of opinion. The anterior loop of the first lower molar (M_1) has a typical characteristic shape in several living species of *Microtus* (Fig. 3.21 a–c), but the intraspecific variation in this character is large and it may be impossible to assign many fossil M_1's to a particular species. Fossil assemblages which, as is often the case, contain more than one *Microtus* species can therefore present considerable problems.

The M_1's in *M. agrestis* and *M. arvalis* are identical in shape, but fortunately the second upper molar (M^2) of *M. agrestis* has an extra loop (Fig. 3.21h, i) which also distinguishes this species from all other Palaearctic *Microtus* species. Hall and Yalden (1978) have stressed the likelihood that many fossil *Microtus* M_1's have been misidentified. Canonical

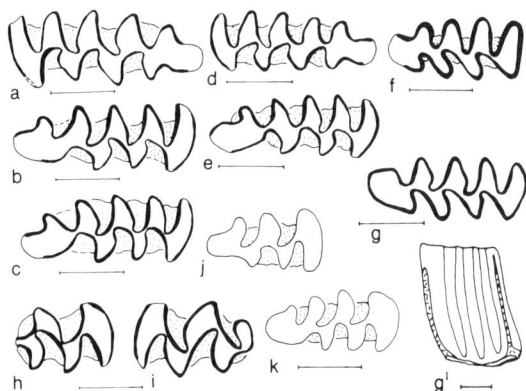

Fig. 3.21. Small-vole molars (crown views except g′). (a) right M₁ *Microtus* agrestis (Ipswichian, Swanton Morley, Norfolk); (b) left M₁ *Microtus oeconomus* (early Flandrian, Nazeing, Essex); (c) left M₁ *Microtus gregalis* (Middle Devensian, Isleworth, London); (d) right M₁ *Pitymys arvaloides*; (e) left M₁ *Pitymys gregaloides* (both Cromerian, West Runton, Norfolk) – note broad connection of first two triangles in genus *Pitymys*; (f) left M₁ *Clethrionomys glareolus* (Cromerian, Sugworth, near Oxford); (g) left M₁ *Pliomys episcopalis*; (g′) buccal view showing roots (Cromerian, Sugworth; (h) left M² *Microtus* sp. (Middle Devensian, Isleworth); (i) right M² *Microtus agrestis* (Ipswichian, Swanton Morley) – note extra posterior angle diagnostic of this species; (j), (k), left M³'s (outlines only) of (j), *Microtus nivalis* (recent, Switzerland) and (k) *M. oeconomus* (recent Norway) – note diagnostic simple form in *M. nivalis*. (Scales = 1 mm.)

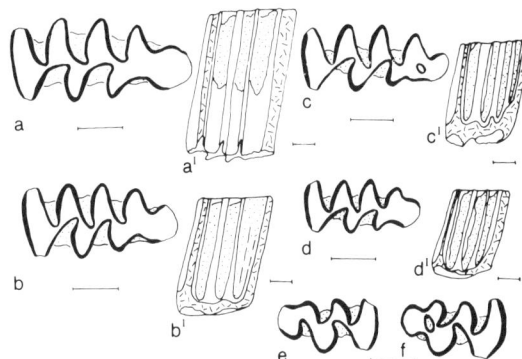

Fig. 3.22. Molars in the voles *Mimomys* and *Arvicola*. (a–f crown views, a′–d′ buccal views). (a, a′), right M₁ *Arvicola terrestris* (early Flandrian, Nazeing, Essex); (b, b′), right M₁ *Mimomys savini* (Cromerian, West Runton, Norfolk); (c, c′), right M₁ *M. pliocaenicus* (Pastonian, West Runton); (d, d′), right M₁ *M. blanci* (Pastonian, West Runton; (e) right M³ *M. savini* (Cromerian, West Runton); (f) right M³ *M. pliocaenicus* (Pastonian, West Runton) – note enamel islet in the latter. (Scales = 1 mm.)

variates analyses of measurements made on samples of modern material of known species by these authors suggests that only *M. oeconomus* can be reliably separated on the M₁, although their measurements probably do not adequately represent the morphology of the anterior loop.

Microtus nivalis (snow vole) has been claimed to occur in the British Pleistocene on the basis of M₁'s (Sutcliffe & Kowalski 1976), but no site has yet yielded a specimen of the simple upper third molar (M³), which is diagnostic of this species (Fig. 3.21j, k). The M₁'s referred to *M. nivalis* are very probably variants of *M. oeconomus* (northern vole).

Cheek teeth of the pine vole, genus *Pitymys*, are distinguished by the broad confluency of the dentine spaces immediately behind the anterior loop (Fig. 3.21d, e). Two species, *P. arvaloides* Hinton and *P. gregaloides* Hinton, have been recognized on the basis of the anterior loop shape on M₁, and con-

trary to the author's earlier opinion (Stuart 1975) this distinction is probably valid. It is possible, however, that *P. arvaloides* is conspecific with the living *P. subterraneus*.

The M₁ in the voles *Mimomys* and *Arvicola* is simpler than in the other genera, with only three closed triangles between the anterior and posterior loops (Figs. 3.20c; 3.22). The Lower Pleistocene species of *Mimomys* have recently been revised by Mayhew and Stuart (in preparation). Of the six taxa recognized, all except *M. newtoni* have thicker enamel on the convex sides of the angles, and in all the molars became rooted at some time in the life of the individual. *M. pliocaenicus* is a large species with abundant crown cementum on the molars. Both M₁ and M³ have enamel islets which persist until after the formation of the roots and M₁ also has a '*Mimomys* fold'. *Mimomys rex* is distinguished from the former mainly by its very large size. *Mimomys blanci* is hypsodont and lacks the enamel islet in M₁ (Fig. 3.22d) although it is present in M³. *Mimomys newtoni* is distinguished by the pattern of enamel thickness, which is as in *Microtus* and *Pitymys*, lack of cementum, and absence of islet on M₁. *Mimomys reidi* has little crown cementum and has both islet and '*Mimomys*' fold on M₁, although the former disappears in early stages of wear in some populations. Lastly, *M. pitymyoides* is characterized by considerable confluency between the dentine spaces.

The genus *Mimomys* survived well into the Cromerian in the form of the advanced species *M. savini* in which the molars are very hypsodont, although they continued to root late in the life of the individual. The '*Mimomys* fold', and very exceptionally even the enamel islet, persist in some unrooted teeth. The M^3 lacks an islet and is as in *Arvicola* (Fig. 3.22d). The genus *Arvicola* is distinguished from *Mimomys* by a complete absence of roots on the molars. The stratigraphically earliest form of *Arvicola*, from the end of the Cromerian interglacial, still retains a '*Mimomys* fold' in most M_1's, as well as thicker enamel on the convex sides of the angles as in *M. savini* – its immediate ancestor. Later forms show loss of the '*Mimomys* fold'. There is a gradual increase in size from the Cromerian to the Early Devensian and the latest forms show variation in different populations between molars with the enamel thicker in the concave side, as in modern *Arvicola terrestris*, through all intermediates to those with the enamel thicknesses as in *Mimomys*. It seems convenient at present to include all these voles under *A. cantiana*, although a case could be made for splitting off the earliest forms. The later Devensian and Flandrian water voles are larger and always have enamel thicker on the concave sides of the angles. These are probably all of modern water vole *A. terrestris*, although the possibility of the other living species *A. sapidus* occurring in the British Pleistocene should be borne in mind. These two species can only be distinguished on the basis of skull morphology (Corbet 1966). For further details see Chapter 11.

The molar pattern and lack of crown cementum in the arctic lemming *Dicrostonyx torquatus* easily distinguish its remains from those of other microtines (Fig. 3.20). The molars of the Norway lemming *Lemmus lemmus* are, however, also paralleled by those of the wood lemming *Myopus schisticolor*, which differs from the former only in its smaller size. Because fossil molars of *Lemmus/Myopus* pattern from Pleistocene deposits seem uniformly large, they have been referred by nearly all authors to *L. lemmus*.

The molars in *Lagurus* have a distinctive open pattern and lack crown cementum (Kowalski 1967).

Mice: Family Muridae (Genera: Apodemus; ?Micromys) (Fig. 3.19)
In Britain, Pleistocene murids appear to be represented by only one indigenous species, the wood mouse *Apodemus sylvaticus*. In England at the present day it is accompanied by another sympatric and very closely related species, the yellow-necked mouse *A. flavicollis* Melchior. The pattern of the cheek teeth in both species is very similar (Fig. 3.23), but differs from that of other species of *Apodemus*. *A. flavicollis* has been reported from certain cave and fissure deposits, probably of Flandrian date (Sutcliffe & Kowalski 1976).

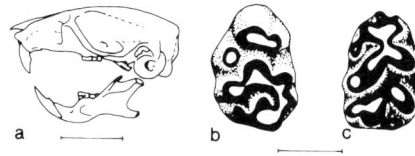

Fig. 3.23. Material of wood mouse *Apodemus sylvaticus*. (a) side view of skull (recent) (Scale = 1 cm.); (b) M^1; (c) M_1 (Ipswichian, Swanton Morley, Norfolk). (Scale = 1 mm.)

The house mouse *Mus musculus* and the two species of rat *Rattus rattus* and *R. norvegicus*, now found in Britain, are of course not native animals, having been unwittingly spread by man from their original homes (see Ch. 10). The status of the last British murid to be considered, the harvest mouse *Micromys minutus*, is also uncertain. It is unknown as a fossil in good stratigraphical context. This might simply reflect rarity of preservation, or alternatively introduction by man in the Flandrian.

Carnivores: Order Carnivora

Dogs: Family Canidae (Genera: Canis, Vulpes; Alopex; Xenocyon) (Fig. 3.24)
Most of the canid fossil specimens from the British Pleistocene are of wolves or foxes. Older finds, mainly from caves, were monographed by Reynolds (1902–12).

The Canidae have a characteristic rather unspecialized dentition which combines blade-like carnassial teeth, for shearing through flesh, with fairly broad post-carnassial molars which can cope with vegetable food.

Fig. 3.24. British Pleistocene canids. (a) extinct dhole *Xenocyon lycaonoides* (restored as recent *Cuon* sp.); (b) wolf *Canis lupus*; (c) red fox *Vulpes vulpes*; (d) arctic fox *Alopex lagopus*. (Scales = 1 m.)

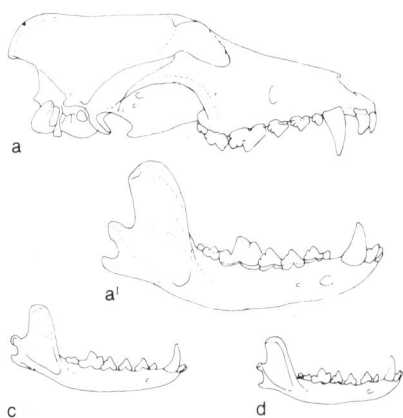

Fig. 3.25. Canid skull and mandibles. (a, a') skull and mandible *(Canis lupus*; (c) mandible of *Vulpes vulpes*; (d) mandible of *Alopex lagopus* (all recent, Europe). (Based on Miller 1912) (Scale = 10 cm.)

The dentitions and skeletons of the wolf *Canis lupus*, red fox *Vulpes vulpes* and arctic fox *Alopex lagopus* differ chiefly in size (Fig. 3.25). The form of *C. lupus* in the Cromerian, and probably also the Hoxnian in England, was smaller than that occurring in the Upper Pleistocene, and has been assigned to the subspecies *C. lupus mosbachensis*.

The earliest material to be referred to domestic dog in Britain comes from the early Flandrian Mesolithic site of Star Carr, Yorkshire, and consists of a partial skull plus a tibia and femur. The skull is distinguished from that of *C. lupus* by its small size and overlapping premolars (Degerbøl 1961).

A large canid mandible from Westbury-sub-

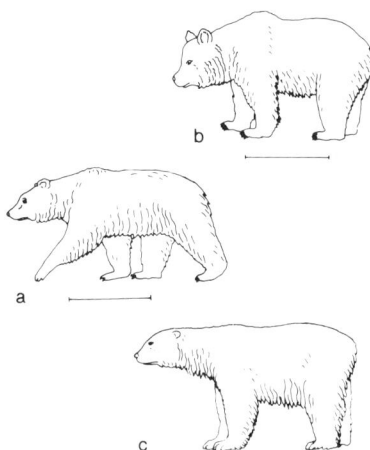

Fig. 3.26. British Pleistocene bears. (a) brown bear *Ursus arctos*; (b) cave bear *U. spelaeus* (sketch restoration); (c) polar bear *U. maritimus*. (Scales = 1 m.)

Mendip has been referred to the extinct genus and species *Xenocyon lycaonoides* by Bishop (1974).

Bears: Family Ursidae (Genus: Ursus) (Fig. 3.26)
Bears are probably the commonest fossil Carnivora in the British Pleistocene, occurring at open sites as well as in caves. The bones are mostly readily distinguished from those of other animals and the large low-crowned, broad, bunodont cheek teeth with their wrinkled enamel (Fig. 3.27) are unlikely to be confused with anything except those of *Sus*, but even here the resemblance is superficial (cf. Fig. 3.53).

The extinct cave bear *Ursus spelaeus* and its only marginally separable precursor *U. deningeri* both show the very distinctive doming of the forehead and loss of the anterior premolars which readily distinguish them from the living brown bear *U. arctos* (Kurtén 1968). (Figs. 3.27–3.29).

Unstratified but rather complete Flandrian material of brown bear *U. arctos* was figured by Reynolds (1902–12).

An ulna of probable Devensian age from Kew, London has been referred by Kurtén (1964) to polar bear *U. maritimus*. It is, however, larger than specimens of any modern bear species and of any European fossil bear. The identification is based on biometrical comparisons and the morphology of the semi-lunar notch and olecranon process.

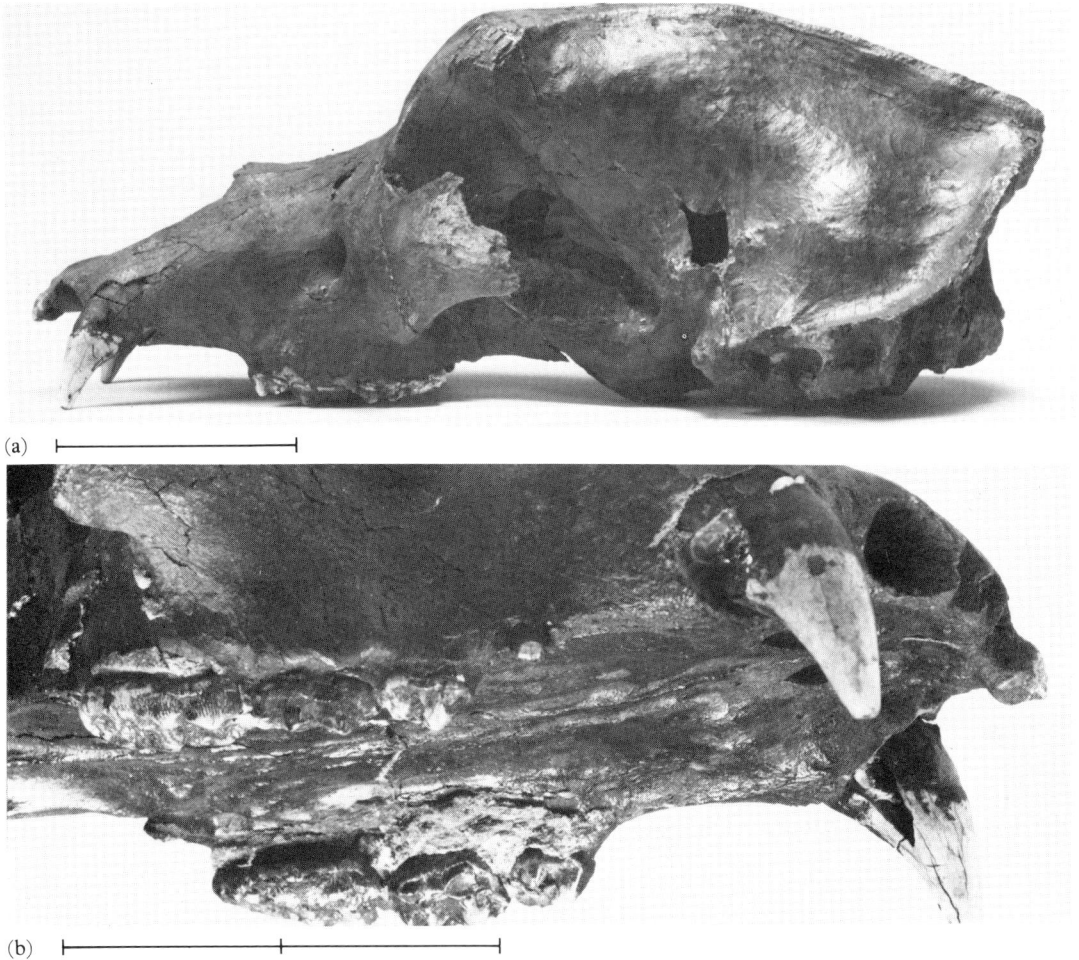

Fig. 3.27. (a) skull and (b) upper dentition of extinct bear *Ursus deningeri* (probably Cromerian, Bacton, Norfolk). (Scale = 10 cm.)

Fig. 3.28. Skull of cave bear *Ursus spelaeus* (Hoxnian, Swanscombe, Kent). (Scale = 10 cm.)

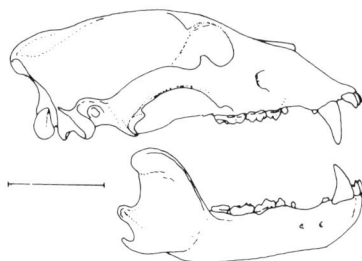

Fig. 3.29. Skull and mandible of brown bear *Ursus arctos* (recent, Europe) (based on Miller 1912). (Scale = 10 cm.)

Mustelids: Family Mustelidae (Genera: Mustela; Martes; Pannonictis; Gulo; Meles; Lutra; Aonyx) (Fig. 3.30)
The Mustelidae are the most varied family within the Carnivora. The predominantly carnivorous species, weasel *Mustela nivalis*, stoat *M. erminea*, martens *Martes* spp., otter *Lutra lutra*, have rather reduced dentitions adapted for slicing flesh, whereas in the more vegetarian forms, glutton *Gulo gulo* and badger *Meles meles*, the molars are broadened for crushing (Fig. 3.31). Illustrations of a number of poorly stratified finds were given by Reynolds (1902–12).

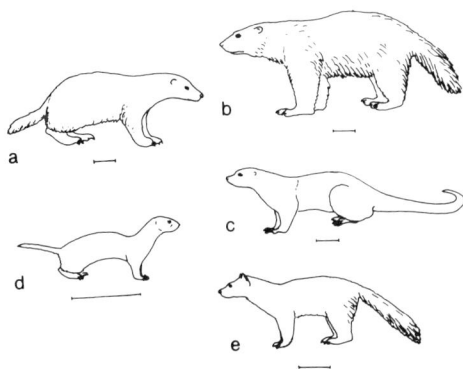

Fig. 3.30. British Pleistocene mustelids. (a) badger *Meles meles*; (b) glutton or wolverine *Gulo gulo*; (c) otter *Lutra lutra*; (d) weasel *Mustela nivalis*; (e) marten *Martes martes*. (Scale = 10 cm.)

Fig. 3.31. Mustelid mandibles. (a) *Gulo gulo* and (b) *Martes martes* (both recent Europe). (Based on Miller 1912) (Scales = 2 cm.)

The Lower and early Middle Pleistocene form of glutton in Europe, *Gulo schlosseri*, has been distinguished from the living species *G. gulo* by the greater size of the latter (Kurtén 1968). The *G. gulo* from Tornewton Cave, Devon, is about the same size as modern Fennoscandian specimens but smaller than those dating from the Last Cold Stage (Kurtén 1973).

According to Kurtén, the marten of the Cromerian interglacial is the extinct *Martes vetus*, which was succeeded in the Upper Pleistocene by the living pine marten *M. martes*.

The clawless otters *Aonyx* spp. differ from Lutra in having broad blunt-cusped teeth adapted for crushing crustaceans and molluscs. The form from the Lower Pleistocene of Bramerton, Norfolk, described as *A. reevei* Newton, is thought by Kurtén (1968) to be possibly conspecific with the Continental Villafranchian (Pliocene or Lower Pleistocene) species *A. bravardi* Pomel. A later form from the Otter Stratum of Tornewton Cave, Devon, has been referred to another extinct species *A. antiqua* Blainville, which according to Kurtén (1968) is more advanced than the Lower Pleistocene form.

The various species of *Mustela* can be distinguished osteologically chiefly by size. Care must be taken, however, in making identifications on this basis since all species show a high degree of sexual dimorphism in size (males are larger).

A single lower canine, from the type Cromerian of West Runton, figured by Newton (1882a) as *Phoca* sp., was referred by Schreuder (1935) to the extinct mustelid genus *Pannonictis*.

Hyaenas: Family Hyaenidae (Genera: Crocuta; Hyaena) (Fig. 3.32)
In both living and fossil spotted hyaena *Crocuta crocuta* the post-carnassial molars are reduced or lost, and the lower carnassial (M_1) is two-cusped as in felids. The canines are rather small but the premolars have been modified into massive conical struc-

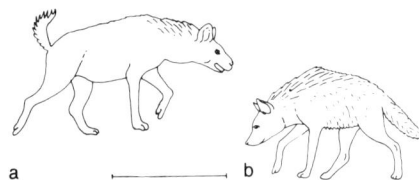

Fig. 3.32. British Pleistocene hyaenas. (a) spotted hyaena *Crocuta crocuta*, and (b) extinct hyaena *Hyaena brevirostris* (restored as recent *H. striata*). (Scale = 1 m.)

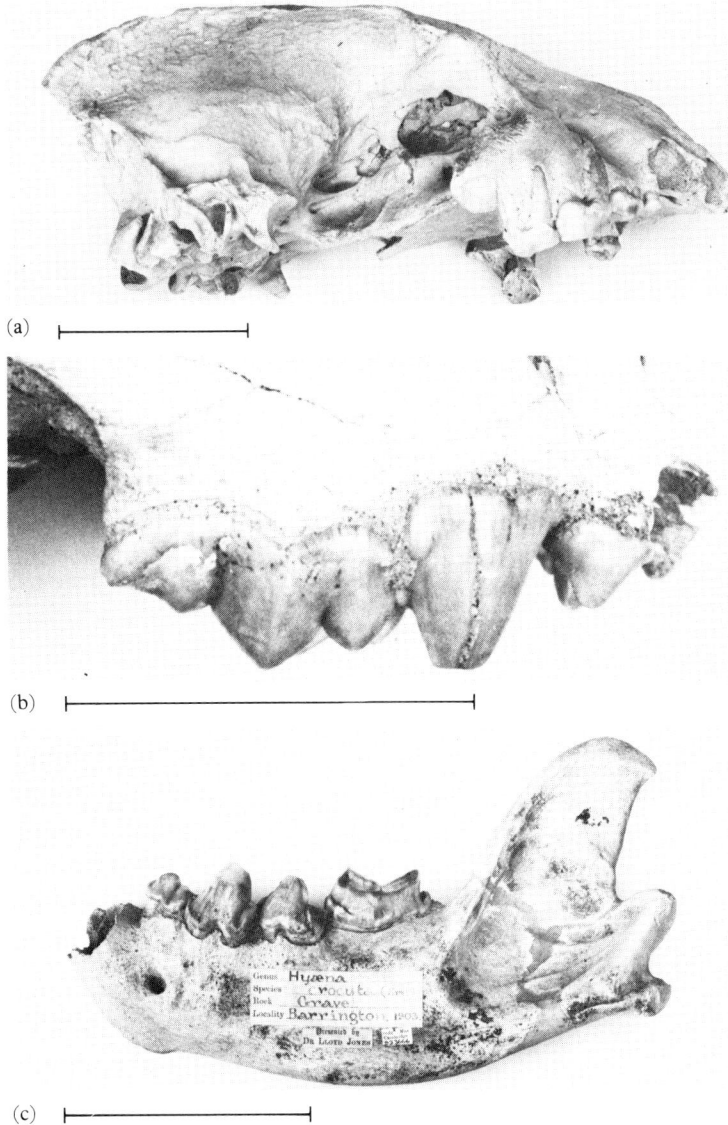

(a)

(b)

(c)

Fig. 3.33. Spotted hyaena *Crocuta crocuta* (Ipswichian, Barrington, Cambridgeshire). (a) skull; (b) right upper dentition; (c) left mandible. (Scales = 5 cm.)

tures adapted for crushing bones (Fig. 3.33). The unity of the British Pleistocene fossil species with living African *C. crocuta* was demonstrated by Kurtén (1958). Kurtén (1967) has shown that in Devensian *C. crocuta* from Kent's Cavern for example the second premolar is shorter, and the third longer than in a sample of Ipswichian age from Tornewton Cave, Hyaena Stratum.

The other extant genus *Hyaena*, is represented by two closely related extinct species *H. perrieri* from the Lower Pleistocene and *H. brevirostris* from the Cromer Forest-bed Formation (Kurtén 1968).

They differ from *C. crocuta* mainly in the less high-crowned premolars (Fig. 3.34).

Cats: Family Felidae (Genera: Panthera; Homotherium; Felis) (Fig. 3.35)

The cats are the most specialized flesh-eaters among the Carnivora, with extreme reduction and loss of the tubercular molars. Also characteristic is the lower carnassial (M_1) which in felids is simplified, by reduction of the trigonid, to a narrow two-cusped blade. They are generally rather rare as Pleistocene fossils. Older finds mainly from caves were illustrated by Dawkins and Sanford (1866–72).

The dentitions of lion *Panthera leo* (Fig. 3.36), leopard *P. pardus*, lynx *Felis lynx* and wild cat *F. sylvestris*, although generally similar, can be distinguished in fossil material mainly on overall size. A single P_4 of a small cat from West Runton (Cromerian) has been identified as *Felis* cf. *lunensis* by Kur-

tén (1965). The mandible of a large cat from West-bury-sub-Mendip has been referred to the extinct leopard *Panthera gombaszogensis* (Bishop 1974).

The extinct sabre-tooths *Homotherium sainzelli* and *H. latidens* show extraordinary modifications of the dentition and mandible (Fig. 3.37). The upper canines are very large, thin sword-like teeth with finely serrated cutting edges. The mandible has a

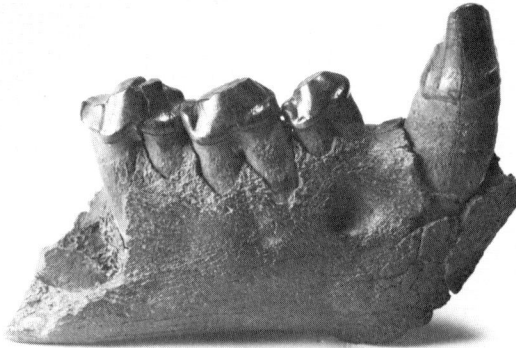

Fig. 3.34. Partial right mandible of extinct hyaena *Hyaena brevirostris* (probably Cromerian, Bacton). (Scale = 5 cm.)

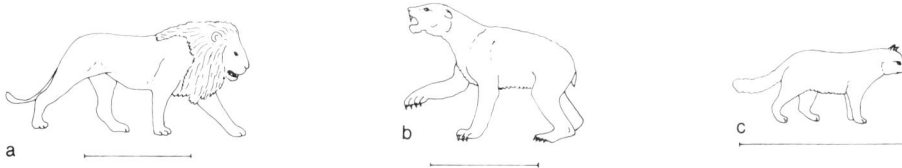

Fig. 3.35. British Pleistocene cats. (a) lion *Panthera leo*; (b) sabre-tooth *Homotherium latidens* (sketch restoration, based on Kurtén; (c) wild cat *Felis sylvestris*. (Scales = 1 m.)

Fig. 3.36. Skull of lion *Panthera leo* (partly restored)? (Ipswichian, Crayford, Kent). (Scale = 10 cm.)

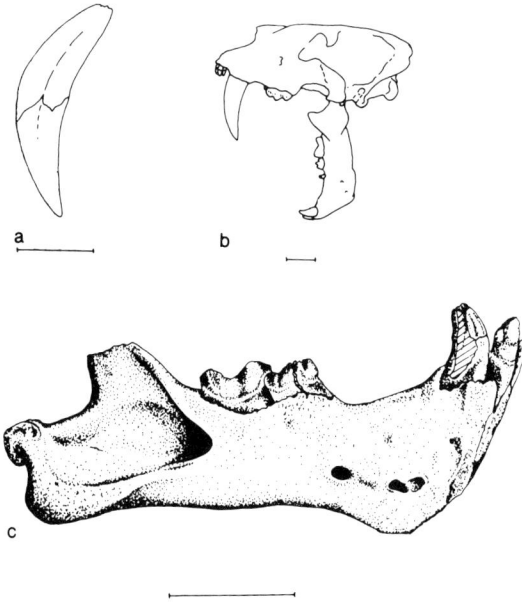

Fig. 3.37. (a) upper canine of sabre-tooth *Homotherium latidens* (Cromer Forest-bed Formation, Bacton, Norfolk) – the tooth is thin and flat with finely serrated cutting edges; (b) skull and mandible of *H. sainzelli* (Lower Pleistocene, Sénèze, France) (Based on Kurtén 1968); (c) right mandible of *H. latidens* (probably Cromerian, Kessingland, Norfolk). (Based on Backhouse 1886). (Scales = 5 cm) – (approx. for b.)

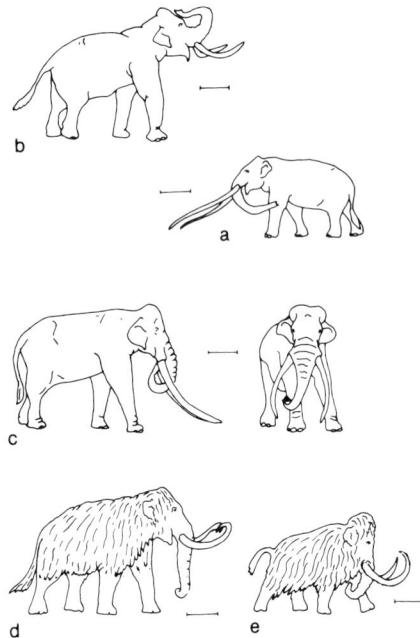

Fig. 3.38. British Pleistocene proboscideans (sketch restorations based on Osborn 1936, 1942). (a) gomphothere mastodont *Anancus arvernensis*; (b) extinct elephant *Archidiskodon meridionalis*; (c) straight-tusked elephant *Palaeoloxodon antiquus*; (d) extinct elephant *Mammuthus trogontherii*; (e) woolly mammoth *Mammuthus primigenius*. (Scales = 1 m.)

flange anteriorly to protect the canines from breakage when the jaws are closed, and the jaw articulation is such that the mouth could probably have been opened to more than 90°, leaving the canines free for slashing and slicing prey. The two Pleistocene species differ only in the size of the upper canines which are smaller in *H. latidens* (Kurtén 1968).

Proboscideans: Order Proboscidea

Gomphothere Mastodonts: Family Gomphotheriidae (Genus: Anancus) (Fig. 3.38)
True mastodons of the genus *Zygolophodon* only survived until the Upper 'Villafranchian' (Upper Pliocene) in Europe, and molar teeth of *Z. borsoni* are confined to the Red Crag Nodule Bed (Pliocene) in Britain.

A fairly common Lower Pleistocene fossil in England, however, is *Anancus arvernensis*, a gomphothere mastodont, which has low-crowned bunodont molars, superficially quite different to those of elephants (Fig. 3.39).

Elephants: Family Elephantidae (Genera: Archidiskodon; Palaeoloxodon; Mammuthus) (Fig. 3.38)
The bones and teeth of elephants are the most spectacular of Pleistocene mammal fossils, but their study presents many problems. The British Pleistocene elephants were monographed in detail by Adams (1877–81), and there has been no such comprehensive study since then. The straight-tusked elephant *Palaeoloxodon antiquus* skeleton found at Upnor, Kent, which is probably of Ipswichian age, was however described and figured in some detail by Andrews (1928).

Much information on fossil Proboscidea is to be found in the two large and formidable volumes published by Osborne (1936, 1942) but the tax-

Fig. 3.39. Molar of gomphothere mastodont *Anancus arvernensis* (Lower Pleistocene, Norwich Crag – stage unknown, Horstead, Norfolk). (Scale = 5 cm.)

onomy and nomenclature is now largely out of date. A more recent revision of the Elephantidae was attempted by Maglio (1973).

Azzaroli (1966, 1977a) has described distinctive skull characters for the four currently recognized species of elephant in the European Pleistocene (Figs. 3.40, 3.41). Unfortunately, fossil elephant skulls are extremely rare and those that have been recovered are generally crushed and distorted to varying degrees, and most work on fossil elephants utilizes the molar teeth, which are far less satisfactory than skulls for taxonomic purposes.

An elephant molar consists of a number of laterally elongated enamel rings each with a dentine core with the intervening spaces packed with crown cementum; the whole forming an efficient shearing and grinding mechanism. Elephants have a peculiar method of tooth replacement, in which as each molar wears down it is displaced by a fresh molar from behind, to a total of six for each jaw half. Two systems of tooth nomenclature are used. In the first of these, the one used here, the molars are simply numbered in succession (e.g. M_1, M_6), whereas in the other method the first three are regarded as deciduous molars (e.g. DM_1, DM_3) and the last three as permanent molars (e.g. M_1, M_3).

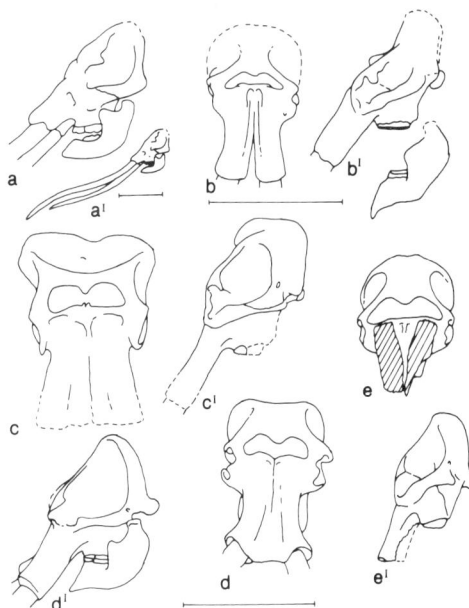

Fig. 3.40. Reconstructions of proboscidean skulls (a, a′), *Anancus arvernensis*; (b, b′), *Archidiskodon meridionalis*; (c, c′), *Palaeoloxodon antiquus*; (d, d′), *Mammuthus trogontherii*; (e, e′), *Mammuthus primigenius*. (a based on Osborne 1936; b–d based on Azzaroli 1966).

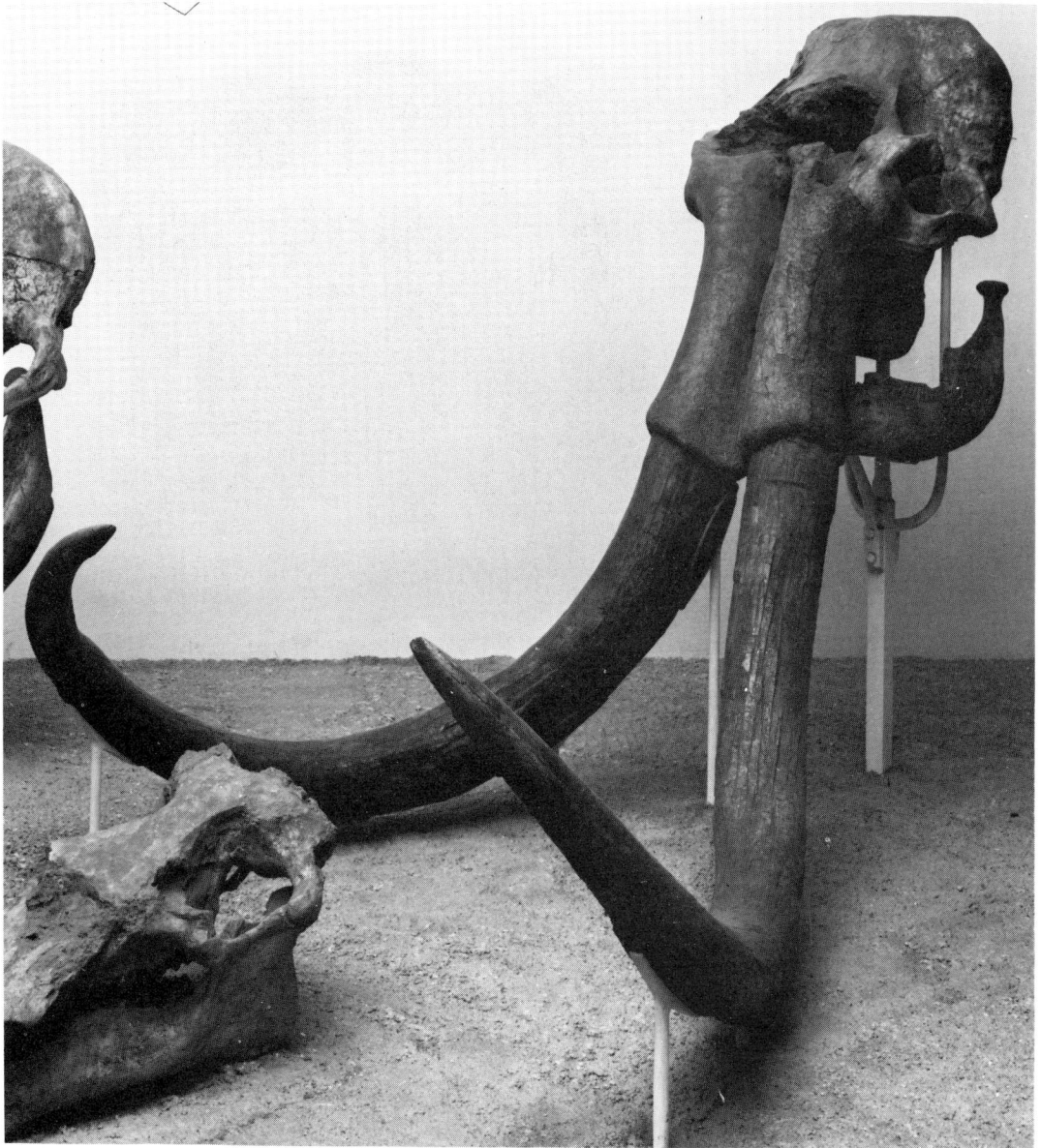

Fig. 3.41. Skull of mammoth *Mammuthus primigenius* (Ipswichian, Ilford, Essex). Base of tusk to crest of occiput is about 1.2 m.

Dental characters can be used to distinguish the molars of the European Pleistocene elephants (Figs. 3.42–3.44), but these teeth are extremely variable and there is a high prevalence of pathologically deformed specimens. The problems of identifying specimens are often further aggravated by the uncertainty of precisely which tooth in the series M^{1-6} or M_{1-6} is represented, especially when the fossil molar is incomplete, as is usually the case.

The large numbers of elephant molars from the Cromer Forest-bed Formation (CF-bF) include specimens referable to *Archidiskodon meridionalis*, *Palaeoloxodon antiquus* and *Mammuthus trogontherii*, with various apparent intermediate forms. This may perhaps in part result from the evolution of the two latter species from *A. meridionalis* within the long periods of time represented by the CF-bF. Unfortunately the CF-bF elephant material comes

Fig. 3.42. Lower molar of extinct elephant *Archidiskodon meridionalis* (Bramertonian, Bramerton, Norfolk). Note the few widely spaced plates and thick enamel. (Scale = 5 cm.)

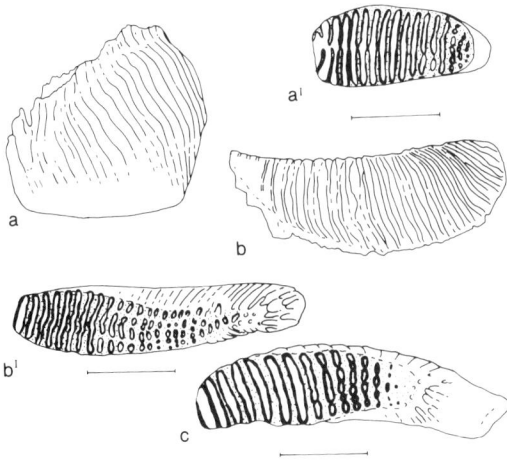

Fig. 3.43. Mammoth molars. (a′, b′) side views rest crown views. (a, a′), right upper molar (M^6) of *Mammuthus primigenius* (probably Devensian, dredged from North Sea); (b, b′) right lower molar (M_6) of *M. primigenius* (Devensian, Broxbourne, Hertfordshire); (c) left lower molar of *M. trogontherii* (early Middle Pleistocene, Süssenborn, East Germany) – note wider spacing of plates in the latter. (Scales = 10 cm.)

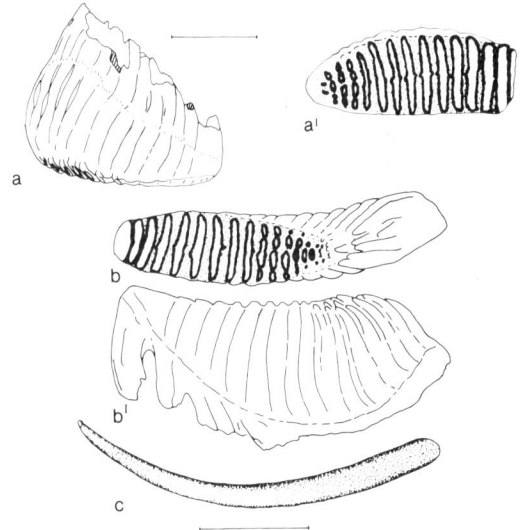

Fig. 3.44. Teeth of straight-tusked elephant *Palaeoloxodon antiquus*. (a, a′), side and crown views of upper molar (M^6); (b, b′) right lower molar (M^6) (both Hoxnian, Clacton, Essex) (Scale = 10 cm); (c) tusk (Hoxnian, Swanscombe, Kent) (Scale = 1 m.)

from several stratigraphical horizons and few specimens have been related to particular stages (Chs. 6, 7).

The gently curved tusks of the straight-tusked elephant *Palaeoloxodon antiquus* are also diagnostic of that species, contrasting with the strongly curved tusks of *Archidiskodon meridionalis* and the even more curved and spirally twisted tusks of *Mammuthus*. Complete tusks are unfortunately also rather rare.

Whole frozen carcasses of the woolly mammoth *Mammuthus primigenius* dating from the Last Cold Stage have been found in northern Siberia (Heintz 1958; Heintz & Garutt 1965), including a calf discovered in 1977. These specimens confirm the general appearance of the animal conveyed by cave paintings from southern France, and in particular the coat of long fur. It is worth mentioning that, as pointed out by Prof. F. E. Zeuner, the reddish-brown coloration of the hair in both woolly mammoth and woolly rhinoceros may not be original, but result from chemical changes in the pigmentation.

Perissodactyls: Order Perissodactyla

Horses: Family Equidae (Genus Equus) (Fig. 3.45)
The taxonomy of the Pleistocene horses of Europe is at present in an unsatisfactory state, being overburdened with a multiplicity of named species, few of which are likely to remain valid in the future. A revision of the British material in particular is badly needed. Taxonomic distinctions are best made on skulls, but with very rare exceptions the student has to be content with isolated teeth, or at best tooth rows in mandibles or maxillae.

The skull of the extinct species *Equus stenonis* from the Upper Villafranchian (late Lower Pleistocene) of Italy differs from the Upper Pleistocene and living horse *E. ferus* in such features as the relatively smaller brain case, longer muzzle and large size of P^1 (Azzaroli 1965) (Fig. 3.46). The upper cheek teeth in *E. stenonis* have a characteristic small ('zebrine') protoconal fold, which serves to identify a number of specimens from the British Lower Pleistocene.

A large Lower Pleistocene horse with a broad ('caballine') protoconal fold has been referred to the extinct *E. bressanus* Viret. The Middle and Upper Pleistocene horses in Britain are all of 'caballine' type and may mostly or entirely belong to *E. ferus* or closely related species (Fig. 3.46). Domesticated

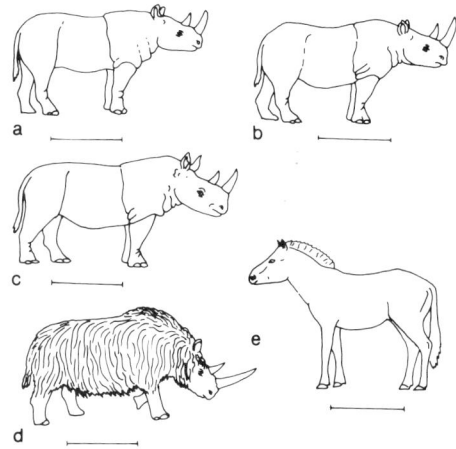

Fig. 3.45. British Pleistocene rhinos and horse. a–d, sketch restorations of extinct rhinos. (a) *Dicerorhinus etruscus*; (b) *Dicerorhinus kirchbergensis*; (c) *Dicerorhinus hemitoechus*; (d) woolly rhino *Coelodonta antiquitatis*; (e) horse *Equus ferus*. (Scales = 1 m.)

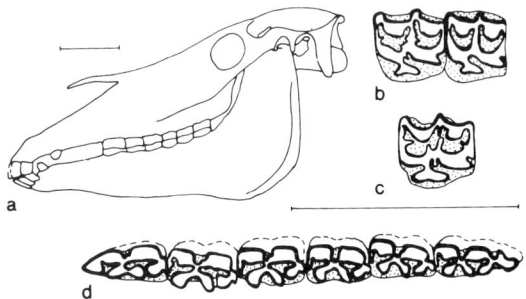

Fig. 3.46. Fossil horse material. (a) reconstruction of skull of extinct horse *Equus stenonis* (late Lower Pleistocene Valdarno, Italy) (Based on Azzaroli 1965); (b) left upper molars of *E. stenonis* (Pre-Pastonian or Pastonian, East Runton, Norfolk); (c) left upper molar *Equus* sp. (caballine) (Cromerian, West Runton, Norfolk); right lower cheek teeth (P_2–M_3 *E. ferus* (Ipswichian, Ilford, Essex). (Scales = 10 cm.)

horse material is not readily distinguished from that of wild *E. ferus*.

Rhinoceroses: Family Rhinocerotidae (Genera: Coelodonta; Dicerorhinus) (Fig. 3.45)
Rhinoceros remains, all of extinct species are often met with in fossil faunas from the British Pleistocene (Woodward 1874). Although the teeth of the woolly rhinoceros *Coelodonta antiquitatis* are easily separable, it is much more difficult to distinguish

those of the three species of *Dicerorhinus*. The skulls of all four species are, however, quite characteristic (Figs. 3.47–3.49), although unfortunately these are rarely found.

The high-crowned cheek teeth of *Coelodonta* have a relatively coarsely corrugated enamel surface, which distinguishes them from those of *Dicerorhinus* spp. in which the enamel is much smoother. Especially characteristic of *Coelodonta* are the isolation of the buccal part of the valley between the

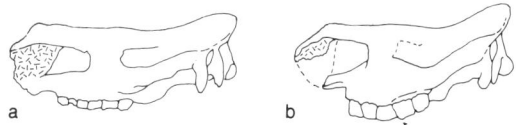

Fig. 3.47. Pleistocene rhino skulls. (a) *Dicerorhinus etruscus*; (b) *D. kirchbergensis* (both early Middle Pleistocene, Mosbach, West Germany). Extent of nasal septum indicated. (Scale = 1 m.)

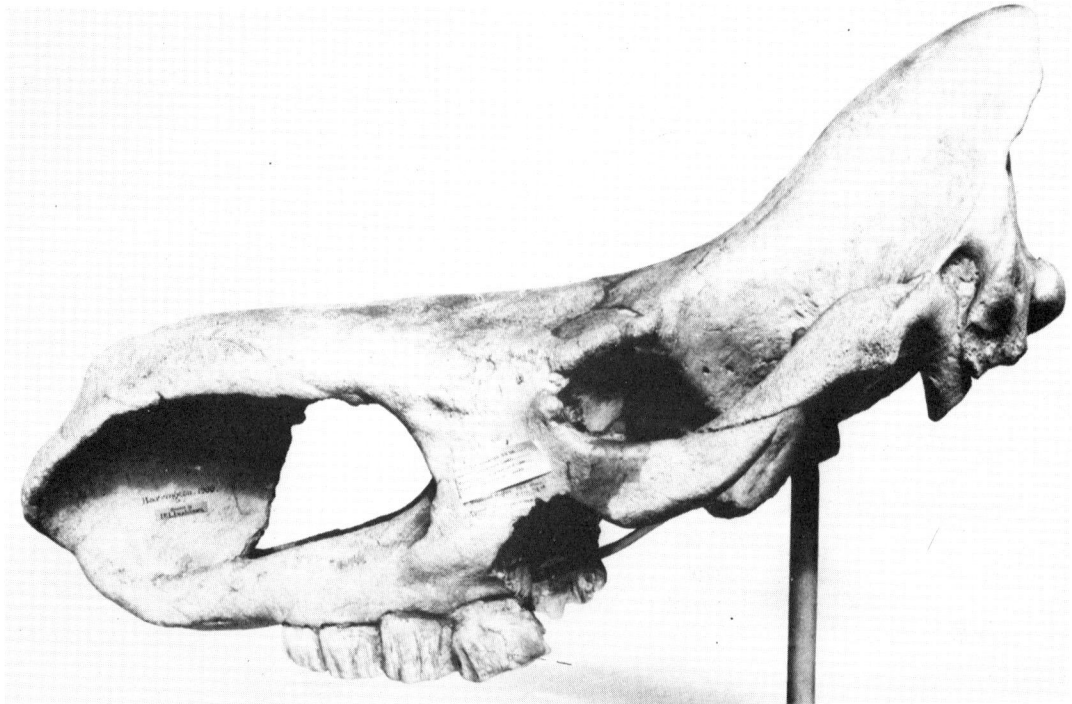

(a)

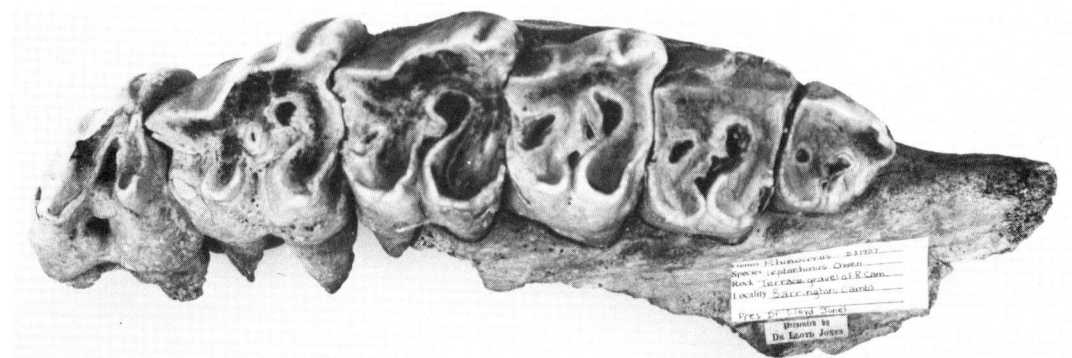

(b)

Fig. 3.48. (a) and (b) [For caption, see over]

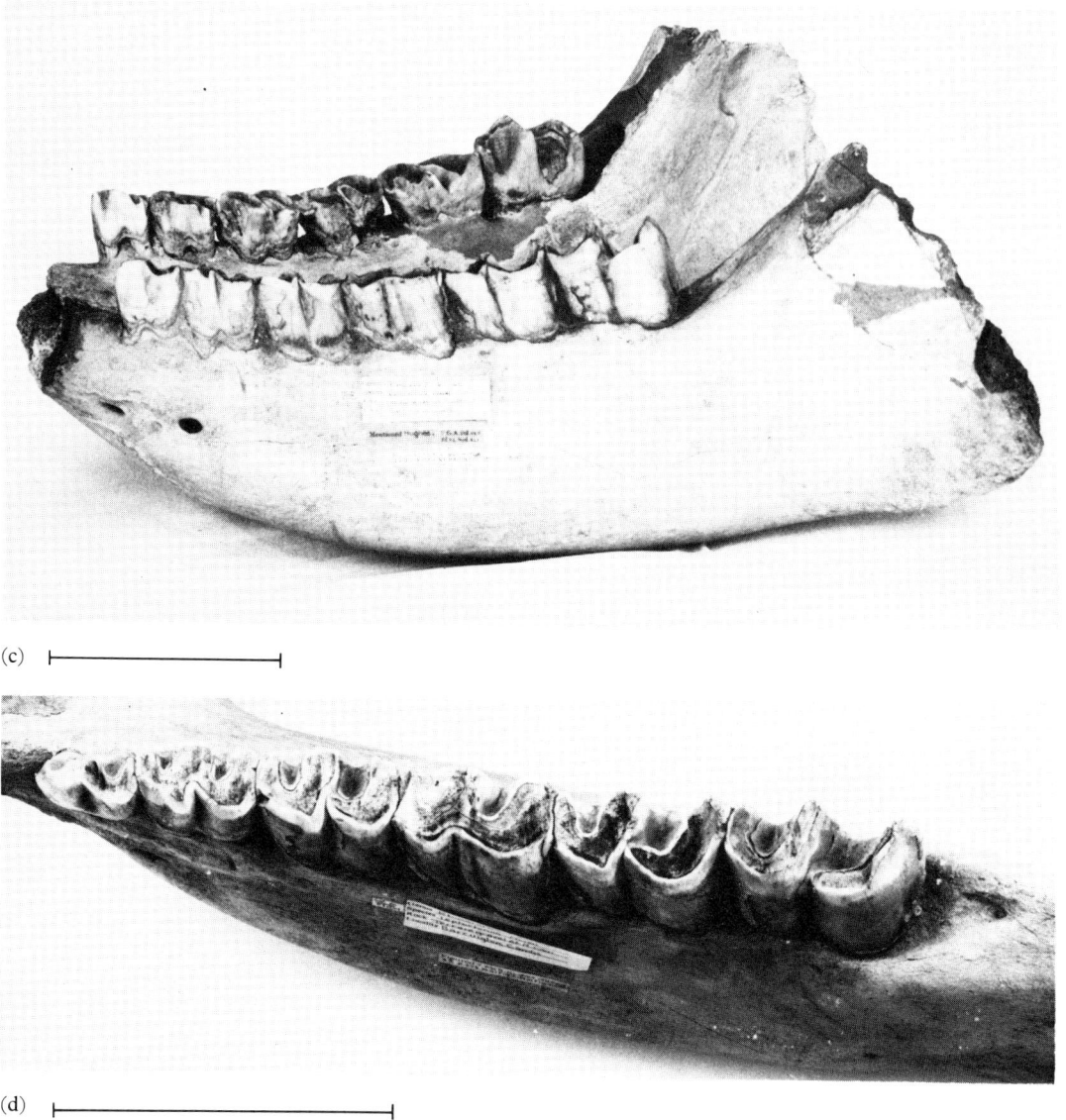

(c) ┣━━━━━━━━━━━━┫

(d) ┣━━━━━━━━━━━━━━━━━━━━┫

Fig. 3.48. Extinct rhino *Dicerorhinus hemitoechus* (Ipswichian, Barrington, Cambridgeshire). (a) skull; note extent of nasal septum. (b) right upper cheek teeth; (c) mandibles; (d) left lower cheek teeth of same specimen. (Scales = 10 cm.)

crista and crochet of the upper molars (Fig. 3.50), and in the skull the presence of a complete bony nasal septum and the fusion of the nasals with the pre-maxilla of the upper jaws. Two finds of entire animals from Starunia Poland, naturally embalmed in salt and petroleum (Stach 1930; Borsuk-Bialynicka 1973) and artistic representations by contemporary man, give a much better idea of the animal in life than could be deduced from the skeleton alone. It is clear that the woolly rhinoceros, of the Last Cold Stage at least, was covered by thick long fur, presumably a protection against cold weather. The position of the exoccipital condyles and the sloping back of the skull suggest that the head was carried fairly low, as in the living African white rhinoceros (*Ceratotherium simum*) – a deduction confirmed by the portrayal of this animal in Upper Palaeolithic art (Zeuner 1932).

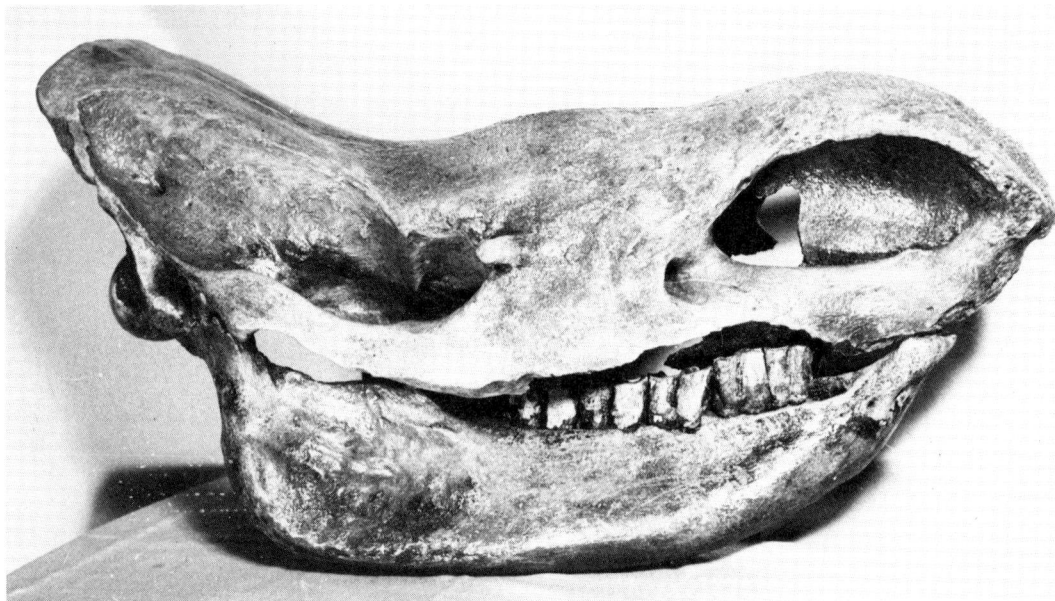

Fig. 3.49. Skull and mandibles of woolly rhino *Coelodonta antiquitatis*. The nasal septum is complete in this species (damaged in specimen shown) (Early Devensian, Coston, Norfolk). (Scale = 20 cm)

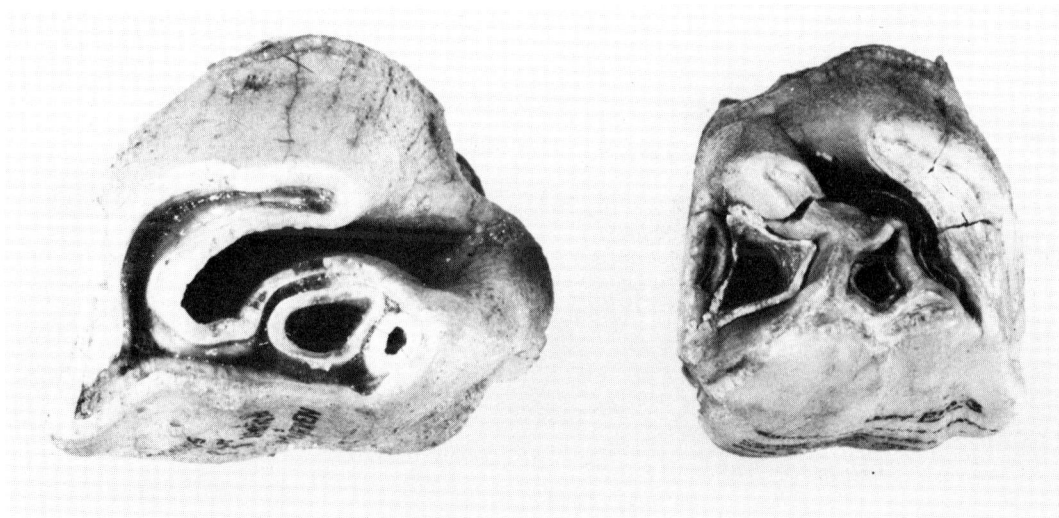

(a)   (b)

Fig. 3.50. Crown views upper cheek teeth of woolly rhino *Coelodonta antiquitatis*. (a) left P^3 (Middle Devensian, Fladbury, Worcestershire); (b) left M^3 (Middle Devensian, Upton Warren, Worcestershire). Note characteristic enamel islet in each. (Scale = 2 cm.)

Problems are encountered in distinguishing the cheek teeth of the three Pleistocene species of *Dicerorhinus* (Dawkins 1866, 1867, 1868). Those of *D. etruscus* are the easiest to recognize, from their small size, brachyodonty and prominent cingula (Figs. 3.48, 3.51). The cheek teeth of *D. kirchbergensis* and *D. hemitoechus* have been separated on conflicting criteria by different authors and the question needs thorough investigation. The skulls are, however, distinctive (Fig. 3.47) and there is no

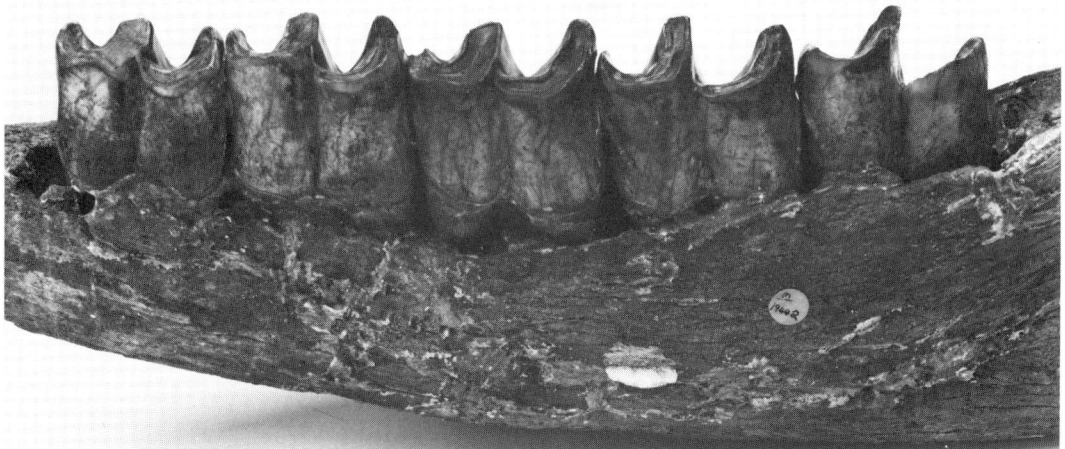

Fig. 3.51. Lower cheek teeth of *Dicerorhinus etruscus* (Cromerian, West Runton, Norfolk). (Scale = 5 cm.)

doubt that three species of *Dicerorhinus* are represented in the Pleistocene of Europe, but it is not certain to what extent *D. kirchbergensis* was present in Britain. The half-dozen or so skulls from the Ipswichian (e.g. Barrington, Ilford) and Hoxnian (Clacton, Swanscombe) interglacials are all of *D. hemitoechus*.

In *D. hemitoechus* the skull shape resembles that of *Coelodonta antiquitatis* and the living *Ceratotherium simum*, indicating that the head was held low, whereas a more upright carriage is implied for *D. kirchbergensis* and *D. etruscus*, resembling that seen in the modern African black rhinoceros *Diceros bicornis*, and the South-East Asian species, *Dicerorhinus sumatrensis*. The latter, Sumatran, rhinoceros is the only species of *Dicerorhinus* alive at the present day. It is, however, much smaller than any of the Pleistocene rhinos of Europe.

Artiodactyls: Order Artiodactyla

Pigs: Family Suidae (Genus: Sus) (Fig. 3.52)
The Middle and Upper Pleistocene pigs of Europe have all been referred to *Sus scrofa*. An older species, *S. strozzii* Meneghini, is recognized in the Lower Pleistocene, but this has not yet been found in Britain except in the Red Crag Nodule Bed.

The tusks of *Sus* are readily distinguished from those of *Hippopotamus*, which are mostly much

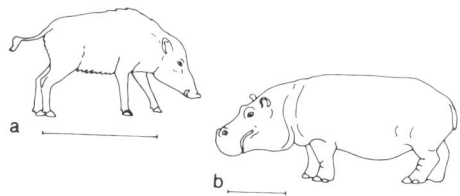

Fig. 3.52. British Pleistocene pig and hippo. (a) wild boar *Sus scrofa*; (b) hippopotamus *Hippopotamus amphibius*. (Scales = 1 m.)

larger, by their triangular cross-section. The cheek teeth are low-crowned and bunodont with complex wrinkles (Fig. 3.53).

European domestic pigs, descendants of *S. scrofa*, show a marked shortening of the skull and much reduced canine tusks.

Hippopotamuses: Family Hippopotamidae (Genus: Hippopotamus) (Fig. 3.52)
Remains of hippopotamuses are known from probably about a hundred localities within England and Wales. The cheek teeth and canine and incisor tusks are unlikely to be confused with those of other animals, and most of the post-cranial bones are also easily identifiable (Fig. 3.54).

According to Blandamura and Azzaroli (1977) two species, widely separated in time, occur in the Pleistocene of Europe. The older, the extinct *Hip-*

Fig. 3.53. Wild boar *Sus scrofa* (Cromerian, West Runton, Norfolk). (a) skull; (b) left upper cheek teeth. (Scales = 10 cm.)

potamus major (= *H. antiquus*?), is found in Lower Pleistocene deposits, whereas the younger, conspecific with the living *H. amphibius*, entered Europe during the Last (Eemian, Ipswichian) Interglacial. *Hippopotamus major* can be distinguished by several skull characters and in the mandible principally by the concave lower border and the anteriorly sloping second premolar with a small gap behind. If these criteria are valid the only complete mandible from the CF-bF of Cromer, Norfolk (Fig. 3.55) should be referred to *H. major*, whereas all Ipswichian finds of mandibles are *H. amphibius* (Fig. 3.54).

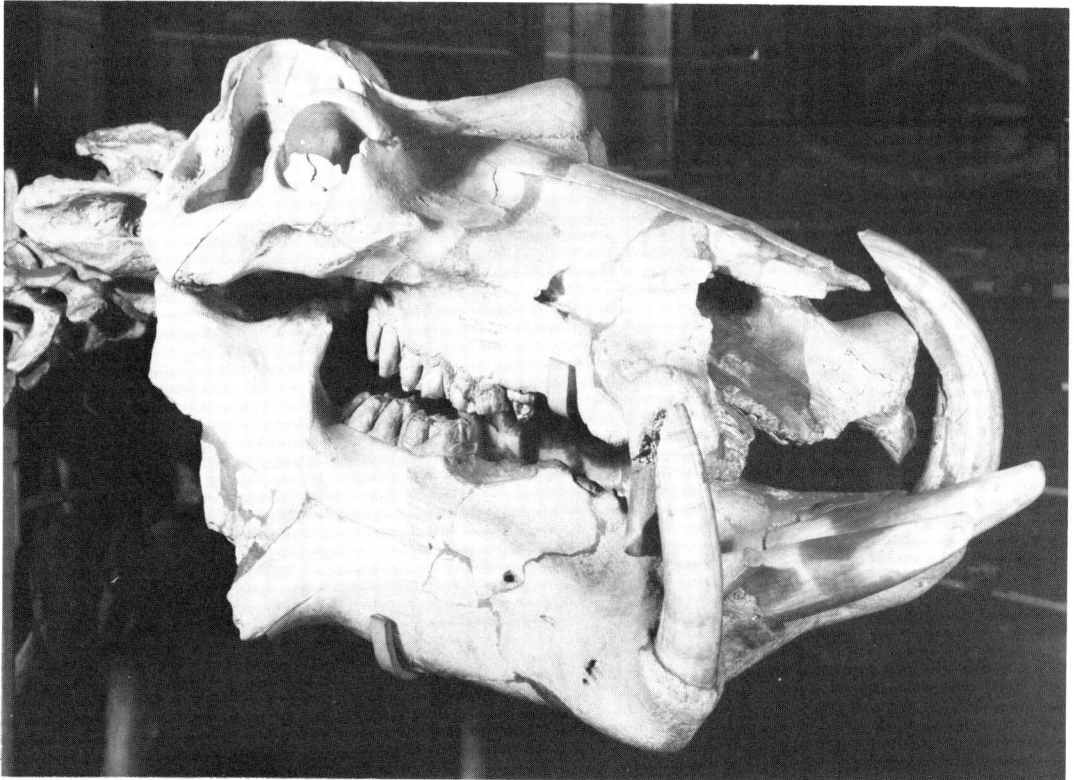

(a)

(b)

Fig. 3.54. Hippopotamus *Hippopotamus amphibius* (Ipswichian, Barrington, Cambridgeshire). (a) skull and mandible; occipital condyle to anterior base of canine is about 61 cm. (b) left lower cheek teeth. (Scale = 10 cm.)

Modern *H. amphibius* material, however, shows variation in these characters. Unfortunately the exact horizon of the Cromer find is unknown and it therefore uncertain whether those *Hippopotamus* finds from the CF-bF which can be dated to the Cromerian are likely to be *H. major* or another species.

The excellent Ipswichian material from Barrington, near Cambridge, has been monographed in detail by Reynolds (1922).

Deer: Family Cervidae (Genera: Cervus; Capreolus; Dama; Megaceros; Eucladoceros; Alces, Rangifer) (*Figs. 3.56, 3.57*)

Deer are probably the most common family of large mammals from the British Pleistocene. The Cromer Forest-bed Formation deer were monographed by Azzaroli (1953), and this publication is still very useful.

Antlers, carried by all male deer and by both sexes in reindeer *Rangifer tarandus* provide the

Fig. 3.55. Left mandible of *Hippopotamus* sp. (Cromerian or late Lower Pleistocene, Cromer, Norfolk). (Scale = 10 cm.)

most obvious characters for distinguishing genera and species (Figs. 3.58–3.64). It should be borne in mind, however, that within a species there is considerable variability, and that since each animal grows and sheds its antlers every year, each set will differ somewhat in size and complexity from the one before. Particular difficulties are encountered in identifying fragments of antler, which are sometimes all that is available from a site.

The cheek teeth of the various species show a strong overall similarity, but differ in such characters as size, degree of molarization of the premolars, details of cusp patterns and surface texture of the enamel (Figs. 3.66, 3.67). The teeth of *Alces* and *Rangifer* are particularly distinctive, whereas those of *Cervus*, *Dama* and *Megaceros* resemble one another in morphology. The postcranial bones are generally also difficult to distinguish, although size can provide a useful clue.

Sexing of fossil material can be a simple matter for nearly all species of deer since, except in *Rangifer*, all antlers represent males. It is, however, especially desirable to be able to sex skulls and antlers of *R. tarandus*, because of the seasonal information that

can be obtained from the antler growth and shedding cycle which is out of phase in male and female reindeer (see Ch. 5). The antlers of mature males are consistently larger than those of females, although those of young males cannot be so distinguished. A very useful sexually diagnostic character is to be found in the fact that in males, a substantial portion of the pedicle is shed along with the antler and remains attached to it whereas in females the break occurs immediately below the burr Bouchud (1966). Skulls can be sexed readily by the pattern of sutures between the frontal and parietal bones (Fig. 3.65).

The red deer *Cervus elaphus* shows marked size changes through the Middle and Upper Pleistocene (A. Lister, 1981). Its dwarfing in the Flandrian is probably due to reduction of its habitat by man (Ch. 11). Continental red deer antlers of approximately Cromerian age (e.g. Mosbach) are acoronate, i.e. they have no cup at the top of their antlers, and such forms have been described as a distinct species *Cervus acoronatus*. The British Cromerian material is insufficient to be certain that the red deer of this stage lacked the 'cup'. In all later forms

Fig. 3.56. British Pleistocene deer (only males figured). (a) giant deer *Megaceros giganteus* (sketch restoration); (b) *Megaceros verticornis* (sketch restoration); (c) red deer *Cervus elaphus*; (d) elk (moose) *Alces alces*; (e) roe *Capreolus capreolus*; (f) fallow deer *Dama dama*; (g) reindeer *Rangifer tarandus* (Scale = 1 m.)

from Britain and Continental Europe the 'cup' is present.

Antlers of a medium-sized deer of Pre-Pastonian/Pastonian age from East Runton, Norfolk, previously described by Azzaroli (1953) as '*Dama*' *nestii*, are here provisionally assigned to *Cervus* sp (Lister, 1981). This taxon will probably prove to be conspecific with one of the late Villafranchian *Cervus* species described from France (Heintz 1970).

Material of roe deer *Capreolus capreolus* is distinguishable from that of other cervids by its very small size. Its antlers are upright with only three points, and highly rugose ornamentation (Fig. 3.59).

The fallow deer *Dama dama*, a medium-sized species with its attractively spotted coat, graceful form and curving palmated antlers, is perhaps the most beautiful of living deer. Specimens of Hoxnian age are rather larger than later forms and the antlers are less palmated with an extra front tine (Leonardi & Petronio 1976) (Fig. 3.61). Such forms have been distinguished by some authors as a separate species *D. clactoniana* but the differences seem to merit only subspecific rank and the name *D. dama clactoniana* can be used.

The extinct giant deer, genus *Megaceros*, are some of the most spectacular and fascinating members of the Pleistocene faunas. All giant deer species are characterized by a strikingly thickened mandible. Three species, *M. verticornis*, *M. dawkinsi* and *M. savini*, are known from the early Middle Pleistocene, whereas only one species, *M. giganteus*, occurs from the Hoxnian onwards. The first two species are probably very closely related. *Megaceros giganteus* and *M. verticornis* were both very large deer whereas the other two species, which are much less well known because of the paucity of material, appear to have been rather smaller.

The antlers in *M. giganteus*, the best-known giant deer species, are extremely large, commonly exceeding 3 m. (see Fig. 8.9) These are, however, no bigger than would be predicted for the body size of the animal, since there is an allometric relationship between the two in nearly all modern deer species (Gould 1974). *Megaceros giganteus* specimens of interglacial age from the Continent show more upright carriage of the antlers than is seen in the open-ground animals from the end of the Last Cold Stage. The interglacial specimens from Britain are all incomplete but the giant deer skulls from the Ipswichian of Barrington, Cambridgeshire, seem to correspond with the Continental material (see Ch. 7).

The extinct deer of the genus *Eucladoceros* (*Euctenoceros*), characterized by their comb-like antlers, are restricted in occurrence to the Lower Pleistocene. Three or four species, *E. falconeri*, *E. sedgwicki*, *E. tetraceros* and perhaps *E. ctenoides*, ranging in size from medium to large, are probably represented by British material (Fig. 3.58), but the group is poorly understood.

In the elks, genus *Alces*, the premolars are more molarized than in other genera of deer, except *Rangifer*, and the cusp pattern of the cheek teeth is distinctive. The antlers are distinctive, with a beam

Fig. 3.57. Life-size model, in concrete, of male *Megaceros giganteus* (made by Waterhouse Hawkins, under the direction of Sir Richard Owen) erected in the grounds of the Crystal Palace, south London, in 1854.

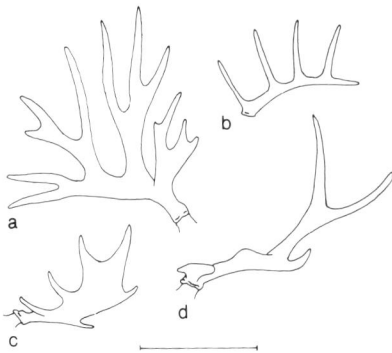

Fig. 3.58. Reconstructions of the antlers of extinct British Pleistocene deer. (a) *Eucladoceros sedgwicki*; (b) *Eucladoceros tetraceros*; (c) *Megaceros dawkinsi*; (d) *Megaceros savini*. (a, c, d based on Azzaroli 1953). (Scale = 50 cm.)

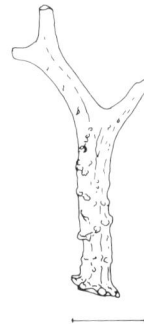

Fig. 3.59. Antler of roe *Capreolus capreolus* (probably Cromerian, Overstrand, Norfolk). (Scale = 5 cm.)

free of tines terminating in a broad palmation (see Fig. 11.1). The Pleistocene elk lineage can be traced from the small *Alces gallicus* with a long beam from the Lower Pleistocene to the very large

A. latifrons of Cromerian age with shorter antlers and finally to the modern and slightly smaller *A. alces* in which the beams are much reduced (Ch. 11). Some specimens of the Cromerian form represent the largest deer known, either fossil or living.

Fig. 3.60. Antler of red deer *Cervus elaphus* (Ipswichian, Ilford, Essex). (Scale = 20 cm.)

Fig. 3.61. Skull and antlers of fallow deer *Dama dama* ('*D. dama clactoniana*') (Hoxnian, Swanscombe, Kent). (Scale = 20 cm.)

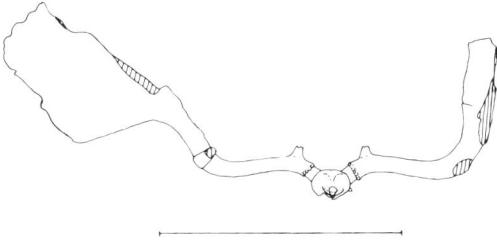

Fig. 3.62. Antlers and part of skull of giant deer *Megaceros verticornis* (rear view) (probably Cromerian, Pakefield, Norfolk). (Based on Harmer 1899). (Scale = 1 m.) Other specimens, from the Continent, are non-palmated.

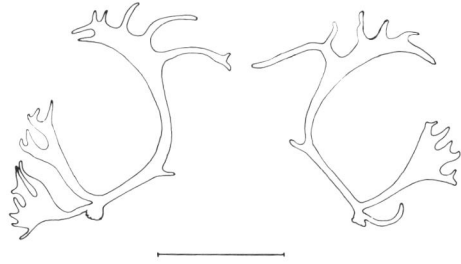

Fig. 3.64. Antlers (attached to skull) of reindeer *Rangifer tarandus* (Late Midlandian/Devensian, Ashbourne, County Meath) (Based on Dawkins & Reynolds 1872–1939). (Scale = 50 cm.)

Fig. 3.63. Antler of extinct deer *Eucladoceros sedgwicki* (Pre-Pastonian or Pastonian, Bacton, Norfolk). (Scale = 20 cm.)

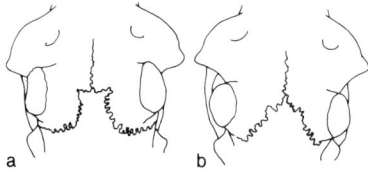

Fig. 3.65. Sexual differences in skulls of reindeer *Rangifer tarandus* (a) male; (b) female. (Based on Bouchud 1966).

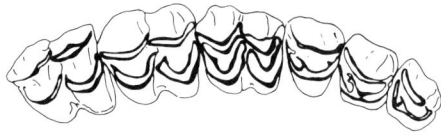

Fig. 3.66. Right upper cheek teeth ($P^2 - M^3$) of fallow deer *Dama dama* (Hoxnian, Swanscombe, Kent). (Scale = 5 cm.)

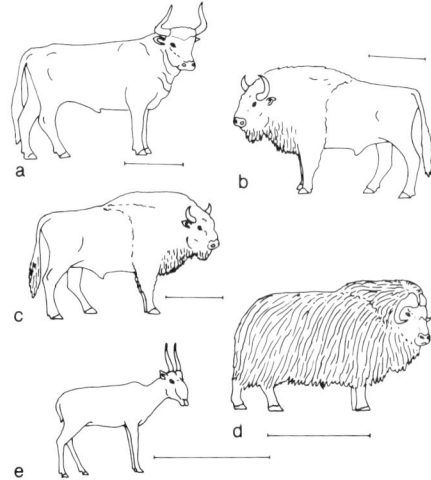

Fig. 3.68. British Pleistocene bovids. (a) aurochs *Bos primigenius* (sketch restoration); (b) extinct bison *Bison priscus* (sketch restoration); (c) extinct bison *Bison schoetensacki* (restored as modern European bison *B. bonasus*); (d) musk ox *Ovibos moschatus*; (e) saiga *Saiga tartarica*. (Scales = 1 m.)

In the reindeer *Rangifer tarandus*, the cheek teeth have a characteristic morphology and the enamel is smooth. The antlers are very variable, quite apart from sexual differences (see above). In modern reindeer the antlers are generally more flattened in the woodland ecotype than in the tundra form.

The metapodials of reindeer can be easily recognized by the presence of a strong posterior groove along most of the length of the bone.

Bovids: Family Bovidae (Genera: Bison; Bos; Ovibos; Praeovibos; Gazella; Saiga; 'Ovis') (Fig. 3.68)
By far the commonest bovids in British Pleistocene deposits belong to the genera *Bos* and *Bison*. The teeth (Fig. 3.71) and limb bones of the two are notoriously difficult to separate, and characters which can be used to distinguish them at one site may fail to work with different populations. The skulls are, however, quite distinct (Figs. 3.69; 3.70) and horn cores alone are also fairly reliable.

Bos is represented solely by *B. primigenius*, but there are two species of *Bison*: *B. schoetensacki* and *B. priscus*. The latter was large with large horn cores in proportion to the skull, whereas the opposite condition prevailed in *B. schoetensacki*. The probably closely related living species *B. bonasus* is known from the late Weichselian (Devensian) of Denmark and elsewhere.

Descriptions of much of the best *Bison* and *Bos* material from the British Isles can be found in Dawkins and Reynolds (1872–1939). Both *Bos* and *Bison* exhibit strong sexual dimorphism which can be demonstrated in bivariate scatters of limb bone measurements (Fig. 3.2).

Domestic cattle first introduced by the Neolithic farmers can be distinguished by their smaller size and reduction in the length of the horn cores.

Fossil musk oxen *Ovibos moschatus* are very rare in Britain. The limb bones and teeth are considerably smaller than in *Bos* and *Bison*, but the skull is

Fig. 3.67. Right lower cheek teeth of red deer *Cervus elaphus* (Hoxnian, Clacton, Essex). Scale = 5 cm.)

Fig. 3.69. Skull of aurochs *Bos primigenius* (Ipswichian, Ilford). (Scale = 20 cm.)

Fig. 3.70. Partial skull of extinct bison *Bison priscus* (Middle Devensian, Tattershall Castle, Lincolnshire). (Scale = 20 cm.)

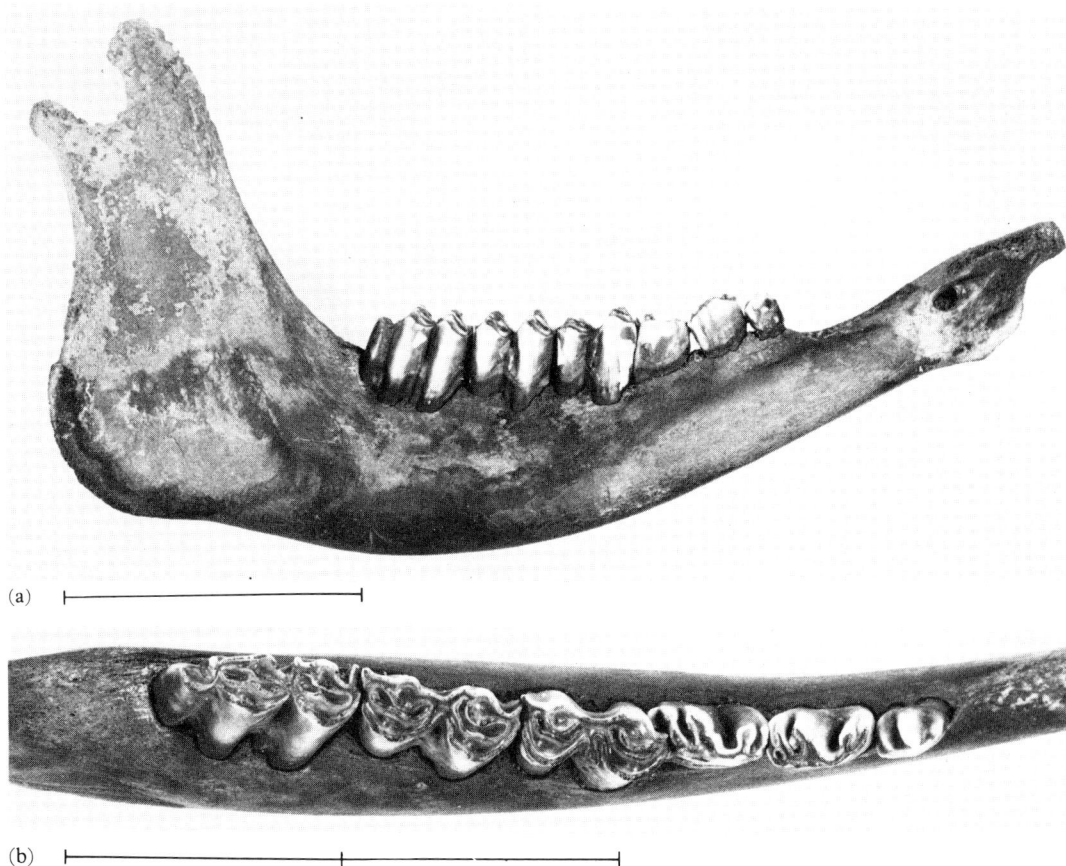

Fig. 3.71. (a) left mandible of *Bison priscus* (Early Devensian, Wretton, Norfolk). (b) occlusal view of cheek teeth. (Scale = 10 cm.)

especially characteristic with the massive thick-based horn cores covering much of the top of the skull and almost meeting in the mid-line (Fig. 3.72). The larger and more lightly built ex-

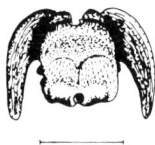

Fig. 3.72. Skull of musk ox *Ovibos moschatus* (posterior view) (? Ipswichian, Crayford, Kent). (Scale = 10 cm.)

tinct species of musk ox *Praeovibos priscus* is recorded in Britain only by part of a skull from the Cromer Forest-bed Formation and its stratigraphical position is unfortunately unknown.

Other very rare small bovids recorded from Britain are a gazelle *Gazella anglica* from the Lower Pleistocene, a sheep or goat '*Ovis*' *savini* from the CF-bF (horizon unknown) (Newton 1882a) and the saiga antelope *Saiga tartarica* from deposits of Middle Devensian age at Twickenham, Middlesex (Dawkins & Reynolds, 1872–1939).

True sheep genus *Ovis* and goats genus *Capra* did not occur in the late Pleistocene of Britain until they were introduced by man.

4 Taphonomy

General

Taphonomy is the study of the processes by which living organisms become converted into fossils. An understanding of these processes is essential in interpreting a fossil assemblage which can give a very distorted picture of the once living communities from which it was derived.

Examples of such distortion in Pleistocene vertebrate assemblages include: the over-representation of Carnivora in cave deposits; the paucity of aerial and arboreal species and the over-representation of aquatic and waterside animals at open sites; and the bias towards favoured prey species when the fossils represent food remains accumulated by various predators.

It should be pointed out, however, that taphonomy studies relevant to Pleistocene vertebrate fossils (Behrensmeyer & Hill 1980), especially in a European context, are still in their infancy and consequently only rather tentative conclusions can be drawn. Fundamentally, fossil vertebrate assemblages are either of autochthonous (*in situ*) or allochthonous (transported) origin. Autochthonous processes include: (a) the incorporation of the remains of animals which lived and died more or less at the depositional site, e.g. fishes in lakes and bears hibernating in caves; and (b) the operation of natural traps, e.g. a cave with a hole in the roof – a pitfall trap – and muddy shallows of lakes and rivers in which large mammals become mired. Allochthonous processes include: (a) transport of animal remains by rivers or marine currents – either as floating carcasses or as disassociated bones and teeth; and (b) transport of small bones and teeth in the digestive systems of predators, subsequently to be expelled in the form of regurgitated pellets in the case of predatory birds, or in the faeces of Carnivora. The latter processes are also discussed from the palaeoecological aspect in Chapter 5.

One over-riding consideration always arises when one is faced with the interpretation of a Pleistocene vertebrate assemblage from marine or freshwater deposits: whether or not it is wholly or partly reworked (derived) from other fossiliferous deposits. It is not uncommon, for example, to find sharks' teeth, and material of other marine vertebrates, reworked from Mesozoic or Tertiary bedrock in the concentrate of small-vertebrate material from Pleistocene fluviatile deposits. These older fossils are, however, generally well-rolled and almost invariably differ in their colour and nature of mineralization to those of Pleistocene age.

It is also apparent that articulated or even associated bones from individual animals and delicate bones and teeth, e.g. fish scales and complete shrew mandibles, could not have been reworked.

It is perhaps fortunate in one sense that Pleistocene deposits with vertebrate fossils are relatively rare, so that reworking of such material probably seldom happens in practice. Nevertheless any suspicions, aroused, for example, by apparently anomalous taxa in a fossil fauna, should be carefully checked for any consistent differences in nature of preservation, amount of abrasion, etc., and the existence of local source deposits for the older fossils should be investigated.

In general, Pleistocene fossil vertebrate remains only occur in sediments with a high alkalinity due to the presence of calcium carbonate, usually in the form of reworked limestone or chalk clasts and/or mollusc shells, algal nodules or oospores and other contemporaneous biogenic carbonate. This carbonate is probably preferentially dissolved by acid groundwaters so that the bones survive rather longer. Large-mammal bones and teeth appear, however, to resist solution and are commonly found in non-calcareous gravels.

With the exception of much of the Lower Pleistocene crag material which is heavily impregnated with iron oxides and bones from caves containing calcium carbonate, most British Pleistocene vertebrate material is evidently only slightly mineralized or unaltered apart from staining – usually to brown or sandy yellow. Collagen still remains in most of the material. The colour pattern of shrew teeth, which in life is white with the cusps a vivid red, is commonly preserved in fossils as brown tipped with black (Fig. 3.9).

Marine environment

Pleistocene marine deposits containing non-marine as well as marine vertebrate fossils are principally represented in Britain by Lower Pleistocene shelly sands and gravels – the 'crags' of East Anglia (Ch. 6). Vertebrate fossils also occur in marine beds within the East Anglian Cromer Forest-bed Formation, interglacial raised-beach deposits in England and Wales, and the interglacial Burtle Beds of Somerset (Ch. 7).

Most of the vertebrate fossils occurring in marine sediments is not surprisingly of marine fishes, marine mammals (Cetacea, Pinnipedia), and occasional sea birds. The presence of terrestrial and freshwater vertebrate fossils in the Lower Pleistocene crags is usually correlated with the occurrence of non-marine mollusc shells, suggesting that both were washed into the sea by rivers. These fossil assemblages are therefore likely to be biased in favour of animals living and dying in and around rivers flowing into the crag seas. The fossils are commonly abraded, reflecting long transport, but other specimens are remarkably well preserved.

At the base of crag deposits of various ages there is usually a pebble bed incorporating the sweepings of a former land surface caught up by the transgression of the sea. Much of the vertebrate material in these pebble beds may be approximately contemporaneous with the sediments, but other material is clearly reworked and of much greater age. The Nodule Bed at the base of the Red Crag includes fossils of late Pliocene age, together with *Hyracotherium* (an extinct perissodactyl) and other vertebrates from the Eocene (Ch. 6). Nodule Bed fossils are invariably well-rolled and highly mineralized so that they have an attractive gloss finish and were much prized by nineteenth-century collectors.

Vertebrates from Pleistocene marine deposits other than the crags have received little attention. Presumably bones, teeth and occasional floating corpses washed in by rivers are the main source of non-marine vertebrate material in all marine deposits. Some material may be incorporated, however, by animals dying on beaches, or falling over cliffs, for example, and other remains may be transported by mudflows and landslips and subsequently washed into the sea.

Lacustrine environment

In lakes and ponds there is no transport of coarse clastic material, so that allochthonous vertebrate remains rarely occur in lacustrine sediments.

Freshwater fishes and Amphibia which live, or at least breed, in lakes and ponds are sometimes very abundant as fossils. Frogs and toads, which hibernate during the winter in the mud at the bottom of ponds, can die in large numbers due to asphyxiation if when they become active in spring there is still ice on the surface (Smith 1969). An early Flandrian *Chara* marl, from near Macclesfield, Cheshire, examined by the author, contained abundant remains, including whole skeletons of common toad *Bufo bufo* and common frog *Rana temporaria*.

Occasionally, complete or partial associated skeletons of large mammals occur in lacustrine deposits, and these clearly represent unfortunate animals which perished in natural traps. At the present day large mammals, including elephants, from time to time become mired in soft mud at the edges of lakes and rivers and are unable to extricate themselves. North American moose *Alces alces* bulls commonly fall through thin ice or lakes and rivers and eventually succumb through exhaustion, weighted down by the ice formed on their antlers (Peterson 1955). Complete skeletons of *Alces alces* recovered from Blackpool, Lancashire, and Neasham, County Durham, both of Late Devensian zone II age, probably died in this way (Hallam *et al.* 1973) (Ch. 8). The Blackpool elk skeleton was slightly dissociated *in situ* – probably the corpse had rotted while floating in the water. The numerous remains of giant deer *Megaceros giganteus* from marls of Late Midlandian (Devensian) age found in Ireland (Ch. 8) probably represent both mired and drowned animals. The disturbance of the sediments noted by some observers certainly suggests the struggles of mired beasts. The Irish skeletons are commonly more or less complete, but sometimes only partial skeletons are found. This again suggests that carcasses floated across the lake and dropped articulated portions of the skeleton as they decomposed.

Archaeological material sometimes occurs in lake deposits, representing accumulated rubbish from lake-side hunting encampments. For example at Star Carr, Yorkshire, Mesolithic hunters camping beside a lake each summer, over a period of several years, discarded into the lake the remains of various mammals and birds that they had eaten, mixed with flint, bone and antler artifacts (Chs. 7, 10). The deposits are notably deficient in remains of small vertebrates, since these were neither part of the Star Carr hunters' diet, nor were they transported by current action.

Fluviatile environment

Vertebrate assemblages in fluviatile, as in lacustrine, sediments include remains of freshwater fishes, amphibians and other vertebrates which lived and died close to the depositional site. The particular feature of fluviatile sediments is that terrestrial vertebrates are also well represented. Fine clastic sediments deposited by slow-flowing water, sometimes yield partial or complete large mammal skeletons, as in the closely similar lacustrine environment. For example, the clays and silts of an Ipswichian river channel at Aveley, Essex, contained superimposed skeletons of straight-tusked elephant *Palaeoloxodon antiquus* (below) and Mammoth *Mammuthus primigenius* (above) (see Fig. 7.13). The apparent coincidence of different species of elephant occurring, in deposits of different pollen zones, at the same spot is probably explicable as follows. The close proximity of these fossils to the margin of the channel suggests that there existed a steep and slippery bank of London Clay, down which the elephants may have fallen and become mired in the soft channel sediments. The author is grateful to Dr A. J. Sutcliffe for the information that the sediment beneath the *M. primigenius* skeleton was disturbed, possibly by the struggles of the trapped animal.

Most remains of terrestrial vertebrates in flu-

viatile sediments are, however, of allochthonous origin – the material arriving at the depositional site either as floating corpses carried downstream or more often as bones and teeth transported as part of the traction load of the river.

These allochthonous processes, although easy to envisage in outline, are far from being understood in detail. Much more research is needed to throw more light on this very important aspect of Pleistocene vertebrate studies.

From time to time animals coming down to a river in order to drink or to feed on the rich flora, would have been trapped and drowned by sudden flooding. The corpses of these and other animals happening to die in the river from different causes, would have been carried downstream until they either broke up or accumulated against obstructions, such as fallen trees or in slack water on meanders or braids. Accumulations of complete or partial skeletons of large mammals, probably originating as described above, are known from fluviatile sediments at Ilford, Essex – elephant, rhinoceros (Figs. 3.41, 3.48) – and Barrington, Cambridgeshire – hippopotamus (Fig. 3.54) and other localities.

It is apparent from the condition of many vertebrate remains that they lay on the ground surface before being incorporated in the river sediments. Large and medium-sized mammal bones from fluviatile deposits sometimes bear tooth and claw marks, and evidence of breakage by carnivorous mammals. Occasionally the marks made by gnawing rodents are seen (Ch. 5). A substantial proportion of the small-mammal material shows the characteristic corrosion suggesting that they have been ingested by, and subsequently regurgitated in the pellets of, diurnal predatory birds (Ch. 5). Similar damage is seen in larger-mammal material passed through in the faeces of carnivorous mammals. Evidence of killing and butchering by man is usually suggested by the association of bones and artifacts, although it cannot be usually assumed that man was responsible for accumulating all the bones at a site. The last three processes involve transport of prey species remains to the depositional site by a predator. It is very difficult to evaluate the bias introduced to a fossil assemblage in this way.

Vertebrate material lying on a land surface is exposed to such destructive forces as frost, desiccation, damage by plant growth and insects, and trampling by large mammals.

The most likely mechanism by which the major-

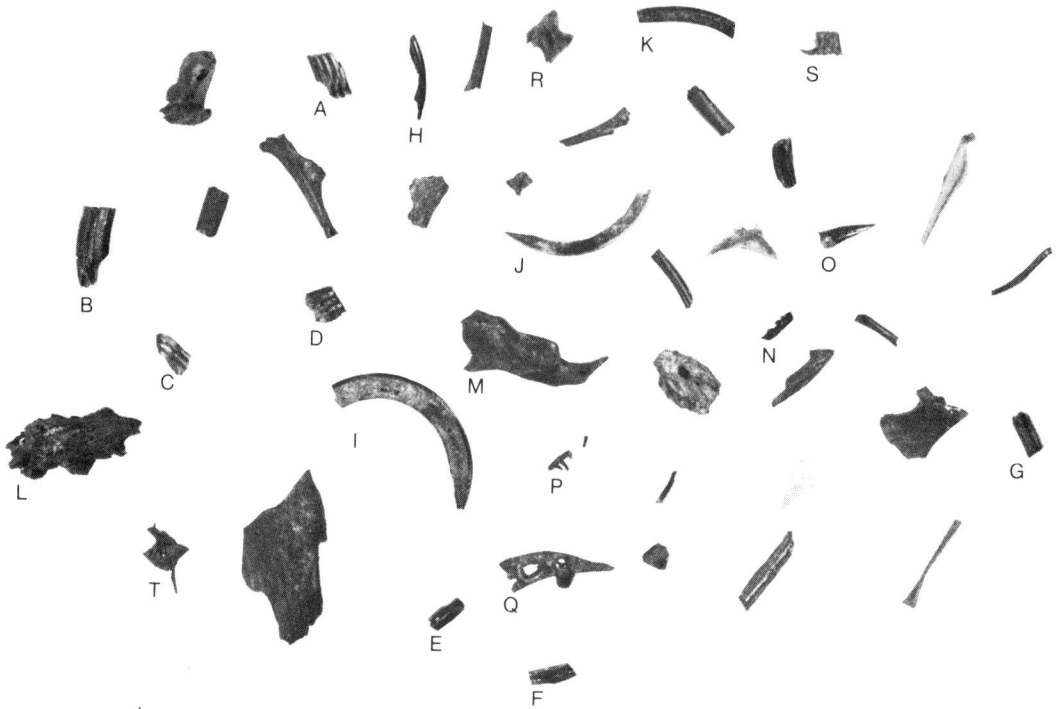

Fig. 4.1. Typical fossil assemblage of small-vertebrate material sorted from fluviatile organic sediments (Ipswichian subzone Ip IIa, Swanton Morley, Norfolk). a–g, vole molars; h–k, small-rodent incisors; (1) vole palate; (m) wood mouse mandible; (n) shrew incisor; (o) pike tooth; (p, q), pharyngeal tooth plates of cyprinid fishes; r–t, fish vertebrae. (Scale = 1 cm.)

ity of dissociated vertebrate remains reach a river is probably by bank erosion as the river migrates across its floodplain or by the constant shifting of multiple channels in a braided river. The highest concentration of terrestrial vertebrate remains in the coarsest basal sediments of the type Cromerian Freshwater Bed at West Runton, Norfolk, support the above deduction (Stuart 1975). All vertebrate material, whatever its origin, once in the river is subject to subsequent transport. The distances involved are unfortunately unknown. Small-vertebrate assemblages (Fig. 4.1) usually include material which has been abraded to different degrees. It is always important to check whether there is any consistent association of amount of abrasion with particular taxa, which would suggest that some material was reworked, or at least transported from different contemporaneous habitats some distance upstream.

Vertebrate assemblages from fluviatile sediments are, not unexpectedly, biased in favour of aquatic and waterside vertebrates, but animals living and dying locally on the river floodplain will be much better represented than those from further away. The West Runton terrestrial small-mammal assemblage, for example, is dominated by grassland voles, living in grassland on the floodplain, while the palaeobotanical evidence indicates regional mixed oak forest at this time (Ch. 7).

Nevertheless, allochthonous fluviatile assemblages reflect the once living communities, from which they were derived, much more closely than assemblages from other types of depositional environment. This is shown, for example, in the relative scarcity of Carnivora, the predominance of small mammals over large, and of Rodentia over Insectivora – reflecting the relative population densities and life spans seen in living communities (Ch. 5).

The various skeletal elements are not equally well represented in fossil small-vertebrate assemblages from fluviatile deposits. There is always a strong bias towards teeth and the more compact bones.

Caves and fissures

Both cave and fissure deposits commonly contain much larger amounts of vertebrate material than deposits representing the other depositional environments discussed above. This is due to several processes which concentrate bones in caves and fissures and to the generally high alkalinity of the deposits which are surrounded by limestone, or at least carbonate-rich, bedrock.

Most of the vertebrate fossils found in caves result from the operation of a natural trap mechanism, were brought in by various carnivores, or are the remains of carnivores, which used the site as a den, and their prey. In some cases material is washed in by streams from the ground surface or from older cave deposits.

Sometimes the configuration of a cave, e.g. with a step within a gallery, may allow animals to venture into a cave but not out again. Other caves have clearly acted as giant pitfall traps, into which unwary animals fell via holes in the roofs, perhaps screened by bushes, e.g. Wirksworth, Derbyshire (Owen 1846, Fig. 130) and Joint Mitnor Cave, Devonshire (Sutcliffe 1960) (Fig. 4.2). The high proportion of Carnivora in the Joint Mitnor assemblage suggests that they were attracted by the cries of injured beasts or the smell of carrion, and in their turn fell into the cave and died.

The principal predators responsible for the accumulation of bones in caves appear to be spotted hyaena *Crocuta crocuta*, wolf *Canis lupus*, various small and medium-sized Carnivora, man, and birds of prey – especially owls.

The use of caves in Britain, during the Pleistocene, as hyaena dens, was recognized as long ago

Fig. 4.2. Artist's restoration of a scene at Joint Mitnor Cave during the Ipswichian interglacial. (Drawing by Maurice Wilson, after Sutcliffe 1960)

as the early nineteenth century, by Buckland (1822) at Kirkdale Cave, north-east Yorkshire, in deposits now considered to be of Ipswichian age. Of several subsequent finds, the Devensian levels of Kents Cavern and the 'Hyaena stratum' of Tornewton Cave (Ipswichian) may be mentioned. At Tornewton Cave the fossil assemblage consisted mainly of the compact foot bones and teeth, the other bones having been destroyed by the hyaenas' powerful jaws and teeth (Sutcliffe & Zeuner 1962). Many of the remains bear tooth marks, and others have been partially dissolved and polished by the hyaenas' gastric juices. All of these features have been found in present day African dens of *C. crocuta*, and the animals have been observed carrying portions of carcasses and bones to these dens (Sutcliffe 1970). Some other Carnivora also accumulate and chew bones, but much less extensively than do hyaenas.

The often very large accumulations of small-mammal remains in caves, sometimes representing many thousands of individuals, and millions in the 'Rodent Earth' of Westbury-sub-Mendip (Ch. 7), probably originate in the main from pellets regurgitated by owls roosting in the caves. Small mammalian carnivores, e.g. red fox *Vulpes vulpes*, also bring small-vertebrate material into caves.

Vertebrate material accumulated by man in caves may show cut marks, and evidence of working, and association with artefacts. Clearly, all predator accumulations are biased towards favoured prey species and may for example under-represent woodland animals, therefore giving a distorted impression of the living communities from which they were derived. A further complication is that any cave assemblage is likely to be of composite origin and it is probably not possible to untangle the sources of particular fossil specimens. For example, evidence that a bone was chewed by hyaenas is no proof that these carnivores were responsible for bringing it to the site.

In many cases, carnivores making their dens in caves add their own remains to those of their prey when they die. Hyaena den assemblages consist of a large proportion of *C. crocuta* bones and teeth, including those of juveniles, duly chewed by other hyaenas. Quantities of the phosphatic coprolities (fossil dung) of hyaenas also occur (Ch. 5).

Remains of bears *Ursus* spp. including juveniles are also very common in cave deposits (e.g. Tornewton Cave Bear Stratum, and Westbury-sub-Mendip) due to their habit of hibernating during the winter months. At the present day bears do not hibernate exclusively in caves, which are in relatively short supply, but more commonly excavate dens beneath trees or rocks, (Ch. 5) but it is mostly the remains of those that died in caves which are preserved. Most deaths probably occur during hibernation when the animal's fat reserves are insufficient.

Other Carnivora fairly common in cave deposits, but significantly rare at open sites, include badger *Meles meles* and other mustelids, and lion *Panthera leo*, wild cat *Felis sylvestris* and other felids. Remains of owls, however, are very rare – presumably they usually die elsewhere.

Bats of course hibernate in caves, and contribute their remains to the bone accumulations, but are less common than might be expected in British caves, occurring however at Westbury-sub-Mendip (Bishop, 1974).

Bones also accumulate in fissures dissolved out of calcareous rocks by surface streams disappearing underground. The assemblages may represent a combination of remains washed in from the ground surface, animals falling into the fissures or material reworked from pre-existing cave deposits. As in caves, the stratigraphy of fissure deposits can be chaotic. Few British examples have been described but the Ightham Fissures, near Sevenoaks, Kent, in Upper Greensand (Cretaceous), have yielded a rich late-Pleistocene fauna (Newton 1894). It is now generally recognized that these deposits represent a considerable period of Devensian and Flandrian time.

5 Palaeoecology

The palaeontologist working on Pleistocene fossils is more fortunate than his colleagues who are concerned with the organisms of earlier geological periods, in that so many of the fossil species or their near relatives are still extant. This clearly facilitates palaeoecological interpretations. Evidence of mode of life can be deduced from the skeletal anatomy for those Pleistocene taxa which are now extinct. Fossil pollen and macroscopic plant remains associated with vertebrate material provide very valuable evidence of the contemporaneous vegetation, and other environmental factors can be deduced from the characteristics of the enclosing sediments.

and faunas, and from the sedimentary environment in which its remains were found.

The distribution maps in this section should be interpreted as giving a broad picture of the range of the animal shown and that each species is limited to particular habitats within these areas, e.g. grassland within forested areas, or conversely forests along rivers in otherwise treeless areas of arid steppe or desert. Aquatic and amphibious animals are obviously restricted to rivers, streams and lakes within the broad distributions shown.

The distributions of many vertebrates at the present day are known to have been drastically modified by human interference (see Ch. 10).

Ecology of individual taxa

When dealing with Pleistocene fossil occurrences of a species which is living at the present day there is usually no reason to suspect that its ecology has changed significantly, especially if it has obvious skeletal adaptations to its mode of life. In very many cases such taxa are recorded as fossils in association with much the same plants and animals as at the present day, although some Pleistocene biotopes, particularly those of cold stages, include floral and faunal associations with no exact modern equivalents.

Occasionally one or two members of a fauna appear out of place in the context of the rest of the fauna and flora. The explanation for this, having of course first ruled out reworking or intrusion of later material, is usually that the species concerned was formerly more widespread in its range of habitats or biotopes.

The ecology of an extinct animal can commonly be reconstructed in outline from the evidence of comparative anatomy, association with fossil floras

Fishes (Osteichthyes)

The study of Pleistocene freshwater fishes in Britain has so far been largely neglected, in spite of the abundance of fossil material. This is a pity because these animals have considerable potential as indicators of climate, and also of local environmental conditions.

As discussed in Chapter 3, many of the few available identifications of fossil fish should be regarded as provisional, until such time as a thorough study can be made. Such taxonomic uncertainties at present obviously limit the possibilities for interpretation of the fossil records.

Valuable summaries of the freshwater fishes of Europe given by Wheeler (1969) and Muus and Dahlstrøm (1971). The distributions of freshwater fishes both on a local and geographical scale is controlled by such factors as: oxygen concentration; temperature – very important for spawning and larval development; whether the water is fast flowing, slow flowing or still; the size of the water body; the presence of weeds or open water; availability of food; predators; and competition from other species.

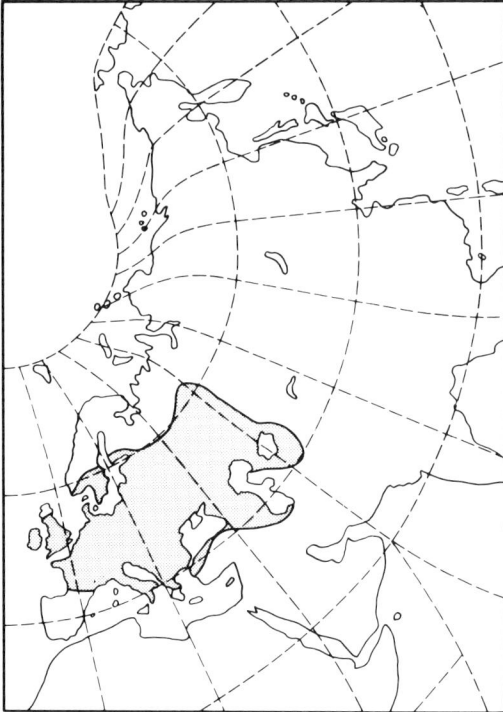

Fig. 5.1. Present distribution of rudd *Scardinius erythropthalmus* (Based on Muus & Dahlstrøm 1971.) Probably introduced in Ireland.

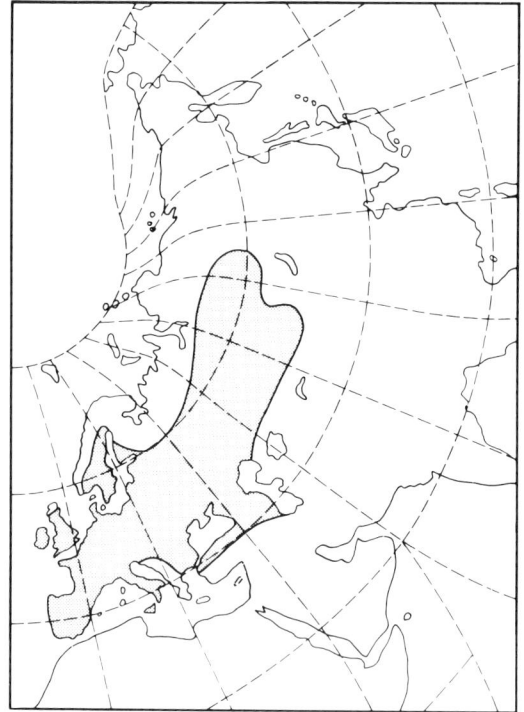

Fig. 5.2. Present distribution of tench *Tinca tinca*. (Based on Muus & Dahlstrøm 1971). Probably introduced in Ireland.

The distributions of the native European freshwater fishes are exclusively Palaearctic or Holarctic. There are no predominantly northern species, but several, including rudd *Scardinius erythropthalmus*, tench *Tinca tinca*, gudgeon *Gobio gobio*, and Chubb *Leuciscus cephalus*, do not occur farther north than the extreme south of Fennoscandia (Figs. 5.1, 5.2).

Most of the Pleistocene fossil fish faunas, from fluviatile deposits, represent the lowland bream zone of a river characterized by a slow current, often turbid water and a rich aquatic flora. The fauna from Brandon, Warwickshire, dating from a Wolstonian interstadial, is of great interest as it includes two fish species, *L. cephalus* and *G. gobio*, which suggest temperate climatic conditions (Ch. 8).

Amphibians (Amphibia)

The Pleistocene amphibians of Britain are poorly known, although there is abundant material, probably representing a modest number of species.

The majority of amphibians are very closely tied to water, laying eggs with a gelatinous coating in water where they hatch into larvae (tadpoles). After a period of feeding the larvae metamorphose to the adult form. They are entirely dependent on external heat for their activity, those in northern Europe hibernating during the winter, and are therefore potentially valuable climatic indicators. The food of most species comprises live invertebrates.

There are no species of Amphibia with exclusively northern distributions, but there is wide variation in the northern limits of many species within Europe, usually without replacement by other species, suggesting a climatic control of distribution. Distribution maps for Europe are given by Arnold and Burton (1978) and for the Soviet Union by Bannikov *et al.* (1977).

Of the very few fossil taxa so far reliably recorded in Britain, the common frog *Rana temporaria* is widespread in Europe to the far north of Fennoscandia. The common toad *Bufo bufo* is, however, absent from Ireland and northern Fennoscandia (Arnold & Burton 1978). Both species are recorded from interglacials and *R. temporaria* is known from the Devensian cold stage.

Reptiles (Reptilia)

In common with the other lower vertebrates the British Pleistocene, reptiles have generally received scant attention, with the exception of the European pond tortoise *Emys orbicularis*.

Reptiles are dependent on external temperatures not only for their activity but also, excepting the few oviviparous species, for their eggs to hatch, as certain minimum temperatures are necessary. The eggs are either hard shelled and laid in dry places, or soft shelled and deposited in more moist situations. With the exception of the tortoises, which are vegetarian, all of the European reptiles feed exclusively on live prey, mostly vertebrates. There are about eighty species of reptile now living in Europe. As with the other lower vertebrates there are no exclusively northern species, but many have distributions which strongly indicate climatic controls.

The viviparous (more accurately oviviparous) lizard *Lacerta vivipera* occurs in Ireland and ranges to the extreme north of Fennoscandia, whereas the northern limits of the adder *Vipera berus* and the grass snake *Natrix natrix* are found progressively further south within Fennoscandia (Arnold & Burton 1978).

The European pond tortoise *Emys orbicularis* frequents ponds, lakes and rivers with still or slow-flowing water, and feeds on aquatic invertebrates together with fish and amphibian larvae. In turn it is eaten by otters and herons and other predators. Females are commonly drowned during the rather brutal courtship, and during particularly hard winters individuals not buried to sufficient depth are killed by frost (Rollinat 1946).

The eggs are laid in light soil exposed to the warmth of the sun. Near the northern limit of its breeding range in central France, eggs may fail to hatch in particularly cool and damp summers.

The pond tortoise is the most northerly-breeding chelonian in the world, reaching to about latitude 55° N in central Europe (Fig. 5.3). The northern limit of the breeding range appears to be controlled by the degree of warmth and cloudiness during the summer months. A mean July temperature exceeding 17–18 °C combined with a considerable amount of sunshine with few damp, cloudy or rainy days seem to be necessary for the eggs to

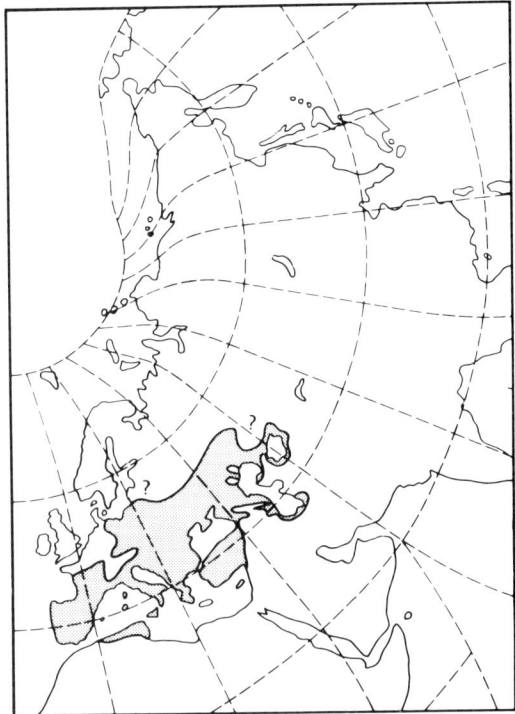

Fig. 5.3. Present distribution of European pond tortoise *Emys orbicularis*. (Based on Anderson 1979; Arnold & Burton 1978; Bannikov *et al.* 1977)

hatch. Because of the long lifespans of pond tortoises, individuals can wander some distance beyond the breeding range. Introduced animals live in Britain and elsewhere outside the natural range, but do not reproduce.

The fossil occurrences of *E. orbicularis* in the British Pleistocene have been discussed by Stuart (1979). Records are available from each interglacial, from the Cromerian (Westbury) to the Flandrian (Ch. 7). They demonstrate that for long periods within each of these stages the summers were drier, sunnier and at least 2 °C warmer than now. The Ipswichian finds show that high summer temperatures were maintained until late in the interglacial. The Flandrian records, from a single site – East Wretham in Norfolk, have been pollen-dated to zone VIIa (Fl IId), known from other palaeontological evidence to have been warmer than at the present day.

The numerous Flandrian finds, spanning a much longer period of time, from Denmark and Scania, reflect the more continental climate prevailing further east.

Several of the fossil finds appear to represent whole animals, found in fine-grained sediments, which either perished during mating or winter hibernation.

Birds (Aves)

In recent years there has been a resurgence of interest in Pleistocene birds in Britain, although as discussed in Chapter 3, considerable difficulties occur in identifying fossil bird material.

Bird bones are fairly common in cave deposits, but extremely rare in the fluviatile deposits which have yielded most of the fossils of other vertebrate classes known from open sites. Avian remains do however occur in archaeological contexts, e.g. Star Carr, and in Fenland peats. Not unexpectedly, most material from open sites represents bird species now closely associated with water.

Like mammals, the natural modern distributions of birds appear to be controlled by a variety of climatic and vegetational factors combined with interspecific competition. Distributions of breeding birds within the Palaearctic region are given by Voous (1960), and for the British Isles by Sharrock (1976). Both summer and winter ranges for western Palaearctic species are depicted in Heinzel *et al.* (1972).

The distributions of many birds have been much reduced by man within historic times, especially within the last two hundred years, e.g. pelicans *Pelecanus* sp. Others may have expanded their ranges in response to human modifications of the environment, especially deforestation and drainage of wetlands. (Ch. 10).

Unlike most mammals, the majority of birds undergo seasonal migrations, individuals in the western Palaearctic commonly flying some hundreds or even a few thousand kilometres southwards or south-westwards from the summer (breeding) to winter ranges. This means that in many cases the identification of a fossil bird gives little ecological information since it is not usually possible to determine at what time of year the particular species of bird was at the site.

Many of the species of birds found as fossils in the British Pleistocene at the present day do not occur further north than southern Scandinavia (Fig. 5.4) and these fossil occurrences therefore imply summers at least as warm as those of temperate Europe today.

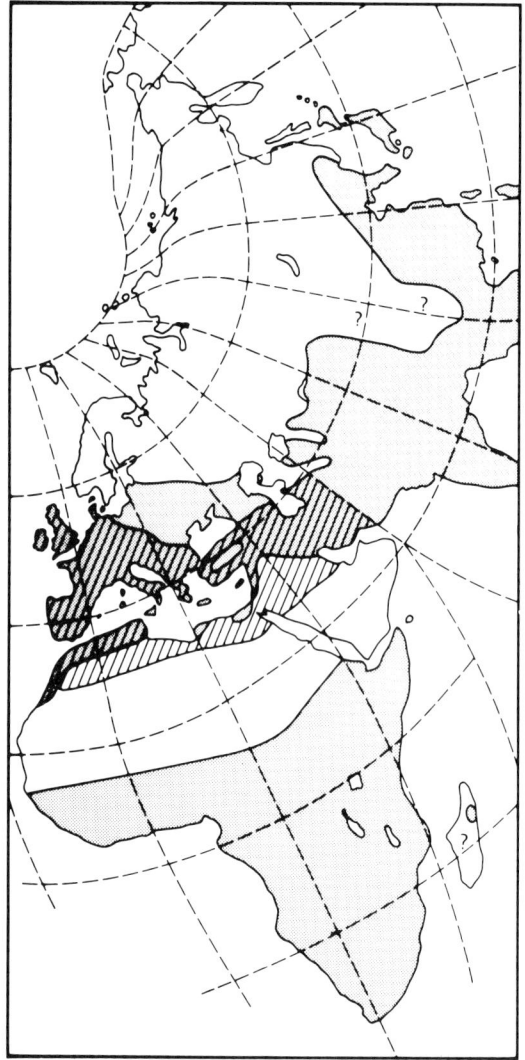

Fig. 5.4. Approximate present-day breeding (summer) range of little grebe *Tachybaptus ruficollis*. (Based on Voous 1960.) Winter range in western Palaearctic only (hatched). (Based on Heinzel *et al.* 1972.)

The ptarmigan *Lagopus mutus*, a non-migratory species, now occurs in the Holarctic tundra, the taiga of eastern Siberia, and the mountains of Scandinavia and Scotland, with isolated relict montane populations further south (Fig. 5.5). It is recorded from a few cave sites in England of Devensian age (Bramwell 1977; Harrison 1980). The occurrence of jungle fowl *Gallus* sp. in the Cromerian and Ipswichian interglacials (Ch. 7) implies changes in

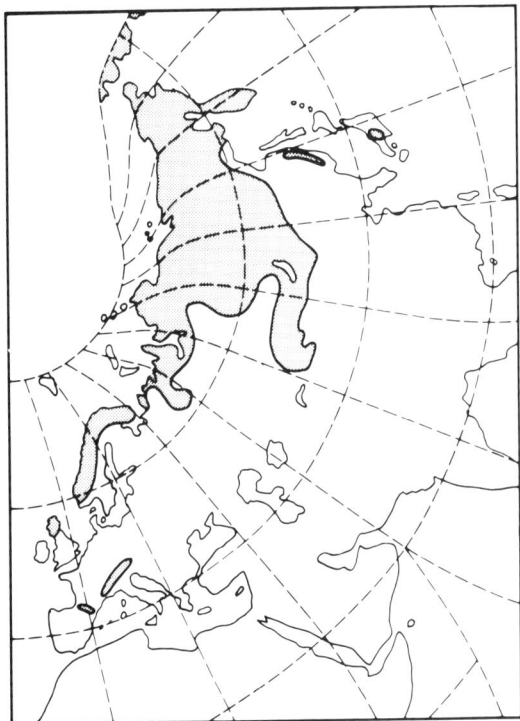

Fig. 5.5. Present distribution of ptarmigan *Lagopus mutus*. (Based on Voous 1960.) (Also in N. America.)

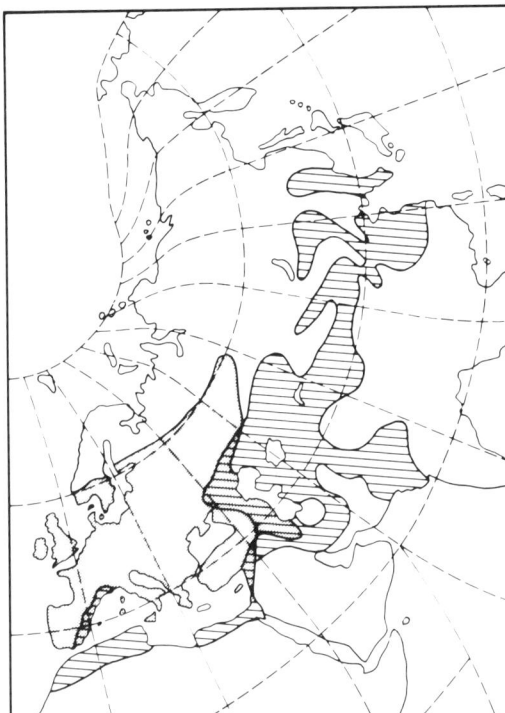

Fig. 5.6. Present distribution of European hedgehog *Erinaceus europaeus*, and other *Erinaceus* species (hatched). (Based on Corbet 1978.)

distribution comparable with those seen in mammals, since its near relative *G. gallus*, perhaps conspecific, is now restricted as a wild animal to the Indian subcontinent. Similarly, the mandarin duck *Aix galericulata* recorded from the Cromerian (Ch. 7) now occurs naturally in China, and the sarus crane *Grus antigone* from the Ipswichian interglacial is nowadays restricted to India, Burma and Thailand.

Mammals (Mammalia)

Like birds, mammals can maintain a constant body temperature (homoiothermy, endothermy) and are therefore less influenced by direct climatic factors than are the lower vertebrates. The present broad distributions of mammal species, allowing for modification by man, commonly approximate to a biotope characterized by a particular regional vegetation type, e.g. steppe, tundra, taiga, but in other cases they correspond much more closely to climatic divisions. Important limiting climatic fac-

tors appear to include snowfall, temperatures of the coldest month, and overall precipitation and its seasonal distribution. These climatic and vegetational conditions may not directly limit the distribution of a given species, but are effective in that they confer a strong disadvantage in the face of competition from other animals, better adapted to a different combination of environmental factors.

As has already been stressed, mammals are by far the most intensively studied of Pleistocene vertebrates, and are therefore considered here in more detail than the other groups. Fossil taxa, known only from finds which have yielded little or no useful ecological information, have however been omitted.

Hedgehogs (Insectivora: Erinaceidae)
European hedgehog *Erinaceus europaeus* occurs in the deciduous and mediterranean woodland zones of Europe and western Asia (Fig. 5.6). It eats a wide variety of invertebrates plus small vertebrates, carrion and fruit. It is rarely preyed on because of

the protection offered by its spines. Although a familiar and conspicuous animal, it actually occurs in very low population densities compared with other small mammals, and is extremely rare as a fossil. It is, however, recorded from the Cromerian, in association with mixed oak forest, and from the early Flandrian with birch and pine woodland (Ch. 7).

Shrews (Insectivora: Soricidae)

Shrews of the genus *Sorex*, to which most of the fossil species belong, are distributed widely in the Palaearctic and all have generally similar ecology. The diet consists of a variety of invertebrates, to which the teeth are clearly adapted. They occur in a wide variety of habitats – the only essentials for most species being food and adequate ground cover. They are heavily predated by birds of prey but occur in large population densities and breed rapidly. They are common in Pleistocene small-mammal assemblages.

White-toothed shrews *Crocidura* spp. are ecologically similar to *Sorex* spp. but their distributions are more southerly (Fig. 5.7). Their extremely rare occurrences in the British Pleistocene appear to be correlated with a climate rather warmer than that of the present day, in the Ipswichian interglacial (Ch. 7).

Present day water shrews *Neomys* spp. are mainly, but not exclusively associated with water. They are scarce compared with other shrews at the present day, and are scarce as fossils.

Beremendia cf. *fissidens*, known in Britain from only one site of Cromerian age (Ch. 7), was a very large shrew. Since the genus is extinct, its ecology can only be conjectured. Presumably it could have fed on a wide range of invertebrates.

Moles (Insectivora: Talpidae)

Common mole *Talpa europaea* is an entirely subterranean burrowing species and occurs in the deciduous and mixed woodland zones of Europe and western Asia (Fig. 5.8). Its distribution is likely to be limited by temperature, especially in avoiding areas with soils permanently or seasonally frozen. Moles are densest in soils with high humus content,

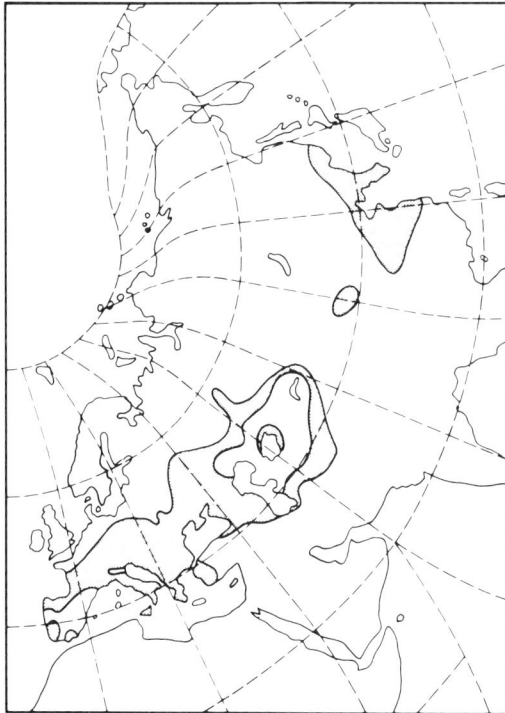

Fig. 5.7. Present distribution of lesser white-toothed shrew *Crocidura suaveolens* (Based on Corbet 1978)

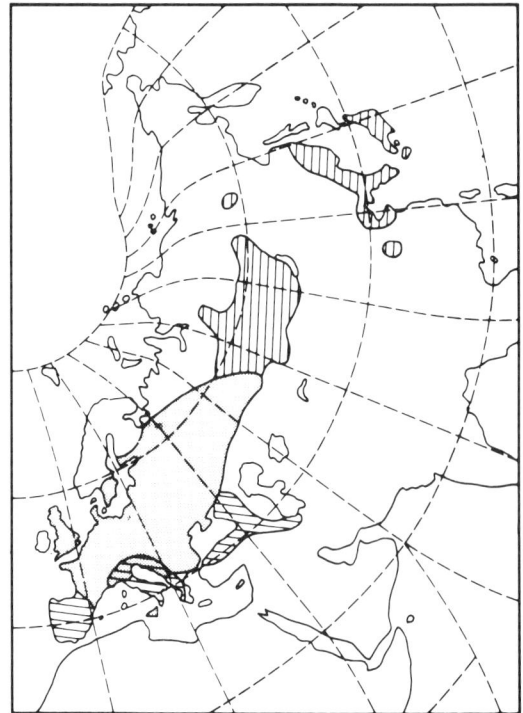

Fig. 5.8. Present distribution of common mole *Talpa europaea*, blind mole *T. caeca* (horizontal hatching) and other *Talpa* species (vertical hatching). (Based on Corbet 1978.)

and occur in deciduous woodland and meadows as well as cultivated ground (Corbet 1966). They eat mostly earthworms and insect larvae and are preyed on by tawny owls *Strix aluco* at such times as they emerge above ground or make very shallow runs.

A smaller species, *T. caeca*, with presumed similar ecology, replaces *T. europaea* in much of the Mediterranean area with some overlap. Two species, *T. europaea* and *T. minor*, of different sizes, co-existed in Britain and elsewhere during the Cromerian but only *T. europaea* was present in the Upper Pleistocene (Ch. 7). Presumably there was some sort of niche separation between the two species.

Moles are quite common in British Cromerian deposits, but are strangely rare in faunas from later stages. *Talpa europaea* occurs mostly, as would be expected, in interglacials, but there is one find from Tornewton cave which suggests that it was present also during some part of the Devensian cold stage (Ch. 8).

Desmans (Insectivora: Talpidae)

The living Russian desman *Desmana moschata*, nowadays occurs only in a limited area in the Ukraine (Fig. 5.9). It is always closely associated with water, preferring the stagnant or slow-flowing waters of river pools, oxbows and lakes, and avoiding rapid currents (Ognev 1928). It burrows into the banks and feeds on small aquatic animals, including various invertebrates, fishes and frogs, and some plant food. It has few predators. Another smaller desman *Galemys pyrenaicus* is found in upland and mountainous areas in the Pyrenees and northern Iberia. Its ecology is generally similar to that of *D. moschata*, with the important difference that it occurs in fast-flowing mountain streams (Corbet 1966). Both are anatomically highly adapted to an aquatic and burrowing mode of life.

The few British Pleistocene records of *D. moschata* are all from interglacials (Ch. 7) and the sediments in which they were found do not indicate fast-flowing water. This, or closely related species, are recorded from interglacials on the Continent, but surprisingly it also occurs in the Late-Weichselian of northern Germany (Degerbøl 1964) (Ch. 8).

The only other, as yet unnamed, Pleistocene desman known from Britain is recorded from the Pastonian temperate stage (Ch. 6).

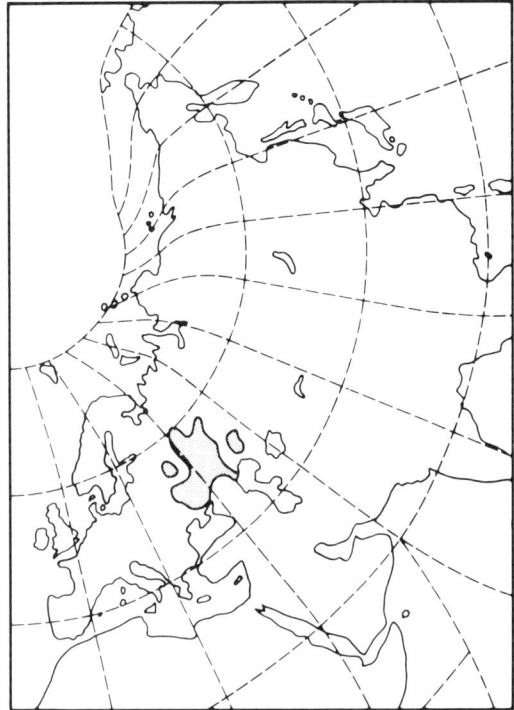

Fig. 5.9. Present distribution of Russian desman *Desmana moschata*. (Based on Corbet 1978.)

Bats (Chiroptera)

Bats are very rare fossils in the British Pleistocene. They are entirely unknown from open sites but do occur in some cave deposits. Most records of bats are not well stratified, and none have so far been described in detail.

There are about seventy species of bat (*Microchiroptera*) in the Palaearctic, with a marked concentration in the west of the region, in Europe and south-west Asia. Bats are absent from the tundra and also most of the taiga (see maps in Corbet 1978).

They are nocturnal, navigating by means of echolocation, and feed on insects caught in flight. They roost, and in winter hibernate in caves, hollow trees and buildings. The deaths of most animals occurs at the roosting sites, so that their remains tend to accumulate in cave deposits.

Monkeys (Primates: Cercopithecidae)

The modern Barbary ape *Macaca sylvana* is limited in occurrence to north-west Africa, and to Gibraltar, where it may or may not be native. Other species of *Macaca* occur in southern and eastern

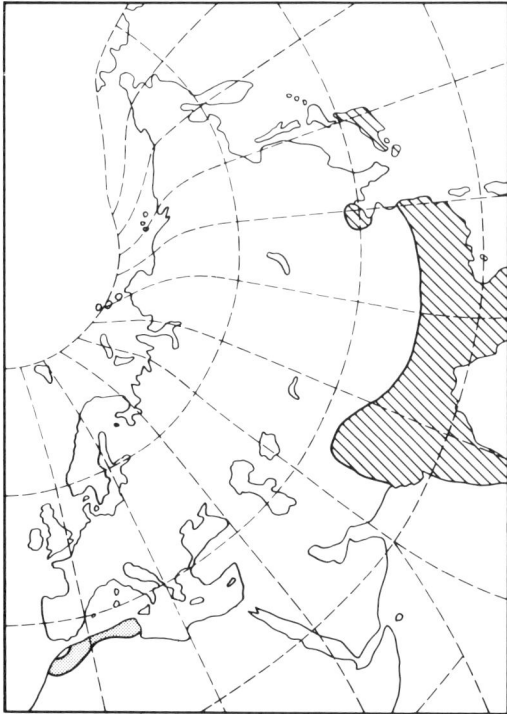

Fig. 5.10. Present distribution of Barbary ape *Macaca sylvana*, and other species of *Macaca* (hatched). (Based on Corbet 1978.)

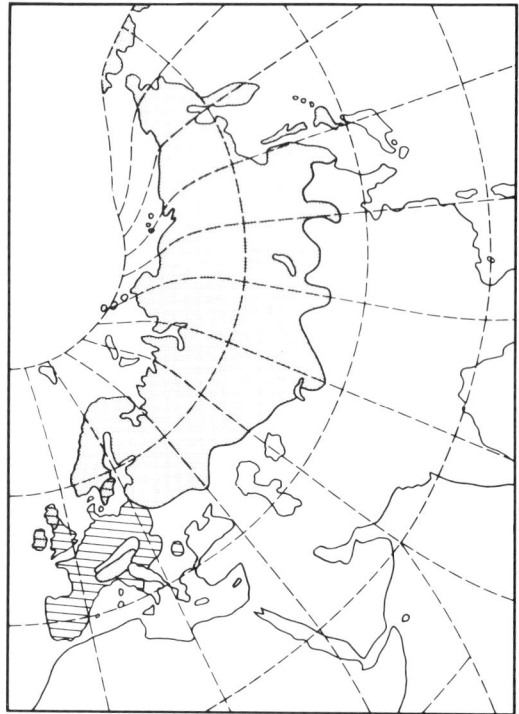

Fig. 5.11. Present distribution of arctic hare *Lepus timidus* and rabbit *Oryctolagus cuniculus* (hatched). (Based on Corbet 1978.) (*Lepus timidus* also in N. America.) The distribution of *O. cuniculus* has been considerably influenced by man.

Asia (Fig. 5.10). Barbary apes live in troops among rocks or in woodland and are rather awkward on level ground. They feed mainly on plant food including grass, fruits, leaves, roots and bulbs plus some invertebrate food (Hill 1974).

The sparse Cromerian and Hoxnian records of *Macaca* are all in association with temperate forests (Ch. 7).

Lagomorphs (*Lagomorpha*)

Two species of *Lepus* occur in Europe at the present day. The mountain or arctic hare *L. timidus* occurs mainly in the tundra and taiga zones of the Palaearctic and in the tundra of North America (Fig. 5.11). Isolated relict populations are found in the Alps, Scotland and Ireland. The brown hare *L. capensis* replaces *L. timidus* to the south, with some overlap roughly between latitudes 50° and 60° N in Europe. Both species inhabit open or lightly wooded country and eat grasses and other herbs, with bark and browse in winter (Corbet 1966).

Lepus capensis is not definitely recorded from the British Pleistocene, but sparse material of *L. timi-*

dus is known from the Devensian cold stage and from the Hoxnian and Ipswichian interglacials Chs. 7, 8).

During the postglacial the rabbit *Oryctolagus cuniculus* is generally thought to have been confined to Iberia until its fortunes were dramatically improved by man, from *c.* 2 000 years ago, who introduced it to much of north-west Europe (Fig. 5.11) and subsequently to many parts of the world. Like the hares, it is a species of open woodlands and grassland. It burrows extensively and feeds on grasses and herbs, and bark in winter (Corbet 1966).

Rabbits have been identified in England from the Hoxnian interglacial by Mayhew (1975), and there is a single find dated to the early Flandrian (Wymer 1962) (Ch. 7). If the latter find is accepted, it appears probable that it subsequently died out and was reintroduced as a domesticated animal in Norman or Plantagenet times, since there are no well-stratified records from Roman sites, for example (see Ch. 10).

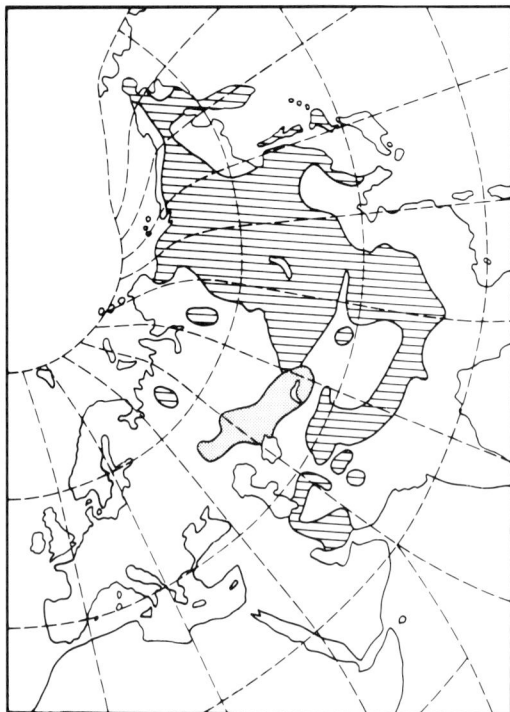

Fig. 5.12. Present distribution of steppe pika *Ochotona pusilla*, and other species of *Ochotona* (hatched). (Based on Corbet 1978.)

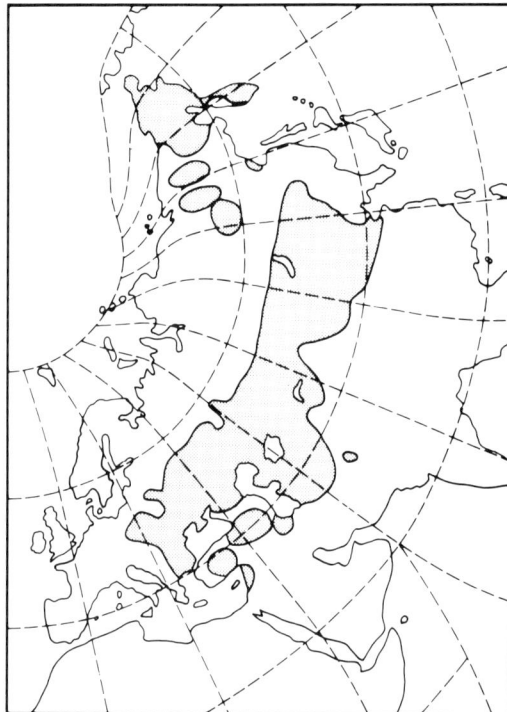

Fig. 5.13. Present combined distributions of species of ground squirrels (or susliks) *Spermophilus* spp. (Based on Corbet 1978.) (Also in N. America.)

The steppe pika *Ochotona pusilla* is restricted to the central part of the Palaearctic steppe. Other species of *Ochotona* occur in mountains (including screes and areas of coniferous forest), steppe and tundra in eastern Eurasia (Fig. 5.12). Pikas live in large colonies, burrow extensively, and feed on herbs, twigs and grasses which are spread out to dry and stored.

In the British Pleistocene, *Ochotona* sp. is recorded from Westbury, several Late-Devensian cave sites, and there is one record from the early Flandrian (Chs. 7, 8). They may represent a steppe component in the faunas from these sites, especially if *O. pusilla* is the species involved. The Flandrian find, however, if *in situ*, is associated with coniferous forest.

Squirrels (Rodentia: Sciuridae)

The red squirrel *Sciurus vulgaris*, a tree squirrel, is found throughout the forested zones of the Palaearctic as far north as the birch scrub between taiga and tundra. It eats conifer seeds, acorns, beech mast, hazelnuts and some animal food, and is preyed on by martens *Martes* spp. and several birds of prey. In common with other arboreal animals *Sciurus* is very poorly represented in the fossil record. The few British Pleistocene occurrences are all in association with forest floras.

The taxonomy of modern ground squirrels or susliks *Spermophilus* spp. is difficult, and their relationships with Pleistocene fossil species has yet to be properly worked out. Nowadays a number of species occur in the Eurasian steppes across to the coniferous forests of eastern Siberia, where they are mostly restricted to locally open areas, and into the tundras and prairies of North America (Fig. 5.13). They are generally characteristic of open grasslands and are very rarely found in forests. All *Spermophilus* spp. live in colonies and make extensive burrows. They feed mainly on grasses and other green plants and seeds, and these are stored underground for use during the winter.

Most of the few British Pleistocene records of *Spermophilus* are from cold stages in association with faunal or palaeobotanical evidence for herb-dominated vegetational conditions (Ch. 8). At Crayford, however, a species of *Spermophilus* appears to have been present towards the end of the Ipswichian interglacial (Ch. 7). It may perhaps have lived along the floodplain meadows of the river, or in a generally open boreal forest.

Beavers (*Rodentia: Castoridae*)

The beaver *Castor fiber* until recently occurred along all the rivers of the forested areas of the Palaearctic and North America. Beavers are well known for their habit of felling trees to build dams across rivers and streams, creating ponds about one metre deep which provide safe storage for and access to winter food. In summer they feed on aquatic and waterside plants, but for the rest of the year the staple food is bark of deciduous trees from stored branches, plus rhizomes, etc. (Corbet 1966).

Since its mode of life is so closely dependent on trees, fossil records of *C. fiber* would only be expected from interglacial and woodland interstadial periods, although so far they are only known from the former (Ch. 7). Beaver-gnawed branches have been found in the CF-bF (McWilliams 1967), which confirms a similar mode of life at least as far back as the Cromerian.

The mode of life of the extinct beaver *Trogontherium cuvieri* has been convincingly reconstructed by Mayhew (1978) on the basis of a thorough study of its skeletal anatomy together with palaeobotanical and sedimentological evidence. Its incisors, with rounded cross-section and thin enamel wear surface on the uppers, were clearly not adapted to felling trees, but may have served to prise off bark. In the living beaver *Castor fiber*, which actively cuts wood and fells trees, the incisors have flat enamel faces and a quite different type of wear.

The abundance of *T. cuvieri* remains in fluviatile and lacustrine deposits indicates that the animal was closely associated with water, and the large hind feet are thought to have been webbed. At sites in Britain and Europe with fine-grained deposits, *T. cuvieri* material tends to outnumber that of *Castor*, suggesting that the former favoured more slow-flowing or stagnant waters, when both animals occurred together.

All stratified records of *T. cuvieri* are from interglacial, or Lower Pleistocene temperate stages (Chs. 6, 7). Several occurrences are associated with regional temperate forest but the species was also present in association with largely coniferous forest at the close of the Dutch Tiglian TC5 (Lower Pleis-

tocene), and it is recorded from late in the Hoxnian stage – its last occurrence in the British Pleistocene.

Mayhew suggests that the living South American coypu *Myocastor coypus* provides the closest recent analogue to *T. cuvieri*.

Hamsters (*Rodentia: Cricetidae*)

The large common hamster *Cricetus cricetus* (not to be confused with the golden hamster *Mesocricetus auratus*) is primarily a species of the Eurasian steppe; but avoiding the more arid parts. It extends westwards into central Europe on cultivated ground (Fig. 5.14). It is found in grassland, including field margins and river banks, and it eats mainly seeds but also roots and insects. Common hamsters burrow extensively and store food for the winter (Corbet 1966). They are preyed upon by several mammalian carnivores.

Cricetus cricetus is very rare in the British Pleistocene. It occurs in apparent association with *Lagurus lagurus*, another steppe species, in the Glutton Stratum at Tornewton Cave, and rather unexpectedly in association with mixed oak forests and a temperate fauna in the Cromerian at West

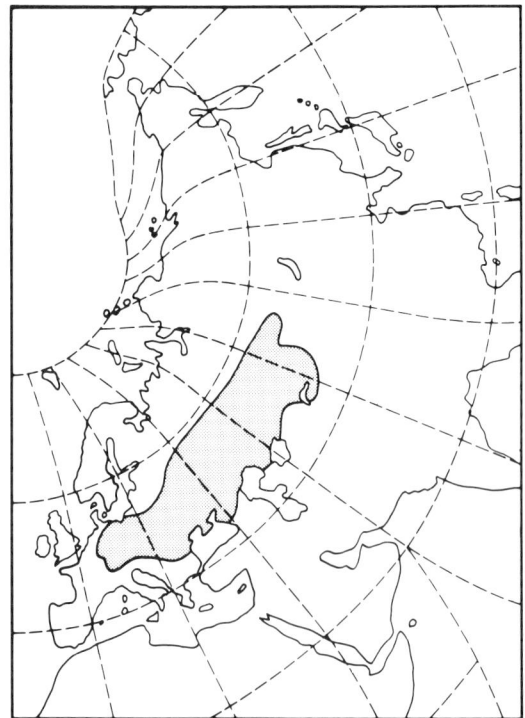

Fig. 5.14. Present distribution of common hamster *Cricetus cricetus*. (Based on Corbet 1978.)

Runton (Chs. 7, 8). It is also recorded from deposits of similar age and fossil content at Voigtstedt, East Germany (Ch. 7). These records indicate that in the Cromerian, *C. cricetus* probably penetrated further west into the temperate forest zone than it does today, perhaps in the main along river valleys where there was local grassland.

The occurrences of small hamsters at Tornewton Cave (Glutton and Bear Strata), and one or two other sites may perhaps reflect steppe-like environments.

Voles and lemmings (Rodentia: Cricetidae)

The voles and lemmings are the most commonly found small mammals in British Pleistocene deposits. Their lifespans are very short, only one to two years, and they commonly occur in very high population densities, attracting the attentions of a wide range of mammalian and avian predators.

The living bank vole *Clethrionomys glareolus* is found throughout the deciduous woodland and most of the taiga of the western Palaearctic, but is replaced by other species of *Clethrionomys* in the far north (Fig. 5.15). It lives in a variety of habitats but characteristically occurs where there is a shrub layer, i.e. mainly in woodland or on woodland margins under natural conditions. It has a much more varied diet than other voles, eating the green parts of various plants plus fruit, seeds, buds, bark, bulbs, roots and insects (Corbet 1966). This dentally non-demanding diet is reflected in the rather low-crowned cheek teeth, which unlike those of most modern voles are rooted and therefore do not continue to grow throughout life.

Bank voles are fairly common in interglacial faunas, often in association with palaeobotanical evidence for woodland (Ch. 7). The relative abundance of *C. glareolus* in small rodent faunas tends to be correlated with that of wood mouse *Apodemus sylvaticus*, and both to proximity of woodland to the depositional site.

The extinct vole *Pliomys episcopalis* is recorded in Britain only from Westbury-sub-Mendip and from the Cromerian of Sugworth, Berkshire (Ch. 7). The latter occurs in association with palaeobotanical evidence for temperate forest, and the relative abun-

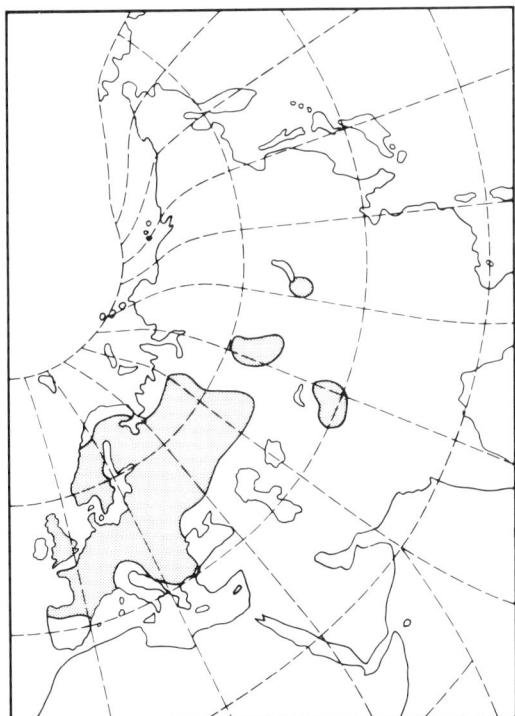

Fig. 5.15. Present distribution of bank vole *Clethrionomys glareolus*. (Based on Corbet 1978.) (Also introduced in south-west Ireland.)

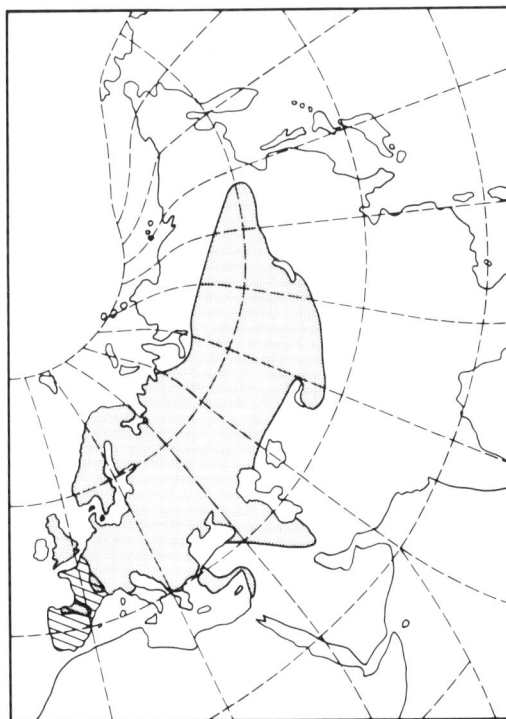

Fig. 5.16. Present distribution of water vole *Arvicola terrestris* and south-western water vole *A. sapidus* (hatched). (Based on Corbet 1978.)

dance of rodent species in the fossil assemblage suggests that there was little open ground close to the depositional site (see Fig. 5.33). The cheek teeth of *Pliomys* were high crowned but not permanently growing and moreover lacked cement (see Ch. 3), and are therefore unlikely to have been able to cope with grass. It was probably a woodland rodent, and may have resembled *C. glareolus* in its ecology.

The water vole *Arvicola terrestris* is widely distributed in the Palaearctic, but is replaced in most of France and Iberia by the south-western water vole *A. sapidus* (Fig. 5.16). *Arvicola sapidus* and generally *A. terrestris* are both closely associated with water, frequenting lakes and slow-flowing rivers with well-vegetated banks. In central Europe and the Alps, however, is found a form of *A. terrestris* which is much more terrestrial, living in grassland. These animals are small and have pro-odont incisors used in burrowing (Corbet 1966).

Arvicola sapidus and most *A. terrestris* feed on green waterside vegetation including reeds, other grasses, sedges and rushes. They are preyed on by otters, herons and some of the larger birds of prey.

The permanently growing cheek teeth of the living water voles are adapted to coping with abrasive grasses, as well as other plants, and it is reasonable to suppose that the extinct species *A. cantiana* had a similar diet. Its immediate ancestor *Mimomys savini*, however, has been distinguished generically on the basis that its cheek teeth were not permanently growing, so that presumably its diet was less demanding. In Lower Pleistocene *Mimomys* species such as *M. pliocaenicus* the cheek teeth were less hypsodont than in *M. savini*, and these voles probably ate little or no grass.

The high proportion of remains of *Arvicola* spp. or *M. savini* in many fossil small-mammal assemblages from fluviatile deposits is consistent with an amphibious mode of life, but some populations could have led a more terrestrial existence.

The smaller size of *Mimomys* spp. and *A. cantiana*, in comparison with modern British *A. terrestris*, would probably have made them vulnerable to predation by smaller avian and mammalian carnivores.

The genus *Microtus* is represented by about twenty-four species in the Palaearctic region (and many more in North America), but of these only four have been demonstrated to occur in the Pleistocene of Britain.

The field or short-tailed vole *Microtus agrestis* is found in the temperate forests and taiga of Europe,

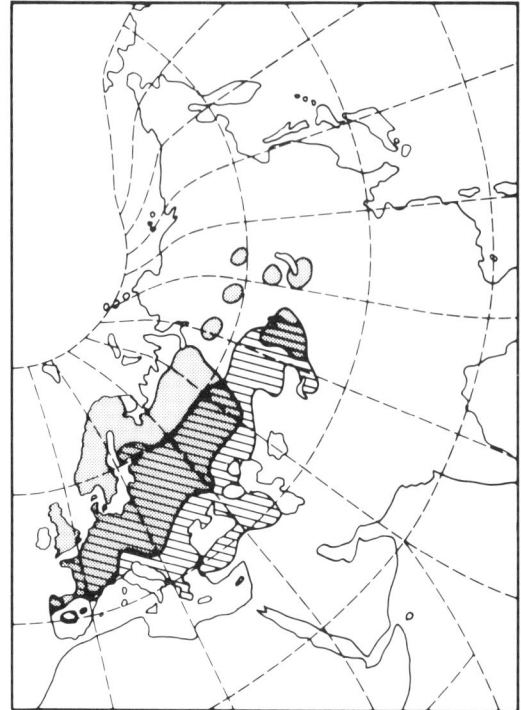

Fig. 5.17. Present distribution of field vole *Microtus agrestis* and common vole *Microtus arvalis* (including *M. subarvalis*) (hatched). (Based on Corbet 1978.)

with discontinuous populations eastwards to Lake Baikal, but is largely absent from the tundra. In the south of its range it is montane (Fig. 5.17) and it is replaced southwards by other species of *Microtus*.

The common vole *M. arvalis* and the very closely-related *M. subarvalis*, are distributed further south, largely avoiding the taiga, but there is a large area of overlap with *M. agrestis* (Fig. 5.17).

The northern vole *M. oeconomus* is widely distributed throughout almost the entire tundra and taiga zones of the Palaearctic, extending to northern Germany and the Netherlands in the west, and southwards to the more wooded parts of the steppe zone (Fig. 5.18). It also occurs in the western part of the North American tundra. The tundra or narrow-skulled vole *M. gregalis* has a curiously disjunct distribution, occurring throughout much of the tundra, in the far north, and again in the wooded steppes of central Asia (Fig. 5.18). It, or a closely-related species *M. miurus*, also occurs in the tundra of Alaska. All of these species of *Microtus* feed largely on herbaceous vegetation, particularly

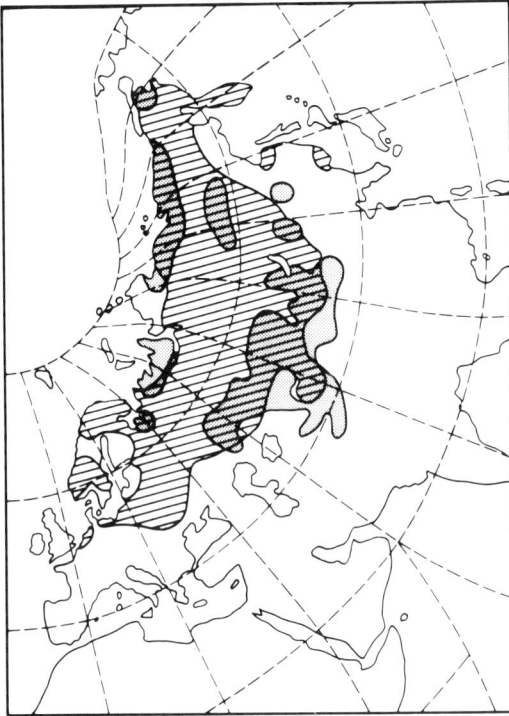

Fig. 5.18. Present distribution of tundra vole *Microtus gregalis* and northern vole *Microtus oeconomus* (hatched). (Based on Corbet 1978.) (Both species also in N. America.)

grasses. Their permanently growing cheek teeth are well adapted for coping with the latter. Roots, rhizomes and bark, where available, are consumed in winter. *Microtus agrestis* is characteristic of long grass, in areas ungrazed by large herbivores, and occurs especially on wet ground with rushes and sedges. It makes prominent runs through the grass. *Microtus arvalis* is more subterranean than *M. agrestis* and is found in association with short grazed grassland. *Microtus oeconomus* again burrows more extensively than *M. agrestis*, but like the latter species is characteristic of wet grassy and marshy habitats (Corbet 1966). *Microtus gregalis* leaves the wetter habitats to *M. eoconomus* where the two species occur together.

Microtus species can occur in very high population densities and sometimes show cycles of abundance with a periodicity of a few years. They attract a wide range of predators, including especially owls, diurnal raptors, foxes, mustelids and small cats.

Microtus remains are very common as Pleistocene

fossils, and are usually the most numerous single component of small-mammal assemblages, whether from open sites or caves – a reflection of relatively high population densities. Most cave material, and probably much of that from open situations as well, appears to have been transported to the depositional sites by predatory birds (see Ch. 4).

Field vole *M. agrestis* is recorded from interglacials from the Hoxnian onwards, and from the Devensian and probably Wolstonian cold stages (Chs. 7, 8). It occurs in association with all types of regional vegetational conditions from mixed oak forests to open herbaceous vegetation. During interglacials field voles probably frequented the local areas of herbaceous vegetation to be found along rivers in forested regions. Their tolerance of wet ground may enhance their relative abundance in fossil assemblages from fluviatile deposits.

Common vole *M. arvalis*, or related species, appears to have been present in the Cromerian and Hoxnian interglacials in association with regional temperate forests, living in local grassland habitats (Ch. 7).

Northern vole *M. oeconomus*, like *M. agrestis* perhaps over-represented in fossil assemblages due to its tolerance of wet ground, is known both from cold stages, in association with herb-dominated vegetation, and more rarely from interglacials, particularly from the opening and closing phases, in direct or inferred association with coniferous forests (Chs. 7, 8). As discussed in Chapter 11 the cold-stage forms are considerably larger than those from temperate stages.

Tundra vole *M. gregalis* is fairly common in deposits of Devensian age, and is recorded in association with herb-dominated vegetational conditions. It also occurs in the Wallingford Fan gravels of Anglian (or perhaps Wolstonian) age. It is absent from interglacial deposits, with the possible exception of Westbury-sub-Mendip (Chs. 7, 8).

The pine voles, genus *Pitymys*, have a southern distribution in the Palaearctic (Fig. 5.19). *Pitymys subterraneus*, the European pine vole, is the commonest and most widespread species, being found mostly in the southern half of the temperate forest zone and eastwards to the steppe. It may be conspecific with the Pleistocene species *P. arvaloides*. Other *Pitymys* species replace *P. subterraneus* in the Mediterranean zone and in parts of south-west Asia and the Himalayas, but the taxonomy of these has not yet been satisfactorily sorted out.

Pitymys subterraneus, and probably also the other

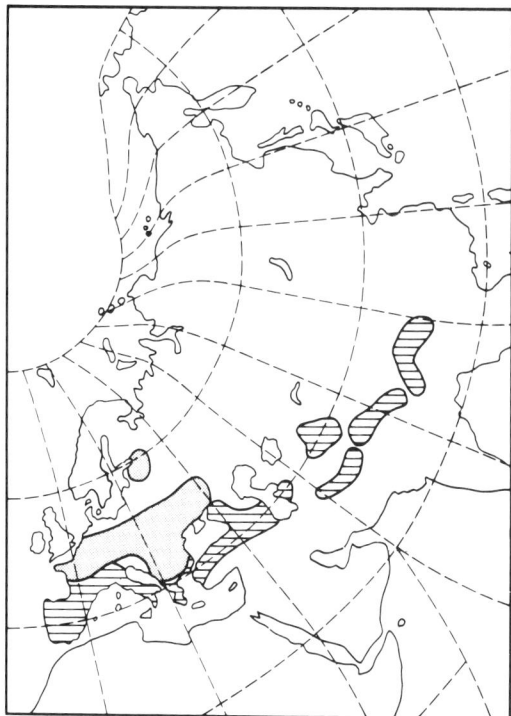

Fig. 5.19. Present distributions of European pine vole *Pitymys subterraneus*, and other species of *Pitymys* (hatched). (Based on Corbet 1978.)

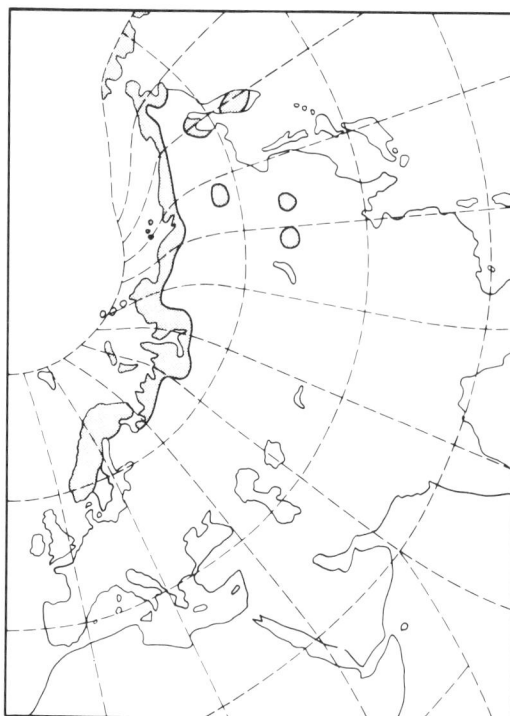

Fig. 5.20. Present distribution of Norway lemming *Lemmus lemmus*. NB the species east of the White Sea is often distinguished as *L. sibericus* and that of the Amur mountains as *L. amurensis*. (Based on Corbet 1978.)

species of *Pitymys*, frequent open grassland in which they make extensive burrows and lead a largely subterranean life, like *M. arvalis* (Corbet 1966).

The extinct pine vole *Pitymys arvaloides* is recorded from both the Cromerian and Hoxnian interglacials (Ch. 7). The Cromerian West Runton occurrences are in association with evidence of regional temperate forest and probably local grassland. *Pitymys gregaloides*, if a valid separate species, occurs also at West Runton and Westbury-sub-Mendip.

The Norway lemming *Lemmus lemmus* occurs over the entire Palaearctic tundra and southwards into the willow and birch woodland transitional to the taiga (Fig. 5.20). It also occurs in the mountains of Scandinavia and the upper Amur basin (*L. amurensis*) and in North America. Norway lemmings dig extensive tunnels in the tundra soil and beneath the snow in winter. Where the arctic lemming *Dicrostonyx torquatus* is also present, *L. lemmus* frequents the wetter low ground. The diet

consists of grasses, sedges, Ericaceae, mosses, lichens and fungi (Corbet 1966).

In 'lemming years' when the Norway lemming populations are at their peak, there are large-scale migrations far south into the coniferous forests of Fennoscandia.

The arctic lemming *Dicrostonyx torquatus* occurs throughout the Palaearctic tundra, including Greenland, but is absent from Fennoscandia (Fig. 5.21). It is also found in the tundra of North America west of Hudson's Bay. It frequents the drier habitats (see above). In summer it digs shallow burrows in the soil and nests under the snow in winter. The diet comprises grasses and sedges in summer, and buds, twigs and bark of willows in the winter. The arctic lemming, like the Norway lemming, shows dramatic fluctuations in population density. Both species of lemming are heavily predated by tundra birds of prey, including the snowy owl *Nyctea scandiaca* and by mammalian carnivores, especially foxes (Corbet 1966).

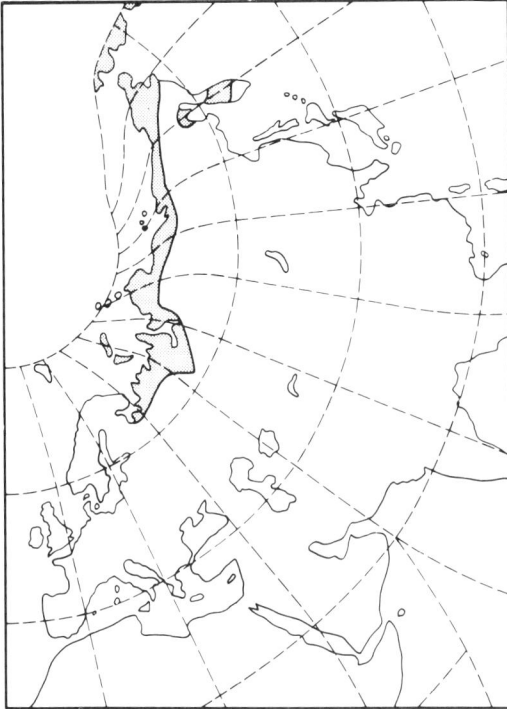

Fig. 5.21. Present distribution of arctic lemming *Dicrostonyx torquatus*. (Based on Corbet 1978.) (Also in N. America.)

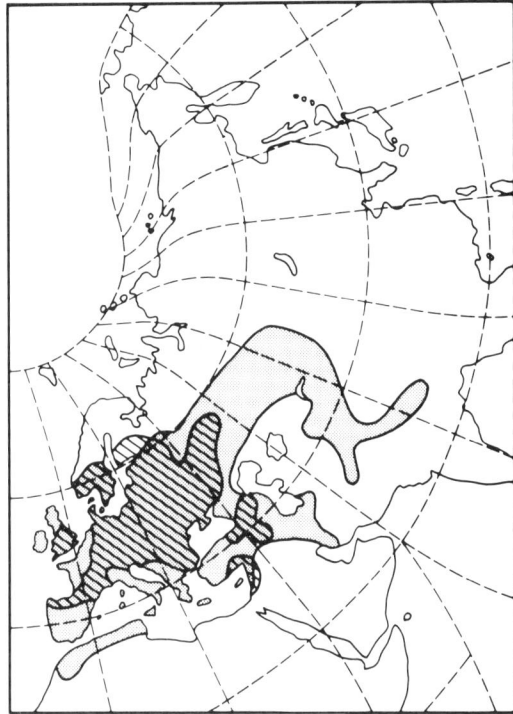

Fig. 5.22. Present distribution of wood mouse *Apodemus sylvaticus* and yellow-necked mouse *A. flavicollis* (hatched). (Based on Corbet 1978.)

Both species are recorded from cold stages in association with herb-dominated vegetational conditions (Ch. 8). *Dicrostonyx torquatus* and *L. lemmus* are, however, both recorded at Crayford, which is thought to date from the end of the Ipswichian stage when the regional vegetation was probably open coniferous forest. *Lemmus lemmus* is also recorded from the end of the Hoxnian or beginning of the Wolstonian at Hoxne, Suffolk and Swanscombe, Kent, and from Westbury-sub-Mendip, perhaps of late Cromerian age (Ch. 7).

The steppe lemming *Lagurus lagurus* is recorded in Britain only from the Glutton and Bear Strata of Tornewton Cave, Devon, probably dating from the Wolstonian Cold Stage (Ch. 8). *Lagurus lagurus* is nowadays found in the steppes from central Asia to the Ukraine.

Mice (Rodentia: Muridae)
The wood mouse *Apodemus sylvaticus* is primarily a species of the deciduous woodland, steppe and Mediterranean zones of the western Palaearctic

(Fig. 5.22). The closely related yellow-necked mouse *A. flavicollis* appears to have a more restricted distribution.

Both species are highly characteristic of woodland, but also frequent more open habitat with scattered shrubs where they are, however, greatly outnumbered by voles. They eat mostly seeds, nuts, fruit, buds and insects, and food is stored for the winter. They are preyed on by a large number of birds and mammals (Corbet 1966).

All of the well-stratified occurrences of *Apodemus* in the British Pleistocene so far are from interglacials (Ch. 7), although they will probably turn up in woodland interstadial deposits as well. Most of the records are in association with temperate deciduous woodland, but some are in association with coniferous forests.

Cats (Carnivora: Felidae)
The range of the lion *Panthera leo* is now restricted to sub-Saharan Africa and an isolated population in the Gir Forest in India. It has however been ex-

terminated by man within the last hundred years or so in much of the Middle East, north-central India and southern Africa. Approximately 2 000 years ago its range was even more extensive (Fig. 5.23).

The African lion is found in open and lightly wooded grassland, montane grassland, and sometimes subdesert but only exceptionally in dense forest (Dorst & Dandelot 1970). Its habitat in the Gir Forest is extensive scrub and stunted trees (Prater 1965). Lions live in prides of up to thirty animals and prey on a variety of medium to large herbivores, including even young hippopotamus and elephant.

Panthera leo is recorded from the Hoxnian and Ipswichian interglacials and from the Middle Devensian, and occurs in association with regional or local open herbaceous vegetation. It was probably also present in the Cromerian (Ch. 7).

As in the case of *Crocuta crocuta*, the present day southern distribution of *P. leo* does not appear to

be related to climatic factors, since it appears to have been present in England during rather cold phases of the Devensian Cold Stage (Ch. 8). Open habitats and abundant large herbivores are probably its main ecological requirements.

The enormous dagger-like upper canines of the extinct sabre-tooths *Homotherium* spp. may have been an adaptation for preying on thick-skinned herbivores such as elephants, rhinoceroses and hippopotamuses. Unfortunately none of the British Pleistocene finds is well-stratified or has a good associated flora or fauna.

The wild cat *Felis sylvestris* is found in the deciduous woodland, Mediterranean, savanna and steppe zones of the Palaearctic, India and Africa (Corbet 1978). It hunts small mammals, especially mice and shrews, but also squirrels, rabbits and hares. In Britain it is recorded from the Flandrian and Hoxnian interglacials, and a related form *Felis* cf. *lunensis* from the Cromerian of West Runton, Norfolk (Ch. 7).

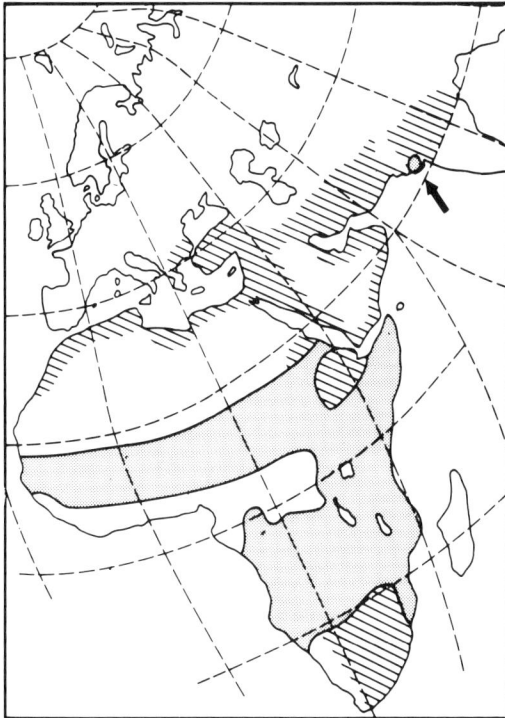

Fig. 5.23. Present distribution of lion *Panthera leo* (based on Dorst & Dandelot 1970). Note also the surviving population in India (arrowed). The hatched area gives a general impression of the areas in which the species has become extinct in the last 2 000 years or so.

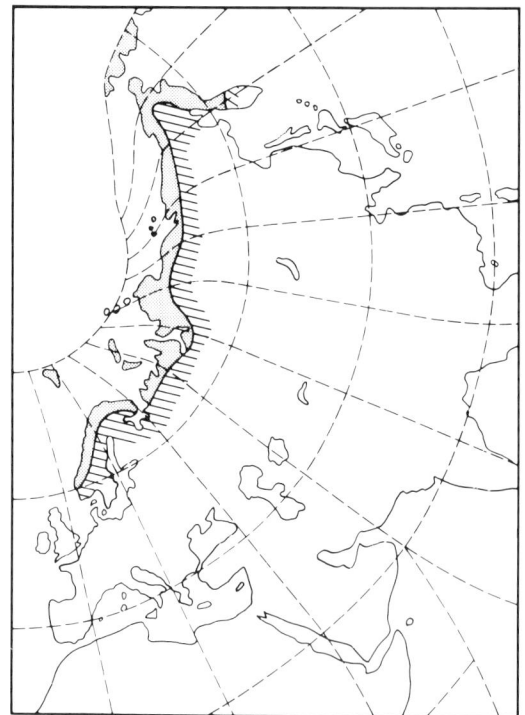

Fig. 5.24. Present distribution of arctic fox *Alopex lagopus*. The hatched area indicates the extension of range in winter. (Based on Corbet 1966, 1978.) (Also in N. America.)

Dogs (Carnivora: Canidae)

The wolf *Canis lupus* originally occupied nearly all of the Palaearctic and Nearctic, extending well into the tundra, but avoiding deserts. It has been exterminated by man in most of western Europe. Wolves occur in most Palaearctic terrestrial habitats, hunting in packs and taking a wide range of prey up to the size of reindeer and elk.

Canis lupus, and in the Lower Pleistocene *C. etruscus*, are among the most common carnivorous mammals in the British Pleistocene, being known from both cold stages and interglacials (Chs. 7, 8).

The red fox *Vulpes vulpes* is another very widespread Holarctic species, being absent only from desert, steppe and parts of the Siberian tundra (Corbet 1978). The smaller arctic fox *Alopex lagopus*, on the other hand, is restricted to the tundra, extending its range into the northern part of the boreal forest in winter (Fig. 5.24). *Vulpes vulpes* eats a variety of small mammals and birds plus insects, fruit and carrion, whereas *A. lagopus* feeds mainly on voles and lemmings.

Both species occur in the British Pleistocene but neither is very common. *Vulpes vulpes* is recorded from both cold stage and interglacial faunas whereas *A. lagopus* is known only from the Devensian (Chs. 7, 8).

Bears (Carnivora: Ursidae)

Bears are probably the commonest fossil Carnivora in the Pleistocene of Britain.

The brown bear *Ursus arctos* was present in historical times throughout the forested zones of the Palaearctic and western North America. It is now extinct in most of western Europe and North Africa (Fig. 5.25).

Ursus arctos is an omnivorous and very versatile feeder, changing its diet with the seasons. The long list of food taken includes roots and tubers, nuts, fruit, honey, fish, carrion, birds and mammals from voles to deer and wild boar. In winter brown bears hibernate in a den in a cave or excavated under a rock or tree.

Ursus arctos is known from the Ipswichian and Flandrian interglacials and from the Devensian in Britain (Chs. 7, 8). The Devensian records suggest that this species did not always occur in association with forests. The bears recorded from earlier stages are the extinct *U. deningeri* (late Lower Pleistocene? and Cromerian) and the very similar, but larger cave bear *U. spelaeus* (Hoxnian). According to Kurtén (1968) the dentition of the cave bear indicates a

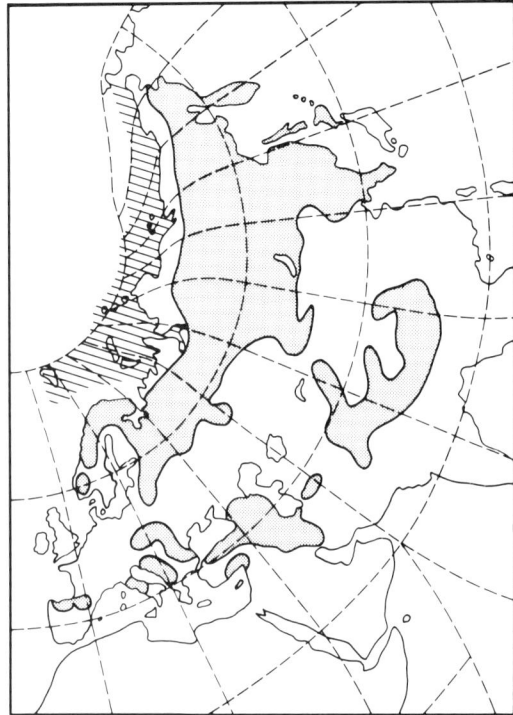

Fig. 5.25. Present distributions of brown bear *Ursus arctos* and polar bear *Ursus (Thalarctos) maritimus* (hatched). (Based on Corbet 1978.) *Ursus arctos* has been recently exterminated in most of W. Europe and N. Africa. (Both species also in N. America.)

much more herbivorous diet than that of the brown bear. *Ursus spelaeus* survived until the Last Cold Stage (Weichselian, Devensian) in central and eastern Europe and perhaps also in Britain. All three species occur, often in large numbers, in European cave deposits, and these probably represent animals that died during hibernation when their fat reserves were low.

The polar bear *Ursus (Thalarctos) maritimus* has a circumpolar distribution and is essentially a marine animal confined to the sea ice and coasts bordering the Arctic Ocean (Fig. 5.25). Polar bears do, however, occasionally reach as far as Iceland and Japan on ice flows (Corbet 1978) and animals do also penetrate some tens or hundreds of kilometres inland (Banfield 1974). Seals are the principal prey.

Polar bears are extremely rare as fossils, which is not surprising in view of their present day mode of life. The single, poorly dated Devensian record from Kew, London, (Ch. 8) presumably represents an individual that wandered far from the nearest sea which, with the considerable drop in sea level during the Last Cold Stage, would have been at least some 140 km away to the south (see Fig. 2.7).

Mustelids (*Carnivora: Mustelidae*)

The Mustelidae are the largest group of Palaearctic Carnivora and are reasonably well represented as Pleistocene fossils.

The glutton, or wolverine *Gulo gulo* occurs throughout the taiga of the Holarctic, moving northwards to the southern part of the tundra in summer (Corbet 1966). The diet consists of carrion, small birds and mammals, fruit and berries.

Gluttons are surprisingly rare as fossils, but records include those from the Glutton Stratum (?Wolstonian) of Tornewton Cave and from the Devensian (Ch. 8). An earlier species *Gulo schlosseri* is known from the CF-bF and may be of Cromerian or early Anglian age. There is no reason to think that it was restricted to boreal environments.

The badger *Meles meles* occurs throughout the woodland and steppe zones of the Palaearctic, except North Africa, northern Fennoscandia and north-east Siberia (Corbet 1978) where it avoids the areas of permafrost. It frequents open woodlands and open country, and in detail its distribution is governed by availability of suitable soils, usually sand, in which it burrows. Badgers are social animals and have a highly varied omnivorous diet.

They are extremely rare as Pleistocene fossils but are recorded from the Glutton Stratum of Tornewton Cave (Ch. 8), and from the middle of the Ipswichian interglacial at Barrington near Cambridge in association with regional mixed oak forest, but an extensively deforested floodplain. They are also recorded from the early Flandrian in association with birch and pine woodland (Ch. 7).

The pine marten *Martes martes* occurs over most of Europe except the tundra, steppe and Iberia, and is replaced by other species of *Martes* in Asia. The beech marten *M. foina* has a more southerly distribution which largely overlaps that of *M. martes*, but it is absent from the British Isles (Corbet 1978).

Both species are mainly arboreal, although rocky ground is also frequented. They prey on small mammals and birds.

Martes sp. is recorded from the Cromerian interglacial (in association with temperate forest), the Hoxnian interglacial and the early Flandrian (Ch. 7).

The stoat *Mustela erminea* and the weasel *M. nivalis* both occur throughout the Palaearctic (except that the former is absent from North Africa) and into North America (Corbet 1978). Their modes of life are very similar except that each takes prey appropriate to its size. The principal habitat requirement is good ground cover to protect them from predatory birds. Their prey ranges from shrews and small rodents to water voles, and rabbits in the case of the stoat. The weasel in particular is sufficiently small and numerous to be preyed on in turn by numerous mammalian and avian carnivores.

There are a few, mostly poorly stratified, records of these two species in the British Pleistocene. *Mustela nivalis*, however, occurs in association with temperate forest in the Cromerian (Ch. 7).

The common otter *Lutra lutra* is very widely distributed in the Palaearctic, wherever there is water, avoiding only deserts and the Siberian tundra (Corbet 1978). The clawless otters genus *Aonyx* are distributed in Africa and southern Asia. The ecology of *Lutra* and *Aonyx* is very similar; both feeding on aquatic animals, mostly fish. *Lutra* is recorded from the Cromerian and *Aonyx* from the Glutton Stratum of Tornewton Cave (Ch. 8).

Hyaenas (*Carnivora: Hyaenidae*)

The living spotted hyaena *Crocuta crocuta* is restricted to Africa south of the Sahara, avoiding the heavily forested regions (Fig. 5.26). It inhabits savannas and semideserts and is rare in dense forests. It scavenges the kills of other predators, mainly lions and hunting dogs, but is also an active predator in its own right, hunting in groups and killing animals up to the size of zebra and young elephant. The powerful jaws and very sturdy teeth are adapted to crushing bones which are then eaten (Dorst & Dandelot 1970).

In the British Pleistocene *C. crocuta* is known from the Cromerian and Ipswichian interglacials with associated floras generally indicative of regional forests, with in some cases rather extensive open herbaceous vegetation along river floodplains, but one occurrence at Swanton Morley, Norfolk, in subzone Ip IIa was in association with forest (Ch. 7). None of the cold-stage occurrences have associated floras, but open herbaceous vegetational conditions are likely to have been present (Ch. 8).

Large-mammal bones damaged by hyaenas are known from several open sites and excavations of caves have demonstrated that many were used as hyaena dens during the Ipswichian and Devensian

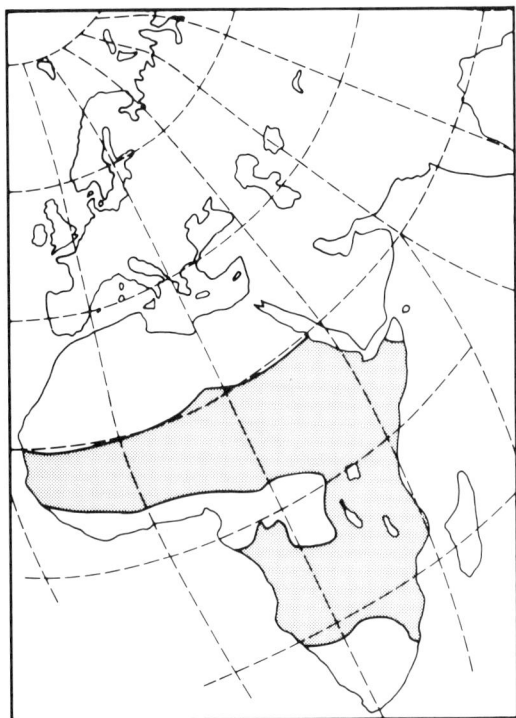

Fig. 5.26. Present distribution of spotted hyaena *Crocuta crocuta*. (Based on Dorst & Dandelot 1970.)

stages. In the British Pleistocene *C. crocuta* evidently collected bones even more enthusiastically than does the living African animal (Ch. 4).

There is little exact stratigraphical information on the occurrences of the extinct hyaena *Hyaena brevirostris* from the early Middle Pleistocene. The two living species of *Hyaena*, *H. striata* and *H. brunnea*, are more strictly scavengers than is *C. crocuta*.

Gomphotheres (*Proboscidea: Gomphotheriidae*)

There are several records of the extinct gomphothere mastodont *Anancus arvernensis* from the Lower Pleistocene in England, although it is absent from the latest stages (Ch. 6). The low-crowned bunodont molars strongly suggest a diet of browse and possibly other fairly soft plant food rather than grasses. The Bramerton and Easton Bavents finds record *A. arvernensis* in association with either temperate or coniferous forests.

Elephants (*Proboscidea: Elephantidae*)

None of the extinct European Pleistocene elephants appears to be very closely related to either of the modern species, but the latter can still throw some light on the likely ecology of the fossil animals.

Both the African elephant *Loxodonta africana* and the Indian elephant *Elephas maximus* live in herds, and require vast quantities of vegetable food. *Loxodonta africana*, nowadays confined to sub-Saharan Africa but formerly present also in North Africa, is found in montane forest to subdesert, but is mostly characteristic of forested savanna, usually not far from water. Extensive migrations can occur in times of drought (Dorst & Dandelot 1970). When population densities are very high, African elephants can cause serious deforestation.

Elephas maximus occurs naturally in the forests of India and south-east Asia, and is found in every type of forest from humid jungle to cool montane woodlands (Prater 1965).

A consideration of the molar teeth would suggest that *E. maximus*, which has closer-packed enamel lamellae, includes a higher proportion of grass in its diet than *L. africana*, which would be expected to be more specialized towards browsing. There is, at first sight however, apparently no clear correlation of dentition and diet. Both species eat a wide variety of plant food including leaves, twigs, shoots, bark, roots and fruits, but grass can constitute most of the large volume of food intake. It appears however that modern *L. africana* has been forced to subsist largely on grass due to habitat destruction by man, and that orginally this species was predominantly a browser (Haltenorth & Diller, 1980).

There is little information from the British Pleistocene on the ecology of *Archidiskodon meridionalis* or *Mammuthus trogontherii*, but the later species, the straight-tusked elephant *Palaeoloxodon antiquus* and the mammoth *Mammuthus primigenius*, are known from a number of well-stratified finds, often with associated fossil floras.

Palaeoloxodon antiquus, with one possible exception (Ch. 8) is confined to interglacials, and the Hoxnian and Ipswichian records show that it was associated with temperate forests (Ch. 7). Its diet probably included both grass and browse.

Mammuthus primigenius occurs mostly in cold-stage faunas associated with open grassy vegetational conditions, but was also present in boreal forest in the Chelford interstadial, and in temperate deciduous forests and coniferous forests in the second half of the Ipswichian interglacial, where for some time it co-existed with *P. antiquus*. The Ipswichian occurrences appear to be associated with a general opening out of the forest during the second half of this interglacial (Chs. 7, 8).

The molars of mammoth have very densely packed lamellae (Ch. 3), far more so than in *E. maximus*, and are very probably an adaptation to coping with a high proportion of grass in the diet. The stomach contents of the frozen mammoth cadaver found at Beresovka, Siberia, show that this animal fed on grasses and other herbs (Heintz 1958; Heintz & Garutt 1965).

Horses (*Perissodactyla: Equidae*)

The wild horse or tarpan *Equus ferus* is now almost extinct as a wild animal, being restricted to a small area on the border of south-west Mongolia and Sinkiang, but was originally probably present over most of the steppe zone from Mongolia to eastern Poland and Hungary (Corbet 1978). It may also have been present in the forests of western Europe until within the last few hundred years (Groves 1974), although this question is confused by the presence of feral domestic horses.

The six or so other living species of *Equus* – the zebras of Africa and the asses, etc., of Asia and North Africa, are all closely associated with grasslands. Because of their hooves, horses are intolerant of soft marshy ground and deep snow. On the other hand, they can thrive on a diet of coarse, low-quality grasses.

In common with most horses, *E. ferus* is or was a grazing species living in herds. It is the ancestor of the domestic horse. Horses are among the commonest Pleistocene mammal fossils in Britain and Europe, but unfortunately their taxonomy is rather confused, especially for the Lower and early Middle Pleistocene forms (Ch. 3). *Equus ferus* or a similar species is known from cold-stage faunas, including several of Devensian age with associated regional herb-dominated vegetational conditions (Ch. 8). The species is also, however, recorded in numerous interglacial faunas, in association with both regional temperate and coniferous forests, although it is entirely absent from the well-known assemblages of zone Ip II age (Ch. 7). The reasons for the latter phenomenon are not obvious, and horses were present in Germany and elsewhere in the middle of the Eemian interglacial. In Britain *E. ferus* appears to have become extinct at the very beginning of the Flandrian as it did in Denmark and North Germany (Degerbøl 1964).

At every interglacial site where horses have been found with associated flora, there is evidence for either open woodland or at least local herb-dominated vegetation which would have provided the necessary grazing.

Lower Pleistocene horses, including both caballine species and the extinct *Equus stenonis*, are again recorded in association with temperate forests (Ch. 6).

Rhinoceroses (*Perissodactyla: Rhinoceratidae*)

None of the species of rhinoceros from the Pleistocene of Europe survives today, although the genus *Dicerorhinus* is represented by the living Sumatran rhinoceros *D. sumatrensis*. The varied structure and ecology of the other four present day rhino species can also throw light on the fossil forms.

Dicerorhinus sumatrensis was until recently present from eastern India through Burma and Malaya to Sumatra and Borneo (Prater 1965). It is a very small rhino, confined to forested areas where it browses on twigs and shrubs.

Something of the mode of life of each fossil species of *Dicerorhinus* can be deduced from its skull morphology (Zeuner 1932) (Ch. 3) and its dentition, by comparison with the modern species, plus associated flora and fauna. Thus *D. etruscus* recorded from the Cromerian interglacial and the Lower Pleistocene, with its low-crowned cheek teeth and horizontal carriage of the head, was probably mainly a browser. Palaeobotanical evidence suggests that it lived in forest rather like its smaller living relative. *Dicerorhinus kirchbergensis*, thought to have been present in the Hoxnian, was similar, although larger with higher-crowned teeth, and it too appears to have been associated with forests (Ch. 7). It may have been a browser, or a browser-grazer like the living African black rhinoceros *Diceros bicornis*. In *Dicerorhinus hemitoechus* however, a Hoxnian and Ipswichian species, the skull was habitually carried low, rather as in the modern African white rhinoceros, which suggests that the extinct animal fed largely on low-growing herbaceous vegetation. Although present in interglacials, it appears to have frequented rather open woodlands and locally deforested areas along river valleys.

The skull morphology of the extinct woolly rhinoceros *Coelodonta antiquitatis* is very similar to that of *D. hemitoechus*, and like this species it, too, almost certainly fed mainly on low-growing grasses and other herbs. *Coelodonta antiquitatis* is recorded mainly from cold stages, but also from the end of the Ipswichian interglacial (Chs. 7, 8). Associated fossil floras and faunas generally indicate open herbaceous vegetation, but it occurs in association with boreal forest in the Chelford Interstadial, and at the end of the Ipswichian.

Pigs (Artiodactyla: Suidae)
The wild boar *Sus scrofa* was present until a few hundred years ago over the deciduous woodland and Mediterranean zones of Europe, North Africa and the southern half of Asia (Fig. 5.27). It has been locally exterminated by man in many parts of Europe. It is a rather solitary animal, generally characteristic of broad-leaved forests, and is an omnivore feeding largely on bulbs, roots, acorns, beechmast with some animal food. Although a formidable animal with its large tusks, wild boar is preyed upon by such large carnivores as wolf *Canis lupus*, brown bear *Ursus arctos*, and in southern Asia tiger *Panthera tigris*.

All British Pleistocene records of *Sus scrofa* are from interglacials, generally in association with

temperate forests, but early Flandrian finds show that it was present in association with birch and pine woodland.

Hippopotamuses (Artiodactyla: Hippopotamidae)
The hippopotamus *Hippopotamus amphibius* is at the present day restricted to sub-Saharan Africa, although in historical times it also occurred throughout the Nile Valley (Fig. 5.28). The other, much smaller, living hippopotamus *Choeropsis liberiensis* is not closely related to the European Pleistocene hippopotamuses.

Hippopotamus amphibius is a gregarious animal and lives in rivers and lakes bordered by grassland. Hippos spend the daylight hours in the water and come out only at night to feed. The diet consists largely of grass and aquatic plants, and the habitat within a kilometre or so on either side of a river or lake is usually much modified by their grazing and trampling activities which open up short grassland communities, and even areas of bare ground (Lock 1972). The possible bias to pollen spectra from

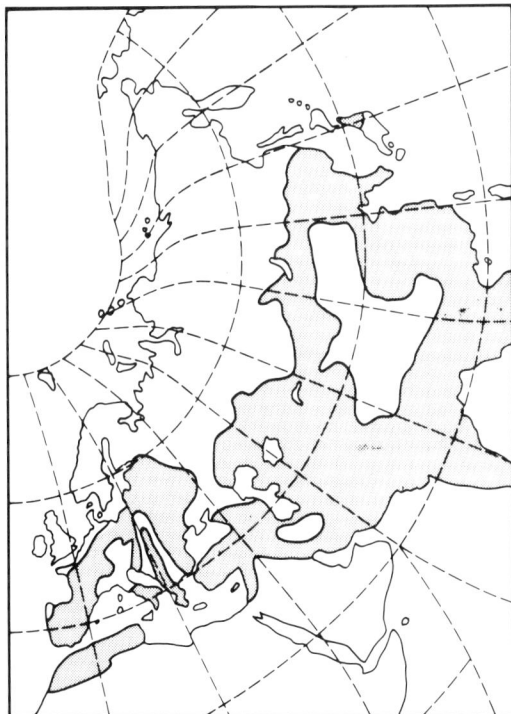

Fig. 5.27. Present distribution of wild boar *Sus scrofa*. (Based on Corbet 1978.) (Also occurred over most of western Europe including Britain within the last 300 years or so.)

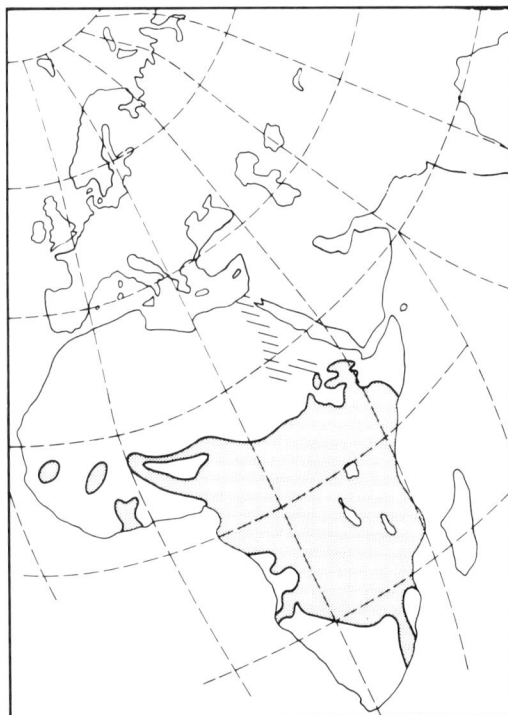

Fig. 5.28. Present distribution of hippopotamus *Hippopotamus amphibius*. (Based on Dorst & Dandelot 1970.) Distribution *c.* 500 years B.P. in Nile Valley (hatched).

such deposits caused by their habit of feeding on land and defaecating in the water is discussed in Chapter 7.

The occurrences of hippopotamuses in the British Pleistocene are discussed in detail by Stuart (1982). During part of the Last Interglacial the European distribution of *H. amphibius*, probably included the Mediterranean area and extended northwards through France to Britain. There are probably about ninety post-Anglian sites with hippopotamus in England and Wales, and all of these appear to be of Ipswichian age (Ch. 7). The pollen-dated finds, and many others with associated faunas, indicate that hippos were present in zone II and the very beginning of zone III but not later in the stage. The most northerly record in the world for hippopotamus is from Stockton-on-Tees, latitude 54° 35′ N, and it is quite possible that the species extended considerably further north than this.

At the few Ipswichian hippopotamus sites which have also yielded pollen, it is clear that the animals were associated with regional temperate forests, but that at some, but not all, of the sites there was extensive local deforestation with herb floras, e.g. including high plantain *Plantago*, characteristic of grazed and trampled grassland. The resemblance to modern hippopotamus habitats is further enhanced by the highly mineragenic content of the sediments from Barrington, Cambridgeshire, where subzone Ip IIb pollen spectra consisted of over 90 per cent herb pollen (Gibbard & Stuart 1975) (Ch. 7), suggesting inwash of soils from bare trampled ground.

The presence of hippopotamus remains in Victoria Cave, Settle, Yorkshire (latitude 54° 05′ N) shows that these animals occurred at at least 440 mm O.D. The site is over 2 km from, and about 290 m above the flood plain of the modern River Ribble, which appears to have been the nearest large body of water in the Ipswichian, as it is today. The hippos probably left the river at night and climbed the valley slopes to graze on the rich limestone herb flora.

During the early Middle Pleistocene hippopotamuses (*Hippopotamus* cf. *major*) were present in England and extended further eastwards into central Europe than in the Last Interglacial, occurring at Mosbach, Mauer and other localities in West Germany.

The English finds, from the Cromer Forest-bed Formation, appear to be mostly or entirely of Cromerian age (Ch. 7). Pollen spectra from sediment adhering to hippopotamus material indicates

that they date from surprisingly late in the stage (zones Cr IIIb–IV) when the temperate forest of the middle of the interglacial was giving way to coniferous forests. There is no indication of extensive herbaceous vegetation in these spectra.

It is difficult to disentangle the factors controlling the past and present distributions of hippopotamuses. The present day absence of these animals from Europe could be due to climate, to human interference or to distributional barriers in the Mediterranean area. It is possible that hippopotamuses are restricted by climate in that they would need an impossibly high food intake to maintain body temperature when immersed in the very cold waters of European lakes and rivers during the winter at the present day.

Deer (Artiodactyla: Cervidae)

The times of shedding of deer antlers are shown in Fig. 5.34.

The distribution of the fallow deer *Dama dama* has been much interfered with by man, who in particular was responsible for introducing this deer to much of central and northern Europe. Its original range was probably Mediterranean, including North Africa, across to Asia Minor and Iran (*D. dama mesopotamica*). It lives in small groups and favours rather open deciduous woodland with grassy glades. Fallow deer are browser-grazers, eating grasses, other herbs, shrubs, and tree foliage plus acorns, etc. (Corbet 1966).

In the British Pleistocene *D. dama* is restricted to interglacials (Ch. 7) and is one of the most reliable indicators of interglacial conditions in a British Pleistocene fauna. Where associated plant fossils are available, temperate forests are indicated, although the species appears to have survived until late in the Hoxnian interglacial. On the other hand, it does not occur later than zone II of the Ipswichian.

The red deer *Cervus elaphus* is a highly adaptable species, being present over most of the deciduous and Mediterranean woodland zones of western Europe, extending eastwards along the forested strips of the Asiatic mountain ranges and along wooded water courses in otherwise treeless steppe and semidesert areas (Fig. 5.29). It does not extend appreciably northwards into the taiga, probably in the main because of the heavy winter snowfalls which prevent access to food.

Red deer are social animals. They are browser-grazers, also eating lichens, berries and fungi. In

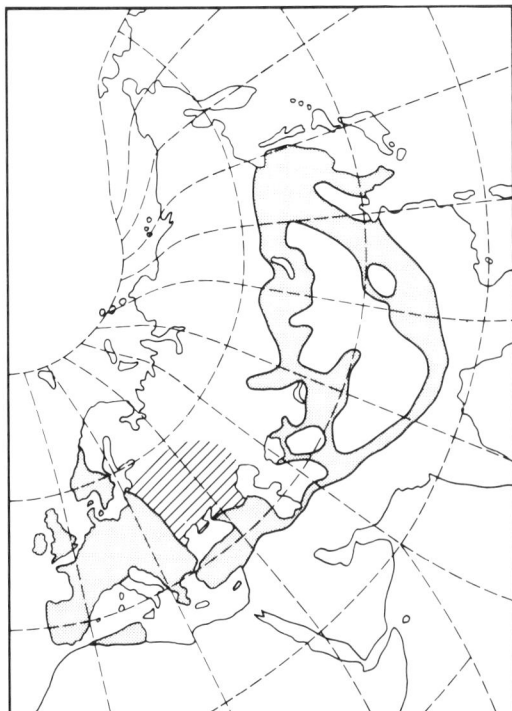

Fig. 5.29. Present distribution of red deer *Cervus elaphus*. (Based on Flerov 1952) It also probably occurred in the area shown hatched until a few hundred years ago. (Also in N. America.)

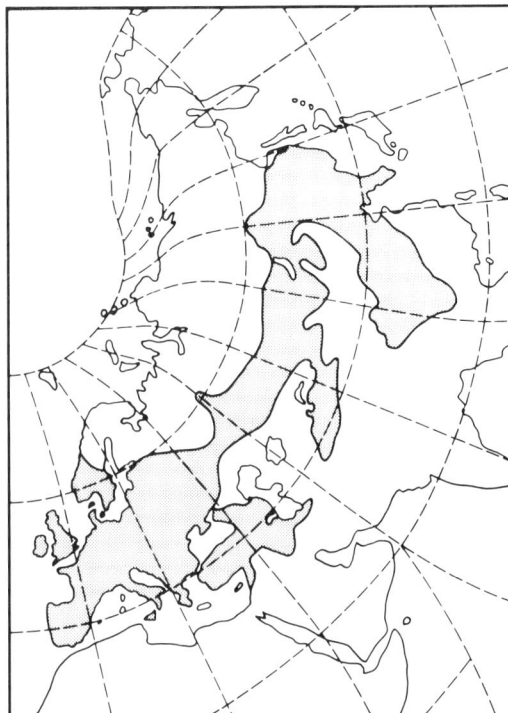

Fig. 5.30. Present distribution of roe deer *Capreolus capreolus*. (Based on Flerov 1952.)

open country such as the Scottish moors they eat grasses, heather, bilberry and lichens (Corbet 1966). Adults are preyed on by wolves, and the young by various carnivores including the larger birds of prey.

Cervus elaphus is one of the most ubiquitous mammals in the British Pleistocene, occurring apparently throughout each of the Middle and Upper Pleistocene interglacials in association with both temperate and coniferous forests (Ch. 7). It is recorded from the Late Anglian cold stage in association with treeless herbaceous vegetation and appears to have occasionally been present during the Middle Devensian cold stage, but the latter records are not accurately dated (Ch. 8). It is also recorded in association with boreal forest from the Chelford interstadial of the Early Devensian. The cold stage, interglacial and interstadial occurrences of red deer in association with coniferous forest or treeless 'steppe tundra' vegetational conditions, may be indicative of the absence of heavy snowfalls.

The roe deer *Capreolus capreolus* is widely distri-

buted in Europe and central Asia, although like the red deer it does not extend very far north into the taiga (Fig. 5.30). It is a small, rather solitary species, closely associated with woodland. It feeds mainly by browsing on trees and shrubs, but also eats grasses, berries, fungi, acorns, etc. (Corbet 1966).

Capreolus capreolus is recorded only from the Middle and Upper Pleistocene interglacials in Britain, and it appears to have been rare or absent in the Ipswichian (Ch. 7). It occurs in association with regional deciduous and coniferous forests.

The elk *Alces alces* is mainly confined to the taiga of Eurasia and North America (where it is called 'moose') but extends southwards into the northern part of the temperate forest zone, and extended westwards across northern Germany and France within the last one to two thousand years (Fig. 5.31). The elk, the largest of living deer, is fond of water, frequenting marshy forest country. It feeds on herbaceous aquatic and waterside plants and the foliage of deciduous trees, and in winter on shoots and bark. Elk are generally solitary for much of the year. Northern populations migrate south-

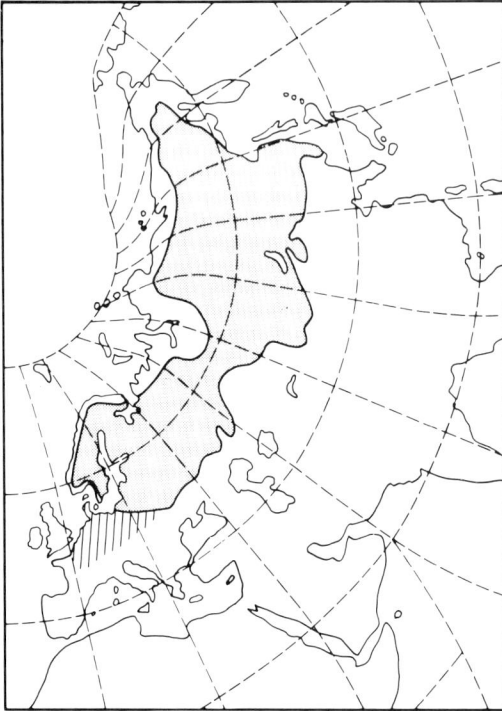

Fig. 5.31. Present distribution of elk *Alces alces*. (Based on Flerov 1952.) The hatched area gives an impression of its former range in north-west Europe, *c*. 2 000 years B.P. (Also in N. America.)

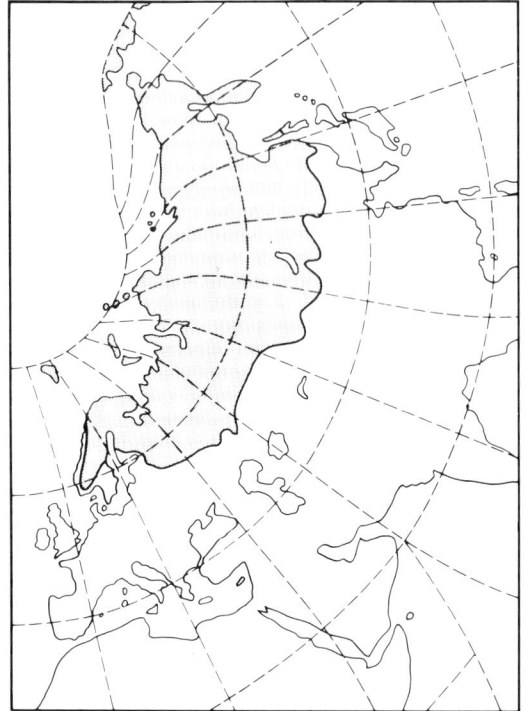

Fig. 5.32. Present distribution of reindeer *Rangifer tarandus* in Eurasia. (Based on Flerov 1952). The Fennoscandian reindeer are mostly domesticated, but probably occupy more or less the natural range. (Also in N. America.)

wards in the winter. The main predators are wolf and bear, but usually only young or sick animals are taken.

In Britain *Alces alces* is known from the Late Devensian, zone 1 De II, in association with scattered birch woodland (Ch. 8), as is now found in the transition from taiga to tundra, and from the early Flandrian in association with birch and pine woodland.

There is no record of *Alces* from the Hoxnian or Ipswichian in Britain, although it is recorded from eastern Germany in the Eemian, in association with a temperate forest flora. The Cromerian elk *Alces latifrons*, even larger than modern *A. alces*, is recorded in association with regional pine–elm–birch woodland or mixed oak forest in England (Ch. 7). In *A. alces*, the antlers are small in proportion to body size – evidently to facilitate movement through forests, whereas the antlers of *A. latifrons*, and its Lower Pleistocene precursor *A. gallicus*, are very large with long beams and are outspread (see Fig. 11.1). Presumably the males would have

needed to avoid dense forest during much of the year when they were carrying antlers. Perhaps, however, their occurrences indicate that the interglacial forests were not generally very dense.

The reindeer *Rangifer tarandus* occurs throughout most of the tundra and taiga of Eurasia and North America (Fig. 5.32). Determining its natural distribution is a little complicated by the presence of domesticated animals on the southern boundary in Eurasia. There are woodland and barren-ground ecotypes which can be distinguished by their antlers. They are highly gregarious, congregating in herds of many tens of thousands of individuals for the great southward migrations in winter, which may involve journeys of several hundred kilometres. In summer they eat herbaceous plants, and in winter the diet is mostly lichens – obtained by scraping off the snow from the ground, or from trees in woodland, plus buds and shoots of shrubs (Corbet 1966). Their broad spreading hooves allow them to walk over soft snow – a considerable advantage in northern latitudes.

In the British Pleistocene, *R. tarandus* records are strictly confined to cold stages, generally, where fossil floras are known, in association with treeless 'steppe-tundra' vegetation (Ch. 8). Reindeer also appear to have been present during the Chelford interstadial in association with boreal forest.

There is little information on the ecology of the extinct Lower Pleistocene deer of the genus *Eucladoceros*, except that their elaborate antlers (see Fig. 3.58) would have restricted access to dense forests (Ch. 6).

In the Cromerian the extinct giant deer *Megaceros verticornis* is recorded in association with regional temperate forest. The antlers were large and outspread and the same arguments regarding movement in forests apply as previously discussed for *Alces latifrons*.

A later species of *Megaceros*, *M. giganteus*, was present during the Hoxnian and Ipswichian interglacials and also at rare times within cold stages, especially near the end of the Late Devensian (Chs. 7, 8). The interglacial animals appear to have had antlers deflected upwards to some extent, probably an adaptation to the problem of movement in forest. In contrast, the Late Devensian zone l De II finds of giant deer stags, of which very many are known from Ireland, although they also occur elsewhere in Europe, are of animals with enormous outspread antlers often with spans of 3 m or more. These animals were living in open environments with rich herbaceous vegetation but with few or no trees, which placed no external restrictions on antler size or form. These antlers with their broad palmations were scarcely ever damaged in life. Almost certainly the antlers were used solely as visual signals to intimidate rival males when maintaining a harem during the rut, and thus large and showy antlers would have been strongly selected for in the cold-stage ecotype of *M. giganteus*. It has been suggested that predators were absent during zone l De II in Ireland, so that the giant deer were able to indulge the luxury of sexual selection for antlers (Coope 1973) but there is no evidence that the fossil antlers of the same age from other geographical areas, where predators were present, are any smaller. The large numbers of *M. giganteus* remains from Ireland may be due to unusual circumstances of taphonomy and preservation (Chs. 4, 8) and need not necessarily imply that giant deer were exceptionally abundant there.

The extinction of *M. giganteus* in north-west Europe appears to have coincided with the renewed cold and vegetational changes at the onset of Late Weichselian zone III (= Late Devensian zone III) times. It is not obvious, however, why the species should have become extinct elsewhere (Chs. 8, 9).

Bovids (Artiodactyla: Bovidae)

Bison remains are among the most common Pleistocene fossils, but they represent extinct species which, however, can be usefully compared with their living relatives.

The European bison *Bison bonasus* has been only narrowly saved from extinction. Approximately 2 000 years ago it appears to have been present across central Europe, southern Sweden, and east to the Volga and Caucasus, but it now survives only as protected herds in Poland and the Caucasus. *Bison bonasus* is predominantly a browser, rarely eating grasses (Corbet 1966).

The American bison *Bison bison* was originally found across most of central North America, mostly in prairie grasslands but also eastwards into the deciduous forests and northwards into the boreal forest zone. It is a highly gregarious animal normally living in groups of four to twenty animals, but sometimes combining in herds of many thousands (Banfield 1974). It is probable that before interference by man all populations migrated 300 km or so southwards every winter. The habitat of *B. bison* ranges from arid plains to parklands, river valleys, meadows and coniferous forest. They are primarily grazers, and predators include wolf, mountain lion and grizzly bear.

The late Lower Pleistocene and Cromerian bison in Britain, the small *B. schoetensacki*, is recorded in association with regional pine–elm–birch woodland or mixed oak forest in the Cromerian interglacial (Ch. 7).

The Upper Pleistocene bison *B. priscus* is represented by a small form in the Devensian, and probably also in the earlier cold stages, and by a larger form in the Ipswichian interglacial. These may have been distinct ecotypes. The interglacial form occurs at a number of Ipswichian sites, in association with either locally deforested environments in the middle of the interglacial, or the generally more open forest later in the stage. The absence of *B. priscus* from the Hoxnian interglacial may perhaps be correlated with a generally denser forest cover (Ch. 7).

Bison priscus is known from numerous finds of Early and Middle (Upton Warren Interstadial) Devensian age but has been found more rarely in later horizons (Ch. 8). At most sites it is associated with regional herbaceous vegetation but occurs with a boreal forest flora of Chelford interstadial age. During cold stages the bison herds probably underwent seasonal migrations.

The aurochs *Bos primigenius* is the ancestor of domestic cattle, but has otherwise been extinct since the seventeenth century when the last surviving Polish population died out. Approximately 3 000 years ago it appears to have been present throughout most of Europe, including Britain and southern Scandinavia, North Africa and the Near East. Judging from its domestic descendants, *B. primigenius* was probably primarily a grazer, although browse may have been important as well.

The numerous British Pleistocene records of *Bos primigenius* are all from interglacials, including the Flandrian, and it occurs to the exclusion of *Bison* in the Hoxnian, and in the Flandrian when the latter was already extinct (Ch. 7). It is possible that *B. primigenius* favoured more forested habitats than *Bison priscus*, especially when both species occurred together.

The musk ox *Ovibos moschatus* no longer occurs naturally in the Palaearctic (although it has been re-introduced by man in a few areas), but is confined to the arctic tundra of Canada and Alaska and the coastal areas of Greenland. It is absent from Baffin Island and east of Hudson Bay (Banfield 1974).

It is a gregarious animal, living in herds up to a hundred individuals. In summer it frequents the river valleys, lakeshores and meadows, but in winter it moves to higher ground and slopes blown free of snow. Musk oxen feed on grasses, sedges, rushes and other herbs, dwarf shrubs and willows. They are preyed upon by wolves and more rarely grizzly bears. When attacked they form the well-known defensive ring and it is usually only isolated sick or old animals that are taken.

Ovibos moschatus is known in England from the Wolstonian and Devensian cold stages, and apparently also from the end of the Ipswichian interglacial (Chs. 7, 8). Its extreme rarity in cold-stage deposits may indicate that it generally occurred in Britain only during the more arctic climatic phases, as is suggested by the single available radiocarbon date of 18 213 years B.P. which, if reliable, places one find within the coldest part of the Late Devensian. The occurrence of musk ox at Crayford, in association with several temperate

species, is therefore enigmatic. Perhaps this Ipswichian record represents a distinct ecotype. The CF-bF record of *Praeovibos priscus* is unstratified.

The saiga antelope *Saiga tartarica* is nowadays widely distributed through the central and eastern Eurasian steppe. There is a single find of probable Middle Devensian age from Kew, London (Ch. 8).

A gazelle *Gazella anglica* is known from the Lower Pleistocene Norwich Crag (Ch. 6). The genus is now widespread in the steppe and desert zones of central Asia, to East Africa and India (Corbet 1978). The former presence of gazelles in western Europe is an example of subsequent Pleistocene contraction of range in the face of competition from other groups, in this case probably deer.

Virtually nothing is known concerning the precise stratigraphical horizon or the taxonomic relationships of '*Ovis*' *savini* from the CF-bF.

Communities and populations

At the present day the relative population densities of particular species of mammals are mainly correlated with body size and whether they are primary or higher-order consumers. For example, in the case of herbivores (primary consumers) representative population densities per square kilometre range from tens of thousands of voles, to tens for deer, to less than one for elephants. The insectivorous shrews occur in densities of thousands per square kilometre, i.e. they are less numerous than voles, whereas the larger hedgehog *Erinaceus europaeus*, although a conspicuous animal, only reaches densities of tens per square kilometre. The population densities of carnivores are uniformly much lower than those of herbivores of equivalent body size. Values per square kilometre range from tens, in the case of the smallest mustelids, to less than one for the lion *Panthera leo*. This considerable disproportion in the availability of material of different species for potential fossilization is further accentuated by the large range in longevity shown between different species of mammals, which is strongly correlated with body size. For example, small rodents and shrews live only 1–2 years, whereas deer live to 10 years or so and elephants to 60 years and sometimes considerably longer.

As discussed in Chapter 4 fossil assemblages

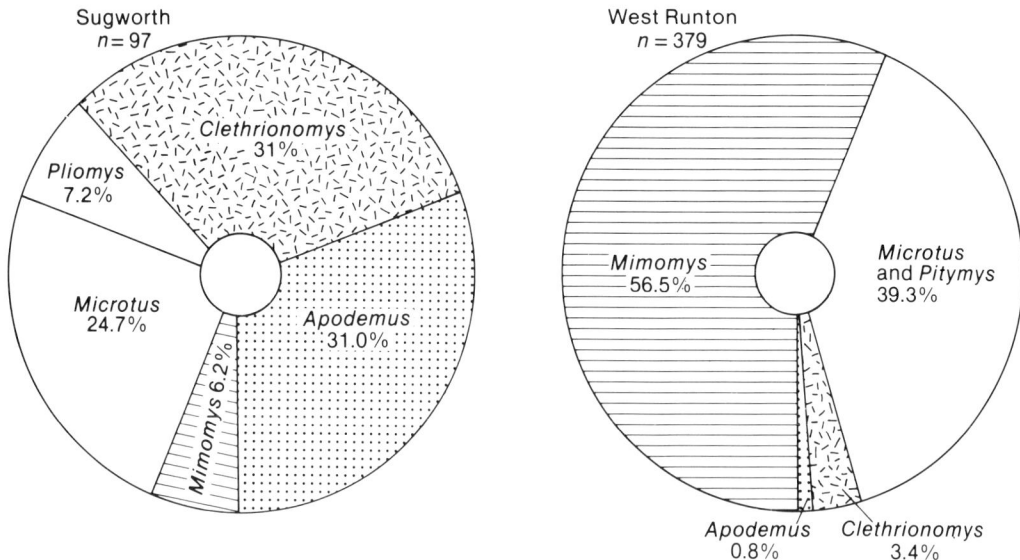

Fig. 5.33. Pie diagrams comparing the relative abundance of rodents, as percentages of total molars, in two deposits of Cromerian age. (After Stuart 1980)

from cave deposits are usually strongly biased in favour of Carnivora. On the other hand, the relative proportions of various taxa in fossil assemblages from fluviatile deposits are generally in agreement with what would be expected from the relative numbers of animals dying per unit time in modern situations. There is, however, also a bias in favour of animals living and dying in or close to the depositional site, and a less readily explained scarcity of arboreal and aerial species.

At many cave sites and at a few open sites, sufficient fossils have been recovered to make meaningful quantitative assessments of relative abundance of taxa. For example, the proportions of small rodents, represented by molars, in material collected by bulk sieving of sediments from two Cromerian sites which have been studied show marked contrasts (Fig. 5.33). At Sugworth there is a strong bias towards woodland rodents, and *Mimomys savini*, a probable water vole, is unusually rare, while the West Runton sample comprises mainly *M. savini* and grassland voles. These differences have been interpreted as due to differences in local habitat structure, but could conceivably have been influenced by bird-of-prey transport of rodent remains (Stuart 1975, 1980a).

Table 5.1 shows mammalian faunal compositions, by orders at selected sites, compared with modern European faunas. The absence or scarcity

as fossils of bats, well-represented in the modern faunas, is particularly striking. The scarcity of small-mammal remains at some fossil sites is due to biased collecting methods. Note the relatively good representation of Carnivora and poor representation of large herbivores in the cave assemblages. The reduced species diversity in cold-stage faunas when compared with the faunas of interglacials is apparent. The overall decrease in the diversity of interglacial faunas from the Cromerian to the present day is discussed in Chapter 9. The palaeoecology of vertebrate communities at particular sites is discussed in Chapters 7 and 8.

Seasonality

Seasonal changes in weather, abundance of food, day length and other factors, profoundly affect the lives of animals living in northern latitudes, and some of their responses to these changes are discernible in the fossil record.

Annual paired growth bands occur in the skeletons of fishes, and are especially well seen in the scales and vertebrae, and also in the calcium carbonate otoliths. Similar annual structures can be seen in the bones of many mammals (the mandible

Table 5.1. A comparison of the composition of fossil-mammal assemblages, by numbers of species in each order, at selected sites. The compositions of the modern faunas of the British Isles and the adjacent Continent are also shown (see text).

	Interglacial			Cold Stage			Modern	
	W Runton freshwater bed (Cr)	Swanscombe Lwr gravel/loam (Ho)	Joint Mitnor (Ip)[1]	Wretton (E-De)	Tattershall Castle (M-De)	Picken's Hole 3(M-De)[2]	British Isles	Belgium, north-east France
Insectivora	7	1	0	0	0	0	5	7
Chiroptera	0	0	0	0	0	0	11	13
Primates	0	2	0	0	0	1	1	1
Lagomorpha	1	1	1	0	0	0	2	1
Rodentia	10	5	5	1	1	2	9	13
Carnivora	9	5	7	2	2	4	9	10
Proboscidea	1	1	1	1	1	1	0	0
Perissodactyla	2	3	1	2	2	2	0	0
Artiodactyla	7	6	6	2	2	3	4	5
Totals	37	24	21	8	8	13	41	50

1. Pitfall trap assemblage
2. Hyaena den assemblage

being particularly useful in this respect) and in the tooth cementum. These growth bands can be used to determine the age of an individual animal (Morris 1972). Since the broad bands represent rapid growth in the summer and the thin bands slower winter growth, in principle the season of death can also be found (Spiess 1976).

Deer exhibit an annual cycle of antler development and shedding. The antler cycles for the five species of living deer recorded from the British Pleistocene are shown in Fig. 5.34. The timing is regulated principally by day length and the cycle is shifted forwards a little with decreasing latitude (Chapman 1975). In most species the younger males retain their antlers longer than the mature animals. Note that in reindeer both sexes bear antlers and that these are retained much longer by the females.

The young of mammals and birds in temperate and northern latitudes are born mainly in spring and early summer, again largely in response to changing day length. In reindeer the shedding of antlers in the female is associated with parturition.

A number of modern large mammals, including reindeer *Rangifer tarandus*, undergo seasonal migrations of some hundreds of kilometres. Some smaller mammals such as arctic fox *Alopex lagopus* also show seasonal shifts in distribution, but of a lesser magnitude. The seasonal migrations of many birds now occurring in Europe are well known. Generally they travel southwards and/or westwards for the winter, sometimes over distances of thousands of kilometres.

Information on seasonal migrations of animals at various times in the Pleistocene can be obtained by examining vertebrate material from different sites for evidence of the season of death, using the characters discussed above. For example, Sutcliffe and Zeuner (1962) deduced from the large numbers of small shed reindeer antlers (probably of females

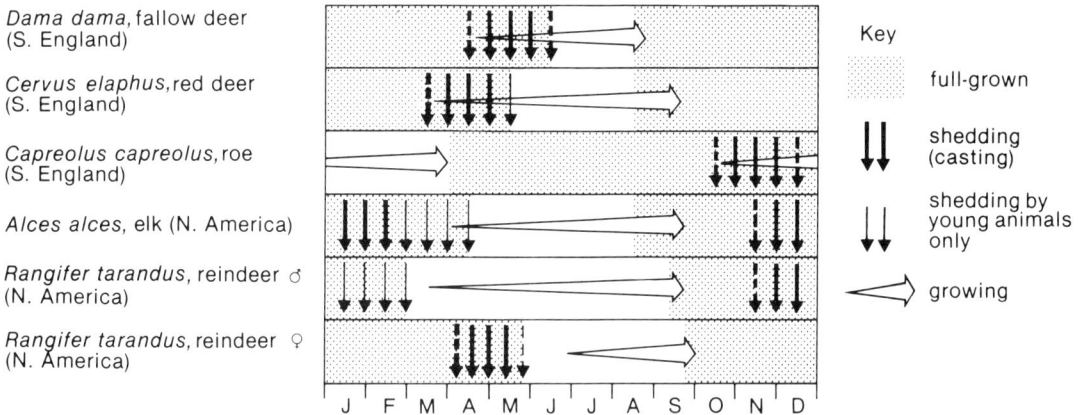

Fig. 5.34. The antler cycle in selected living species of deer. (Data from Chapman 1975; Banfield 1974.)

and perhaps young males) in the Reindeer Stratum (Devensian) of Tornewton Cave, Devon, that the animals were present there in the summer months. This conclusion was supported by the occurrence of the mandible of a very young reindeer which probably died in the summer.

Fossil remains yielding evidence of the season in which death occurred for particular animals, can also be very useful for determining seasonal occupations of sites by early man and seasonal patterns of hunting.

The antlers of the elk *Alces alces* skeleton from Blackpool (Late Devensian) were about to be shed when the animal died, after being injured by hunting weapons (see Palaeopathology section below), indicating, since it was a mature stag, that it had been hunted at a time during the winter months, between November and February.

The final seasonal phenomenon to be considered is hibernation, which is undergone by amphibians, reptiles, and some mammals, notably: the hedgehog *Erinaceus europaeus*, dormice, e.g. *Muscardinus avellanarius*, and the brown bear *Ursus arctos*.

Frogs and toads *Rana* spp. *Bufo* spp., and the pond tortoise *Emys orbicularis* commonly spend the winter hibernation buried in the mud at the bottom of a pool, and this behaviour probably accounts for the occasional Pleistocene finds of fairly complete skeletons of these animals in fine-grained sediments. Animals are likely to die during hibernation if the reserves of food in their bodies is insufficient, or in the case of sub-aquatic hibernators if when they awake the surface is still frozen over.

Similarly, large accumulations in caves of the bones of the brown bear *Ursus arctos* and the extinct species *U. spelaeus* and *U. deningeri* probably represent animals dying over the years during winter hibernation. Weak or diseased individuals unable to build up sufficient fat reserves from spring to autumn would have been especially vulnerable.

The season (or seasons) of occupation of a site by carnivores or man may be determinable by examination of seasonal structures in the prey remains.

Tracks and signs

Fossil tracks and signs ('trace fossils') provide direct evidence of animal activity in the past. An excellent account of the tracks and signs of modern European wild mammals and birds is given by Bang and Dahlstrøm (1974).

Tracks

Horizons with fossil footprints have only rarely been found in the British Pleistocene. Well-preserved examples representing bovids, horses and deer were, however, recorded from the top of the Lower Loam at Swanscombe, Kent (Fig. 5.35). All of these animals are also represented by skeletal remains in adjacent horizons. Beds showing disturbance in detail, probably due to trampling by large

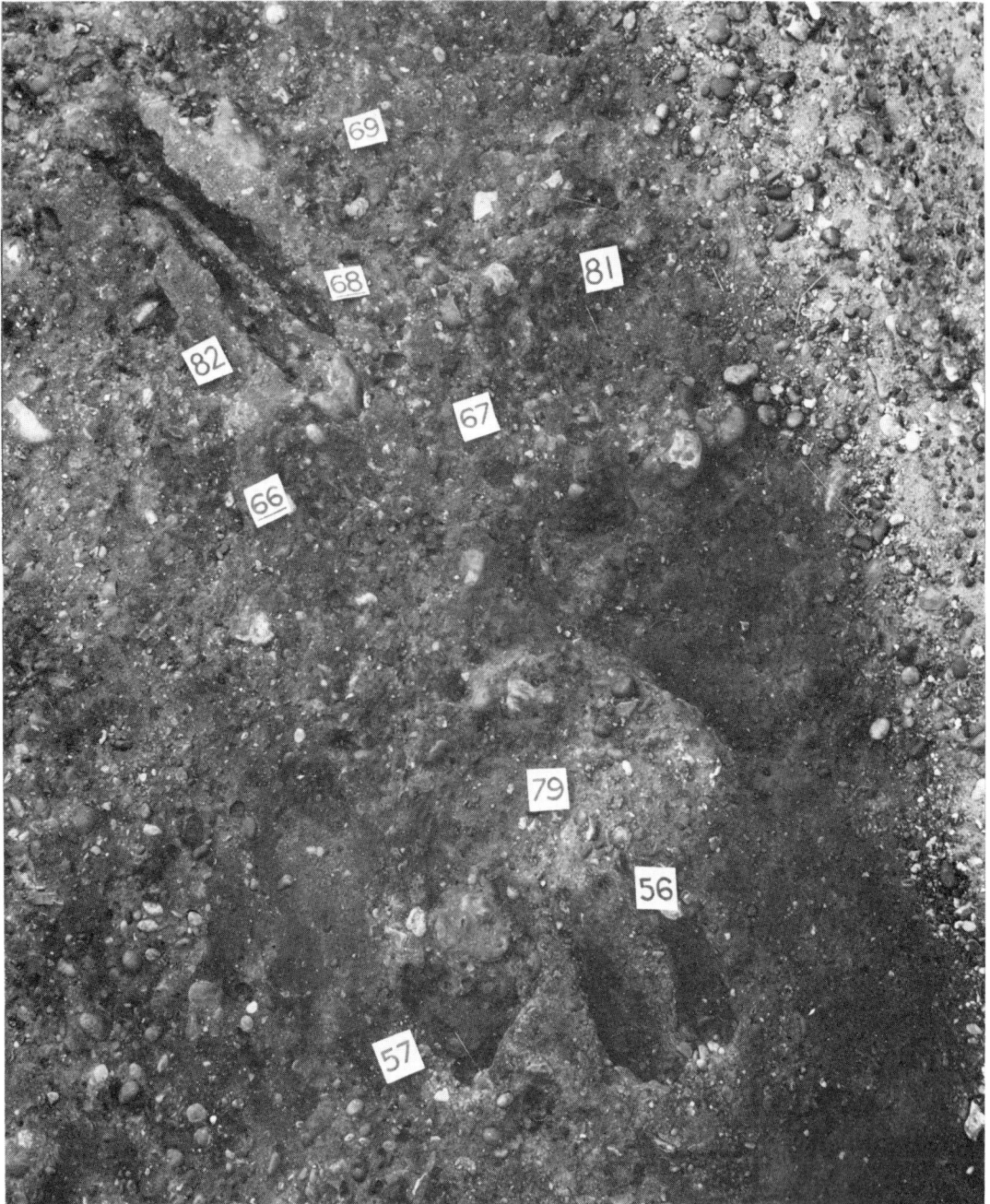

Fig. 5.35. The surface of the Lower Loam at Swanscombe, Kent (Hoxnian) excavated by Dr J. Waechter, showing footprints of a large bovid, probably *Bos primigenius*: 56 and 68 (skid mark).

mammals, are known from Aveley, Essex, in association with a skeleton of mammoth *Mammuthus primigenius*, and from elsewhere.

Tooth and claw marks

Bones damaged by mammalian carnivores are common in Pleistocene fossil assemblages, especially

(a)

(b)

Fig. 5.36. Examples of bones damaged by spotted hyaena *Crocuta crocuta* from Ipswichian deposits at Swanton Morley, Norfolk. (a) distal end of left femur shaft of medium-sized deer showing scalloping of chewed edge produced by the bite of the conical premolars; (b) distal end of aurochs *Bos primigenius* metatarsal snapped off by twisting, probably when still attached to the carcass, and showing tooth-pressure and tooth-scratch marks (Scales = 2 cm.)

from caves which were used as carnivore dens (see Ch. 4), but also from open sites, e.g. Barrington, Cambridgeshire, and Swanton Morley, Norfolk. The wolf *Canis lupus* and especially the spotted hyaena *Crocuta crocuta* appear to be the main agents responsible. Studies of bone damage by modern *C. crocuta*, in East Africa (Sutcliffe 1970) provide detailed comparisons with fossil examples. Typically cancellous bone at the epiphyses is chewed and ingested leaving only the shafts, which consist of compact bone, with one or both ends missing. Tooth marks, including scalloping of broken surfaces, produced by the crushing premolars are very characteristic, as is also the type of fracture produced in limb bones when a limb is twisted off from a carcass (Fig. 5.36). Other marks seen include sinuous gnaw marks, and scratches probably made by claws. It is not possible in many cases to determine which carnivore was responsible for particular bone damage observed, but only *C. crocuta* is capable of breaking, for example, the thick-walled metapodials of large bovids, and the scalloping mentioned above is also characteristic (Fig. 5.36) (Coxon *et al.* 1980).

Damage to teeth and bones resulting from ingestion by carnivores are considered below.

Several species of deer have been observed to chew and ingest bones and antlers, which provide an important source of phosphate. Sutcliffe (1973, 1977) has studied this phenomenon, and pointed out the dangers of mistaking such deer-chewed material for artifacts manufactured by early man. Typically the ends of deer-chewed long bones and antler beams and tines have forked ends. Material chewed by reindeer commonly has surprisingly regular zig-zag margins which should be recognizable in fossil material.

The incisor teeth of rodents produce characteristic paired short grooves on antlers or bones gnawed by these animals, but few examples are known from the British Pleistocene. Wood gnawed by beaver *Castor fiber*, with broad paired incisor marks, has been found in the Cromer Forest-bed Formation, horizon unknown, at Bacton, Norfolk (McWilliams 1967).

Various rodents and birds tackle cones and nuts in different ways, so that the feeding remains show damage which can usually be assigned to the particular animal responsible (Bang & Dahlstrøm 1974). Spruce *Picea* cones handled by squirrels are known from the Cromer Forest-bed Formation of Bacton, Norfolk (McWilliams 1967), and hazel

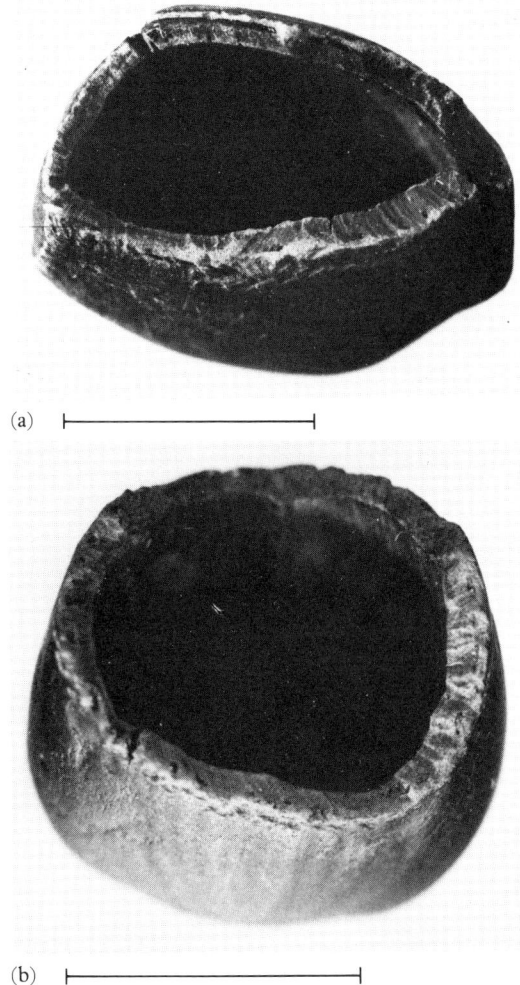

(a)

(b)

Fig. 5.37. (a, b), Hazelnuts (*Corylus avellana*) showing gnawing by wood mouse *Apodemus sylvaticus* (Ipswichian, Swanton Morley, Norfolk). (Note additional row of tooth-marks on outside of the shells parallel to gnawed edge of hole, which distinguishes this from the work of bank vole *Clethrionomys glareolus*). (Scale = 1 cm.)

nuts *Corylus* opened by field mouse *Apodemus sylvaticus*, or yellow-necked mouse *A. flavicollis*, have been described from the Ipswichian of Swanton Morley, Norfolk (Coxon *et al.* 1980) (Fig. 5.37).

Droppings and pellets

Fossil droppings or faeces (coprolites) are known from several occurrences in the British Pleistocene.

Fig. 5.38. Coprolite of spotted hyaena *Crocuta crocuta* from the Freshwater Bed of West Runton, Norfolk (Cromerian). (Scale = 1 cm.)

Small cylindrical droppings with rounded ends, probably produced by arctic lemmings *Dicrostonyx torquatus*, were found in Devensian deposits at Angel Road, North London, in association with skeletal remains of this animal. Droppings formerly attributed to elk *Alces alces*, reported from Bronze Age peats at Ugg Mere, Cambridgeshire, appear to represent a smaller species of deer (Ch. 7).

The high phosphate content of the faeces of spotted hyaena *Crocuta crocuta* allows them to be commonly preserved as fossils. Most finds are from caves used as hyaena dens, but there are also a few finds from open sites, e.g. Swanton Morley (Ipswichian) and West Runton (Cromerian) (Fig. 5.38), both in Norfolk.

Bone fragments ingested by modern spotted hyaenas and subsequently regurgitated, show evidence of corrosion by gastric juices such as polished surfaces, often sharp edges and characteristically circular holes (Sutcliffe 1970). Such fragments are quite common in assemblages from fossil hyaena dens.

Mellet (1974) has suggested that a large proportion of the small and medium-sized mammal remains, and some larger material found as fossils have been ingested by small and medium-sized Carnivora, and passed out with the faeces. He investigated recent material from the droppings of several North American Carnivora, and found that it was identical in appearance to fossil assemblages with which it was compared. The assemblages include longitudinally split long bones, broken-off femoral heads, isolated teeth and undamaged compact bones such as calcanea and phalanges. Mellet considers that the largely fragmentary condition of much fossil bone is itself a strong indicator of origin from Carnivore droppings. Trampling by large mammals may, however, also be an important agent in breaking bones, especially as many are far too large to have been passed through the gut of another animal, or to have been broken by its teeth. The question needs much further investigation in view of its implications for the taphonomy of vertebrate assemblages (Ch. 4).

Small-mammal bones from the pellets regurgitated by modern diurnal birds of prey (raptors) show corrosion, which appears to be of a characteristic type and can be matched in Pleistocene fossil assemblages (Mayhew 1977). Mayhew describes and illustrates a number of recent and fossil examples. In vole molars, for example, corrosion is confined to the enamel ridges near the crowns, the rest of the tooth having been protected by the bone of the jaw.

Material recovered from the pellets of owls shows no such corrosion and little breakage, and is therefore not readily recognizable in fossil assemblages. Nevertheless, most of the fossil small-mammal bones and teeth from cave deposits at least almost certainly originated from pellets dropped by owls. Occasionally, discrete patches of fossil small-mammal material have been observed, sometimes with traces of organic matter, evidently representing owl pellets, as at Angel Road, North London (Devensian). The pellets contained bones and teeth of arctic lemming *Dicrostonyx torquatus* in an excellent state of preservation (Hinton 1912).

Palaeopathology

Pathological abnormalities are occasionally observed in Pleistocene fossil mammal material. For example, Wells and Lawrence (1976) describe a metatarsal of giant deer *Megaceros verticornis*,

from the Cromerian of West Runton, Norfolk, which has a large bone tumour, with a central pit, on the antero-medial surface. The lesion is thought most likely to have been caused by ossification of a sub-periosteal haematoma resulting from injury.

Pathological elephant molars, showing twisting, distortion and eruption at abnormal angles, are fairly common. Bone tumours and direct injury have been cited as causes of these lesions (McWilliams 1967).

Lesions due to physical injury by weapons have been described in detail from Star Carr, Yorkshire (early Flandrian), and Blackpool, Lancashire (Late Devensian). Two scapulae, one of red deer *Cervus elaphus*, the other of elk *Alces alces*, from Star Carr, show partly-healed fractures produced by flint-tipped projectile weapons or barbed points (Noe-Nygaard 1975). A complete elk skeleton from Blackpool (Ch. 8) bears a variety of unhealed lesions resulting from the impact of flint-tipped projectile weapons, together with what appear to be axe cuts on one of the metacarpals, all dating from immediately prior to the death of the animal. In addition, however, there are a few lesions with accompanying reaction – osteoporosis of the bone due to bacterial infection which must have dated from some time before the elk's death. In particular, a barbed bone projectile point was excavated *in situ* resting in a broad groove in the distal end of the left metatarsal (Hallam *et al.* 1973) (see Figs 8.6, 8.7). The groove had evidently been eroded by the point which was embedded in the animal's foot, an estimated two to three weeks before death. Noe-Nygaard's (1975) dismissal of the lesions as caused by earth pressure and by damage during excavation appears to be based on misunderstandings of the nature of the site and the state of preservation of the bones (Stuart 1976b).

6 Lower Pleistocene faunas

With the exception of one cave assemblage, the Lower Pleistocene vertebrates of the British Isles come from the predominantly marine crags of East Anglia. The record is therefore not surprisingly patchy and unsatisfactory in comparison with the 'Villafranchian' faunas of southern and eastern Europe.

Due to the combination of sparse material and imprecise stratigraphical information for many finds, there is little prospect of detecting faunal changes within stages for the Lower Pleistocene. The overall faunal history for the period is discussed in Chapter 9.

The main sites with Lower Pleistocene vertebrate faunas are shown in Fig. 6.1

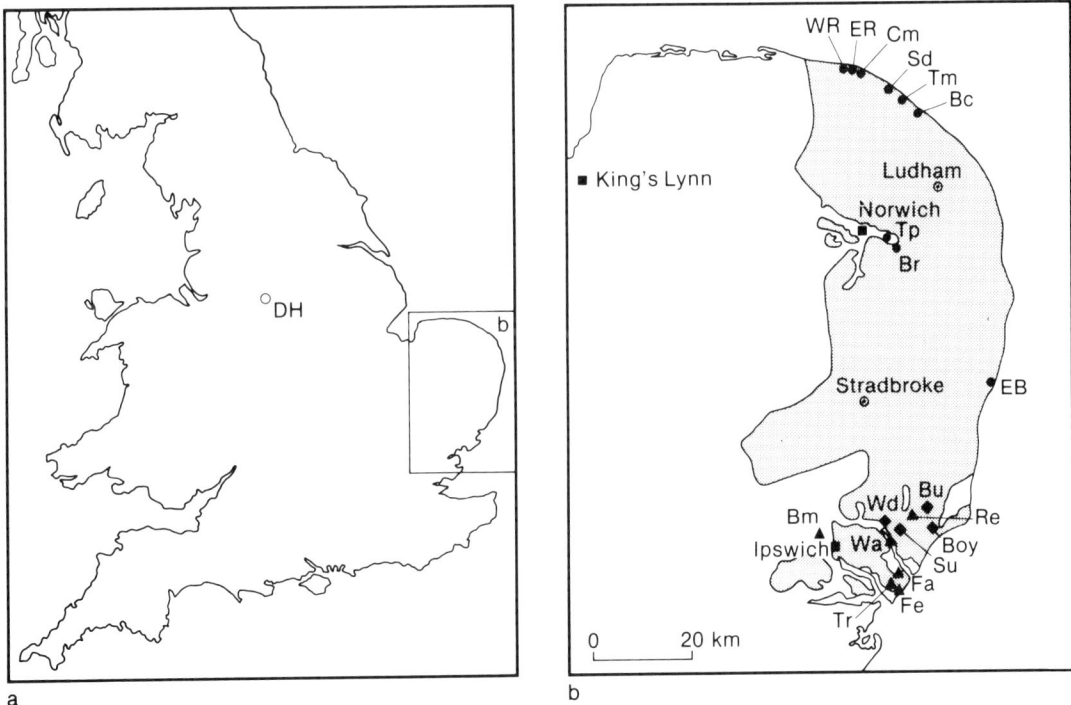

Fig. 6.1. Location map of the main Pliocene and Lower Pleistocene vertebrate sites. ◆, Red Crag Nodule Bed (Pliocene); ▲, Red Crag; ●, other crags; ○, cave sites. The extent of the Pliocene Coralline Crag (hatched) and the Lower Pleistocene crags (stippled) are indicated, together with the locations of the Ludham and Stradbroke boreholes. Bc, Bacton; Bm, Bramford; Boy, Boyton; Br, Bramerton; Bu, Butley; Cm, Cromer; DH, Doveholes; EB, Easton Bavents; ER, East Runton; Fa, Falkenham; Fe, Felixstowe; Re, Rendlesham; Sd, Sidestrand; Su, Sutton; Tm, Trimingham; Tp, Thorpe, Norwich; Tr, Trimley; Wa, Waldringfield; Wd, Woodbridge; WR, West Runton.

Upper Pliocene (Red Crag Nodule Bed)

The Red Crag occurs over much of south-east Suffolk and as small outliers in north-east Essex. At its base at a number of localities, (notably Woodbridge, Boyton, Sutton and Butley, all in Suffolk) is found a condensed deposit – comprising flint pebbles and phosphatic nodules. Vertebrate fossils from this horizon are generally heavily mineralized, and often well rolled and polished, imparting an attractive glass, so that specimens were much prized by nineteenth-century, and later, collectors.

Some of the fossil vertebrate material has clearly been reworked from much older strata. In particular, remains of *Coryphodon* and *Hyracotherium* were derived from Eocene London Clay which occurs over much of the area. Comparison with Continental faunas suggests that the bulk of the vertebrate material is of broadly Upper Pliocene ('Lower Villafranchian') age. The Pliocene age strictly puts the Red Crag Nodule Bed fauna outside the scope of this chapter, but it is nevertheless briefly considered here as a prelude to the faunas of the Lower Pleistocene. Little modern work has been done on this material, which was, however, extensively described and figured by Newton (1891).

Taxa recorded include porcupine *Hystrix* sp., beaver *Castor fiber*, a small beaver-like rodent *Trogontherium minus*, a bear-like carnivore *Agriotherium* sp., extinct hyaena *Hyaena perrieri*, an extinct panda *Parailurus anglicus*, gomphothere mastodont *Anancus arvernensis*, true mastodon *Zygolophodon borsoni*, extinct elephant *Archidiskodon meridionalis*, horse *Equus* sp., extinct three-toed horse *Hipparion* sp., extinct tapir *Tapirus arvernensis*, extinct rhinoceros *Dicerorhinus megarhinus* and an extinct bovid cf. *Leptobos* sp.

Marine vertebrate remains also occur abundantly. Taxa represented include fishes, turtles, a sirenian, a walrus and several whales (Newton 1891).

Pre-Ludhamian Stage (Red Crag)

Comparison of the foraminifers and marine molluscs from surface outcrops of Red Crag, with faunas from the Ludham and Stradbroke boreholes strongly suggest that the Red Crag was deposited largely or entirely within the first stage of the British Pleistocene, the Pre-Ludhamian (Funnell & West 1977). Most fossil terrestrial vertebrates recorded from the Red Crag probably originate from the Red Crag Nodule Bed. A few specimens appear from their less mineralized condition, and/or where they were found, to have come from the Red Crag proper (Spencer 1964, 1966) and are therefore probably of Pre-Ludhamian age, if not reworked from older strata. Taxa represented include beaver *C. fiber*, gomphothere *Anancus arvernensis*, extinct elephant *Archidiskodon meridionalis*, horses including both *Equus* cf. *stenonis* and a 'caballine' species *Equus bressanus*, a deer *Eucladoceros* sp., a gazelle *Gazella* sp., and albatross *Diomedea* sp. Marine vertebrates are also recorded (Newton 1891).

Antian and Baventian Stages (Norwich Crag, in part)

It is uncertain to what extent the Ludhamian and Thurnian stages, which occur in the Ludham and Stradbroke boreholes, can be recognized in surface exposures of deposits assigned to the Red or Norwich Crag. Vertebrate records from the Norwich Crag so far available can be assigned to one or more of the stages from the Antian to the Pre-Pastonian.

The cliff section at Easton Bavents, north of Southwold, Suffolk, includes at least 2.8 m of Norwich Crag (Fig. 6.2), overlain by more than 2 m of laminated grey and blue clays (Funnell & West 1962). Pollen analyses of silt bands within the basal metre of crag indicates temperate forests with hemlock *Tsuga*, and the deposits are assigned to the Antian Stage with Easton Bavents as the type locality. A single pollen spectrum obtained from the upper part of the crag is of intermediate character and was assigned to the early part of the Baventian (zone Lp4a of Ludham). The crag therefore ranges from the Antian to the early Baventian in age.

The marine mollusc faunas (Norton & Beck 1972) record changes within the crag from open-coast littoral conditions at the base to sublittoral conditions towards the top.

Fig. 6.2. Shelly marine sands ('crag') of Antian/early Baventian age at Easton Bavents, Suffolk.

Marine fish material is common in the crag, but remains of non-marine vertebrates are sparse, and much of our knowledge results from patient collecting over many years by Mr T. H. Gardner. Taxa recorded from the rarely exposed 'Lower Shell Bed', of probable Antian age, include *Equus* cf. *stenonis* and *Archidiskodon meridionalis*. Large mammals from the 'Upper Shell Bed' of early Baventian, or late Antian age, include *E.* cf. *stenonis*, *A. meridionalis*, *Eucladoceros falconeri*, *Eucladoceros* sp. and *Anancus arvernensis*. Teeth of the extinct water vole *Mimomys pliocaenicus* were described by Carreck (1966), and more recently collected material includes also the smaller species *Mimomys blanci* (Mayhew & Stuart, in preparation).

Bramertonian Stage and Pre-Pastonian *a* Substage (Norwich Crag, in part)

The pit at Bramerton Common, near Norwich, Norfolk, has long been regarded as the type section for the Norwich Crag, and dates from the early nineteenth century. A later excavation, Blake's Pit, 300 m to the east, was first noted in 1870. The stratigraphy, pollen, foraminifers and marine molluscs from both localities have recently been described in detail by Funnell, Norton and West (1979).

At Bramerton shelly sands with silt bands overlie Chalk. Pollen analyses from silty bands within the

6 m of crag at Blake's Pit allow the recognition of an *Alnus-Quercus-Carpinus* pollen assemblage zone, covering the bottom 4 m, indicating temperate forest. These spectra are assigned to a new stage, the Bramertonian with Blake's Pit as the type locality. A single sample from about 5 m above the Chalk is assigned to a *Pinus-Ericales-Gramineae* pollen assemblage zone, representing heath and herbaceous communities and a cold climate, and is correlated with the Pre-Pastonian *a* substage of the Norfolk coast succession.

The foraminiferan and molluscan assemblages at Blake's Pit confirm the climatic history based on pollen evidence and also allow a fairly firm correlation with the Bramerton Common section. The Mollusca indicate littoral and sublittoral depositional environments, with periods with brackish sheltered tidal flat conditions marked by a 'fluvio-marine' molluscan assemblage which includes non-marine taxa washed in to the sea.

Most of the vertebrate material from Bramerton was found during the last century, notably by Reeve. The exact localities and horizons of most specimens are unclear, but most of the material probably comes from Bramerton Common pit. It seems fairly certain, however, that specimens from the 'Lower Shell Bed' at either pit are of Bramertonian age, whereas those labelled 'Upper Shell Bed' are likely to date from the Pre-Pastonian *a* substage, or perhaps from the end of the Bramertonian.

Recently a very valuable collection of vole material has been made from the type Bramertonian Lower Shell Bed of Blake's Pit by P.G. Cambridge.

The faunal list from the 'Lower Shell Bed' (based on Mayhew 1979) includes the voles *Mimomys pliocaenicus*, *Mimomys reidi* and *Mimomys newtoni*, the extinct clawless otter *Aonyx reevei*, and from the basal stone bed the extinct elephant *Archidiskodon meridionalis* and deer *Eucladoceros* cf. *sedgwicki*. Taxa recorded from the 'Upper Shell Bed' include *Aonyx reevei*, *M. pliocaenicus* and the large vole *Mimomys rex*. The horizon of the gomphothere *Anancus arvernensis* is unfortunately unknown. The vole *Mimomys blanci*, known from several Lower Pleistocene localities, is strangely absent at Bramerton. Marine fishes and a seal *Phoca* sp. are also recorded.

One of the best available collections of crag vertebrates is from the Norwich Crag of Thorpe Norwich, collected during the last century, mainly by Fitch. The crag at this locality, which is only 5 km

from Bramerton, is probably of approximately Bramertonian/Pre-Pastonian age. Taxa recorded include the extinct beaver *Trogontherium cuvieri*, voles *M. pliocaenicus*, *M. newtoni*, *M. blanci* and *M. reidi*, horse *Equus stenonis*, deer *Eucladoceros falconeri* and gazelle *Gazella anglica*.

Pre-Pastonian Stage ('Weybourne Crag' facies of Cromer Forest-bed Formation, in part)

Most of the older Cromer Forest-bed Formation finds unfortunately can be only broadly assigned to the Pre-Pastonian and Pastonian stages. These include the fine antler of *Eucladoceros sedgwicki* from Bacton, Norfolk, much of the large-mammal material from East Runton, Norfolk, where beds of both ages occur together. At a few sites, however, the stratigraphical evidence is good enough to assign finds to particular stages or substages.

At Sidestrand, Norfolk, locality SSB (West 1980a) shelly crag overlying chalk (Fig. 6.3) yielded teeth of the voles *Mimomys pliocaenicus*, *Mimomys reidi* and *Mimomys blanci*. Associated pollen spectra have been correlated by West with the Pre-Pastonian *a* substage, and a cold climate park-tundra vegetation is indicated.

A molar of the extinct elephant *Archidiskodon meridionalis*, found by R. G. West at West Runton cemented on to the surface of the Stone Bed, is probably of Pre-Pastonian *a* age and an antler of extinct elk *Alces gallicus* from West Runton is also attributable to this stage. At East Runton, Norfolk, teeth of voles *M. pliocaenicus*, *M. newtoni*, *M. blanci*, *M. reidi* and *Mimomys pitymyoides* are recorded from the 'Weybourne Crag'. This crag is overlain by freshwater muds giving a Pre-Pastonian *d* spectrum (West 1980a) and is almost certainly of Pre-Pastonian age.

Pastonian Stage (Cromer Forest-bed Formation, in part)

At East Runton a bed of clay conglomerate, (Bed e) probably 2–3 m thick containing marine shells,

Fig. 6.3. Section in deposits of the Cromer Forest-bed Formation at Sidestrand, Norfolk. The Pleistocene deposits overlie domes of Chalk which have been thrust upwards by several metres. Pre-Pastonian and Pastonian crag and sands are unconformably overlain by Cromerian sediments, which are seen to channel into the older beds in the left of the photo, about halfway up the cliff. Site SSB, which yielded vole teeth from Pre-Pastonian crag immediately overlying the Chalk, is near the extreme right of the picture (see text).

rests on an eroded surface of the crag described in the previous section, and is in turn overlaid conformably by marine silts yielding Pastonian zone Pa II pollen spectra. Bed *e* is therefore probably of Pastonian age. Antlers of deer are reported to have come from this horizon by Reid (1882), but unfortunately it is not clear to which specimens he was referring. A few vole teeth recorded from East Runton appear to have come from this horizon.

Excavations for sea defences at West Runton in 1975 exposed up to 2 m of shelly crag (bed d) (Fig. 6.4), the upper part of which was seen to interdigitate with Pastonian (zone Pa II) marine silts and must therefore be of this age (West 1980a). Samples of small-vertebrate remains were collected from both this horizon, and the crag beneath. The former is therefore of Pastonian age, and the latter could be of Pre-Pastonian or Pastonian age, although a Pastonian is much more probable. Taxa

recorded include an unnamed species of desman, and the voles *Mimomys pliocaenicus, Mimomys newtoni, Mimomys blanci, Mimomys reidi* and *Mimomys pitymyoides* (Mayhew & Stuart, in preparation). On the assumption that there has been no reworking, all these species probably lived in association with regional temperate forest. Marine fishes also occur.

Cave Sites

An assemblage of Pleistocene mammal, remains from a cave, at about 351 m O.D., in carboniferous limestone at Doveholes, Bibbington, Derbyshire, was originally described by Dawkins (1903). The fauna, recently reassessed and figured by Spencer and Melville (1974), includes a hyaena

Fig. 6.4. Marine silts and crag of Pastonian age exposed beneath the beach, in the course of constructing sea defences at West Runton, Norfolk, to the west side of Woman Hythe. (Cromerian freshwater deposits occur at a higher level in the base of the cliff – see Figs. 7.2, 7.3, 7.4).

Hyaena sp., sabre-tooth *Homotherium sainzelli*, gomphothere mastodont *Anancus arvernensis*, extinct elephant *Archidiskodon meridionalis*, extinct horse *Equus* cf. *bressanus*, and a deer. The presence of *A. arvernensis* indicates an age not later than Bramertonian.

Comparison with Continental faunas

The 'Villafranchian' deposits of southern Europe are subdivided, on the basis of their mammalian faunas, into Lower ('Pliocene'), Middle (earlier Lower Pleistocene) and Upper (later Lower Pleistocene) units. Finer divisions are also made using faunas of individual sites. The earliest Villafranchian faunas (Triversa Faunal Unit) of Italy (Azzaroli 1970, 1977b; Azzaroli & Vialli 1971) include mastodon *Zygolophodon borsoni*, the vole *Mimomys polonicus*, and other characteristically Pliocene taxa.

The later Lower Villafranchian fauna (Montopoli fauna) lacks these elements, but includes the earliest elephant and horse in Italy. The Suffolk Red Crag Nodule Bed assemblage may therefore include a mixture of fossils of broadly Lower Villafranchian age.

The Middle Villafranchian, not found in Italy, is represented by the French Saint Vallier fauna. Azzaroli (1977b) equates it with that of the English Red Crag. The earliest faunas from Italy attributed to the Late Villafranchian (Olivola Faunal Unit) still include the gomphothere mastodont *Anancus arvernensis*, but this species is absent from the later faunas (Tasso and Farneta Faunal Units). This corresponds to the pattern of faunal change seen in the British Lower Pleistocene. An interesting feature of the Italian faunas is the occurrence of the extinct hippopotamus *Hippopotamus major*.

The deer faunas from Villafranchian localities in France and Spain (Heintz 1970) show considerable change from the Pliocene through the Lower Pleistocene. In particular, *Eucladoceros* spp. occur only in the Middle and Upper Villafranchian (Lower

Pleistocene) and *Alces* (*Libralces*) *gallicus* is restricted to the Upper Villafranchian only, again corresponding to the British sequence. Villafranchian records of other taxa can be found in Lumley (1976).

The Upper Pliocene and Lower Pleistocene assemblages of central and eastern Europe are known mainly from cave and fissure deposits, and are generally restricted to small-mammal material.

The fauna from the Tegelen Clay, south Netherlands, is of great importance because it can be dated to the late part of the Tiglian temperate stage in the detailed pollen-biostratigraphical scheme for the Dutch Lower Pleistocene. The large mammals need revision, but include *Anancus arvernensis*, ex-

tinct tapir *Tapirus arvernensis* (both dating from the beginning of the succeeding Eburonian cold stage), and a species of *Eucladoceros* (*E. tegelensis*) resembling the British *E. tetraceros* (Kortenbout van der Sluijs & Zagwijn 1962). The small mammals (from Tiglian zone Tc 5) include *Mimomys reidi*, *Mimomys blanci* and *Mimomys pliocaenicus* (Freudenthal *et al.* 1976). The fauna indicates a probable correlation with the Antian or Bramertonian temperate stages of the East Anglian sequence.

A. correlation of European Lower Pleistocene deposits based on pollen biostratigraphy, palaeomagnetic data and vertebrate faunas is given by Zagwijn (1974).

7 Middle and Upper Pleistocene interglacial faunas

General

As discussed in Chapter 2 the interglacial periods appear to have been relatively short, each of the order of 10–20 000 years, compared with the Middle and Upper Pleistocene as a whole. It should be stressed that the various interglacials were not all of the same duration.

Each interglacial had a broadly similar vegetational cycle with the development of temperate deciduous forests in the middle of the stage (pollen zones II, III – see Ch. 2), when warm summers and mild winters are indicated from the evidence of various fossil invertebrates and plants. Coniferous and birch woodland and more extensive herbaceous vegetation characterize the beginning and end of each interglacial (zones I and IV).

Faunal change within the stage largely reflecting climatic and vegetational changes can be detected for each of the interglacials, but is particularly evident in the Ipswichian, which is also represented by a comparatively large number of sites.

The faunas from the middle and generally warmest parts (pollen zones II and III) of the interglacials from the Cromerian to the present day each comprise a mixture of species nowadays either: (a) extinct; (b) widespread in the Palaearctic and commonly beyond; (c) characteristic of the temperate regions only; or (d) restricted to areas to the south of the British Isles. Although the general character of the faunas from each of the interglacials is similar, they nevertheless differ in detail, reflecting complex patterns of evolution, extinction and immigration.

Faunas dated more or less certainly to the closing phases of the Cromerian, Hoxnian and Ipswichian interglacials, each seem to show the appearance of nowadays arctic-boreal taxa in association with surviving temperate and southern taxa. This phenomenon may be related to the prevalence of continental climatic conditions with warm summers and cold winters.

Notwithstanding the higher sea levels reached in earlier interglacials, compared with that of the presend day (Flandrian), Britain appears to have remained connected to the Continent throughout the Cromerian and Hoxnian interglacials. There is evidence, however, that England was separated from France by sea during part of the Ipswichian interglacial (Ch. 2), and the Flandrian flooding of the Straits of Dover probably dates from a time within pollen zone VI (Fl II).

It is not known whether or not Ireland was connected (presumably via south-west Scotland) to Britain during interglacials before the Flandrian. The Flandrian separation from Britain was probably as early as zone IV (Fl Ia).

Cromerian Stage

Sites and Faunas (Fig. 7.1, Table 7.1)

The Cromer Forest-bed Formation (CF-bF) has been famous for its fossil mammal remains since the early part of the last century, but unfortunately few finds can be accurately related to particular stages (see Ch. 2), largely because the exact locations and horizons of the fossils were not recorded at the time of discovery. Nevertheless a rich fauna is accurately recorded from the type locality of the Cromerian stage at West Runton, Norfolk, a few fossils have been found *in situ* at other CF-bF localities and it has proved possible to date certain other finds by pollen analyses of adhering sediment.

The West Runton Freshwater Bed occupies a broad shallow channel, cut in sands and gravels, more than 400 m across in section and crops out at the base of the cliff east of Woman Hythe (West Runton) (Figs. 7.2, 7.3). The channel filling with a maximum thickness of about 2 m constitutes the type section for the Cromerian Stage.

Table 7.1. Pollen-dated records of Cromerian mammals.

Sites:	West Runton	West Runton	West Runton	Sugworth	Trimingham	Mundesley Bacton		Ostend
Cromerian Pollen zones	?Ia	Ib–IIb	IIIa	IIIb	?IIIb	?IV		IV
MAMMALIA								
Insectivora								
1. *Erinaceus* cf. *europaeus* L., hedgehog	–	+	–	–	–	–	–	–
2. *Sorex* cf. *minutus* L., pigmy shrew	–	–	–	+	–	–	–	–
3. *Sorex runtonensis* Hinton, extinct shrew	–	+	–	–	–	–	–	+
4. *Sorex savini* Hinton, extinct shrew	–	+	–	+	–	–	–	+
5. *Neomys newtoni* Hinton, extinct water shrew	–	+	–	–	–	–	–	–
6. *Beremendia* cf. *fissidens*	–	–	–	+	–	–	–	–
7. *Talpa europaea* L., mole	–	+	–	–	–	–	–	+
8. *Talpa minor* Freudenberg, extinct mole	–	+	–	+	–	–	–	–
9. *Desmana moschata* Pallas, Russian desman	–	+	–	–	–	–	–	+
Primates								
10. *Macaca* sp., macaque monkey	–	–	+	–	–	–	–	–
Lagomorpha								
11. *Lepus* sp., hare	–	+	–	–	–	–	–	–
Rodentia								
12. *Sciurus whitei* Hinton, extinct squirrel	–	–	+	–	–	–	–	–
13. *Sciurus* sp., a squirrel	–	–	–	–	–	–	–	+
14. *Trogontherium cuvieri* Fischer, extinct beaver	–	+	–	–	–	–	–	+
15. *Castor fiber* L., beaver	–	+	–	–	–	–	–	–
16. *Cricetus cricetus* (L.), common hamster	–	+	–	–	–	–	–	–
17. *Clethrionomys glareolus* (Schreber), bank vole	–	+	–	+	–	–	–	+
18. *Pliomys episcopalis* Méhely, extinct vole	–	–	–	+	–	–	–	–
19. *Mimomys savini* Hinton, extinct water vole	+	+	+	–	–	–	–	–
20. *Arvicola cantiana* (Hinton), extinct water vole	–	–	–	–	–	–	–	+
21. *Pitymys arvaloides* Hinton, extinct pine vole	–	+	–	–	–	–	–	–
22. *Pitymys gregaloides* Hinton, extinct pine vole	–	+	–	–	–	–	–	–
23. *Microtus* cf. *arvalis* (Pallas), common vole	–	+	–	+	–	–	–	+
24. *Microtus oeconomus* (Pallas), northern vole	–	+	–	–	–	–	–	–
25. *Apodemus sylvaticus* (L.), wood mouse	–	+	+	+	–	–	–	–
Carnivora								
26. *Canis lupus* L., wolf	–	+	–	–	–	–	–	–
27. *Ursus deningeri* v. Reichenau, extinct bear	–	+	–	–	–	–	–	–
28. *Mustela nivalis* L., weasel	–	+	–	–	–	–	–	–
29. *Martes* sp., marten	–	+	–	–	–	–	–	–
30. *Pannonictis* sp., extinct mustelid	–	+	–	–	–	–	–	–
31. *Lutra* sp., otter	–	+	–	–	–	–	–	–
32. *Crocuta crocuta* Erxleben, spotted hyaena	–	+	–	–	–	–	–	–
33. *Felis* cf. *lunensis* Martelli, extinct cat	–	+	–	–	–	–	–	–
34. Undetermined large felid	–	+	–	–	–	–	–	–
Proboscidea								
35. cf. *Mammuthus trogontherii* Pohlig, extinct elephant	–	–	–	–	–	–	–	+
36. Undetermined elephant	–	+	–	–	·	–	–	–
Perissodactyla								
37. *Equus* sp. (caballine), a horse	–	+	–	–	–	–	–	+
38. *Dicerorhinus etruscus* (Falconer), extinct rhinoceros	–	+	–	–	–	–	–	–
Artiodactyla								
39. *Sus scrofa* L., wild boar	–	+	–	–	–	–	–	–
40. *Hippopotamus* sp., hippopotamus	–	–	–	–	+	+	+	–
41. *Megaceros verticornis* Dawkins, giant deer	–	+	–	–	–	–	–	–
42. *Megaceros dawkinsi* (Newton), extinct giant deer	–	–	–	–	–	–	–	–
43. *Megaceros* sp., giant deer	–	–	–	+	–	+	–	–
44. *Dama dama* (L.), fallow deer	–	+	–	–	–	–	–	–
45. *Cervus elaphus* L., red deer	–	+	–	+	–	–	–	–
46. *Alces latifrons* Johnson, extinct elk	–	+	–	–	–	–	–	–
47. *Capreolus capreolus* (L.), roe deer	–	+	–	–	–	–	–	+
48. *Bison* cf. *schoetensacki* Freudenberg, extinct bison	–	+	–	+	–	–	–	–

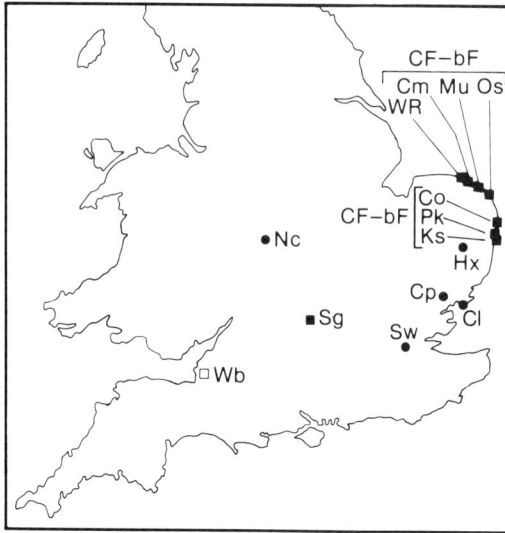

Fig. 7.1. Location map of Cromerian and Hoxnian vertebrate sites. ■, Cromerian; ●, Hoxnian; (cave site shown by open symbol). Cl, Clacton; Cm, Cromer; Co, Corton; Cp, Copford; Hx, Hoxne; Ks, Kessingland; Mu, Mundesley; Nc, Nechells Birmingham; Os, Ostend near Bacton; Pk, Pakefield; Sg, Sugworth; Sw, Swanscombe and Ingress Vale; Wb, Westbury-sub-Mendip; WR, West Runton.

The basal bed of the channel filling, West's Bed a, comprising marls and detritus muds, is of Late Beestonian and Cromerian subzone Cr Ia age (West 1980a). On its eroded surface rest beds c–e: comprising fluviatile shelly sands and organic muds containing lumps of marl reworked from the underlying deposit. Pollen analyses demonstrate that these beds essentially cover subzones Cr Ib to Cr IIa. The bulk of the West Runton Freshwater Bed consists of detritus muds, leached at the top, and covers subzone Cr IIb.

These deposits have yielded a rich vertebrate fauna (Table 7.1), although the records of the larger mammals are based on relatively sparse material. Much of the collecting was done by A. C. Savin, a local amateur, from about 1880 to 1945. These finds can be dated only rather broadly to the range subzones Cr Ib to Cr IIb (i.e. not restricted to Cr II as previously stated, e.g. Stuart 1975), since vertebrate remains are extremely rare in the earlier horizon. It is apparent, however, both from material collected *in situ* by the author, and examination of museum material with attached sediment matrix, that all large-mammal finds come from the coarser

basal units. With minor exceptions, therefore, the age of the vast majority of the fauna can be narrowed to subzones Cr Ib to Cr IIa. Bulk samples of small vertebrates were collected by the author from three separate lithological units, corresponding fairly closely with subzones Cr Ib, Cr IIa and Cr IIb, at West's locality AJS. All three assemblages are almost identical, although the concentration of terrestrial vertebrate material for a given weight of sediment decreases sharply from bottom to top (Stuart 1975).

The fossil pollen and macroscopic plant remains (West 1980a) record changes from a pine–elm–birch woodland with extensive herb vegetation and restricted fen and reed swamp in subzone Cr Ib (*Pinus–Ulmus* pollen-assemblage biozone: p.a.b.), to a more diverse woodland with oak and other thermophilous genera more widespread, persistent local open habitats with herbaceous vegetation, and fen and reedswamp, in subzone Cr IIa (*Pinus–Quercus–Ulmus* p.a.b.). During subzone Cr IIb (*Quercus–Ulmus–Tilia* p.a.b.) mixed oak forest dominated, but again with persistent local open herb vegetation and even indications of heath. A rich aquatic and reedswamp flora is indicated.

Taking the sedimentological and palaeontological evidence together, one can picture a slow-flowing river, rich in aquatic plants and fringed by fen, supporting a wide variety of fishes, such as is found in a typical English lowland river today, plus frogs and toads, grass snake *Natrix* sp., water birds, and mammals of waterside habitats, including Russian desman *Desmana moschata*, beaver *Castor fiber*, extinct beaver *Trogontherium cuvieri* and extinct water vole *Mimomys savini*. Local herb-dominated vegetation on the floodplain appears to have supported grassland voles *Microtus* spp. and *Pitymys* spp., and common hamster *Cricetus cricetus*.

Two species of mole, *Talpa europaea*, and the smaller extinct *T. minor*, made their tunnels in the floodplain.

Much of the fauna, including wood mouse *Apodemus sylvaticus*, bank vole *Clethrionomys glareolus*, extinct rhinoceros *Dicerorhinus etruscus*, wild boar *Sus scrofa*, fallow deer *Dama dama* and roe deer *Capreolus capreolus*, is consistent with the presence of temperate forest, although many of these animals probably obtained much of their food at the forest edge on the floodplain, or in glades within the forest. The presence of the large deer *Megaceros verticornis* and *Alces latifrons*, in which the males carried enormous outspread antlers,

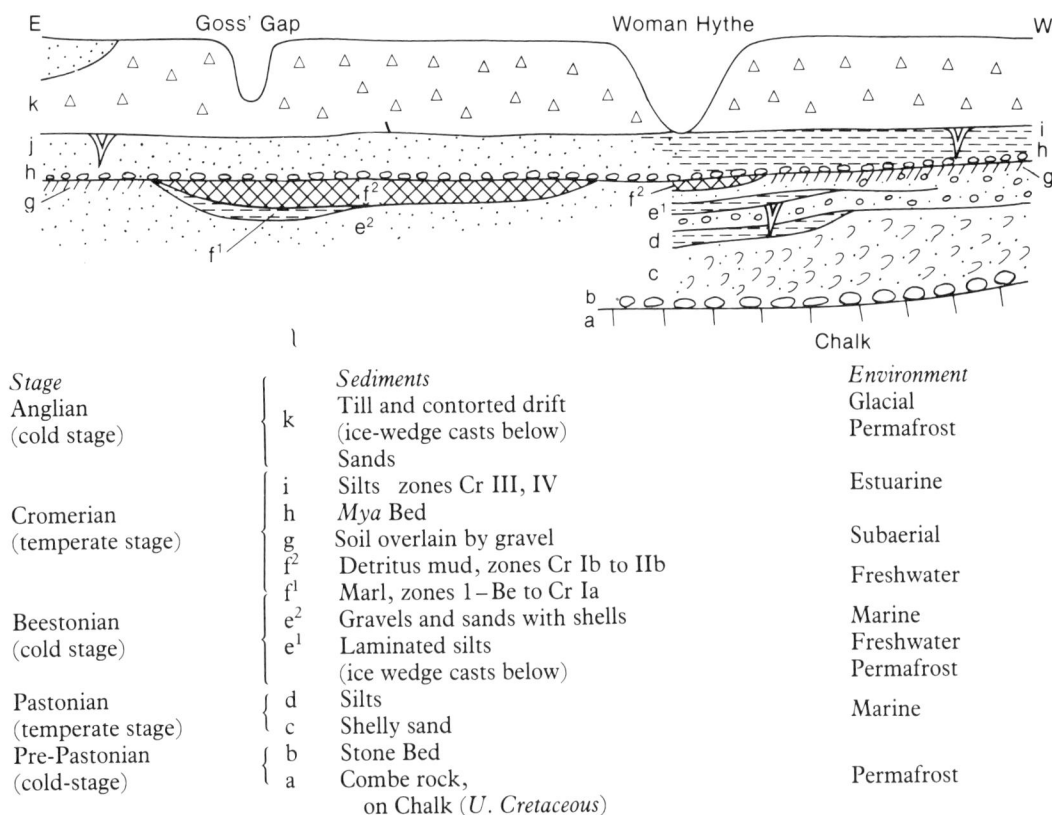

Stage		Sediments	Environment
Anglian (cold stage)	k	Till and contorted drift (ice-wedge casts below) Sands	Glacial Permafrost
Cromerian (temperate stage)	i	Silts zones Cr III, IV	Estuarine
	h	*Mya* Bed	
	g	Soil overlain by gravel	Subaerial
	f^2	Detritus mud, zones Cr Ib to IIb	Freshwater
	f^1	Marl, zones 1 – Be to Cr Ia	
Beestonian (cold stage)	e^2	Gravels and sands with shells	Marine
	e^1	Laminated silts (ice wedge casts below)	Freshwater Permafrost
Pastonian (temperate stage)	d	Silts	Marine
	c	Shelly sand	
Pre-Pastonian (cold-stage)	b	Stone Bed	
	a	Combe rock, on Chalk (*U. Cretaceous*)	Permafrost

Fig. 7.2. Sketch section at West Runton, Norfolk (not to scale). (Adapted from West 1977a) Length of section approximately 450 m; depth of deposits below till approximately 7 m. The V-shaped vertical structures are ice-wedge casts. Vertebrates are recorded from beds b, c, f^2 and h.

together with horse *Equus* sp. and probably certain other large-mammal taxa, suggests that the forest was not very dense. Carnivores preying on the wide variety of available herbivores included wolf *Canis lupus*, the omnivorous extinct bear *Ursus deningeri*, weasel *Mustela nivalis*, spotted hyaena *Crocuta crocuta*, extinct cat *Felis* cf. *lunensis* and an undetermined large cat (Stuart 1975, 1981).

A sparse fauna is recorded from the marine or estuarine gravel which immediately overlies the West Runton Freshwater Bed (Fig. 7.4). This horizon ('Monkey Gravel' of Hinton 1908) is overlain by marine silts with pollen of subzones Cr IIIa and Cr IIIb (West 1980a). The faunal list includes *Mimomys savini*, *Apodemus sylvaticus*, and two taxa not recorded from the older bed: macaque monkey *Macaca* sp. (Hinton 1908) and extinct squirrel *Sciurus whitei* (Hinton 1914, 1915). The pollen spectra from the overlying deposits indicate that

these animals probably lived in temperate forest (West 1980a).

Harrison (1979a) records 20 bird taxa from the West Runton Freshwater Bed. These comprise water fowl and others closely associated with water, e.g. cormorant *Phalacrocorax carbo*, Bewick's swan *Cygnus bewicki*, greylag goose *Anser anser* and various ducks (genera *Anas*, *Netta*, *Athya*, *Bucephala* and *Mergus*). The only non-British species recorded are mandarin duck *Aix galericulata*, nowadays indigenous to China, and an eider duck considered by Harrison to represent an extinct species *Somateria gravipes*.

The Rev. C. Green and Anna Gurney collected a limited fauna, mainly small mammals, from Ostend near Bacton, Norfolk, in the early part of the last century. Taxa recorded (Table 7.1) include extinct shrews *Sorex runtonensis* and *S. savini*, *Desmana moschata*, extinct water vole *Arvicola cantiana* and

Fig. 7.3a. View of cliff at West Runton, Norfolk, looking eastwards from Woman Hythe. The Cromerian Freshwater Bed can be seen as a dark band at the foot of the cliff.

Fig. 7.3b. Cliff section showing the Cromerian West Runton Freshwater Bed (subzones Cr Ib–IIb) resting on lacustrine marls of Late Beestonian and early Cromerian (subzone Cr Ia) age.

Fig. 7.3c. Detail of base of West Runton Freshwater Bed, showing reworked marl lumps and non-marine molluscan shells.

sparse large mammals. Pollen analyses of sediment matrix of some of the specimens showed that they dated from pollen zone Cr IV (Stuart & West 1976). The contemporary vegetation, towards the end of the interglacial, had reverted to coniferous forest. Of particular interest is the occurrence at Ostend of *Arvicola cantiana*, an extinct water vole with permanently growing (rootless) cheek teeth, replacing the earlier species *Mimomys savini* in which the cheek teeth became rooted (see Ch. 11). Harrison (1979a) records an extinct species of jungle fowl *Gallus europaeus* from this locality.

Pollen obtained from sediment within fossil *Hippopotamus* bones from the CF-bF has shown that this animal was present in England during pollen zones Cr IIIb and Cr IV (Gibbard, in Stuart 1982). The inferred contemporaneous vegetation was regional conifer-dominated forest with only local areas of herb vegetation.

An antler of the extinct giant deer *Megaceros dawkinsi* from Mundesley has similarly been assigned to zone Cr III or Cr IV.

As mentioned above, the majority of CF-bF finds

do not have accompanying stratigraphical data. Nevertheless, the faunas of the Pre-Pastonian and Pastonian stages (Ch. 6) include few taxa which also occur in the Cromerian and *vice versa* so that, for example, nearly all specimens of *Megaceros verticornis* probably date from the Cromerian, with perhaps some from the Beestonian and Early Anglian stages. Moreover, at a few sites, e.g. Pakefield, Corton, Kessingland, Mundesley, most of the recorded fauna is of Cromerian type so that at these localities the earlier deposits are probably not very fossiliferous.

The following taxa, not included in Table 7.1 because they lack precise stratigraphical data, may be in part of Cromerian or approximately Cromerian age: extinct glutton *Gulo schlosseri* (Mundesley); extinct hyaena *Hyaena brevirostris* (Mundesley); lion *Panthera leo* (Pakefield); sabre tooth *Homotherium latidens* (Kessingland); straight-tusked elephant *Palaeoloxodon antiquus* (e.g. Corton, Mundesley); extinct elephant *Archidiskodon meridionalis* (Mundesley); extinct giant deer *Megaceros savini* (Mundesley, Pakefield) and extinct musk ox *Praeovibos priscus* (Walcott).

Fig. 7.4. Cliff section showing estuarine gravel and alternating sands and silts (Cromerian zone Cr III) resting on the West Runton Freshwater Bed.

Until a few years ago no fossil vertebrate sites of definite Cromerian age were known outside East Anglia. In 1972, however, fossiliferous sediments filling a river channel cut in the Jurassic Kimmeridge Clay were discovered at Sugworth near Oxford, 40 m above the modern River Thames (Briggs *et al*: 1975). The palaeontological evidence taken together indicates a Cromerian age, and the pollen and macroscopic plant remains indicate pollen assemblage subzone Cr IIIb (Gibbard & Pettit 1978). The vegetation is interpreted as regional mixed coniferous-deciduous forest in the river valley with alder fen carr bordering the river. Both wet and dry ground herb communities probably grew on the floodplain immediately adjacent to the river and on the point bar.

The collection of Sugworth vertebrate material (Stuart 1980) is much less extensive than that from West Runton, as the deposits were only ex-posed for a short time. The fish and amphibian fauna is consistent with West Runton, but several small mammals, pigmy shrew *Sorex minutus*, large extinct shrew *Beremendia* cf. *fissidens* and extinct vole *Pliomys episcopalis*, are not recorded from West Runton, although the rest of the Sugworth mammals, including *Sorex savini*, *Mimomys savini* and *Dicerorhinus etruscus*, have been found at the type site.

In contrast to West Runton, the Sugworth small-mammal assemblage, with high percentages of *Apodemus sylvaticus* and *Clethrionomys glareolus*, is consistent with forested habitats predominating close to the depositional site (see Ch. 5).

In 1969 extensive cave deposits containing very large numbers of vertebrate fossils were discovered in the course of quarrying the Carboniferous limestone near Westbury-sub-Mendip, Somerset (Fig. 7.5). The stratigraphy and fauna are being

Fig. 7.5. View of quarry face at Westbury-sub-Mendip showing fossiliferous early Middle Pleistocene cave deposits (foreground and middle distance) in the carboniferous limestone.

studied by Bishop (1974, 1975, 1982) and also by a team from the British Museum (Natural History), London, directed by P. Andrews. The stratigraphy of the deposits is extremely complex and at present the only reliable evidence for the relative age of these deposits seems to be the vertebrate assemblage itself.

Disregarding the lowest beds ('Siliceous Group' Bed 1 of Bishop 1974) which have a fauna no younger than Cromerian in age, the bulk of the deposits ('Calcareous Group', including the 'Rodent Earth' Beds 3–10) will be considered here as a whole. The deposits, however, may span a considerable period of time.

The fauna includes many elements occurring at West Runton, e.g. *Sorex savini*, *Desmana moschata*, *Ursus deningeri*, *Dicerorhinus etruscus* and extinct pine vole *Pitymys gregaloides*. However, it also includes *Pliomys episcopalis*, recorded elsewhere only at Sugworth, and significantly *Arvicola cantiana*, which has been found in the CF-bF only at Ostend, Norfolk (zone Cr IV), although very rare specimens attributed to *Mimomys*

savini do occur in Bed 1 (Bishop, 1982). Like many cave assemblages, the Westbury fauna is rich in Carnivora. These include extinct leopard *Panthera gombazogensis*, extinct dhole *Xenocyon lycaonoides* – both unique records for the British Pleistocene, and sabre-tooth *Homotherium latidens*. Unfortunately, large herbivores are rather sparsely represented, complicating comparisons with open-site faunas.

Other interesting records from Beds 3–10 include the now arctic-boreal Norway lemming *Lemmus lemmus* and arctic lemming *Dicrostonyx torquatus*, the steppe-dwelling pika *Ochotona pusilla*, and in contrast European pond tortoise *Emys orbicularis* (Stuart 1979) which requires mean July temperatures in excess of 17–18 °C for its eggs to hatch (Ch. 5).

This mixture of temperate and cold-stage elements seems to characterize the ends of interglacial periods, and it is tempting to place Westbury at the end of the Cromerian, especially in view of the occurrence of *Arvicola cantiana*, suggesting an approximate correlation with the Ostend zone Cr

IV fauna. It is, however, possible that the West-bury deposits represent in part one or more inter-stadials within the Anglian, or even, as has been suggested on the grounds that many of the species are larger than at West Runton (Bishop, 1982), a distinct interglacial period. The available evidence does not, however, appear to be sufficient to justify the latter conclusion. The most economical solution for the present seems to be to provisionally place the main Westbury fauna within a period at the end of the Cromerian and perhaps also extending into beginning of the Anglian.

It is especially desirable to determine the age of the deposits because Westbury provides the earliest plausible evidence of man in the British Pleistocene (Bishop 1975) (Ch. 10).

Cromerian faunal history

Generally speaking there are rather few accurately dated records for the Cromerian (Table 7.1) on which to base an account of faunal history through the stage. It is difficult, for example, to judge whether the differences in small-mammal faunas between sites, particularly Sugworth and West Runton, are reflecting local habitat differences, or have some temporal or geographical significance. Faunal change through the interglacial is, however, suggested by the presence of *Hippopotamus* sp. and *Megaceros dawkinsi* in pollen zones Cr IIIb and IV, when these are absent from the rich fauna of temperate aspect from the type site, of Cr II age. Similarly, the replacement of *Mimomys savini*, recorded from zones Cr II, Cr III, by the phylogenetically more advanced *Arvicola cantiana* in zone Cr IV at Ostend may have regional significance. It is, however, possible that populations of both species co-existed in Britain and Europe at this time. We have no evidence for assuming that the replacement of one species by another was geologically instantaneous, even within a limited geographical area.

If all of the main Westbury deposits are considered to be of late Cromerian age, then lemmings and *Ochotona pusilla* had arrived before the close of the interglacial. The occurrence of *Emys orbicularis*, however, indicates that summer temperatures remained high.

Since there is no trace of undoubted man-made artefacts from the CF-bF or earlier, the Westbury material suggests that man first arrived in England towards the end of the Cromerian interglacial, and

that at this period the human population was very sparse (Ch. 10).

Comparison with Continental faunas

Vertebrate faunas which can be broadly correlated with the type Cromerian are known from a number of localities in Continental Europe, especially from Germany (Kahlke 1975a).

The rich mammal fauna from Voigtstedt, San-gerhausen, Thüringia, East Germany (Kahlke 1965) comes from a restricted horizon immediately overlain by organic sediments yielding 'pollen spectra which can be correlated with zones Cr III and Cr IV of the type Cromerian. The Voigtstedt fauna is therefore virtually contemporaneous with that of the West Runton Freshwater Bed, and they are correspondingly remarkably similar (Stuart 1981). Two species, an extinct suslik *Spermophilus dietrichi* and extinct flying squirrel *Petauria voigtstedtensis*, which have not been found at West Runton, may reflect the more eastern continental situation of Voigtstedt.

The vertebrate material from another classic Thüringian locality, Süssenborn near Weimar, described in a series of papers edited by Kahlke (1969), includes reindeer *Rangifer tarandus* and musk ox *Ovibos moschatus* – both arctic species, as well as temperate Cromerian forms, and probably covers part of the preceding cold stage as well.

Comparison with the British sequence suggests that the rich faunas from the main vertebrate horizons at Mosbach, Wiesbaden, West Germany which include an extinct hippopotamus *Hippopotamus antiquus* and *Rangifer tarandus* (Kahlke 1975a; Brüning 1978) date from the end of the Cromerian interglacial and the beginning of the Elsterian (Anglian) cold stage. The more strictly temperate fauna from Mauer near Heidelberg, West Germany, also with *H. antiquus*, but including one of the earliest finds of man in Europe, a mandible attributed either to an advanced *Homo erectus* or an early form of *H. sapiens* may date rather earlier in the second half of the Cromerian. Other important faunas of approximate Cromerian age are known from Stránská Skála, Brno, Czechoslovakia, Vértess-zöllös, Tata, Hungary, and Tiraspol, Moldavia, USSR. Vértesszöllós is of particular importance for its record of early man, both from bones and artefacts. The faunas of these and many other sites are listed by Kretzoi (1965), Kahlke (1975a) and Jánossy (1975).

Table 7.2. Records of mammals and *Emys orbicularis* from the Hoxnian (N.B. most records can only be tentatively or imprecisely related to pollen zones).

Site:	Clacton	Swanscombe a.	Hoxne a.	Hoxne b.	Ingress Vale	Hoxne c.	Hoxne d.	Swanscombe b.
Pollen zone:	c.IIb (I–IIIa)	?II	II	IIc	?III	?III–IV	?IV	
MAMMALIA								
Insectivora								
Sorex araneus L., common shrew	–	–	–	–	–	+	–	–
Talpa cf. *minor* Freudenberg, extinct mole	–	+	–	–	–	–	–	–
Desmana moschata Pallas, Russian desman	–	–	–	–	–	–	+	–
Primates								
Macaca sp., macaque monkey	–	+	–	–	–	+	–	–
Homo sp., man (skull)	–	–	–	–	–	–	–	+
Homo sp., man (artefacts) – C: Clactonian; A: Acheulian	C	C	–	A	A	A	A	A
Lagomorpha								
Oryctolagus cuniculus L., rabbit	–	+	–	–	–	–	–	–
Lepus timidus L., mountain hare	–	–	–	–	–	–	–	+
Rodentia								
Trogontherium cuvieri Fischer, extinct beaver	+[1]	–	+	–	+	+	+	–
Castor fiber L., beaver	?	+	–	–	–	+	–	–
Lemmus lemmus (L.), Norway lemming	–	–	–	–	–	–	+	+
Clethrionomys glareolus (Schreber), bank vole	+	–	–	–	+	–	–	
Arvicola cantiana (Hinton), extinct water vole	+	+	–	–	+	+	+	–
Pitymys arvaloides Hinton, extinct pine vole	–	+	–	–	–	–	–	–
Microtus cf. *arvalis* Pallas, common vole	(+)[1]	+	–	–	–	–	–	+
Microtus agrestis (L.), field vole	–	–	–	–	–	+	–	–
Microtus oeconomus (Pallas), northern vole	–	+	–	–	–	–	–	+
Apodemus sylvaticus (L.), wood mouse	–	–	–	–	+	–	–	–
Carnivora								
Canis lupus L., wolf	–	+	–	–	+	–	–	+
Ursus spelaeus Rosenmüller & Heinroth, (extinct) cave bear	–	+	–	–	–	–	–	–
Martes martes L., marten	–	+	–	–	–	–	–	–
Panthera leo (L.), lion	+	+	–	–	+	–	–	+
Felis sylvestris Schreber, wild cat	–	+	–	–	–	–	–	–
Proboscidea								
Palaeoloxodon antiquus Falconer & Cautley, (extinct) straight-tusked elephant	+	+	–	+	+	–	–	+
Perissodactyla								
Equus ferus Boddaert, horse	+	+	–	+	+	+	+	+
Dicerorhinus kirchbergensis (Jäger), extinct rhinoceros	+	+	–	–	+	–	–	+
Dicerorhinus hemitoechus (Falconer), extinct rhinoceros	+	+	–	–	–	–	–	–
Artiodactyla								
Sus scrofa L., wild boar	+	+	–	–	+	–	–	–
Megaceros giganteus Blumenbach, (extinct) giant deer	–	+	–	–	–	+	–	+
Dama dama (L.), fallow deer	+	+	–	–	+	+	–	+
Cervus elaphus L., red deer	+	+	–	–	+	+	–	+
Capreolus capreolus L., roe deer	–	+	–	–	–	+	–	–
Bos primigenius Bojanus, (extinct) aurochs	+	+	–	–	+	–	–	+
Bos sp., aurochs or *Bison* sp., bison	–	–	–	–	–	+	+	–
REPTILIA								
Chelonia								
Emys orbicularis L. European pond tortoise	–	–	–	–	+	–	–	–

1. Clacton Golf Course Excavation

Hoxnian

Sites and faunas (Fig. 7.1, Table 7.2)

Fossil vertebrates of Hoxnian age are known in abundance from a very limited number of sites, and have mostly been obtained in conjunction with archaeological excavations. Unfortunately, in most cases there are problems in attempting to determine the exact stratigraphical horizons of these fossils. Nevertheless, a few pollen-dated records are available, and it is possible to assign at least tentatively most of the fossil assemblages to pollen zones using other palaeontological or stratigraphical evidence.

Interglacial fluviatile deposits of the 'Clacton Channel', comprising silts and sands with organic horizons and rich in artefacts and mammal bones, were formerly exposed in the cliffs and foreshore at Clacton-on-Sea, Essex (Warren 1951, 1955). These freshwater deposits are overlain by estuarine clays and silts which occupy much of the cliff. Pollen analyses by Pike and Godwin (1952) showed that these deposits are of Hoxnian interglacial age. The uppermost estuarine beds were assigned to zone Ho IIIb and the top freshwater loamy organic sands to zone Ho IIIa. Subsequent investigations by Turner and Kerney (1971) demonstrated that the freshwater deposits date from at least as far back as zone Ho IIb, the latter date appertaining to bed y of Warren, from which he obtained the majority of artefacts and bones. It is probable therefore that the majority of the fauna relates to subzone Ho IIb, but some fossils could be from pre-Ho IIb horizons, or as late as subzone Ho IIIa.

Recent archaeological excavations at the Clacton Golf Course site have produced many more artefacts and some vertebrate remains from fluviatile gravels (Singer *et al.* 1973). These authors tentatively consider that this horizon pre-dates zone Ho I, i.e. belongs within the preceding Anglian Cold Stage, but the pollen analyses on which this view is based may be questioned, especially as primary pollen is unlikely to be preserved in gravels. Moreover, the occurrence of beech (*Fagus*) pollen raises the suspicion that the deposits contain Flandrian pollen, as this tree is not recorded from other stages in the British Pleistocene. It seems more likely that the Golf Course deposits are part of the 'Clacton Channel' complex, and that the artefacts and fauna are of much the same age as the other material.

The pollen and plant macrofossil analyses for the subzone Ho IIb samples (Turner, in Kerney 1971) indicate a river floodplain with marshland and occasional dry grassland habitats, with fairly dense mixed oak forest on higher ground. The non-marine mollusc analyses are consistent with this picture, and show considerable similarities with the Lower Loam faunas of Swanscombe.

The mammalian fauna, listed by Sutcliffe (1964), with additions from the Clacton Golf Course Site (Singer *et al.* 1973), is given in Table 7.2. It is very similar to, but less rich than, the Swanscombe Lower Gravel and Lower Loam faunas, with woodland elements such as straight-tusked elephant *Palaeoloxodon antiquus*, wild boar *Sus scrofa*, and fallow deer *Dama dama*. The presence of lion *Panthera leo*, horse *Equus ferus*, and an extinct rhinoceros *Dicerorhinus hemitoechus*, which probably fed on low-growing vegetation (Ch. 5), is consistent with the palaeobotanical evidence for areas of herbaceous vegetation on the floodplain.

Numerous flint tools, from which the Clactonian industry is named, and a wooden spear have been recovered from the 'Clacton Channel' deposits (Ch. 10).

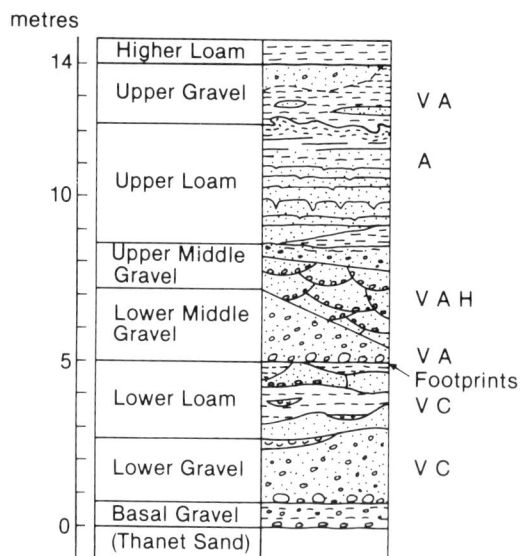

Fig. 7.6. Generalized section of Hoxnian and early Wolstonian deposits at Barnfield Pit, Swanscombe (modified and simplified from Conway & Waechter, in Shephard-Thorn & Wymer 1977). Note ice wedge casts (V-shaped) in upper beds. V, vertebrate fossils; H, human skull; C, Clactonian artefacts; A, Acheulian artefacts.

Fig. 7.7. Section in the lower part of the sequence of Hoxnian deposits at Barnfield Pit, Swanscombe, showing Lower Gravel (beneath figure) overlain by Lower Loam and Lower Middle Gravel. Note horizon rich in bones on surface of Lower Gravel.

At Barnfield Pit, Swanscombe, Kent – the famous human-skull site – a series of fluviatile gravels, sands and silts occupy a broad channel cut by an early River Thames (Figs. 7.6, 7.7). The stratigraphy, archaeology and palaeontology of the site were described in some detail in the memoir edited by Ovey (1964).

Subsequent excavations (1968–72) have been directed by J. Waechter and the findings are

summarized by Conway and Waechter (in Shephard-Thorn and Wymer 1977).

As discussed in Chapter 2, the archaeology and vertebrate and molluscan faunas strongly suggest that at least the bulk of the sequence belongs within the Hoxnian Interglacial, and Kerney (1971) attempted to assign the beds to particular Hoxnian pollen zones. He suggested that the Lower Gravel and Lower Loam were deposited in zone Ho II, whereas the Middle Gravels did not begin to accumulate until the end of zone Ho III, and deposition probably continued into the early part of the succeeding cold stage (Wolstonian).

The mammal faunas are listed in full (Table 7.2) based on data in Sutcliffe (1964) and material from the recent excavations. Artefacts are numerous in the deposits and show a succession from Clactonian flakes and cores in the Lower Gravel and Lower Loam, with Acheulian hand axes in the later deposits (Ch. 10). Some of the faunal material may be human food debris, but much of it was probably incorporated by natural processes and subsequently water-transported, as were the assemblages from other fluviatile deposits (Ch. 4).

According to Kerney, the terrestrial mollusc fauna of the Lower Gravel and most of the Lower Loam indicates reedswamp and fen, close to the depositional site, with drier open ground, and dry open woodland, probably of hazel (*Corylus*).

The mammalian fauna (Table 7.2, Swanscombe a) is consistent with regional mixed oak forest, including such woodland elements as macaque monkey *Macaca* sp., beaver *Castor fiber*, pine marten *Martes martes*, wild cat *Felis sylvestris*, *Palaeoloxodon antiquus*, *Sus scrofa*, *Dama dama* and *Capreolus capreolus*. Taxa consistent with probably rather local, more open habitats include rabbit *Oryctolagus cuniculus*, extinct pine vole *Pitymys arvaloides*, voles *Microtus* spp., *Panthera leo*, *Equus ferus*, *Dicerorhinus hemitoechus* and giant deer *Megaceros giganteus*.

From the vertebrate point of view, one of the most exciting results from the 1968–72 excavations was the discovery of an horizon of fossil footprints at the eroded junction between the weathered surface of the Lower Loam and the overlying gravels. A 5 m square yielded 92 prints mostly deer, but also including horse, bovid, rhino and elephant (see Fig. 5.35). Presumably these represent animals living immediately prior to the deposition of the Middle Gravels, that trampled the river bank when visiting the river to drink.

The terrestrial molluscs from the base of the Lower Middle Gravel suggest a more closed forest with subordinate open ground, whereas those from the Upper Middle Gravel indicate damp open grassland, which Kerney suggests belongs to the closing phases of the Hoxnian interglacial. Unfortunately, although fossil vertebrates occur in the Lower Middle Gravel, they were not collected separately from material from the higher beds. The Upper Middle Gravel mammal fauna (Table 7.2, Swanscombe b) is on the whole very similar to that of the Lower Gravel and Lower Loam. The smaller number of species recorded is probably due to the fact that far fewer fossils have been collected from the Upper Middle Gravel.

Contrary to the mollusc evidence, the records of *Palaeoloxodon antiquus* and especially *Dama dama* strongly suggest forest (and therefore a date within the interglacial), although other woodland indicators recorded from the older horizons may be absent. Most of the indicators of more open vegetational conditions, e.g. horse, giant deer, do however continue from the Lower Gravel and Lower Loam, joined by mountain hare *Lepus timidus* and the now arctic-boreal Norway lemming, *Lemmus lemmus*.

The fragments of human cranium were found about one metre above the base of the Upper Middle Gravel, at the same horizon as a number of pointed Acheulean hand axes.

The Swanscombe Lower Gravel has also yielded remains of pike *Esox lucius* (Patterson in Ovey, 1964), and birds identified as shoveller *Anas clypeata*, red-breasted merganser *Mergus serrator*, garden warbler *Sylvia borin* and others (Harrison 1979b). Cormorant *Phalacrocorax carbo*, eagle owl *Bubo bubo* and serin *Serinus serinus* are recorded by Harrison from the Lower Loam.

Shelly sands in Dierden's Pit, Ingress Vale, about 400 m north-west of Barnfield Pit, have also produced an abundance of vertebrate material. Kerney (1971) considered that the mollusc assemblage suggested a zone Ho III age. The mammal fauna (Sutcliffe 1964) (Table 7.2) is very similar to that of the Swanscombe Lower Gravel and Lower Loam, and to the Clacton Channel. It includes extinct beaver *Trogontherium cuvieri*, recorded from Clacton and other Hoxnian sites, but not Swanscombe. The find of a dolphin *Tursiops* sp. vertebra may represent an individual which swam up the river and perhaps became stranded.

Of particular interest is the record from Ingress Vale of European pond tortoise *Emys orbicularis* (Stuart 1979). Frog and/or toad bones, and teeth of cyprinid fishes, have also been found. Capercaillie *Tetrao urogallus* is recorded from this locality by Harrison (1979b).

At Hoxne, Suffolk, the type site for the Hoxnian Interglacial stage, organic lacustrine deposits occupy a basin in the Anglian Chalky Boulder Clay and are overlain by a series of fluviatile, lacustrine and solifluction deposits (Gladfelter & Singer 1975; Wymer 1974) (Table 7.3).

Table 7.3. Stratigraphical succession at Hoxne, Suffolk. (Based on West 1956; Gladfelter & Singer 1975; Turner, in West 1977c)

Beds (nomenclature after West 1956 (C to G); Gladfelter & Singer 1975 (1–10)).		Thickness (m)	Stage/pollen zone
9–10	Sand, gravel, silt	0.5–2.5	Wolstonian
7–8	Sands with ice-wedge casts	1.8	Wolstonian
6	Gravel	0.3	? Wolstonian
5	Sandy silt	0.5	? Wolstonian
1–4 (= C in part)	Silts and clays with seams of fine Chalk gravel, brecciated clay and clay-mud pebbles (Main faunal and archaeological horizon at base of Bed 1)	3.5	? Hoxnian, Ho III–IV
D	Lacustrine detritus mud	0.4	Hoxnian, Ho IIIa
E	Lacustrine clay-mud	6.5	Hoxnian, Ho IIa–c
F	Lacustrine clay-mud and marl	0.5	Late Anglian to Hoxnian Ho I
G	Chalky till (chalky boulder clay)	7.5	Anglian (glaciation)

Of the few vertebrates recovered from the lake deposits, *Trogontherium cuvieri* is recorded from Bed E (zone Ho II) and a mandible of *Palaeoloxodon antiquus* and bones of teeth of *Equus ferus* from the same bed can be dated more precisely to subzone Ho IIc. Flint flakes and an Acheulian hand axe, apparently in primary context, were also recovered from this subzone (Ch. 10). The palaeobotanical evidence (West 1956) indicates regional mixed oak forest throughout most of zone Ho II, with very limited open ground. Both the straight-tusked elephant and artefacts, however, come from an horizon within subzone Ho IIc, the 'Hoxne high non-tree pollen phase', marked by a temporary decline in forest and spread of herb communities (West 1956).

Abundant, but generally fragmentary, vertebrate remains have been recovered from two main horizons within the upper sequence. The lower horizon (Bed 1) has vertebrate and archaeological material, apparently in primary context, and immediately overlies lake muds of subzone Ho IIIa age, so that its age may lie within zones Ho IIIb to Ho IV. The fauna is being studied at present and only preliminary determinations are given here.

The mammal fauna (Table 7.2 – Hoxne c) includes *Macaca* sp., *Castor fiber Dama dama* and *Capreolus capreolus* indicative of forest. A number of flint blades, flakes, cores, scrapers and Acheulian hand axes have been recovered from this horizon. Bird and frog and/or toad bones were also found, together with a number of fishes including

pike *Esox lucius*, three-spined stickleback *Gasterosteus aculeatus* and cyprinids.

Vertebrates recorded from Beds 4 and 5 are generally similar to those recorded from the lower archaeological horizon, Bed 1, with e.g. *Macaca* sp., *Trogontherium cuvieri* and *Equus ferus*, but Russian desman *Desmana moschata* and the nowadays arctic-boreal *Lemmus lemmus* also occur.

Archaeological material includes cores, scrapers, flakes and hand axes.

The faunal assemblage, with juxtaposed forest elements and *Lemmus lemmus*, may represent the closing phases of the interglacial (i.e. zone Ho IV), perhaps an interstadial within the early Wolstonian.

Lacustrine deposits at Copford, Essex, have yielded pollen characteristic of the Hoxnian interglacial (Turner 1970). Fossils found during the last century include a bear *Ursus* sp. and *Trogontherium cuvieri*. Fishes recorded from Hoxnian lacustrine deposits at Nechells, Birmingham, include rudd *Scardinius erythrophthalmus*, roach *Rutilus rutilus*, bleak *Alburnus alburnus*, pike *Esox lucius* and perch *Perca fluviatilis* (Shotton & Osborne 1965).

Hoxnian faunal history

The small number of sites and the stratigraphical uncertainties preclude any detailed analysis of the faunal history of the Hoxnian Stage. Nevertheless the appearance of *Lemmus* late in the interglacial, perhaps in response to opening out of the forest, parallels the situation in the Ipswichian and probably Cromerian interglacials. The most striking observation on the Hoxnian faunal succession is that *Dama dama* and *Palaeoloxodon antiquus* evidently persisted until late in the stage (? zone Ho IV), whereas in the Ipswichian they disappeared much earlier. Other characteristics of the Hoxnian which contrast with the Ipswichian, include the presence of the rhinoceros *Dicerorhinus kirchbergensis* in addition to *D. hemitoechus*, and the apparent absence of mammoth *Mammuthus primigenius*, extinct bison *Bison priscus*, and spotted hyaena *Crocuta crocuta*.

The single record of *Emys orbicularis* indicates that summer temperatures in southern England, at least in the middle part (? zone Ho III) of the interglacial, were higher than those of the present day.

Comparison with Continental faunas

On the European Continent faunas which can be attributed with reasonable confidence to the Holsteinian (= Hoxnian) Interglacial are rare. River gravels at Steinheim, Würtemburg, in southern Germany have yielded a fauna resembling those of the Lower Gravel and Lower Loam at Swanscombe and of the Clacton Channel, with the interesting additions of extinct bison *Bison priscus* and extinct buffalo *Buffelus murrensis* Burkemer (Adam 1954, 1975). This is also the locality of the famous human skull which compares closely with the much less complete specimen from Swanscombe (Ch. 3). Buffalo occurs also at Schönebeck, East Germany, in association with a temperate fauna. The assemblage from a cave deposit at Heppenloch, Swäbische Alb, West Germany, has also been attributed to the Holsteinian (Adam 1975). The species recorded compare closely with those of Steinheim and Swanscombe, with the interesting addition of an extinct dhole *Cuon alpinus*.

Lacustrine clays, dated by pollen spectra to the Holsteinian interglacial, occur at Neede, Netherlands. Vertebrate finds include the extinct beaver *Trogontherium cuvieri* (Hooijer 1959). Conspicuously absent from all European faunas of this stage are spotted hyaena *Crocuta crocuta* and hippopotamus *Hippopotamus* sp. Of considerable interest is the lack of bison *Bison priscus*, buffalo *Buffelus murrensis* and mammoths *Mammuthus* spp. in the British Hoxnian. This and the corresponding lack of aurochs *Bos primigenius* in central Europe indicates

some geographical differences in faunas relating to the degree of oceanity or continentality of the climate.

Ipswichian

Sites and faunas (Fig. 7.8, Table 7.4)

From the vertebrate point of view the Ipswichian is by far the best known of the interglacials, only excepted the Flandrian. Vertebrate records from a large number of open sites, generally with fluviatile deposits, can be assigned with varying degrees of precision to particular pollen assemblage zones or subzones (Table 7.4). In addition, on the assumption that *Hippopotamus amphibius* is diagnostic of

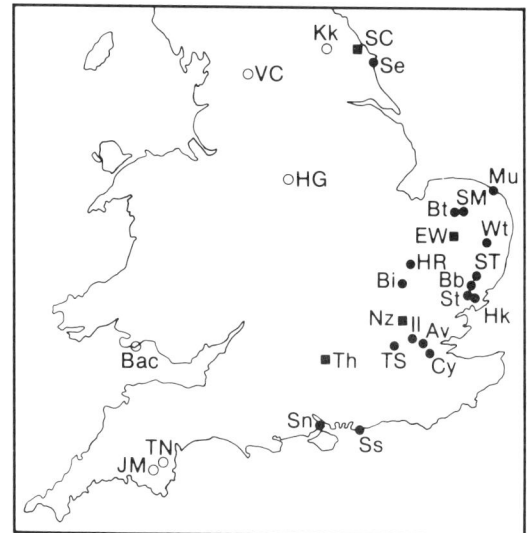

Fig. 7.8. Location map of Ipswichian and Flandrian vertebrate sites. ●, Ipswichian; ■, Flandrian; (cave sites shown by open symbols). Av, Aveley; Bac, Bacon Hole; Bb, Bobbitshole, Ipswich; Bi, Barrington; Bt, Beetley; Bur, Burwell; Cy, Crayford; EW, East Wretham near Thetford; HG, Hoe Grange Cave; Hk, Harkstead; HR, Histon Road; Il, Ilford; JM, Joint Mitnor Cave; Kk, Kirkdale Cave; Mu, Mundesley; Nz, Nazeing; SC, Star Carr; Se, Sewerby; SM, Swanton Morley; Sn, Stone; Ss, Selsey; St, Stutton; ST, Stoke Tunnel; Th, Thatcham; TN, Tornewton Cave (Hyaena Stratum); TS, Trafalgar Square; VC, Victoria Cave; Wt, Wortwell.

Fig. 7.9. View of fossiliferous Ipswichian organic deposits (subzones Ip IIa, b), overlain by Devensian gravels, at Swanton Morley, Norfolk.

the Ipswichian, rather than the Hoxnian, a number of cave and open-site faunas lacking pollen can also be dated fairly confidently to the Ipswichian interglacial. The small-mammal fauna is, however, less well known than might be expected from the lists of larger mammals.

The faunas from most of the important Ipswichian sites were previously discussed by the author (Stuart 1976a). The opportunity is taken here of revising and up-dating this account.

Horse *Equus ferus* is recorded from freshwater deposits covering the end of the Late Wolstonian to Ipswichian subzone Ia at Selsey, Sussex (West & Sparks 1960). During these zones birch woodland and pine replaced the late-glacial herb-dominated vegetation. Later horizons, zones Ib to early IIb, have yielded typical mid-Ipswichian taxa, plus evidence of man (Ch. 10).

So far the only recorded fauna of definite subzone Ip IIa age comes from Swanton Morley, Norfolk (Fig. 7.9), in association with palaeobotanical evidence for temperate mixed coniferous-deciduous

forest and local herb-dominated communities (Coxon *et al.* 1980). This fauna resembles faunas of Ip IIb age from a number of sites, except that European pond tortoise *Emys orbicularis* (not definitely recorded from subzone Ip IIb) and northern vole *Microtus oeconomus* are recorded from this subzone Ip IIa horizon. The fossil assemblage includes large-mammal bones chewed by spotted hyaena *Crocuta crocuta*, and hazelnuts opened by wood mouse *Apodemus sylvaticus* (Ch. 5).

The same locality has yielded a sparse and unremarkable zone Ip IIb fauna, and the sole record (two individuals) of *Hippopotamus amphibius* from early in zone Ip III.

The best pollen-dated fauna of subzone Ip IIb age is from Barrington, Cambridgeshire, where around the turn of the century a spectacular assemblage of mammal bones were recovered from calcareous fluvial sediments of a tributary of the River Cam (Gibbard & Stuart 1975) (Fig. 7.10). The pollen spectra indicate regional mixed oak forest, but the extraordinarily high herb pollen levels suggest that

Table 7.4. Pollen-dated records of Ipswichian mammals and *Emys orbicularis* (N.B. no pollen spectra have been obtained from Crayford, which is only tentatively assigned to zone Ip IV). (Modified from Stuart 1976a) Wo; Wolstonian

Site: Pollen zones:	Selsey IWo–Ia	Selsey Mundesley Ib–early IIb
MAMMALIA		
Insectivora		
1. *Sorex araneus* L., common shrew	–	– –
2. *Sorex minutus* L., pigmy shrew	–	– –
3. *Neomys fodiens* (Pennant), water shrew	–	– –
4. *Crocidura* cf. *suaveolens* (Pallas), lesser white-toothed shrew	–	– –
Primates		
5. *Homo sapiens* L., man (artefacts)	–	+ –
Rodentia		
6. *Spermophilus* sp., suslik	–	– –
7. *Castor fiber* L., beaver	–	+ –
8. *Dicrostonyx torquatus* (Pallas), arctic lemming	–	– –
9. *Lemmus lemmus* (L.), Norway lemming	–	– –
10. *Clethrionomys glareolus* (Schreber), bank vole	–	– –
11. *Arvicola cantiana* (Hinton), extinct water vole	–	– –
12. *Microtus agrestis* (L.), field vole	–	– –
13. *Microtus oeconomus* (Pallas), northern vole	–	– –
14. *Apodemus sylvaticus* (L.), wood mouse	–	– –
Carnivora		
15. *Canis lupus* L., wolf	–	– –
16. *Ursus arctos* L., brown bear	–	– –
17. *Meles meles* (L.), badger	–	– –
18. *Crocuta crocuta* Erxleben, spotted hyaena	–	– –
19. *Panthera leo* (L.), lion	–	– –
Proboscidea		
20. *Palaeoloxodon antiquus* Falconer & Cautley, (extinct) straight-tusked elephant	–	+ +
21. *Mammuthus primigenius* Blumenbach, (extinct) Mammoth	–	– –
Perissodactyla		
22. *Equus ferus* Boddaert, horse	+	– –
23. *Dicerorhinus hemitoechus* (Falconer), extinct rhinoceros	–	+ –
24. *Coelodonta antiquitatis* Blumenbach (extinct) woolly rhinoceros	–	– –
Artiodactyla		
25. *Hippopotamus amphibius* L., hippopotamus		
26. *Megaceros giganteus* Blumenbach, (extinct) giant deer	–	– –
27. *Dama dama* (L.), fallow deer	–	– –
28. *Cervus elaphus* L., red deer	–	– –
29. *Bos primigenius* Bojanus, (extinct) aurochs	–	– –
30. *Bison priscus* Bojanus, extinct bison	–	– –
31. *Bos* sp., aurochs, or *Bison* sp., bison	–	– –
32. *Ovibos moschatus* (Zimmerman), musk ox	–	– –
REPTILIA		
Chelonia		
33. *Emys orbicularis* L., pond tortoise	–	+ +

Bobbitshole	Swanton Morley	Beetley	Beetley	Barrington	Trafalgar Square	Stone	Wortwell	Swanton Morley	Aveley	Swanton Morley	Aveley	Stutton	Harkstead	Ilford	Lexden	Stoke Tunnel	Crayford
IWo–IIb	IIa	IIa–IIb	IIb							early III		III (?–IV)	?III (?–IV)		?IV		
−	+	−	−	−	−	−	−	−	−	−	−	+	−	−	−	−	−
−	+	−	−	−	−	−	−	−	−	−	−	+	−	−	−	−	−
−	−	−	−	−	−	−	−	−	+	−	−	−	−	−	−	−	−
−	−	−	−	−	−	−	−	−	−	−	−	+	−	?	−	+	+
−	−	−	−	−	−	−	−	−	−	−	−	−	−	−	−	−	+
+	−	−	−	−	−	−	−	−	−	−	−	+	−	+	−	−	−
−	−	−	−	−	−	−	−	−	−	−	−	−	−	−	−	−	+
+	+	−	−	−	−	−	−	+	+	−	−	−	−	−	−	−	+
+	+	−	−	+	−	−	−	+	+	−	+	+	+	+	−	+	−
(+)	+	−	−	+	−	−	−	(+)	(+)	−	−	+	−	−	−	+	−
−	+	−	−	−	−	−	−	−	−	−	−	+	−	−	−	+	+
+	+	−	−	−	−	−	−	+	−	−	−	+	−	−	−	−	−
−	−	−	−	+	−	−	−	−	−	−	−	−	−	−	−	+	+
−	−	−	−	+	−	−	−	−	−	−	−	−	−	+	−	(+)	+
−	−	−	−	+	−	−	−	−	−	−	−	−	−	−	−	−	−
−	+	−	−	+	−	−	−	−	−	−	−	−	−	−	−	−	−
−	−	−	−	+	+	−	−	−	−	−	−	+	−	+	−	+	+
−	−	+	−	+	+	+	+	+	+	−	−	+	+	+	−	−	−
−	−	−	−	−	−	−	−	−	−	−	+	+	+	+	+	+	+
−	−	−	−	−	−	−	−	−	−	−	+	+	+	+	−	+	+
−	−	−	−	+	(+)	−	−	−	−	−	−	−	−	+	+	−	+
−	−	−	−	−	−	−	−	−	−	−	−	−	−	−	−	+	+
−	−	−	+	+	+	−	−	−	−	+	−	−	−	−	−	−	−
−	−	(+)	−	+	+	−	−	−	−	−	−	+	−	+	−	−	+
−	(+)	−	−	+	+	−	−	+	−	−	−	−	−	−	−	−	−
−	+	+	−	+	+	−	−	−	−	−	+	+	+	+	−	+	+
−	+	−	−	+	+	−	−	−	−	+	−	−	−	+	−	−	+
−	−	−	−	+	+	−	−	−	−	−	−	−	−	+	−	−	+
−	+	−	−	−	−	−	−	−	+	−	+	+	+	−	?	+	−
−	−	−	−	−	−	−	−	−	−	−	−	−	−	−	−	−	+
+	+	−	−	−	−	−	−	−	−	−	−	−	+	−	−	+	−

Fig. 7.10. Excavating a rhinoceros *Dicerorhinus hemitoechus* skull from Ipswichian marls, sands and gravels at Barrington, Cambridgeshire, in 1900.

the broad river valley was largely deforested, probably due to the activities of large herbivores. Thus situation appears to be reflected in the fauna, which includes *Crocuta crocuta* and lion *Panthera leo*, neither of which favour dense forest at the present day (Ch. 5). The presence of a number of fossils, including two skulls of *C. crocuta*, a species generally very unusual in faunas from open sites, perhaps suggests that the hyaenas were scavenging close to the river, and were occasionally drowned. The presence of a giant deer *Megaceros giganteus* in which the males had enormous outspread antlers, is consistent with an open or lightly wooded environment. The extinct rhinoceros *Dicerorhinus hemitoechus* appears to have fed on grasses and other low-growing herbs rather than leaves, and the ex-

tinct *Bison priscus* was also probably a grazer (Ch. 5). *Hippopotamus amphibius* at Barrington presumably fed on grasses and probably other herbs, for which it may have travelled for a considerable distance away from the river, as do the living African animals.

Species more at home in the forest, including badger *Meles meles*, fallow deer *Dama dama*, and probably also straight-tusked elephant *Palaeoloxodon antiquus*, were however also present. Interestingly enough there is no trace of horse *Equus*, even though the local habitat would appear to have been very suitable.

Several other pollen-dated faunas and isolated records are available for this subzone (Table 7.4). It should be pointed out, however, that the associated

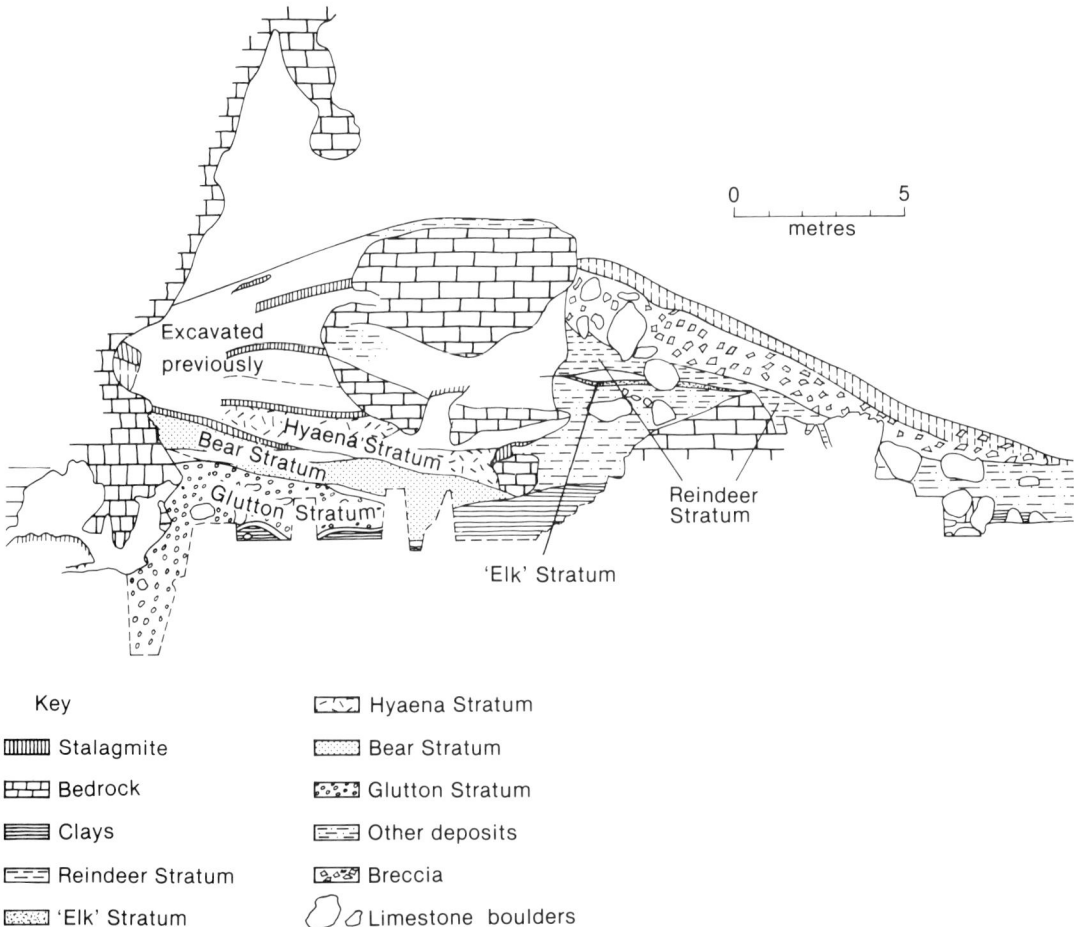

Fig. 7.11. Simplified schematic section of the deposits in Tornewton Cave, Torbryan, Devonshire. (Modified from Sutcliffe & Zeuner 1962)

herb pollen levels are extremely variable but generally very much lower than those recorded from Barrington. *Palaeoloxodon antiquus*, *Emys*, *orbicularis* and a skeleton of red-throated diver *Gavia stellata* were found in deposits of zone Ip Ib-IIb age at Mundesley, Norfolk (Newton 1883). Large-mammal faunas including *Crocuta crocuta*, *Palaeoloxodon antiquus*, *Dicerorhinus hemitoechus*, *Hippopotamus amphibius*, *Dama dama*, etc., but lacking *Equus ferus*, i.e. resembling faunas pollen-dated to subzone Ip IIb, are known from a number of open and cave sites in England and Wales. They probably date from zone Ip II or possibly, in part, even from zone I, since comparative dated faunas from the early part of the stage are almost unknown.

The faunas from two carefully excavated cave sites, Joint Mitnor Cave (Sutcliffe 1960) and Tornewton Cave (Hyaena Stratum) (Fig. 7.11). Sutcliffe & Zeuner (1962), both in Devon, include taxa not so far recorded from pollen-dated sites, namely a hare *Lepus* sp., red fox *Vulpes vulpes*, wild cat *Felis sylvestris* and wild boar *Sus scrofa*. Roe deer *Capreolus capreolus* is recorded only from Hoe Grange Cave, Derbyshire, in cave deposits of probable Ipswichian age (Bemrose & Newton 1905).

The rich fauna from a single thin horizon at Kirkdale Cave, Kirkby Moorside, Yorkshire, is of considerable historical importance, having first been described by Buckland (1822) (see Ch. 1). The faunal list revised by Boylan (1972; and in Catt 1977) is very similar to that of Joint Mitnor Cave, and can similarly be attributed to the middle of the Ipswichian interglacial.

Victoria Cave, near Settle, Yorkshire (latitude 54° 05′ N) is the most northerly site so far discovered to yield an Ipswichian-type fauna, including *Hippopotamus amphibius*, *Palaeoloxodon antiquus* and *Dicerorhinus hemitoechus* (Boylan, in Catt 1977). The cave is in a prominent Carboniferous Limestone cliff (Langcliffe Scar) at a height of 440 m O.D. The isolated record of *H. amphibius* from Stockton-on-Tees (latitude 54° 35′ N), however, marks the northernmost known occurrence of any of these species (Ch. 5).

'Hippopotamus faunas', probably dating from the middle of the Ipswichian, but possibly dating from earlier within this interglacial, are known from numerous sites in England and Wales. Significantly, all of the localities (Fig. 7.12) are south of the maximum limit of advance of the Devensian ice sheets, except for some caves in which the fossiliferous deposits were protected from glacial erosion, and the raised beach deposits at Sewerby, exposed in coastal section beneath Devensian till (Boylan 1967a).

Interglacial deposits north of the Devensian glacial ice limit would have mostly either been destroyed or buried beneath glacial deposits.

At Aveley, Essex, fluviatile organic deposits containing pollen characteristic of subzone Ip IIb yielded much of a skeleton of *Palaeoloxodon antiquus* (West 1969). The horizon has otherwise produced a sparse vertebrate assemblage which, however, includes the only British Pleistocene recorded of lesser white-toothed shrew *Crocidura* cf. *suaveolens*. The pollen spectra indicate temperate mixed oak forest vegetation. Immediately above the first elephant was found a second skeleton, this time of mammoth *Mammuthus primigenius* in sediments of zone Ip III age (Fig. 7.13), with pollen indicating a less dense forest cover. *Equus ferus* is also recorded. The situation of the elephant skeletons, marginal to the river channel cut in London Clay (Eocene), suggests that they became mired in the soft sediments and were unable to extricate themselves because of the steep slippery clay bank.

Unoxidized sediments with plant fossils are un-

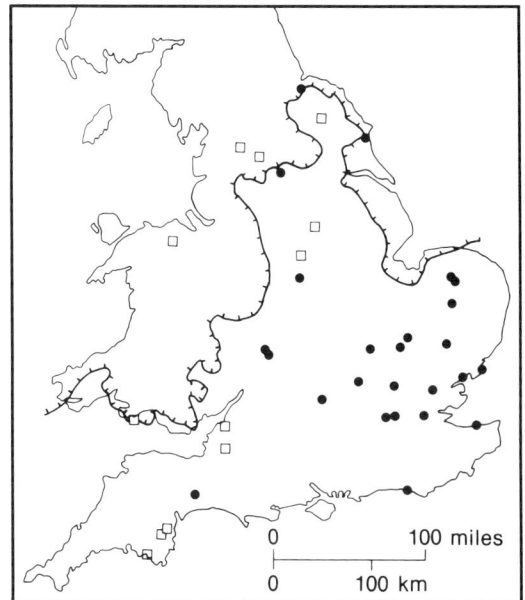

Fig. 7.12. Map showing representative finds of hippopotamus *Hippopotamus amphibius* either dated to, or presumed to date from, the Ipswichian Interglacial (cave sites are shown by open squares). The Devensian till limit is also shown.

(a)

(b)

Fig. 7.13. *For caption, see over*

(c)

Fig. 7.13. Excavations of skeletons of straight-tusked elephant *Palaeoloxodon antiquus* and mammoth *Mammuthus primigenius* found in Ipswichian deposits, channelled into London Clay, at Aveley, Essex. (a) general view; (b) excavating the skeletons – *P. antiquus* below (subzone Ip IIb), *M. primigenius* above (zone Ip III); (c) skeleton of *M. primigenius* after excavation.

fortunately rather rare from the second half of the Ipswichian, so that it is difficult to assign many vertebrate assemblages to precise pollen zones. For example, the fauna from Stutton, on the Stour Estuary, Suffolk, comes from oxidized sandy silts ('brickearths'), often rich in non-marine Mollusca (Fig. 7.14), about 1–2 m above the horizon of a single pollen spectrum, fortunately highly characteristic of zone Ip III (Sparks & West 1963). Taxa recorded include *Palaeoloxodon antiquus, Mammuthus primigenius, Equus ferus* and *Microtus oeconomus*. A similar fauna with the addition of *Emys orbicularis* is known from similar deposits at the same height at nearby Harkstead. The general stratigraphical position of the Stutton fauna is confirmed by an almost identical fauna from several pits in 'brickearths' at Ilford, Essex (Cotton 1847; Woodward & Davies 1874). The Ilford vertebrate assemblages appear to post-date subzone Ip IIb organic deposits occupying a channel at Seven Kings, Ilford (West *et al.* 1964) (see Ch. 2). Harrison and Walker (1977) record a swan *Cygnus* sp., white-fronted goose *Anser albifrons*, greylag goose *Anser anser*, mallard *Anas platyrhynchos* and a large crane '*Grus primigenia*' (sarus crane *Grus antigone*). The latter is nowadays restricted to India, Burma and Thailand. The sparse fauna from Histon Road, Cambridge, formerly attributed to a zone Ip III–IV horizon (Stuart 1976a), is now known to include fallow deer *Dama dama* (Lister 1981) which suggests that some material comes from an earlier horizon.

Mammalian fossils were recovered from the base of terrace gravels of the River Stour at Brundon, Suffolk, in association with artefacts of Levalloisian type (Moir & Hopwood 1939). The fauna includes *Palaeoloxodon antiquus, Mammuthus primigenius, Equus ferus, Cervus elaphus, Megaceros giganteus, Bos primigenius* abd *Bison priscus*. The height relationships and mollusc fauna suggest correlation

Fig. 7.14. Detail of sandy silts ('brickearth') of late Ipswichian age, rich in molluscan shells, including *Corbicula fluminalis*, and small vertebrates, at Stutton, Suffolk.

with Stutton, i.e. approximately zone Ip III, and this is supported by the close similarity of the vertebrate faunas of the two sites.

An extensive series of pits in Thames terrace 'brickearths' and sands in the area of Grays and West Thurrock, Essex, yielded large quantities of mammalian remains, chiefly during the last century. Deposits of more than one interglacial appear to be present in this area, but most of the faunal material is probably of Ipswichian age. The fauna from the Tunnel Cement Works Quarry, West Thurrock, was listed by Abbot (1890) and the surviving material revised by Carreck (1976), who attributed the deposits at this site to the later part of the Ipswichian. The fauna appears to be similar to that of Ilford.

Evidence for the faunas at the very end of the Ipswichian is provided mainly by the assemblages from Crayford, Kent (Kennard 1944), and Stoke Tunnel, Suffolk (Layard 1920). The 'brickearths' from the former site are at a similar height to the 'brickearths' of Ilford, Aveley and other Lower

Thames localities. The fauna, however, which includes a suslik *Spermophilus* sp., lemmings, woolly rhinoceros *Coelodonta antiquitatis*, and musk ox *Ovibos moschatus*, together with more typically interglacial species, appears to be transitional to a typically Devensian fauna and would therefore be rather later than the other interglacial sites. A similar but less rich assemblage from Stoke Tunnel, which however also includes *Emys orbicularis*, is associated with organic sediments within a sequence of 'brickearths' and gravels. A preliminary pollen analysis by C. Turner (Turner, in West 1977c) is not inconsistent with a zone Ip IV age. Harrison and Walker (1977) record smew *Mergus albellus*, jungle fowl *Gallus gallus* and coot *Fulica atra* from Crayford.

At Bacon Hole Cave, on the coast of Gower, South Wales, a series of about 8 m of sands, clays, cave earths and breccias have yielded a succession of faunas at a single site, apparently covering much of the Ipswichian interglacial (Stringer 1975, 1977). The lower beds contain much marine mollusc material, while its absence from the younger beds suggests recession of the sea from the vicinity of the cave. The oldest beds ('orange and grey sands') contain horse *Equus ferus* and a large form of northern vole *Microtus oeconomus* (Ch. 11) and may date from the Late Wolstonian or early Ipswichian. The next group of beds ('sandy breccio-conglomerate' and 'sandy cave earth') have yielded a temperate fauna including *Palaeoloxodon antiquus*, *Cervus elaphus*, lion *Panthera leo*, wood mouse *Apodemus sylvaticus*, bank vole *Clethriononomys glareolus*, field vole *Microtus agretis* and water vole *Arvicola cantiana*, but *Microtus oeconomus* is virtually absent. These beds may date from about the middle of the interglacial. The faunas from the succeeding beds ('grey clays, silts and sands', 'coarse brown sands', 'upper cave earth') show the return of *M. oeconomus* in association with a largely temperate fauna, which includes spotted hyaena *Crocuta crocuta*. Mammoth *Mammuthus primigenius* occurs in the 'grey clays and sands', while *P. antiquus* occurs in the 'upper cave earth'. This part of the sequence may represent much of the second half of the Ipswichian, but not the final phases.

Ipswichian faunal history

A summary of the important changes in the Ipswichian vertebrate fauna is given in Fig. 7.15.

Equus ferus is known from the very beginning of the Ipswichian (or the very end of the Wolstonian) in association with probable open birch and pine woodland or open grassland. No other zone Ip I fauna is available, and a subzone Ip IIa fauna is known from one site only. The latter, however, suggests that most of the elements of the subzone Ip IIb faunas were already present by Ip IIa, in association with regional mixed coniferous-deciduous forest. The occurrence of *Emys orbicularis*, assuming that the fossils represent breeding populations, indicates that summer temperatures in subzone Ip IIa were rather higher than at the present day.

The classic Ipswichian faunal assemblage ('hippopotamus fauna') of subzone Ip IIb age, associated with regional mixed oak forest, but generally also with probably local herbaceous vegetation, includes *Crocuta crocuta*, *Palaeoloxodon antiquus*, *Dicerorhinus hemitoechus*, *Hippopotamus amphibius* and *Dama dama*. *Mammuthus primigenius* and curiously also *Equus ferus* appear to have been ab-

sent from this subzone. Similar fossil assemblages from a number of cave and open sites also lack these taxa, so that it is almost certainly a real phenomenon, perhaps related to the density of the regional forest cover. On the other hand, the apparent absence of man from subzone Ip IIb is less certain (see Ch. 10).

Zone III saw the reappearance of mammoth and horse, possibly reflecting a regional opening out of the forest cover. Neither *Dama dama* nor *Crocuta crocuta* are recorded later than subzone Ip IIb, but the latter species is in any case rare from open sites so that its apparent absence may not be significant.

Hippopotamus amphibius is recorded at one site from the beginning of zone Ip III, but it presumably disappeared shortly afterwards.

By zone Ip IV, rather open coniferous forest had replaced the earlier temperate woodlands. *Palaeoloxodon antiquus* had disappeared, and arctic-boreal species *Dicrostonyx torquatus*, *Lemmus lemmus*, *Ovibos moschatus*, and an extinct characteristically cold-stage species *Coelodonta antiquitatis*, had appeared. Another remarkable addition was *Spermophilus* sp. since this genus is now found in non-forested biotopes including steppe. These taxa were, however, accompanied by several interglacial species including *Bos primigenius* and *Emys orbicularis* – the latter indicative of considerable summer warmth (Ch. 5).

Such a fauna would be consistent with a continental climate, in the sense of large seasonal temperature fluctuations – a conclusion in agreement with the vegetational evidence (Ch. 2).

The faunal succession from Bacon Hole Cave appears, to a large extent, to corroborate the succession pieced together from a number of open sites, and strongly suggests that they all belong to a single (Ipswichian) interglacial (Ch. 2).

Comparison with Continental faunas

The rich fossil vertebrate assemblages from travertine deposits in Thüringia, East Germany, have been described in great detail in a series of publications edited by Kahlke (1974, 1975c, 1977, 1979). The faunas from Weimar Ehringsdorf (Lower Travertine), Taubach near Weimar, and Burgtonna are remarkably similar to one another. The presence of vertebrates, molluscs and macroscopic plant fossils of temperate character indicates interglacial conditions, and the deposits very probably

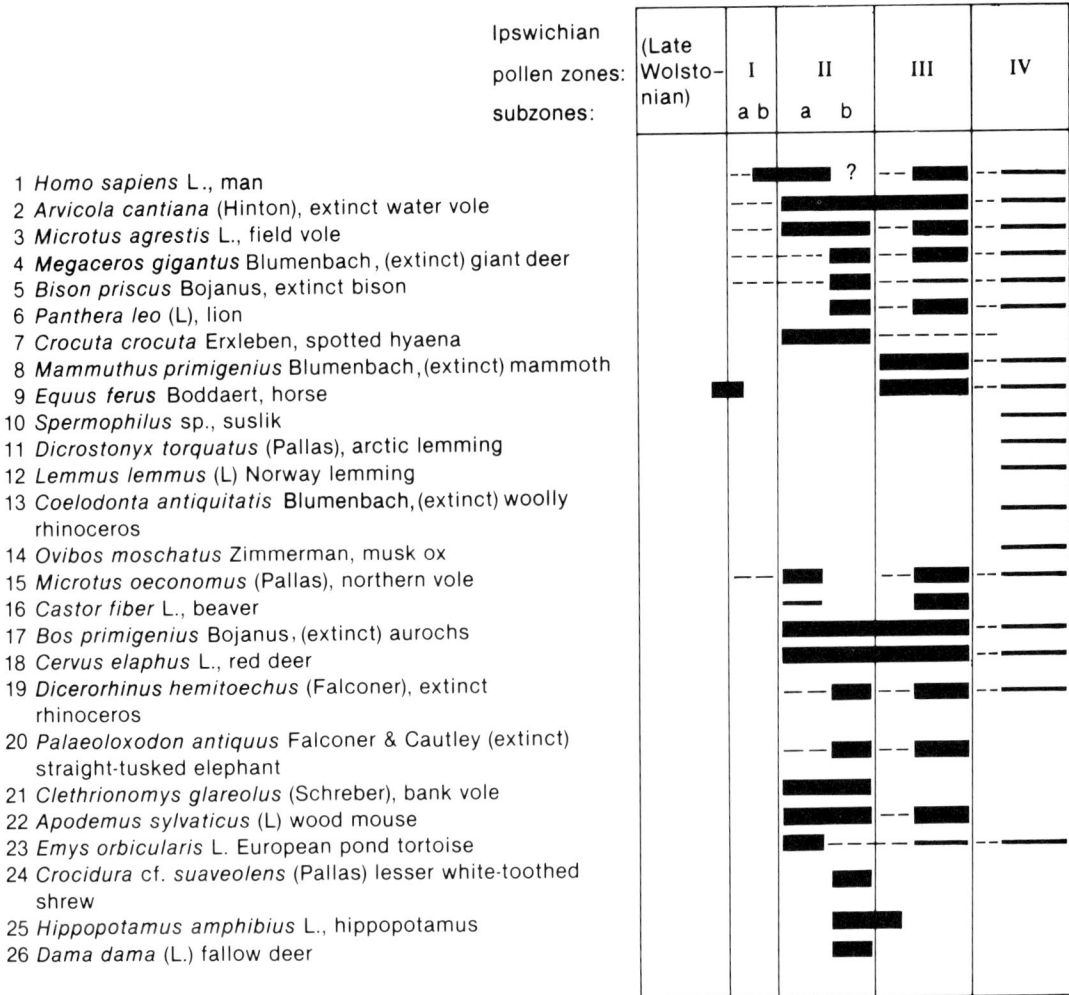

Ipswichian pollen zones: subzones:	(Late Wolsto-nian)	I		II		III	IV
		a b	a		b		

1 *Homo sapiens* L., man
2 *Arvicola cantiana* (Hinton), extinct water vole
3 *Microtus agrestis* L., field vole
4 *Megaceros gigantus* Blumenbach, (extinct) giant deer
5 *Bison priscus* Bojanus, extinct bison
6 *Panthera leo* (L), lion
7 *Crocuta crocuta* Erxleben, spotted hyaena
8 *Mammuthus primigenius* Blumenbach,(extinct) mammoth
9 *Equus ferus* Boddaert, horse
10 *Spermophilus* sp., suslik
11 *Dicrostonyx torquatus* (Pallas), arctic lemming
12 *Lemmus lemmus* (L) Norway lemming
13 *Coelodonta antiquitatis* Blumenbach,(extinct) woolly rhinoceros
14 *Ovibos moschatus* Zimmerman, musk ox
15 *Microtus oeconomus* (Pallas), northern vole
16 *Castor fiber* L., beaver
17 *Bos primigenius* Bojanus,(extinct) aurochs
18 *Cervus elaphus* L., red deer
19 *Dicerorhinus hemitoechus* (Falconer), extinct rhinoceros
20 *Palaeoloxodon antiquus* Falconer & Cautley (extinct) straight-tusked elephant
21 *Clethrionomys glareolus* (Schreber), bank vole
22 *Apodemus sylvaticus* (L) wood mouse
23 *Emys orbicularis* L. European pond tortoise
24 *Crocidura* cf. *suaveolens* (Pallas) lesser white-toothed shrew
25 *Hippopotamus amphibius* L., hippopotamus
26 *Dama dama* (L.) fallow deer

Key

■■■ Pollen-dated records

▬▬▬ Probable occurrences based on less certainly dated records

– – – occurrences inferred

Fig. 7.15. Summary of faunal changes during the Ipswichian Interglacial in southern England.

date from the middle of the Last (Eemian, Ipswichian) Interglacial. The faunas closely resemble those of Ipswichian zone Ip II age from England, with certain very interesting exceptions. *Hippotamus amphibius* and *Bos primigenius*, common in English faunas, are unknown from Germany, while conversely an elk, referred to a subspecies of *Alces*

latifrons, and common hamster *Cricetus cricetus* are present in Germany but not England. Moreover, horse *Equus ferus*, abundant at the German sites, is absent from Ipswichian zone II in England. These differences probably reflect regional distributions of species in response to the degree of oceanity or continentality of the climate.

Aesculapian snake *Elaphe* cf. *longissima*, now found considerably further south in Europe, is present in the German Eemian faunas, implying rather higher summer temperatures in the past.

Neanderthal man *Homo sapiens neanderthalis*, is represented by both bones and artefacts at Ehringsdorf, and artefacts only at Taubach. The apparent absence of man from the mid-Ipswichian in Britain is not readily explicable (Ch. 10).

Faunas of probable Eemian age and resembling those of the mid-Ipswichian in England, including *Hippopotamus amphibius*, are recorded from Spain (e.g. Olazagutia Cave, Yacimiento de Coscobilo, Navarra, France (e.g. Grotte du Prince, Ligurie italienne) and Italy (Saccopastore, Porta Pia, Rome) (Kahlke 1975a; Segre 1948). The last site, like Ehringsdorf, has also yielded artefacts and skeletal remains of Neanderthal man.

The '25 foot' raised beach at Belle Hougue Cave, Jersey, Channel Islands, has yielded remains of a very small red deer *Cervus elaphus*. These finds, of probable Last Interglacial age, appear to represent a dwarf island form (Zeuner 1946).

Flandrian

Sites and faunas (Figs. 7.8, 7.16)

The Flandrian falls well within the range of radiocarbon dating, and is in fact defined as the period post-dating 10 000 radiocarbon years B.P. (Ch. 2). In addition, both the vegetational history and archaeological sequence of cultures are known in far greater detail than for earlier stages.

The history of the wild vertebrate fauna through the stage has not been comprehensively studied, however, and would undoubtedly repay a thorough investigation. None the less, a great deal can be gleaned from the available information, since fortunately there exist good well-dated faunas from the very beginning of the stage and the modern fauna is of course well known. There is also documentary evidence for the existence of several nowadays extinct large mammals in historical times, together with a number of dated records of isolated finds, but few faunas, scattered throughout Flandrian time, which help to build up an overall picture of Flandrian faunal history. An attempt to synthesize the available evidence is given in Fig. 7.16.

At Thatcham, near Newbury, Berkshire, algal marls overlying gravels of the River Kennet yielded Mesolithic bone and flint artefacts together with numerous vertebrate remains (Wymer 1962; Churchill 1962). Both the pollen spectra, representing zones IV to VIa (Fl Ia–IIa), and the series of radiocarbon dates, ranging from 10 365 ± 170 to 8 480 ± 160 years B.P., show that the deposits cover a long period of time. Nevertheless, the bulk of the artefacts and fauna were found in the lower deposits of broadly zone IV (Fl Ia) age, when the region was probably clothed by birch and pine forest, with areas of herbaceous and marsh vegetation around the depositional site.

Lacustrine muds at Star Carr, East Yorkshire, with radiocarbon dates of 9 488 ± 350 years B.P. and 9 557 ± 210 years B.P., have produced spectacular evidence of lake-side occupation by Mesolithic hunter-gatherers. The deposits have yielded numerous flint and antler artefacts together with animal bone food debris (Clark 1954). Pollen analyses indicate occupation within the later part of zone IV (Fl Ia). Closed birch and pine woods clothed the dry land but a few open herb communities probably grew between the forest and the water's edge. Narrow reedswamp fringed the shore and aquatic plants grew in deeper water (Godwin, in Clark 1954).

At both sites the fossil assemblages are made up almost entirely of the remains of animals killed by Mesolithic hunters, and are therefore a biased sample of the fauna of that time, especially in the scarcity of small vertebrates. The Thatcham and Star Carr mammal faunas are very similar (Table 7.5). Of particular interest are the records of domestic dog (Degerbøl 1961; Wymer 1962), which are among the earliest in the world. The occurrence of hedgehog *Erinaceus europaeus*, badger *Meles meles*, wild boar *Sus scrofa* and aurochs *Bos primigenius*, in association with regional birch-pine forest is also noteworthy (see below). Other important records from Thatcham only, are of rabbit *Oryctolagus cuniculus*, which the excavators stress was sealed by algal marl and therefore not a modern intrusion, and horse *Equus ferus*, probably associated with generally open vegetational conditions at the beginning of pollen zone IV (Fl Ia), or from the very end of the Late Devensian, pollen zone L-De III.

Not surprisingly, most of the bird species recorded nowadays frequent lakes and fens.

Wheeler (1978) has interpreted the absence of

Pollen zones (England & Wales)

F I I		F I II			F I III		
IV	V	VI	VII a		VII b		VIII

Thousands radiocarbon years B. P.

| 10 | 9 | 8 | 7 | 6 | 5 | 4 | 3 | 2 | 1 | 0 |

Archaeology

| Mesolithic | Neo-lithic | Bronze Age | Iron age | Romano-British to present day |

MAMMALIA

Insectivora
1 *Erinaceus europaeus* L., hedgehog
2 *Sorex araneus* L., common shrew
3 *Sorex minutus* L., pigmy shrew
4 *Neomys fodiens* (Pennant), water shrew
5 *Talpa europaea* L., mole

Primates
6 *Homo sapiens* L., man

Lagomorpha
7 *Oryctolagus cuniculus* (L.) rabbit
8 *Lepus capensis* L., brown hare
9 *Lepus timidus* L., mountain hare
10 *Ochotona pusilla*, steppe pika

Rodentia
11 *Sciurus vulgaris* L., red squirrel
12 *Castor fiber* L., beaver
13 *Muscardinius avellanarius* (L.) dormouse
14 *Clethrionomys glareolus* (Schreber) bank vole
15 *Arvicola terrestris* L., water vole
16 *Microtus agrestis* L., field vole
17 *Microtus oeconomus* (Pallas) northern vole
18 *Apodemus sylvaticus* (L.) wood mouse
19 *Apodemus flavicollis* (Melchior), yellow-necked mouse
20 *Micromys minutus* (Pallas) harvest mouse

Carnivora
21 *Canis lupus* L., wolf
22 *Vulpes vulpes* (L.) red fox
23 *Ursus arctos* L., brown bear
24 *Martes martes* (L.) pine marten
25 *Mustela nivalis* L, weasel
26 *Mustela erminea* L., stoat
27 *Mustela putorius* L., polecat
28 *Meles meles* (L.) badger
29 *Lutra lutra* (L.) otter
30 *Felis sylvestris* Schreber, wild cat

Perissodactyla
31 *Equus ferus* Boddaert, horse

Artiodactyla
32 *Sus scrofa* L., wild boar
33 *Cervus elaphus* L., red deer
34 *Capreolus capreolus* (L) roe deer
35 *Alces alces* L., elk
36 *Bos primigenius* Bojanus (extinct) aurochs

REPTILIA
Chelonia
37 *Emys orbicularis* L., pond tortoise

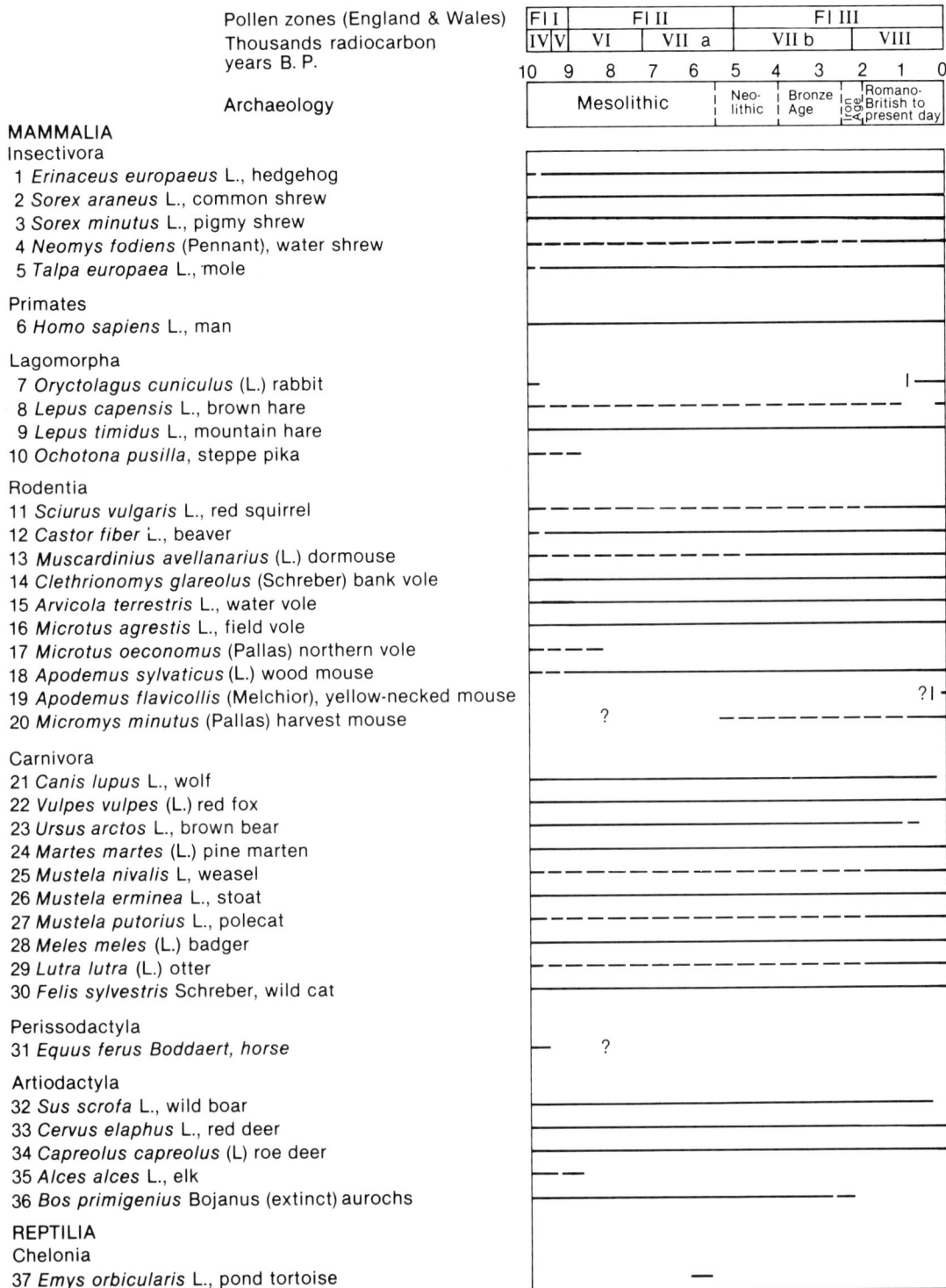

Fig. 7.16. Summary of faunal changes during the Flandrian in Britain. [1] introduced

Table 7.5 Early Flandrian Faunas from Thatcham and Star Carr.

	Thatcham	Star Carr
MAMMALIA		
Insectivora		
Erinaceus europaeus L., hedgehog	+	+
Sorex araneus L., common shrew	+	−
Talpa europaea L., mole	+	−
Primates		
Homo sapiens L., man (humerus)	+	−
Homo sapiens L., man (artefacts)	+	+
Lagomorpha		
Lepus sp.	−	+
Oryctolagus cuniculus (L.), rabbit	+	−
Rodentia		
Castor fiber L., beaver	+	+
Arvicola terrestris L., water vole	+	−
Carnivora		
Canis lupus L., wolf	+	+
Canis (domestic), dog	+	+
Vulpes vulpes (L.), red fox	+	+
Martes martes (L.), pine marten	+	+
Meles meles (L.), badger	+	+
Felis sylvestris Schreber, wild cat	+	+
Perissodactyla		
Equus ferus Boddaert, horse	+	−
Artiodactyla		
Sus scrofa L., wild boar	+	+
Cervus elaphus L., red deer	+	+
Alces alces L., elk	+	+
Capreolus capreolus (L.) roe deer	+	+
Bos primigenius Bojanus, (extinct) aurochs	+	+
AVES		
Graviiformes		
Gavia stellata (*Pontoppidan*), red-throated diver	−	+
Podicipediformes		
Podiceps cristatus L., great crested grebe	−	+
Podiceps ruficollis Pallas, little grebe	−	+
Ciconiiformes		
cf. *Ciconia ciconia* L., white stork	−	+
Anseriformes		
Anas platyrhynchos (L.), mallard	+	−
Anas sp. (small species), a duck	+	−
Bucephala clangula (L.), golden eye duck	+	−
Mergus serrator L., red-breasted merganser	−	+
Falconiformes		
Buteo buteo L., buzzard	−	+
Ralliformes		
Grus grus L., common crane	+	+
Charadriformes		
Vanellus vanellus L., lapwing	−	+
Passeriformes		
Turdus sp., blackbird or thrush, etc.	+	−

fish remains at Star Carr, as indicating that by zone IV (Fl Ia) fishes had not yet penetrated the Vale of Pickering via the River Derwent.

'Surface MX' at Nazeing, Essex, in the flood-plain deposits of the River Lea, yielded material of common shrew *Sorex araneus*, pika *Ochotona pusilla*, bank vole *Clethrionomys glareolus*, water vole *Arvicola terrestris*, northern vole *Microtus oeconomus* and wood mouse *Apodemus sylvaticus* (Allison et al. 1952). The pollen spectra from immediately above this horizon indicate pine-birch woodland and a zone V (Fl Ib) age. The fauna is generally consistent with a woodland environment, but the occurrence of *Ochotona pusilla* – a survival from the Late Devensian – is interesting as this species now occurs only in the Palaearctic steppe (Ch. 5).

Bones of wild boar *Sus scrofa* and red deer *Cervus elaphus* are recorded from sands overlying peat and beneath estuarine clays at Belfast Lough; all apparently dating from the early Flandrian (Savage 1964, 1966). These finds suggest that both species are native to Ireland.

Vertebrate material dating from later in the Flandrian is available from such deposits as the peats of the East Anglian Fenland and from archaeological sites. Many finds are in need of critical reassessment, with regard to both identification and stratigraphy. Only the more interesting records will be considered here.

The peats of the Fen margins north of Cambridge (Godwin 1978) date from the second half of the Flandrian, i.e. subzone VIIa (Fl IId, about 7 000 years B.P.) and later. Most of the bones collected from this area (villages of Burwell, Swaffham and Reach) during the last century are probably of zone VIII age (Fl IId, early Fl III). Mammals recorded include wolf *Canis lupus*, brown bear *Ursus arctos*, otter *Lutra lutra*, beaver *Castor fiber*, roe deer *Capreolus capreolus*, red deer *Cervus elaphus* and aurochs *Bos primigenius*. Birds include bittern *Botaurus stellaris*, mute swan *Cygnus cygnus*, whooper swan *Cygnus olor*, white-tailed eagle *Haliaetus albicilla*, common crane *Grus grus* and razorbill *Alca torda* (Northcote 1980b).

The record of elk *Alces alces*, based on droppings from peat at Ugg Mere, Cambridgeshire, and radiocarbon dated to about 3 260 years B.P. (Godwin, 1975), is now known to be incorrect. Re-examination of the material by A. Lister has shown that the droppings are too small for *A. alces*. There are no other records of this animal from later than the early Flandrian.

Vertebrae of a pelican *Pelecanus* sp. were recovered from peat near King's Lynn, Norfolk, radiocarbon dated to 3 915 ± 120 years B.P. (Forbes *et al*. 1958). Dalmatian pelican *Pelecanus crispus* is recorded from several localities in the Cambridgeshire Fens, and also from the Iron Age Lake village at Glastonbury, Somerset (Northcote 1980b).

The sole record of European pond tortoise *Emys orbicularis*, from the Flandrian of the British Isles, is based on remains of three individuals from mere peats at East Wretham, near Thetford, Norfolk (Stuart 1979). Pollen analysis of a peat sample preserved with the finds indicate a subzone VIIa (Fl IId) age.

Northern vole, not recorded from later than the early Flandrian on the mainland, occurs in Bronze or Iron Age deposits at Nornour, Isles of Scilly (Pernetta & Handford 1970).

Written sources provide most of the evidence for survival into historical times of many species which subsequently became extinct in Britain (see Table 7.6).

Flandrian faunal history

The history of the wild vertebrate fauna during the Flandrian (Fig. 7.16) is complicated by factors, not important in earlier interglacials:
(a) isolation of Britain from the Continent early in the Flandrian – preventing further immigration of terrestrial and freshwater vertebrates;
(b) extinctions, mainly of large mammals due to human activities; and
(c) the introduction by man of alien vertebrates to Britain (Ch. 10).

The availability of good early Flandrian faunas is particularly valuable because the faunas of pollen zone I age from earlier interglacials are almost unknown. *Ochotona pusilla*, *Microtus oeconomus* and perhaps *Equus ferus* as a native species were restricted to the early Flandrian, in association with regional birch and pine forests, and probably extensive open habitats. They can be regarded as survivals from the Late Devensian. On the other hand, the earliest Flandrian faunas (zone IV – Fl Ia) already include several taxa nowadays associated with the regional temperate forest biotope, and not extending further north than southern Fennoscandia: mammals – *Erinaceus europaeus*, *Talpa europaea*, *Meles meles*, *Sus scrofa* and *Cervus elaphus*;

and birds – *Podiceps cristatus*, *Podiceps ruficollis* and *Ciconia ciconia*. This phenomenon may reflect a rapid amelioration of climate early in the Flandrian.

The record of *Oryctolagus cuniculus* from the very early Flandrian is remarkable in that this species is generally thought to have been restricted to parts of Iberia during the postglacial until its fortunes were dramatically reversed by man from Roman times onwards, when it was introduced to northern Europe. Confirmation of the Thatcham record would be desirable. It is, however, possible that the rabbit became extinct in Britain at some time after the early Flandrian and was re-introduced in Norman or Plantagenet times.

The single record of *Emys orbicularis* (three individuals) of zone VIIa (Fl IId) age, at the climatic optimum of the Flandrian, is particularly significant as there are no less than six records from the previous and generally warmer Ipswichian interglacial, and numerous Flandrian finds from Denmark and southern Sweden. The abundance of Scandinavian records is very probably related to the prevalence of warmer summers further east.

The extinction of a number of wild mammals and birds within the last 2 000 years or so is clearly related to hunting coupled with destruction of the forests and later draining of the wetlands by man. The subject is discussed in Chapter 10.

Comparison with Continental faunas

It is especially interesting to compare the Flandrian vertebrate faunal succession in Denmark and adjacent areas, as reviewed by Degerbøl (1964), with that seen in England. Important differences include the records of horse *Equus ferus* from Swedish deposits pollen-dated to zone V (Fl Ib), and the survival of elk *Alces alces* in Denmark until at least zone VIIb (early Fl III). The European pond tortoise *Emys orbicularis* is represented by numerous fossils from Denmark and southern Sweden, covering pollen zones V (Fl Ib) to VIIb (early Fl III). (Degerbøl & Krog 1951; Stuart 1979). This disparity between the numbers and stratigraphical ranges of Scandinavian and English finds reflects the warmer summers in the east, while the species was probably near the limits of its range in Britain with its cooler and more cloudy maritime climate (Ch. 3).

The modern fauna

The present-day native vertebrate fauna of the British Isles comprises about 200 breeding birds, 41 non-marine mammals (including 5 species extinct within the last 2 500 years) and 11 breeding bats, 19 primary freshwater fishes, 6 reptiles and 6 amphibians (Table 7.6).

Table 7.7 demonstrates the way in which the present-day vertebrate faunas of Britain and Ireland become progressively impoverished according to their remoteness from Continental Europe. For example, voles and snakes are native to Britain but not Ireland, and green lizard *Lacerta viridis* and garden dormouse *Eliomys quercinus* are absent from the British Isles, but are found on the adjacent part of the Continent. This phenomenon is in part due to climatic factors and a reduced variety of habitats in Ireland, but for terrestrial and freshwater species it is largely related to the timing of Flandrian land/sea level changes. These changes may have isolated Ireland from Britain (formerly connected via southwest Scotland) as early as about 9 500 years B.P., and then Britain from the Continent (formerly connected via the southern North Sea and Straits of Dover) perhaps a thousand years later (Ch. 2).

Vertebrate species occurring on the adjacent Continent at the present day, but absent from the British Isles, are almost entirely those with southern, or sometimes eastern, distributions in Europe. Presumably they were not able to advance sufficiently far north, in response to the Flandrian climatic amelioration, before Britain became isolated by the rise in sea level. It is possible, however, that a few such species did manage to reach Britain, but subsequently became extinct due to climatic or other changes, as did *Emys orbicularis*.

Significantly, the fall in species from France to Britain to Ireland is least marked in the aerial birds and bats, whose distribution is likely to be little affected by sea barriers. As far as the birds are concerned there are actually more breeding species in Britain than in the rather small area of the Continent used for comparison, which has a less varied range of habitats. Similarly, the more restricted availability of habitats, and, to a lesser extent, climatic conditions account for the rather lower numbers of breeding birds and bats in Ireland compared with Britain.

The restricted distributions within the British Isles of many native vertebrate species can be attri-

Table 7.6. Present day native British fauna of terrestrial vertebrates (*, also occurs in Ireland; †, extinct).

AMPHIBIA (Smith 1969)
 Triturus cristatus (Laurenti), warty newt
**Triturus vulgaris* (L.), smooth newt
 Triturus helveticus (Razoumoski), palmate newt
 Bufo bufo (L.), common toad
*Bufo calamita Laurenti, natterjack
*Rana temporaria L., common frog

REPTILIA (Smith 1969)
 Anguis fragilis L., slow-worm
 Lacerta agilis L., sand lizard
*Lacerta vivipara Jacquin, viviparous lizard
 Natrix matrix (L.), grass snake
 Coronella austriaca Laurenti, smooth snake
 Vipera berus (L.), adder

MAMMALIA (modified from Corbet & Southern 1977)
(Includes species extinct within last 2 500 years,
shown by †)
Insectivora
 Sorex araneus L., common shrew
*Sorex minutus L., pigmy shrew
 Neomys fodiens (Pennant), water shrew
**Erinaceus europaeus* L., hedgehog? Introduced in
 Ireland
 Talpa europaea L., mole
Lagomorpha
 Lepus capensis L., brown hare. Introduced
recently in Ireland.
*Lepus timidus L., mountain hare

Rodentia
*Sciurus vulgaris L., red squirrel ?Introduced in
Ireland
†*Castor fiber* L., beaver. Extinct twelfth century or
 later
 Muscardinus avellanarius (L.), dormouse
 Clethrionomys glareolus (Schreber), bank vole.
 Introduced in Ireland (probably very recently)
 Arvicola terrestris L., water vole
 Microtus agrestis (L.), field vole
 Micromys minutus (Pallas), harvest mouse
**Apodemus sylvaticus* (L.), wood mouse
 Introduced in Ireland
 Apodemus flavicollis (Melchior), yellow-necked
 mouse

Carnivora
†*Canis lupus L., wolf. Extinct eighteenth century
 *Vulpes vulpes (L.), red fox
† *Ursus arctos* L., brown bear. Extinct about tenth
 century
 *Martes martes (L.), pine marten
 *Mustela erminea L., stoat
 Mustela nivalis L., weasel
 Mustela putorius L., polecat
 *Meles meles (L.), badger
 *Lutra lutra (L.), otter
 Felis sylvestris Schreber, wild cat

Artiodactyla
†*Sus scrofa L., wild boar. Extinct probably
 seventeeth century
 *Cervus elaphus L., red deer
 Capreolus capreolus (L.), roe deer
 †*Bos primigenius* Bojanus, aurochs. Extinct by
 2 500 years B.P.?

buted wholly or partly to human interference
(Ch. 10), which complicates the interpretation of
natural distribution patterns determined by climatic and geographical factors. Species of mammals
confined in the British Isles to offshore islands
appear to have been introduced by man from the
Continent (see Ch. 10).

Wheeler (1977) considers that all the primary
freshwater fishes (pike *Esox lucius*; Cyprinidae (e.g.

roach *Rutilus rutilus*, tench *Tinca tinca*); loaches
Cobitis taenia and *Noemacheilus barbatulus*; burbot
Lota lota; perch *Perca fluviatilis*, ruffe *Gymnocepha-
lus cernua*; and miller's thumb *Cottus gobio*) now
found in the British Isles, are only indigenous to
the river catchments bordering the eastern English
Channel and southern North Sea. The fishes are
thought to have entered these rivers when they
were formerly joined in the extensive land area con-

Table 7.7. Numbers of non-marine vertebrate species native to Ireland, England and the adjacent areas of Continental Europe. (Data from Muus & Dahlstrøm 1971; Wheeler 1977; Arnold & Burton 1978; Heinzel *et al.* 1972; Sharrock 1976; Brink 1967)

	Ireland	England	Belgium and north-east France
Fish (primary freshwater species)	0	19	24
Amphibians	3	6	16
Reptiles	1	6	8
Birds (breeding species)[1]	138	182	170+
Mammals (except bats)[2]	14	30	37
Bats (breeding species)	6	11	13

1. British Isles 201, Scotland 181
2. Includes species occurring within last 3000 years (see Table 7.6) and man.

necting England with the Continent in the early Flandrian. The occurrence of many of these primary freshwater species in other parts of the British Isles, is attributed to introduction by man, and the only native fishes in these areas, including Ireland, are the secondary freshwater species which are tolerant of saltwater and penetrated the rivers via the sea. Fossil evidence is needed to confirm or refute this hypothesis.

Two secondary freshwater fishes, the arctic charr *Salvelinus alpinus* and whitefishes *Coregonus* spp., are restricted to isolated occurrences in cold upland lakes in Scotland, Cumbria, North Wales, and lowland lakes in Ireland. They also occur in the Alps and elsewhere. The main present-day distributions of these fishes are, however, in arctic and northern seas, ascending rivers to spawn. The non-migratory freshwater populations are probably the descendants of Late Devensian fishes which became isolated when the main distributions shifted northward with the improved climate of the early Flandrian. A find of salmonid bones and scales, probably attributable to *Salvelinus*, from Esthwaite Water, Cumbria, in a deposit dating from the end of the Late Devensian, lends some support to this interpretation (Freshwater Biological Association 1960; Wheeler 1977).

Similar relict distributions, paralleling those of certain plants, e.g. dwarf-birch *Betula nana*, are shown by the mountain hare *Lepus timidus* and ptarmigan *Lagopus mutus*. *Lepus timidus*, recorded from southern England in the Devensian, is now indigenous only to the Scottish Highlands and Ireland, although introduced to other upland areas. In lowland Britain it is replaced by brown hare *Lepus capensis*, which however is not indigenous to Ire-

land. *Lagopus mutus*, also recorded from Devensian deposits in England, is now restricted to the Scottish Highlands (Sharrock 1976).

The overall distributions of many birds within the British Isles are clearly much influenced by biogeographical factors. Many species are more or less coastal, or favour upland or lowland areas, while others breed only in, for example, southern England or conversely only in Scotland, stressing the importance of climatic controls. The difficulties of disentangling such effects, from those produced by man, however, must again be pointed out (Ch. 10).

Amphibians and reptiles with distributions which, at least in part, reflect climatic factors, include natterjack *Bufo calamita* (restricted to sandy coastal and heath areas in England and south-west Ireland), sand lizard *Lacerta agilis* (restricted to sandy coastal and heath areas in England and Wales), smooth snake *Coronella austriaca* (distribution as in *L. agilis*, but restricted to southern England) and grass snake *Natrix natrix* (absent from Scotland except the Midland Valley) (Arnold 1973). Yalden (1980) has suggested that the disjunct ranges of *B. calamita*, *L. agilis* and *C. austriaca* result from initial early Flandrian colonization of large areas of lowland Britain, followed by a drastic reduction of range to coastal areas as forest replaced open herb vegetation. Climatic deterioration restricted their spread from these refugia when the forests were subsequently cleared by man. Of the mammals, dormouse *Muscardinus avellanarius* and harvest mouse *Micromys minutus* are probably indigenous only to England and Wales, because of climatic limitations.

8 Middle and Upper Pleistocene cold-stage faunas

General

The cold stages are characterized by climates predominantly much colder than those of the present day, but each covers complex sequences of climatic fluctuations. As currently recognized, each cold stage lasted several times longer than any interglacial. Radiocarbon dates on Devensian material show that the duration of this cold stage is at least 60 000 years, perhaps as much as 90 000 or 100 000 years (see Ch. 2).

Each cold stage covers a period in which climatic and vegetational conditions varied widely. For much of the time, however, the vegetation was herb-dominated mainly with grasses and sedges, but there were also milder periods which permitted the growth of tree birch and conifers, and, on the other hand, intensely cold phases with very little fauna or flora ('polar desert') may also have occurred. Some beetle faunas of Devensian age indicate that there were short periods of warm climate which were not accompanied by the establishment of woodland, although perhaps they resulted in a richer herb growth.

During the Devensian the main phase of glaciation appears to have been late in the stage, between about 18 000 and 15 000 radiocarbon years B.P. The relative timings of glaciations within earlier cold stages can only be estimated very roughly (see Ch. 2). There are considerable difficulties in dating fossiliferous deposits to or within particular cold stages older than the Devensian, because such deposits are well beyond the range of radiocarbon dating and, unlike interglacials, also lack a continuous pollen or other biostratigraphical record.

The vertebrate faunas of the Middle and Upper Devensian can be dated by radiocarbon and usually related to fossil floras and beetle faunas. Again, however, there exists no continuous biostratigraphical record for much of the stage, and all too often one is relying solely on the accuracy of radiocarbon dates.

Early Devensian deposits are beyond the range of radiocarbon dating, or near the limits of the method, but fortunately there exists a fairly continuous pollen record for some of this period, and the woodland interstadials can probably be distinguished on their pollen spectra (Ch. 2). A further difficulty with cold-stage vertebrate faunas is that at most open sites the fossils, which often occur in very large numbers, are generally not found in the datable organic horizons but in the sands and gravels above and below.

For the reasons given above it is not possible to reconstruct the history of the vertebrate fauna through the Beestonian, Anglian or Wolstonian stages even in outline. The changes in the mammal faunas during the Devensian, however, can be followed in some detail.

The typical vertebrate faunas of the cold stages, excluding periods with woodland interstadials on the one hand and polar desert on the other, comprise: (a) extinct taxa; (b) taxa now confined to arctic or rarely alpine regions; (c) taxa nowadays characteristic of steppe; and (d) animals now confined to regions further south.

These associations are remarkably similar for the Anglian, Wolstonian and Devensian stages and reflect climatic and vegetational conditions not represented anywhere in the world at the present day.

There is a rather marked reduction in species diversity in cold-stage faunas in comparison with those of interglacial age. On the other hand, the abundance of bones, especially of *Bison priscus*, recovered from many deposits of Devensian age indicates that during certain phases within cold stages the vertebrate biomass may have considerably exceeded that of any time within an interglacial period.

Table 8.1. Mammal faunas from pre-Devensian cold stages. Be, Beeston; Ang, Anglian; Wo, Wolstonian

Stage/substage	West Runton	Beeston	Mundesley	Wallingford	Homersfield	Hoxne	Baginton-Lillington Gravels	Broome Heath	Bakers Hole	Water Hall Farm
	Be	Be	e-Ang	?Ang	?Ang	l-Ang	e-Wo	Wo	Wo	l-Wo
PRIMATES										
Homo sapiens L., man	–	–	–	?	–	–	–	–	+	–
RODENTIA										
Spermophilus sp., suslik	–	–	+	–	–	–	–	–	–	–
Lemmus lemmus (L.), Norway lemming	–	–	–	+	–	–	–	–	–	–
Arvicola cantiana (Hinton), extinct water vole	–	–	–	+	–	–	–	–	–	–
Microtus oeconomus (Pallas), northern vole	–	–	–	–	–	–	–	–	–	+
Microtus gregalis (Pallas), tundra vole	–	–	–	+	–	–	–	–	–	?
CARNIVORA										
Crocuta crocuta Erxleben, spotted hyaena	–	–	–	–	–	–	+	–	–	–
PROBOSCIDEA										
cf. *Mammuthus trogontherii* Pohlig, extinct elephant	–	+	–	–	–	–	–	–	–	–
Mammuthus primigenius Blumenbach, mammoth	–	–	–	–	+	–	+	+	+	–
PERISSODACTYLA										
Equus ferus Boddaert, horse	–	–	–	+	+	–	+	–	+	–
Coelodonta antiquitatis Blumenbach, woolly rhino	–	–	–	–	+	–	+	–	+	–
ARTIODACTYLA										
Megaceros giganteus Blumenbach, giant deer	–	–	–	–	+	–	–	–	–	–
Cervus elaphus L., red deer	–	–	–	–	–	+	–	–	–	–
Rangifer tarandus L., reindeer	–	–	–	+	+	–	+	–	–	–
Indet. deer	·+	–	–	–	–	–	–	–	–	–
Bison sp. or *Bos* sp., bison or aurochs	+	–	–	–	+	–	+	+	–	–

Pre-Devensian Cold Stages (Fig. 8.1, Table 8.1)

The very few available 'cold' faunas for which a pre-Devensian age can be demonstrated are very similar to typical faunas of Devensian age. The implication is that the former are perhaps fairly common, but in general are assumed to be of Devensian age in the absence of clear stratigraphical evidence.

The paucity of faunas and the impossibility of dating deposits precisely within the stage, precludes any attempt at present to reconstruct faunal histories for the Beestonian, Anglian and Wolstonian cold stages.

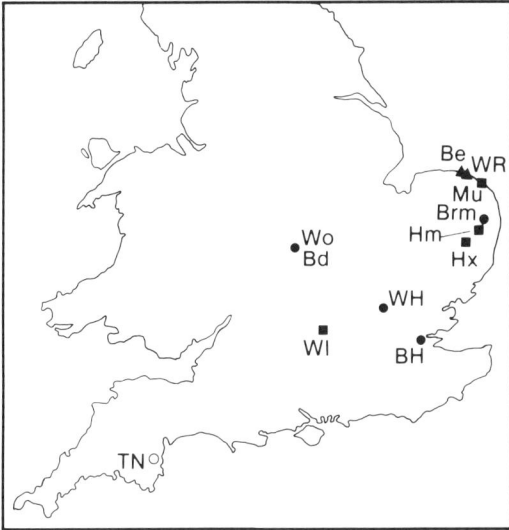

Fig. 8.1. Location map of Beestonian, Anglian and Wolstonian vertebrate sites. ▲, Beestonian; ■, Anglian; ●, Wolstonian; (cave sites shown by open symbols). Bd, Brandon; Be, Beeston; BH, Baker's Hole, Northfleet; Brm, Broome Heath; Hm Homersfield; Hx, Hoxne; Mu, Mundesley; TN, Tornewton Cave; WH, Water Hall Farm; Wl, Wallingford; Wo, Wolston, WR, West Runton.

Beestonian Stage

At present only four fossil mammal specimens can be confidently assigned to the Beestonian Cold Stage. A mandible of an elephant apparently intermediate between *Archidiskodon meridionalis* and *Mammuthus trogontherii*, was found *in situ* in the cliff at Beeston, Norfolk, in marine beach sands and gravels (Bed O), assigned to the Beestonian Stage, and resting on an eroded surface of Pastonian marine silts (West 1980a). Pollen spectra from Bed O consist mainly of grasses, birch and pine, but with some pollen of thermophilous trees probably reworked from the Pastonian. A cool climate and grassy vegetation with stands of birch and pine can be tentatively inferred.

At West Runton, Norfolk, the topmost bed of the pre-West Runton Freshwater Bed (Cromerian) succession (Bed i) consists of sands and silts with marine shells assigned to the Beestonian Stage (West 1980a). *Bison* and a deer are recorded from this bed.

Anglian Stage

A crushed skeleton of a suslik *Spermophilus* sp. was found in freshwater silts ('Arctic Bed') immediately beneath the till in the cliff at Mundesley, Norfolk (Newton 1882b). These silts are now referred to the Early Anglian Cold Stage, and the pollen spectra indicate open grassland and a cold climate (West 1980a). Unfortunately, this constitutes the only known fossil mammal definitely dated to the beginning of this stage. The association of *Spermophilus* with unwooded vegetational conditions is consistent with the ecology of this genus at the present day.

The Wallingford Fan Gravels occur, as remnants of a formerly more extensive sheet, near Benson, Oxfordshire. The deposits, about 6 m thick, mainly comprise chalky flint gravels, thought to have been soliflucted (coombe deposits), and angular flint gravels and sands with seams of sands, calcareous silts and clays, largely deposited under fluviatile conditions (Horton & Whittow, in Shephard-Thorn & Wymer 1977). The stratification has been contorted by cryoturbation, and ice-wedge casts also testify to permafrost conditions during the deposition of these beds. The Wallingford Fan Gravels appear to grade to the level of the Winter Hill or Black Park Terrace of the River Thames, which suggests an Anglian age, but this is by no means certain.

In Hall's Pit near Benson, Dr A. Horton found in the calcareous silt unit (unit ii) non-marine Mollusca and rare vertebrate remains including frog *Rana* sp. and/or toad *Bufo* sp., Norway lemming *Lemmus lemmus*, extinct water vole *Arvicola cantiana*, tundra vole *Microtus gregalis*, horse *Equus ferus*, and reindeer *Rangifer tarandus*.

A single well-dated record of red deer *Cervus elaphus* from the Late Anglian is known from Hoxne, Suffolk. Three foot bones were found resting on the surface of the Anglian till in lacustrine clay mud and marl (Bed F) containing pollen indicative of the Anglian late-glacial (Spencer, in West 1956). The pollen points to open herb-dominated vegetational conditions with sea buckthorn *Hippophaë* scrub. This gives a clear association of *C. elaphus* with unwooded vegetational conditions (Ch. 5).

In the valley of the River Waveney, which is the boundary between Norfolk and Suffolk, two distinct terraces occur above pollen-dated Ipswichian deposits, at Wortwell, Norfolk (see Ch. 2) which are at approximately the level of the modern floodplain (Sparks & West 1968). The higher, and therefore presumably older, Homersfield Terrace surface is at approximately 8 m above the floodplain. In the early 1950s mammalian remains were collected from sands and gravels of this terrace at Homersfield, Suffolk, by Prof. B. Funnell, and the fauna comprises mammoth *Mammuthus primigenius*, woolly rhino *Coelodonta antiquitatis*, horse *Equus ferus*, reindeer *Rangifer tarandus*, giant deer *Megaceros giganteus* and a large bovid *Bison* or *Bos*, and is thus a typical cold-stage fauna, identical to faunas of Wolstonian or Devensian age. Recent work by Coxon (1979) has shown that at nearby Flixton, the Homersfield Terrace deposits are intimately associated with chalky till. This and the height relationships to the type Hoxnian interglacial lake deposits at Hoxne, also in the Waveney Valley area, suggest an Anglian age for this terrace. Previously the terrace had been tentatively ascribed to the Wolstonian Stage by Sparks and West.

Wolstonian Stage

The surface of the Broome Terrace of the River Waveney lies about 3 m above the floodplain. Teeth of mammoth *Mammuthus primigenius*, and bones of a bovid *Bison* sp. or *Bos* sp., have been found in the sands and gravels of this terrace at Broome Heath, and organic deposits at this site have yielded a full-glacial flora of plant macrofossils. The discovery of reworked Hoxnian plant remains at this site by Coxon here confirms the Wolstonian age previously suggested by Sparks and West (1968).

Large-mammal remains have been collected from pits in the fluviatile Baginton-Lillington Gravel in the vicinity of Wolston, Warwickshire (Shotton 1953, 1968). These deposits are the lowest member of the type sequence of the Wolstonian, and most probably date from the very early part of this stage. The fauna is given as: spotted hyaena *Crocuta crocuta*, mammoth *Mammuthus primigenius*, straight-tusked elephant *Palaeoloxodon antiquus*, woolly rhino *Coelodonta antiquitatis*, horse *Equus ferus*, reindeer *Rangifer tarandus* and bison *Bison* sp. or aurochs *Bos* sp. The record of *P. antiquus*, if correct, is unexpected in a cold-stage fauna.

At Brandon, Warwickshire, fossiliferous silts occupying a channel within the Baginton-Lillington

gravels yielded a very interesting fauna of freshwater fishes (Osborne & Shotton 1968). According to H. Greenwood is Osborne & Shotton (1968), the species present include pike *Esox lucius*, gudgeon *Gobio gobio*, possibly minnow *Phoxinus phoxinus*, chub *Leuciscus cephalus*, roach *Rutilus rutilus*, various other undetermined cyprinids, perch *Perca fluviatilis* and three-spined stickleback *Gasterosteus aculeatus*. The beetle fauna is stated to include some southern forms and lacks arctic stenotherms, and the pollen spectra indicate meadow birch woodland Kelly (1968). *Gobio gobio* and *L. cephalus* do not occur further north than southern Scandinavia at the present day.

The general picture is of a cool but not arctic climate, suggesting interstadial conditions within the Early Wolstonian.

At Northfleet, Kent, in a small tributary valley of the River Thames, coombe rock, frost-heaved chalk, soliflucted gravels and loess underlie freshwater silts, attributed to the Ipswichian Interglacial on the basis of temperate non-marine molluscan faunas. Further periglacial deposits occur above (Kerney & Sieveking, in Shephard-Thorn & Wymer 1977). Excavations at the Baker's Hole pit early in the present century (Smith 1911) yielded a few large-mammal remains (Table 8.1) from the earlier periglacial deposits, which appear to be of Wolstonian age – again probably from late in this stage.

Lacustrine stonewort *Chara* marls at Water Hall Farm, Hertfordshire, occur beneath sands and gravels containing *Hippopotamus amphibius* and other mammals indicative of the Ipswichian interglacial. The marls are penetrated by one or more ice-wedge casts which indicate a Wolstonian age, most probably near the end of this stage. Small vertebrates from the deposit include pike *Esox lucius*, frog *Rana* sp. and/or toad *Bufo* sp. and northern vole *Microtus oeconomus*.

In Tornewton Cave, Torbryan, Devon, a series of deposits with vertebrate fossils represents parts of the Wolstonian, Ipswichian, Devensian and Flandrian Stages (Sutcliffe & Zeuner 1962) (see Fig. 7.11). The oldest fossiliferous bed, termed the Glutton Stratum, thought to have been soliflucted into place, contains stalagmite apparently shattered by freeze-thaw processes, and has yielded arctic mammals. The immediately overlying Bear Stratum has much the same fauna but lacks evidence of periglacial conditions. The stratigraphical position of these beds, beneath the Hyaena Stratum with its characteristic Ipswichian fauna, suggests that both the Glutton and Bear Strata are of Wolstonian age; most probably dating from near the end of the stage. Unfortunately, however, there are strong suspicions that the faunal remains from the Glutton Stratum are mixed with material of interglacial age.

Mammals recorded from the Glutton and Bear Strata are bear *Ursus* sp., wolf *Canis lupus*, red fox *Vulpes vulpes*, lion *Panthera leo*, badger *Meles meles*, clawless otter *Aonyx antiqua* Blainville, glutton *Gulo gulo*, mountain hare *Lepus timidus*, horse *Equus ferus*, rhinoceros cf. *Coelodonta* sp., reindeer *Rangifer tarandus* and a small bison or aurochs (Sutcliffe & Zeuner 1962). Small vertebrates include fishes, frogs and/or toads, common hamster *Cricetus cricetus*, a small hamster assigned to the extinct *Allocricetus bursae*, steppe lemming *Lagurus lagurus*, arctic lemming *Dicrostonyx torquatus*, Norway lemming *Lemmus lemmus* and northern vole *Microtus oeconomus* (Kowalski 1967; Sutcliffe & Kowalski 1976. The status of the records of snow vole *Microtus nivalis* from this site have been discussed in Chapter 3. Birds identified from these beds by Harrison (1980) include ducks, kestrel *Falco tinnunculus*, eagle owl *Bubo bubo*, crossbill *Loxia* cf. *curvirostra*, carrion crow *Corvus corone* and raven *Corvus corax*. A fragment found in the Glutton Stratum is the sole basis for the description of the extinct patridge *Alectoris sutcliffei* Harrison. Confirmation of this record with more material would be desirable.

The Glutton and Bear Strata faunas show a mixture of steppe, boreal-arctic, and temperate components as is seen in many Devensian faunas, although the steppe contribution, including hamsters and *Lagurus lagurus*, is especially marked. The presence of the distinctly temperate *Meles meles*, and if correct of *Loxia curvirostra*, a species dependent on coniferous trees, however, either indicates interstadial conditions or may reflect contamination with interglacial material.

Comparison with Continental faunas

Some of the faunas from central Europe (e.g. Stránská Skála, Vértesszöllös, Mauer) which have been ascribed to the Elsterian (Anglian) (Kahlke 1975a), could be more convincingly correlated with the Cromerian Interglacial (Ch. 7). Faunas of probable Elsterian age listed by Kahlke, e.g. Bornhausen and Neuekrug (Harz), West Germany,

include *Mammuthus trogontherii*, *Coelodonta antiquitatis*, *Rangifer tarandus* and *Bison priscus*.

At Steinheim (Murr), West Germany, the 'Main Mammoth Gravels' overlying the gravels with a Holsteinian fauna (Ch. 7) and therefore of probable Saalian age, have yielded a fauna which includes elephants referred to both *M. trogontherii* and *M. primigenius*, *C. antiquitatis*, *Megaceros giganteus* and *B. priscus* (Kahlke 1975a).

Similar faunas assigned to the 'Rissian' (Saalian, Wolstonian) Cold Stage are recorded from the cave sequences of Southern France (Lumley 1976). The southern location, however, is reflected in the occurrence of such temperate species as fallow deer *Dama dama* and aurochs *Bos primigenius* in many of these faunas and the proximity to mountainous areas by the many finds of ibex *Capra ibex* and chamois *Rupicapra rupicapra*.

Devensian stage

An outline of the stratigraphy, climate, vegetation and history of the beetle faunas of this stage is given in Chapter 2.

Sites and faunas (Fig. 8.2, Table 8.2)

The vertebrate faunas of the Devensian are far better known than those of earlier cold stages, and have been found in most areas of the British Isles. Open-site records are mostly from fluviatile deposits, but some of the best-preserved material comes from lacustrine sediments. Most assemblages from caves are also of Devensian age. Unfortunately, however, the majority of finds are neither accurately stratified nor dated.

Early Devensian (pre-50 000 radiocarbon year B.P.)
Early Devensian vertebrate faunas are known so far almost entirely from only two localities, both in Norfolk (Table 8.2).

In the early 1960s excavations for a flood-relief channel along the Fenland margin at Wretton, Norfolk, revealed an extremely complex sequence of Ipswichian and Devensian deposits of the River Wissey (Sparks & West 1970; West *et al.* 1974) (Fig. 8.3). The Devensian sediments record deposition in a wide range of environments. Much of the

Table 8.2. Mammal faunas from well-stratified/dated Devensian open sites. Circled crosses indicate radiocarbon-dated records. Other Middle and Upper Devensian records are more broadly associated with the radiocarbon dates given.

	Early		Middle							Late						
Site	Wretton	Coston	Isleworth	Tattershall Castle	Upton Warren	Fladbury	Kirkby-on-Bain	Brandon	Beckford	Barnwell Stn	e.g. Ballybetagh	Neasham	Blackpool	Flixton	Nazeing	Sproughton
Pollen zone/approx. radiocarbon date (years B.P.)	Herb substage I	Chelford	43 140	43 000	42 000	38 200	34 800	28 200	27 650	19 500	II/.11 000–12 000	III/11 561	II/11 993	III/pre-10 413	III	III/pre-9 880
PRIMATES																
Homo sapiens L., man	–	–	–	–	–	–	–	–	–	–	–	–	⊕	+	–	+
RODENTIA																
Dicrostonyx torquatus (Pallas), arctic lemming	–	–	–	–	–	–	–	⊕	–	–	–	–	–	–	+	–
Lemmus lemmus (L.), Norway lemming	–	–	–	–	+	–	–	–	–	–	–	–	–	–	+[1]	–
Arvicola cantiana (Hinton), extinct water vole	–	+	⊕	–	–	–	–	–	–	–	–	–	–	–	–	–
Microtus oeconomus (Pallas), northern vole	–	–	⊕	⊕	–	–	–	–	+	–	–	–	–	–	+	–
Microtus gregalis (Pallas), tundra vole	–	+	–	–	–	–	–	–	–	–	–	–	–	–	+	–
Microtus agrestis L., field vole	–	–	–	–	+	–	–	–	–	–	–	–	–	–	+	–
Microtus sp., a vole	+	–	–	–	–	–	–	–	–	–	–	–	–	–	–	–
CARNIVORA																
Canis lupus L., wolf	+	–	+	+	–	–	–	–	–	–	–	–	–	–	+	–
Alopex lagopus (L.), arctic fox	+	–	–	–	–	–	–	–	–	–	–	–	–	–	+	–
Ursus arctos L., brown bear	+	–	⊕	+	–	–	–	–	–	–	–	–	–	–	+	–
PROBOSCIDEA																
Mammuthus primigenius Blumenbach, mammoth	+	+	+	+	+	+	+	–	+	+	–	–	–	–	–	–

PERISSODACTYLA
Equus ferus Boddaert, horse
Coelodonta antiquitatis Blumenbach, woolly rhino

ARTIODACTYLA
Cervus elaphus L., red deer
Rangifer tarandus L., reindeer
Megaceros giganteus (Blumenbach), giant deer
Alces alces (L.), elk
Bison priscus Bojanus, extinct bison
Ovibos moschatus Zimmerman, musk ox

---

1. Could be slightly older

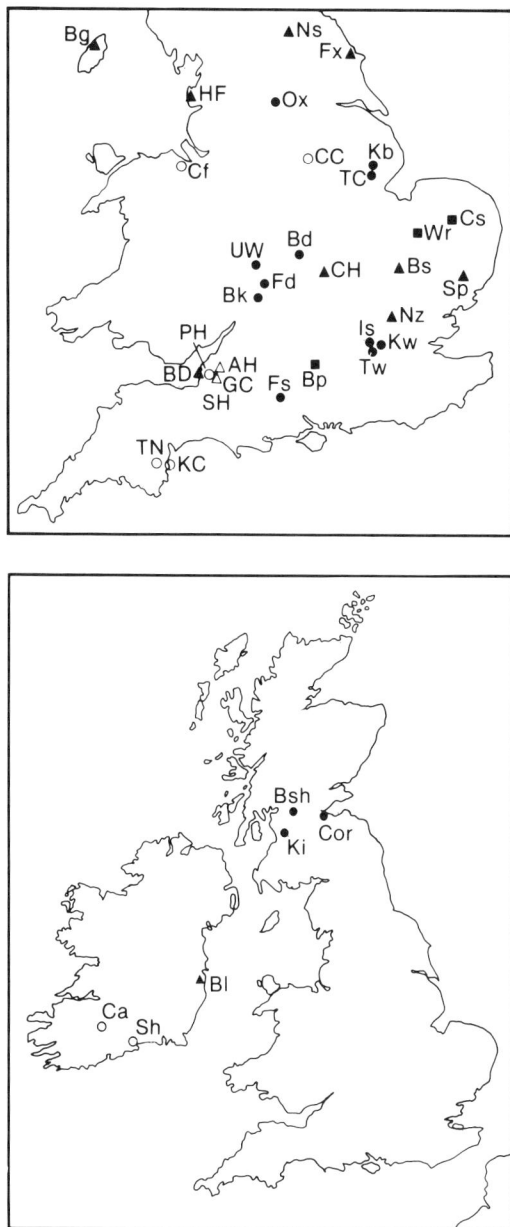

Fx, Flixton; Fs, Fisherton; GC, Gough's Cave; HF, High Furlong, Blackpool; Is, Isleworth; Kb, Kirkby-on-Bain; KC, Kent's Cavern Ki, Kilmaurs; Kw, Kew; Ns, Neasham; Nz, Nazeing; Ox, Oxbow; PH, Picken's Hole; Sh, Shandon Cave; SH, Sun Hole; Sp, Sproughton; TC, Tattershall Castle; TN, Tornewton Cave (Reindeer Stratum); Tw, Twickenham; UW, Upton Warren; Wr, Wretton.

sequence comprises fluviatile sands, silts and gravels, with fine clastic and organic sediments in small enclosed basins thought to have been formed by the melting of ice mounds. Eight local pollen zones A to H, representing three herb substages and two woodland substages (interstadials) were recognized on the basis of pollen spectra. The later interstadial is thought to be equivalent to the Chelford (Cheshire) woodland substage, and the earlier designated as the Wretton woodland substage. These may correlate with the Brørup and Amersfoort interstadials respectively recognized in Denmark, North Germany and the Netherlands.

Bones of wolf *Canis lupus* have been found *in situ* in beds with pollen spectra of herb substage I type (Fig. 8.3b). The majority of the Wretton mammal material was found loose in the mounds of excavated deposits, but all or most of it probably comes from the beds of herb substage I age; a conclusion corroborated by the uniformity of the fauna. The abundant fossils, collected by Dr K. A. Joysey, are now being studied by him in collaboration with the author (Table 8.2).

The extinct bison *Bison priscus* is by far the best-represented taxon, followed by reindeer *Rangifer tarandus*. The other taxa, *Canis lupus*, arctic fox *Alopex lagopus*, bear *Ursus* sp., mammoth *Mammuthus primigenius*, woolly rhinoceros *Coelodonta antiquitatis* and horse *Equus ferus*, are mostly represented only by one or two specimens each. The picture of large herds of grazing bison and reindeer is entirely consistent with the palaeobotanical evidence for a rich herbaceous vegetation. The predominance of male shed antlers at Wretton indicates that reindeer herds were in the area mainly in the winter (see Ch. 5).

Beetle remains recovered from zones A and B of Wretton herb substage I were interpreted as suggesting open, rather marshy, grassland with sandy soils, and a cool but not arctic climate (Coope, in West *et al.* 1974). There is, however, a marked disagreement between the beetle faunas and the pollen

Fig. 8.2. Location map of Devensian vertebrate sites. ■, Early Devensian; ●, Middle Devensian (or uncertain); ▲, Late Devensian; (cave sites shown by open symbols). AH, Aveline's Hole; BD, Brean Down; Bd, Brandon; Bg, Ballaugh; Bk, Beckford; Bl, Ballybetagh; Bp, Brimpton; BS, Barnwell Station, Cambridge; Bsh, Bishopbriggs; Ca, Castlepook Cave; Cor, Corstophine; CC, Creswell Crags (Robin Hood's Cave, Pinhole Cave); Cf, Cefn Cave; CH, Clifford Hill; Cs, Coston; Fd, Fladbury;

(a)

(b)

Fig. 8.3. Early Devensian river terrace deposits at Wretton, Norfolk. (a) general view of flood-relief channel looking eastwards towards Wretton Fen Bridge. The high banks on either side consist of excavated spoil in which many bones were found. *In situ* deposits are exposed in sections above and below water level. (b) section in south bank showing sands and silts, overlain by organic deposits yielding herb substage I pollen spectra (see text). A partial skeleton of wolf *Canis lupus* was found in the sands and silts. The scapula and another bone are visible in the photo to the left and above the trowel.

spectra for zones F and G. According to Coope, the beetles indicate a severe arctic climate, whereas the pollen shows the development of pine *Pinus* and spruce *Picea* forest. This discrepancy has yet to be resolved.

Organic deposits in sands and silts of the second terrace of the River Cam at Sidgwick Avenue, Cambridge, have been attributed to the Early Devensian (Lambert, Pearson & Sparks 1962). Plant macrofossils indicate an open unwooded landscape and a climate colder than today. A skull of *Bison priscus* was recovered from these deposits.

Organic sands and silts beneath gravels at Coston near Barnham Broom, Norfolk, have yielded macroscopic plant remains, molluscs and vertebrate remains. Preliminary pollen analyses by P. L. Gibbard indicate spruce *Picea*/pine *Pinus* forest giving way to an unwooded environment dominated by grasses and sedges. A correlation with the end of the Early Devensian Chelford interstadial seems very probable. Ipswichian interglacial deposits also occur in the gravel pit and a hippopotamus *Hippopotamus amphibius* tooth has been recorded from the site, although not *in situ*.

The majority of large-mammal bones from Coston are of *Bison priscus*. Other taxa, represented by a few specimens each, comprise *Coelodonta antiquitatis*, *Mammuthus primigenius*, *Rangifer tarandus*, and red deer *Cervus elaphus*. All of these species were recorded *in situ* in the organic deposits, although many unstratified finds have also been made. Small-vertebrate remains collected *in situ* by the author include: three-spined stickleback *Gasterosteus aculeatus*, frog *Rana* sp. and/or *Bufo* sp., toad, short-tailed vole *Microtus agrestis* and extinct water vole *Arvicola cantiana*.

A basal antler fragment of *C. elaphus* has been found in deposits attributed to a post Chelford interstadial at Brimpton, Berkshire (Bryant & Holyoak 1980).

Middle Devensian (50 000 to 26 000 radiocarbon years B.P.)

Middle Devensian vertebrate faunas are available from a number of open sites in association with radiocarbon dates, beetle faunas and pollen (Table 8.2).

At Tattershall Castle, Lincolnshire, several metres of fluviatile gravel, deposited by the River Witham, overlie fossiliferous organic deposits dated by pollen analyses to the Ipswichian interglacial (Girling 1974) (Fig. 8.4). A thin silt band near the base of the gravels has yielded a fossil beetle fauna of arctic type and radiocarbon dates of 44 300 $\pm$ $^{1\,600}_{1\,300}$ and 42 100 $\pm$ $^{1\,400}_{1\,100}$ years B.P. (Lab. no. Birm-408, 398. A higher silt band up to 2 m thick has, in contrast, yielded a temperate beetle fauna, and radiocarbon dates of 43 000 $\pm$ $^{1\,300}_{1\,100}$ and 42 200 $\pm$ 1 000 years B.P. (Birm-341, 409). Numerous large-mammal bones have been found at this site, of which as at Wretton the majority are of *Bison priscus*, with *Rangifer tarandus* in second place (Rackham 1978). Bones of both these species have been found *in situ* in the upper silt bed, but most finds are not stratigraphically located and may cover several thousands of years, within which there may have been considerable changes in climate. The presence of abundant shed male antlers at the site indicates that *Rangifer tarandus* was present in the winter months (Ch. 5).

Of particular interest is the occurrence of numerous dung beetles in the upper silt bed coleopteran fauna, indicating the presence of large herbivores in the area during the summer months as well.

Numerous large-mammal remains were discovered in the late 1950s and early 1960s at Willment's Pit, Isleworth, Middlesex, and collected by J. W. Simons. The deposits, laid down by the River Thames, comprise a sequence about 5 m thick of gravels, sands and organic silty clays, the latter giving a radiocarbon date of 43 140 $\pm$ $^{1\,520}_{1\,280}$ years B.P. (Birm-319) (Coope & Angus 1975). The vertebrate fauna (Table 8.2) includes fishes, amphibians, and the voles *Microtus oeconomus* and *Microtus gregalis* from the dated silty clay bed. Of the far more abundant large-mammal remains, bear *Ursus* sp., reindeer *Rangifer tarandus* and bison *Bison priscus* are definitely recorded from the silty clay bed, while the majority of finds are from the gravels and sands, and are therefore less precisely dated.

The vertebrate assemblage is dominated by the remains of *Bison priscus*. Remains of *Rangifer tarandus* are also conspicuous, though much less abundant than *Bison*; but this impression is exaggerated since they include many shed antlers, and each reindeer produces several pairs of antlers in its lifetime. The other taxa are each represented by one or a few specimens only.

The organic silty clay bed has produced a rich beetle fauna, described by Coope and Angus, with representatives of aquatic pool, riparian and terrestrial environments. The latter were interpreted as comprising an adjacent marshy area with lush herbaceous vegetation, and patchy vegetation includ-

Fig. 8.4. Section showing sequence of Middle Devensian deposits at Tattershall Castle, Lincolnshire. A fossiliferous organic rich channel fill (dark) near the base, is succeeded by cross-bedded sands and gravels (the holes were made by sand martins).

ing heath on higher and drier ground. More recent pollen analyses, by P. L. Gibbard, show typical Devensian herb pollen spectra dominated by grasses and sedges. According to Coope and Angus, the beetle fauna consists of temperate species now found in Britain plus a smaller number of more southern or eastern distribution, indicating mean July temperatures of 18 °C or more, i.e. higher than at the present day. The absence of trees was attributed to the climatic amelioration having been too short for trees to immigrate. The possibility of grazing pressure by the large herbivores, preventing tree growth, was also mentioned. Tree growth may, however, have been restricted by severe winters (West 1977b).

It is not known whether *Bison priscus* was present at Isleworth throughout the year. Provisional study of the numerous *Rangifer tarandus* antlers from the site suggests that most of the shed antlers are from males, indicating presence of the herds in the winter months (see Ch. 5).

As at Tattershall Castle the large and varied dung-beetle fauna indicates that large herbivores were present during the summer. Carrion beetles are also recorded.

At Upton Warren, Worcestershire, many bones and teeth of large mammals were found in terrace deposits of the River Salwarpe (Coope, Shotton & Strachan 1961). Silt bands within the sands and gravels yielded pollen spectra indicative of treeless herb-dominated vegetation. One of these silt bands gave a radiocarbon date of 42 100 ± 800 years B.P. (GrN-1245). Only a few remains of three-spined stickleback *Gasterosteus aculeatus* were, however, actually found in this dated silt. Bones assigned to common frog *Rana temporaria*, arctic lemming *Dicrostonyx torquatus* and a vole *Microtus* sp. were recovered from the other silt bands. The large-mammal bones were mostly found by workmen in the sands and gravels so that the majority of records are only broadly associated with the radiocarbon date. Mammoth *Mammuthus primigenius* is much better represented than in the faunas from Isleworth and Tattershall Castle, although both *Bison priscus* and *Rangifer tarandus* are still very abundant.

From the abundance of both dung and carcass beetles, Coope *et al.* suggested that the pools on the floodplain, represented by fossiliferous silt bands, were used as waterholes by large mammals.

An organic silt horizon at Oxbow near Leeds yielded a tusk of *Mammuthus primigenius* together

with insects and pollen and a radiocarbon date of 38 600 ± $^{1\,720}_{1\,420}$ years B.P. (NPL-163B) (Gaunt, Coope & Franks 1970). The pollen indicates a thin herbaceous plant cover with patches of bare ground, and the beetles also point to arctic conditions.

River sands and gravels at Fladbury, Worcestershire, include a peat horizon radiocarbon dated to 38 200 ± 600 years B.P. (GrN-1269). The vertebrate fauna from the gravels comprises only *Mammuthus primigenius*, *Coelodonta antiquitatis* and horse *Equus ferus* (Coope 1962). The beetles from the peat again indicate an arctic environment.

At Kirkby-on-Bain (Tattershall Thorpe) Lincolnshire, only some 4 km from Tattershall Castle in the valley of the River Witham, several metres of sands and gravels (Fig. 8.4) have produced a number of large-mammal bones. A silt band, radiocarbon dated to 34 800 ± 1 000 years B.P. (Birm-250), has yielded an arctic beetle fauna (Girling 1974). Rackham (1978) has listed the fauna (Table 8.2) and pointed out the striking differences when compared with the earlier sites. At Kirkby *Bison priscus* is virtually absent, and no remains of *Rangifer tarandus* have been found. The faunal assemblage is here dominated by remains of mammoth *Mammuthus primigenius* and rarer woolly rhinoceros *Coelodonta antiquitatis*.

At Brandon, Warwickshire, organic silts, radiocarbon dated to about 28 200 years B.P., occur at the base of gravels of the River Avon number 2 terrace (Shotton 1968). They contain plant and insect fossils (Kelly 1968; Coope 1968a) both of which indicate an open, herb-rich, treeless environment. Dwarf birch *Betula nana* and dwarf willow *Salix herbacea* were also present. The beetles imply a severe arctic climate. The single vertebrate record from the silt deposits is of arctic lemming *Dicrostonyx torquatus*.

Organic silt bands within terrace sands and gravels of the Carrant Brook at Beckford, Worcestershire, gave a radiocarbon date of 27 650 ± 250 years B.P. (Birm-293) (Briggs, Coope & Gilbertson 1975). Non-marine molluscs from the silt were thought to suggest marshy ground and exposed open environments with lack of continuous grass cover. The beetle assemblage is of arctic tundra type, again suggesting sparse vegetation. One species of carcass beetle occurs. According to Whitehead (in Shotton, 1977c) the large-mammal bones from the sands and gravels, and therefore only broadly associated with the radiocarbon date, in-

Table 8.3. Devensian radiocarbon-dated mammal records based on bone collagen. (Data from *Radiocarbon* 1959–79; Campbell 1977)

	Lab. and assay no.	Date in radiocarbon years B.P.
Homo sapiens, man		
Paviland, Glamorganshire ('Red Lady')	BM-374	18 460 ± 340
Ursus arctos, brown bear		
Sun Hole, Somersetshire	BM-524	12 378 ± 150
Kent's Cavern, Devonshire	GrN-6203	14 275 ± 120
Robin Hood's Cave, Derbyshire	BM-602	28 500 $\pm^{1\,600}_{1\,300}$
Kent's Cavern, Devonshire	GrN-6202	28 720 ± 450
Mammuthus primigenius, mammoth		
Cae Gwyn Cave, Flintshire	Birm-146	18 000 $\pm^{1\,400}_{1\,200}$
English Channel off Sussex	Gif.-1110	19 300 ± 700
Castlepook Cave, County Cork	D-122	33 500 ± 1 200
Little Rissington, Gloucestershire	Birm-466	34 500 ± 500
Oxbow, near Leeds	NPL-162B	38 600 $\pm^{1\,720}_{1\,420}$
Coelodonta antiquitatis, woolly rhino		
Ogof-yr-Ichen, Caldey Island, Pembrokeshire	Birm-340	22 350 ± 620
Bishopbriggs, Lanarkshire	GX	27 550 $\pm^{1\,370}_{1\,680}$
Kent's Cavern, Devonshire	GrN-6201	28 160 ± 435
Leadenhall Street, London	GrN-4630	29 450 ± 350
Equus ferus, horse		
Robin Hood's Cave, Derbyshire	BM-604	10 590 ± 90
Kent's Cavern, Devonshire	GrN-6324	38 270 $\pm^{1\,470}_{1\,240}$
Megaceros giganteus, giant deer		
Kent's Cavern, Devonshire	GrN-6204	12 180 ± 100
Brandesburton, Yorkshire (reworked)	Birm-55	12 850 ± 250
Rangifer tarandus, reindeer		
Dead Man's Cave, Anston, Yorkshire	BM-440b	9 750 ± 110
Rodden's Port, County Down	LJ-658	10 250 ± 350
Ossoms Cave, Staffordshire	GrN-7400	10 590 ± 70
Cattedown Cave, Plymouth, Devonshire	BM-729	15 125 ± 390
Coygan Cave, Camarthenshire	BM-499	38 684 $\pm^{2\,713}_{2\,024}$
Kilmaurs, Ayrshire	Birm-93	>40 000
cf. *Bison priscus*, extinct bison		
Broadway, Worcestershire	Birm-656	26 600 $\pm^{700}_{650}$
Kent's Cavern	GN-6325	27 730 ± 350
Ovibos moschatus, musk ox		
Clifford Hill, Northamptonshire	BM-725	18 213 ± 310

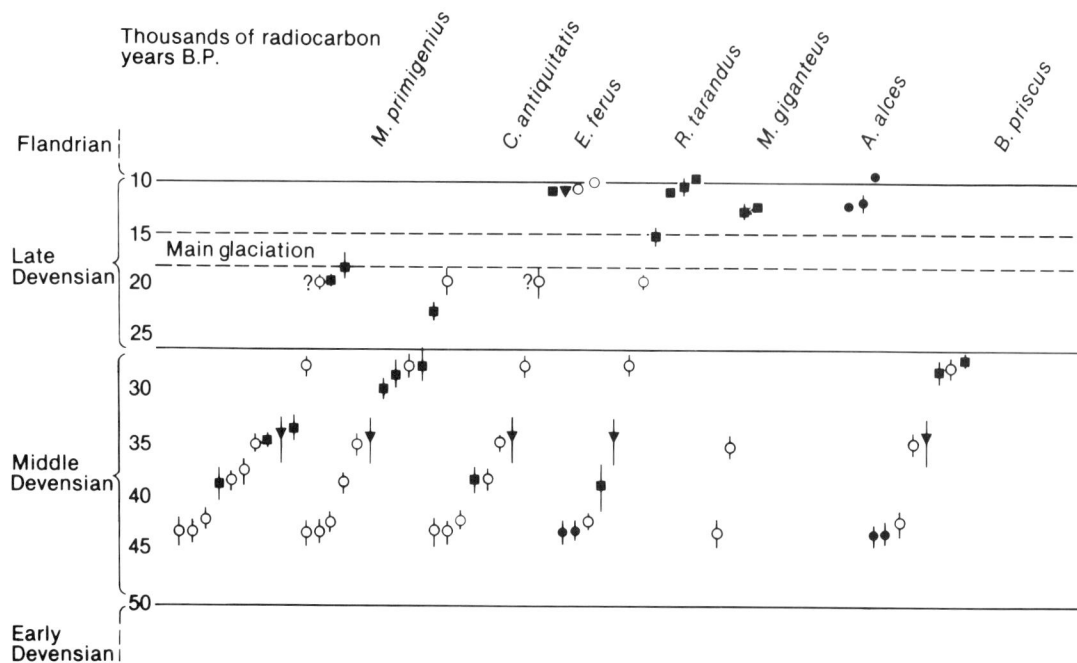

Fig. 8.5. Chart of radiocarbon dates, showing time-stratigraphical ranges of major species of large mammals during the Devensian Cold Stage (data from *Radiocarbon*, and Campbell 1977). ●, date on plant material from same horizon; ○, date on plant material broadly associated with mammal bones; ■, date on bone collagen from this species; ▼, bone collagen date on material from same horizon.

clude *Mammuthus primigenius, Coelodonta antiquitatis, Equus ferus, Rangifer tarandus, Bison priscus,* and one specimen of musk ox *Ovibos moschatus.* Molar teeth of small voles from this site attributed by Sutcliffe and Kowalski (1976) to *Microtus arvalis* are very probably of tundra vole *Microtus gregalis* as suggested by Hall and Yalden (1978).

In addition to the open sites of Middle Devensian age described above, where vertebrate remains have been recovered in good or reasonably well-stratified contexts, there are numerous finds from caves, fissures and open sites where the evidence for dating is rather less satisfactory. Radiocarbon dates on bone collagen are, however, available from some of these sites, and in some cases serve to date many other finds from the same horizon.

Radiocarbon dates on isolated Devensian mammal records are given in Table 8.3, and dated finds of selected large mammals plotted in Fig. 8.5. The possibility of contamination of a sample by younger carbon, and the lack of independent evidence on the age of many finds, means that it is unwise to rely greatly on any single radiocarbon date, although

the overall pattern of dates can be accepted more confidently.

At Tornewton Cave, Devon (Sutcliffe & Zeuner 1962; Sutcliffe & Kowalski 1976), a series of deposits containing cold-stage type faunas, overlie the Hyaena Stratum with its characteristically Ipswichian fauna (see Fig. 7.11). The two main faunas are from the Elk stratum (actually there is no *Alces* material from this site, the name resulting from a misidentification – Lister 1981) and the Reindeer Stratum. The mammals recorded are listed in Table 8.4. Notable occurrences are of red deer *Cervus elaphus* in the Elk Stratum, and of mole *Talpa europaea* and bank vole *Clethrionomys glareolus* in the Reindeer Stratum.

Birds from the latter horizon, according to Harrison (1980), include teal *Anas crecca*, ptarmigan *Lagopus mutus*, willow grouse *Lagopus lagopus*, little bustard *Otis tetrax*, skylark, *Alauda arvensis*, fieldfare *Turdus pilaris*, starling *Turdus vulgaris* and carrion crow *Corvus corone*.

The main agents responsible for accumulating the vertebrate remains were probably spotted

Table 8.4 Mammalian faunas of selected Middle and Upper Devensian cave deposits.

	Tornewton Cave Elk Stratum	Tornewton Cave Reindeer Stratum	Picken's Hole Layer 5	Picken's Hole Layer 3 (34 265 years B.P.)	Castlepook Cave Ireland, (33 500 years B.P.)
Insectivora					
Talpa europaea L., mole	–	+	–	–	–
Primates					
Homo sapiens L., man (B, bones; A, artefacts)	A	A,B	–	B	–
Rodentia					
Spermophilus sp., suslik	–	–	–	+	–
Dicrostonyx torquatus (Pallas), arctic lemming	+	–	–	–	+
Lemmus lemmus (L.), Norway lemming	–	–	–	–	+
Clethrionomys glareolus (Schreber), bank vole	+	+	–	–	–
Arvicola terrestris L., water vole	+	+	–	–	–
Microtus oeconomus (Pallas), northern vole	+	+	+	+	–
Microtus gregalis (Pallas), tundra vole	+	+	+	–	–
Microtus agrestis L., field vole	+	+	–	–	–
Carnivora					
Canis lupus L., wolf	+	–	+	–	+
Alopex lagopus (L.), arctic fox	–	–	–	+	+
Vulpes vulpes (L.), red fox	+	+	+	–	+
Ursus sp., bear	+	+	+	+	+
Mustela erminea L., stoat	–	–	–	–	+
Crocuta crocuta Erxleben, spotted hyaena	+	+	–	+	+
Panthera leo (L.), lion	–	–	–	+	–
Proboscidea					
Mammuthus primigenius Blumenbach, mammoth	–	–	–	+	+
Perissodactyla					
Coelodonta antiquitatis Blumenbach, woolly rhino	+	+	–	+	–
Equus ferus Boddaert, horse	+	+	–	+	–
Artiodactyla					
Megaceros giganteus Blumenbach, giant deer	–	–	–	–	+
Cervus elaphus L., red deer	+	–	+	+	–
Rangifer tarandus L., reindeer	+	+	+	+	+
Bison sp. or *Bos* sp., bison or aurochs	+	+	+	+	–

hyaena *Crocuta crocuta*, which may have used the cave as a den; man, whose presence is attested by some worked flints and teeth; and owls roosting near the cave entrance. No radiocarbon dates are available for these faunas, which on present evidence could date from two phases anywhere within the Devensian earlier than about 18 000 years B.P.

A preliminary account of the stratigraphy and

vertebrate faunas from the cave or rock shelter called Picken's Hole, Compton Bishop, Somerset, was given by Tratman (1964). Revised faunal lists were given by Stuart (1974, 1977a). At this locality two quite distinct cave earths were seen sandwiched between and separated by frost-shattered angular limestone breccias. The fauna of the earlier fossiliferous cave earth, Layer 5, includes wolf *Canis lupus*, red fox *Vulpes vulpes*, bear *Ursus* sp., *C. elaphus* and *R. tarandus*; whereas that of the younger horizon has in addition a suslik *Spermophilus* sp., arctic fox *Alopex lagopus*, hyaena *C. crocuta*, mammoth *Mammuthus primigenius*, woolly rhino *Coelodonta antiquitatis*, and horse *Equus ferus* (Table 8.4). A few nondescript worked flints and some human teeth indicate that man *Homo sapiens* was also present. The Layer 5 assemblage was perhaps partly accumulated by wolves. Bears dying in winter hibernation also contributed their remains. The more species-rich assemblage of layer 3 was, in contrast, largely accumulated by hyaenas, as is shown by the characteristic bone damage (see Ch. 4).

Bone collagen from Layer 3 gave an acceptable radiocarbon date of $34\,265 \pm {}^{2\,600}_{1\,950}$ years B.P. (BM-654), but the date for the earlier fauna from Layer 5 is considerably younger at $26\,650 \pm {}^{1\,700}_{1\,400}$ years B.P. (BM-655A). A further assay made to check this result gave a very similar figure of $27\,000 \pm {}^{1\,850}_{1\,500}$ years B.P. (BM-655B). The reasons for these anomalous results are unclear, but they certainly warn against the uncritical acceptance of isolated radiocarbon dates, especially those based on bone collagen.

In the last century mammalian remains were discovered in 'brickearths' at Fisherton near Salisbury, Wiltshire. Species represented include *Mammuthus primigenius*, *Coelodonta antiquitatis*, *Rangifer tarandus*, *Ovibus moschatus* and a suslik *Spermophilus* sp. (Dawkins & Reynolds 1872–1939; Simons 1962). The fauna is presumably of Devensian age.

A unique and very interesting record of saiga antelope *Saiga tartarica* is known from River Thames gravels at Twickenham, London (Dawkins & Reynolds 1872–1939). The age of these gravels is very probably Middle Devensian, broadly equivalent to the Upton Warren Interstadial (Coope & Angus 1975).

The sole record of polar bear *Ursus maritimus* is based on a specimen from a railway cutting in low terrace gravels of the River Thames near Kew Bridge, London (Kurtén 1964). Bones of *R. tarandus* have also been found in the same general area.

A Middle or Late Devensian age is likely for these finds.

Robin Hood's Cave and Pin Hole Cave, in the Permian Magnesian Limestone of Creswell Crags, Derbyshire, contain abundant vertebrate remains of Devensian age. Radiocarbon dates (Table 8.3) indicate the presence of Late-Devensian horizons, but the deposits date back at least to well into the Middle Devensian. Radiocarbon dates for Kent's Cavern, Torquay, Devon, indicate a similar time range for the younger sequence of deposits at that locality. All three sites have yielded generally similar faunas resembling those of broadly Middle Devensian age from elsewhere. Of particular interest, however, is the presence of a large red deer *Cervus elaphus* at Kent's Cavern and probably also the other two sites, apparently in association with a 'cold' fauna. Even more intriguing are the records of sabre-tooth *Homotherium latidens* from these three sites, since the species is otherwise unknown from Britain and Continental Europe later than the Middle Pleistocene. The Kent's Cavern specimen can be dismissed because deposits of Middle Pleistocene age also occur within the cave, but at Robin Hood's Cave an *H. latidens* canine was excavated (in the presence of W. B. Dawkins), in direct association with material of *M. primigenius*, *C. antiquitatis*, etc., and flint artefacts (Dawkins 1877). Late survival of *H. latidens* in Britain, as suggested by Kurtén (1968), seems highly improbable, however, but a possible explanation is that the specimens are actually of Middle Pleistocene date and being distinctive were collected by man in Devensian times.

Leopard *Panthera pardus* is known from Robin Hood's cave (Dawkins 1877) and also from Banwell and Bleadon Caves, Somerset. Finds attributed to cave bear *Ursus spelaeus*, from Kent's Cavern, Wookey Hole, Mendip, Somerset and elsewhere in south-west England, are probably of Middle or Early Devensian age.

The Devensian mammal faunas of Scotland have not received very much attention and would repay detailed study. Arctic lemming *Dicrostonyx torquatus* is recorded from Corstorphine Edinburgh (Sutcliffe & Kowalski 1976). Delair (1969) lists *M. primigenius*, *C. antiquitatis*, *R. tarandus* and *M. giganteus*, some of which could be of Late Devensian age. A specimen of *C. antiquitatis* from Bishopbriggs, Lanarkshire is dated to near the end of the Middle Devensian (Table 8.3). *M. primigenius* and *R. tarandus* are recorded from beneath till at Kilmaurs, Ayrshire (Gregory & Currie, 1928) (see Table 8.3).

Castlepook Cave, County Cork, provides the principal evidence of pre-Late Devensian vertebrates in Ireland (Scharff, Seymour & Newton 1918). Unfortunately, the fossils were recovered from a series of sands and stalagmite floors and may not all be of the same age. Flandrian mammals including domestic species were found in later deposits within the cave, and the presence of wood mouse *Apodemus sylvaticus* in association with the older fauna strongly suggests contamination with later material. A list of the fauna believed to be of Midlandian (Devensian) age is given in Table 8.4. A radiocarbon date of 33 400 ± 1 200 years B.P. (D-122) on collagen from a mammoth bone suggests a Middle Devensian age for this faunal assemblage, which includes both species of lemming *Dicrostonyx torquatus* and *Lemmus lemmus*, wolf *Canis lupus*, fox *Vulpes vulpes*, arctic fox *Alopex lagopus*, bear *Ursus* sp., spotted hyaena *C. crocuta*, mammoth *M. primigenius*, giant deer *Megaceros giganteus* and reindeer *R. tarandus*. Conspicuously absent at Castlepook, and elsewhere in Ireland, are any species of vole, woolly rhino *C. antiquitatis* and bison *Bison priscus*. Horse *Equus ferus*, although absent at Castlepook, is recorded elsewhere in Ireland at Shandon Cave, County Waterford, in association with mammoth and reindeer (Brenan 1860; Carte 1860).

Lynx *Felis lynx* is recorded from Kilgreany Cave, County Waterford (Savage 1966). The age of the find is uncertain.

Bones and teeth of *M. primigenius*, *C. antiquitatis*, and other cold stage species, are from time to time dredged from the sea bed in the English Channel and southern North Sea, especially from the Dogger Bank. These finds graphically illustrate the depressed sea level of at least certain phases of the Devensian in comparison with that of the present day (Ch. 2).

Late Devensian (26 000 to 10 000 radiocarbon years B.P.)

The present state of knowledge on the Late Devensian vertebrate faunas is far from satisfactory. Most of the material ascribed to this period is from various cave deposits, most of which were not properly excavated, so that it is impossible to be sure which of the species represented actually lived at any given time. More reliable faunal records are, however, available from a few cave sites, often in association with radiocarbon dates, usually based on bone collagen.

There are also a few sparse faunas available from fluviatile deposits in association with radiocarbon dates and/or pollen spectra. Remarkably complete large-mammal material is available in accurately known stratigraphical context from lacustrine deposits in both Britain and Ireland, but the finds are of one or two species only.

Sands and gravels about 1.5 m thick overlying Gault Clay were exposed near Barnwell Station, Cambridge, early in the present century (Marr & Gardner 1916). These deposits form part of the second terrace of the River Cam. Peaty seams within the sands yielded plant macrofossils and beetles. The former were re-examined by Bell and Dickson (1971) and indicate a rich herbaceous vegetation, together with the shrubs *Betula nana* and *Salix* spp. (willows). Coope (1968b) reappraised the beetle fauna, which he says suggests an open habitat devoid of trees. An arctic climate is indicated by the limited number of species and presence of arctic and arctic-alpine beetles. The radiocarbon date of 19 500 ± 650 years B.P. (Q-590) on plant detritus, which puts these deposits into the early part of the Late Devensian, contradicts Coope's correlation of the Barnwell Station Beds with the closing phases of the Upton Warren interstadial complex (i.e. about 28 000 years B.P.). It is possible, as pointed out by Coope, that the radiocarbon date is too young, as it was made on a peat sample stored for many years previously.

Large-mammal remains found by workmen in the sands and gravels and listed by Marr and Gardner include *M. primigenius*, *E. ferus*, *C. antiquitatis* and *R. tarandus* (Table 8.2), of which only the last two species are represented in the collections of the Sedgwick Museum, Cambridge. Red deer *Cervus elaphus* was also mentioned by these authors, but antlers of this species labelled from nearby pits adjacent to Newmarket Road are included in the Sedgwick Museum collection, and significantly Marr omitted this species from the Barnwell Station lists in subsequent publications.

With the principal exception of the Barnwell Station material, nearly all assemblages of Late Devensian age, appear to date from the end of the substage, conveniently termed 'late-glacial' (*c.* 15 000 to 10 000 years B.P.).

In 1970 an entire associated skeleton of a male elk *Alces alces* was found *in situ* in detritus muds, within a sequence of lacustrine sediments, at High

Fig. 8.6. Hind limb bones of elk *Alces alces in situ* in Late Devensian zone II, lacustrine deposits at High Furlong, Blackpool, Lancashire. (Scale in feet)

Furlong, Blackpool, Lancashire (Hallam *et al.* 1973) (Figs 8.6, 8.7). Pollen analyses showed that the sequence represented pollen zones I to III of the Late Devensian plus part of the Flandrian. The detritus mud bed yielded pollen spectra characteristic of zone L-DeII, and gave radiocarbon dates of 11 665 ± 140 and 12 200 ± 160 years B.P. (IGS-C14/134, IGS-C14/135) which are rather too high. The contemporary vegetation appears to have been birch woodland (tree birch leaves were also found) with juniper, grasses, sedges and other open-ground herbs. Two barbed projectile points were found with the skeleton, which also bears numerous lesions due to injuries by weapons (see Ch. 5). The occurrence of the skeleton, which was clearly not butchered by the hunters, in lacustrine deposits suggests that it may have perished by breaking through thin ice and subsequently drowning, as has been observed to happen with modern animals. This hypothesis finds support from the fact that the antlers were nearly parted from the pedicles at the time of death, i.e. were about to be shed, which indicates winter as the season when the animal died (see Ch. 5).

Another skeleton of *A. alces* was discovered in 1939 at Neasham near Darlington, County Durham (Trechmann 1939). Blackburn (1952) later established that, like the Blackpool specimen, this specimen also came from Late Devensian zone II muds of a former pond or lake. Radiocarbon dates of 11 011 ± 230 and 11 561 ± 250 years B.P. (Q-207, Q-208) were obtained from the muds. The Neasham specimen is also male, but in this case the antlers were found firmly united to the skull (see Hallam *et al.* 1973), so that the season of death is uncertain.

The Pleistocene of Ireland is renowned for the many hundreds of giant deer *Megaceros giganteus* skulls and skeletons which have been found beneath the peat bogs (Figs. 8.8, 8.9). The fossils

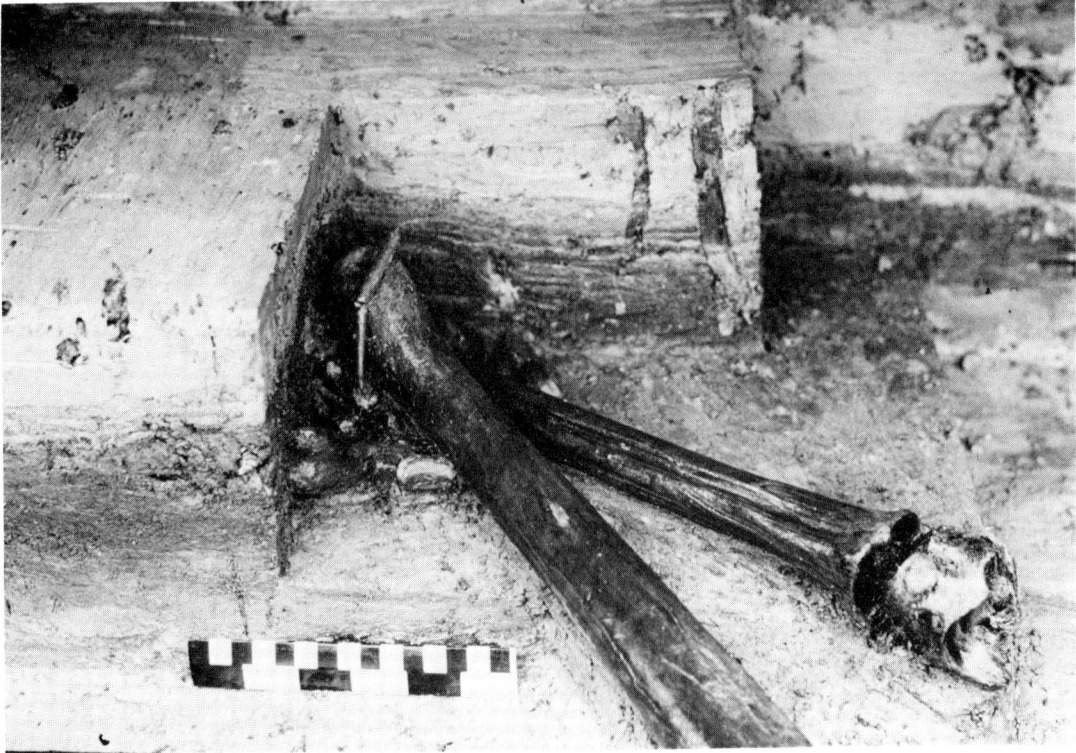

Fig. 8.7. Close-up of metatarsals of High Furlong *Alces alces*, showing barbed projectile point *in situ*.

almost invariably occur in calcareous lacustrine muds which date from Late Midlandian (= Late Devensian) pollen zone II (Mitchell & Parkes 1949). Remains of reindeer *Rangifer tarandus* also occur in the same deposits but are much less common than those of *M. giganteus* (Mitchell 1941). Most specimens were recovered for ornamental purposes, and many are to be seen in Irish country houses as well as in museums throughout the British Isles and elsewhere. Since nearly all the existing specimens are of stags with fine antlers, it is probable that the less spectacular material including skulls of females (the latter probably also confused with domestic horse) was not readily collected. The occurrence of *M. giganteus* remains suggests that the animals perished by being mired in soft mud at the edge of lakes, or perhaps sometimes breaking through thin ice and drowning. This situation would result in a bias towards males which are encumbered by their large antlers, and also explains the relative rarity of *R. tarandus* finds, since the latter are very much smaller and lighter animals. Whole *M. giganteus* skeletons do occur but portions of the skeleton, or detached skull and antlers are usual, suggesting break-up of floating carcasses. The three small bogs in a small steep-sided valley at Ballybetagh near Dublin yielded remains of over 60 individuals, and no doubt more are still entombed in the deposits.

The large numbers of *M. giganteus* remains found have led many authors to conclude that this animal was especially common in Ireland near the end of the Last Cold Stage. This apparent abundance may, however, be simply a result of the widespread existence of such natural traps and the calcareous nature of these lacustrine deposits which has preserved the bones. *M. giganteus* is also recorded from zone L-De II deposits at Ballaugh, Isle of Man (Mitchell & Parkes 1949).

There has been no up-to-date study of an *M. giganteus* find in conjunction with palaeobotanical work, so that the precise history of this animal in Ireland in relation to the vegetational history is unknown. The occurrences of *M. giganteus* and *R. tarandus*, however, most probably correspond to the Gramineae (grass) phase, dating from approximately 12 000 to 10 900 years B.P. The plant assemblage suggests predominant short grassland with small herbs and shrubs and stands of the tree birch *Betula pubescens* (Watts 1977).

Rangifer tarandus, *M. giganteus* and a duck *Anas* sp., mentioned by Jessen and Farrington (1938), are the only taxa of zone II age known from Ireland. A few finds of *R. tarandus* are recorded from overlying horizons, presumably dating from zone III. Very probably, many cave finds also date from the end of the Late Midlandian, although this has yet to be demonstrated since no Irish cave deposits of this age have been properly excavated.

At Flixton near Star Carr, Yorkshire, Late Devensian muds yielded pollen suggesting a date towards the end of pollen zone II. Overlying muds with an early pollen zone III spectrum gave a radiocarbon date of 10 413 ± 210 years B.P. (Q-66). Partial skeletons of three individuals of horse *Equus ferus* were found in the zone II horizon accompanied by a flint point and some bird bones (Clark 1954). The associated pollen spectra indicate open grassy vegetation with perhaps some tree birch.

At Nazeing, Essex, a series of deposits of Late Devensian and Flandrian age occupy a channel cut in Devensian gravels of the River Lea (Allison, Godwin & Warren 1952). The gravels have yielded remains of *M. primigenius*, *C. antiquitatis*, *R. tarandus* and other large mammals. Peat rafts, within these gravels ('Arctic Plant Bed') at Broxbourne near Nazeing, have been radiocarbon dated to about 28 000 years B.P., so that the mammal bones probably represent the late Middle Devensian and the early part of the Late Devensian. Remains of arctic lemming *Dicrostonyx torquatus* and a vole *Microtus* sp. have been found in the same terrace at Angel Road, Edmonton (Warren 1912). The 'Arctic Bed' yielded macroscopic plant fossils indicating a tundra-like flora with sedges, grasses and a variety of other open-ground herbs.

The earliest channel deposits ('peaty muds' of beds AB4, B4) appear to be of Late Devensian pollen zone II age or slightly earlier. Small mammals from this bed include Norway lemming *Lemmus lemmus* and northern vole *Microtus oeconomus*. The pollen indicates grass sedge tundra or park tundra. Overlying calcareous muds (Beds 'M' in part) pollen dated to the end of zone L-De III yielded remains of *D. torquatus*, tundra vole *Microtus gregalis*, *M. oeconomus*, frog *Rana* sp., toad *Bufo* sp. and common lizard *Lacerta vivipara*. Fossil pollen and

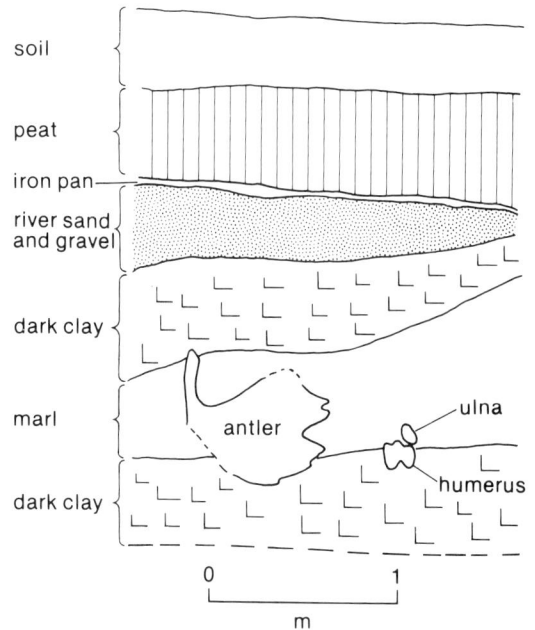

Fig. 8.8. Field sketch (after J. P. O'Connor) showing stratigraphical position of *in situ* find of giant deer *Megaceros giganteus* at Craddanstown, Co. Meath, Ireland, in 1976.

macroscopic plant remains indicate a typical lateglacial flora with many herbs and dwarf birch *Betula nana*.

The faunas of the Flandrian deposits at Nazeing are discussed in Chapter 7.

Gravels and sands of the River Gipping at Sproughton near Ipswich, Suffolk, have yielded barbed projectile points and remains of horse *Equus ferus* and reindeer *Rangifer tarandus* (Wymer *et al.* 1975). A find of the former species was bracketed between radiocarbon dates of 9 880 and 11 370 years B.P., lying stratigraphically much closer to the younger date, i.e. probably towards the end of pollen zone III. The *R. tarandus* finds probably date from zone III or possibly a little earlier.

A fossil vertebrate assemblage of probable Late Devensian age was found in a series of sands and limestone breccias banked up against a 'fossil' Pleistocene sea cliff at Brean Down near Weston–Super-Mare, Somerset (Apsimon, Donovan & Taylor 1961). The fauna includes arctic fox *Alopex lagopus*, horse *Equus ferus* and reindeer *Rangifer tarandus*.

The faunas from a number of cave deposits in England are distinctive in lacking *M. primigenius*, *C. antiquitatis*, etc., whereas the steppe pika *Ocho-*

Fig. 8.9. Excavation of skull of *Megaceros giganteus* at Craddanstown.

tona pusilla is commonly present. Unfortunately, few of these faunas can be relied upon to date from a single horizon, largely because of contamination with younger material, but in a few cases carefully excavated material is available. The fauna from a single horizon in Ossom's Cave in the Manifold Valley, Staffordshire, *identified by D. Bramwell* (personal communication) includes: *D. torquatus; L. lemmus*; several voles, *E. ferus; R. tarandus*; red deer *C. elaphus*; eagle owl *Bubo bubo*; grouse *Lagopus lagopus*; ptarmigan *Lagopus mutus*; black grouse *Lyrurus tetrix*; corncrake *Crex crex*; jackdaw *Corvus monedula*; and missel thrush *Turdus viscivorus*. A radiocarbon date of 10 590 ± 70 years B.P. obtained from bone collagen suggests that the fauna was associated with the harsh climatic conditions of Devensian late-glacial pollen zone III.

Birds of probable Late Devensian age from a number of cave sites were discussed by Bramwell (1960), and more recently the same author has listed the Late Devensian avian and mammalian cave faunas of the Peak District, Derbyshire (Bramwell 1977). Campbell (1977) also lists faunas attributed to Late Devensian horizons from several caves in central and south-western England. These faunal lists generally resemble those from Ossom's Cave and other sites dating from the end of the Late Devensian. The records of temperate taxa, if correctly attributed to this time range, may largely date from the Windermere Interstadial. Remains of glutton *Gulo gulo*, known from a few sites in Britain including: Plas Heaton Cave, N. Wales (Dawkins, 1871); Wetton Mill Rock Shelter, Staffordshire and Chelm's Coombe Rock Shelter, Mendip (Bramwell, 1976); may be entirely or partly of Late Devensian age.

One find of musk ox *Ovibos moschatus* has been dated to the Late Devensian. (Table 8.3). The record from Maidenhead, Berkshire from the low terrace of the River Thames (Owen, 1856) is very probably also of Devensian age.

Devensian Faunal History

The faunal history of the Devensian is much more complex than those of the interglacial stages, because of the much longer time span and the multiple climatic cycles covered by this cold stage.

Of the taxa represented, good fossil records are available for mammoth *Mammuthus primigenius*, woolly rhino *Coelodonta antiquitatis*, horse *Equus ferus*, reindeer *Rangifer tarandus*, extinct bison *Bison priscus* and, to a lesser extent, brown bear *Ursus arctos*. Fossil mammal assemblages from the Early Devensian and the peak of the Upton Warren Interstadial (early Middle Devensian – about 43 000 years B.P.) are dominated by remains of *B. priscus*. *Rangifer tarandus* also occurs but *E. ferus* and *M. primigenius* are only sparsely represented. In faunas from later in the Middle Devensian, however, *B. priscus* becomes much scarcer, with *M. primigenius* and *E. ferus* now abundant, and *B. priscus* may have become extinct in Britain soon after the beginning of the Late Devensian (Fig. 8.5). As noted by Rackham (1978) the relative abundance of *B. priscus* appears to correspond rather closely to the temperature curve inferred from beetle faunas constructed by Coope (see Fig. 2.4). This probably indicates, by analogy with modern species of bison (Ch. 5), that during relatively warm periods a richer growth of herbs was able to support large herds of grazing *B. priscus*, whereas the deteriorating climatic conditions of the later Middle Devensian, and much of the Late Devensian allowed the growth of only poorer quality graze, which was, however, sufficient for *M. primigenius*, *C. antiquitatis* and *E. ferus* (Ch. 5). The amelioration of climate of the Windermere Interstadial was, however, probably not accompanied by the return of *B. priscus*.

Mammuthus primigenius and *C. antiquitatis* are conspicuously absent from the numerous assemblages which can be attributed with varying precision to the end of the Late Devensian ('late glacial'), post-dating the main glaciation of about 18 000 to 15 000 years B.P. Both species, however, appear to have been present immediately prior to this event (Fig. 8.5).

The virtual absence of radiocarbon-dated records, including those of man (Ch. 10), suggests that few vertebrates were able to persist in those areas not covered by ice south of the ice sheets, and that the faunas from the 'late glacial' therefore resulted from re-immigration from the Continent, to which the British Isles would have been broadly connected at this time (Ch. 2).

Mammuthus primigenius and *C. antiquitatis* evidently failed to return after the main glaciation, probably because they had become rare or extinct on the Continent by this late date.

Other species which did not return in the Devensian 'late glacial' include the carnivores lion *Panthera leo* and spotted hyaena *Crocuta crocuta*.

On the other hand, the arctic fox *Alopex lagopus*, lemmings *Lemmus lemmus* and *Dicrostonyx torquatus*, together with *E. ferus* and *R. tarandus* survived until the very end of the Late Devensian (Fig. 8.5), and their disappearance by the beginning of Flandrian can readily be attributed to the amelioration of climate and spread of forests. Northern vole *Microtus oeconomus* lasted into the early Flandrian. Other species with wide tolerances, such as the red fox *Vulpes vulpes*, may have been present in Britain during much of the Devensian, as this animal was throughout the Flandrian.

Two species, the steppe pika *Ochotona pusilla* and elk *Alces alces*, appear to be unique in the Devensian to the period *c.* 15 000 to 10 000 years B.P. The giant deer *Megaceros giganteus*, like *A. alces* apparently restricted in the 'late glacial' to the milder interstadial conditions of zone L-De II in both Britain and Ireland, is however also sparsely recorded from the Middle Devensian (Fig. 8.5). Its scarcity suggests that it may have migrated into the British Isles only during interstadials.

Of particular interest is the Devensian history of red deer *Cervus elaphus*, which also has a sparse fossil record for this stage. It is recorded in association with the boreal forests of the Chelford Interstadial, but also appears to have been present during colder periods (e.g. at Picken's Hole *c.* 34 265 years B.P.). The latter may represent a distinct open-ground ecotype. Equally intriguing is the sparse record of musk ox *Ovibos moschatus*. The single radiocarbon date of 18 213 years B.P. suggests that this animal may have occurred in Britain only during the more arctic phases of the Last Cold Stage. The rarity of lion *Panthera leo*, spotted hyaena *Crocuta crocuta* (and possibly leopard *Panthera pardus*) in faunas of Devensian age also suggests that they also were present only at certain periods within the stage.

The Irish Devensian (Midlandian) faunas show some interesting differences and similarities to those of Britain. In the Middle Devensian, lion *Panthera leo*, *Coelodonta antiquitatis*, *Bison priscus* and the various species of vole were for some reason unable to cross over to Ireland via the link with south-west Scotland, while many other mammals were successful in doing so. Ireland was largely covered by ice within the Late Devensian so that the

Irish 'late glacial' fauna represents a fresh immigration of animals via Britain. Only two species – *Rangifer tarandus* and *Megaceros giganteus* – have been dated to this period, but the high probability that many cave deposits are of 'late glacial' age allows us to infer that certain species, well represented in Britain, were almost certainly absent from Ireland. These include elk *Alces alces*, *Ochotona pusilla*, and all species of voles.

The relative impoverishment of the Irish Devensian faunas in comparison with those of England could be due to climatic differences, or alternatively could reflect topographical, climatic or vegetational conditions in the vicinity of the land connection between Britain and Ireland, which could have filtered out potential immigrants.

Comparison with Continental faunas

Fossil vertebrates dating from the Last Cold Stage are known from numerous sites in Europe across to northern Asia and North America. Broadly similar assemblages with *Mammuthus primigenius*, *Equus ferus*, *Coelodonta antiquitatis*, *Rangifer tarandus*, *Dicrostonyx torquatus*, *Lemmus lemmus* and other species typical of the British Devensian, occur from southern France to Siberia (Klein 1971), but few faunas are precisely dated or can be accurately related to climatic and vegetational changes. Pre–late glacial faunas from central Europe show a stronger steppe component than those from Britain, with, for example, jerboa *Allactaga jaculus*, pika *Ochotona pusilla*, and a greater number of records of saiga *Saiga tartarica* (Kahlke 1975b).

Last Cold Stage ('Würmian') faunas from southern France, well represented in cave deposits, are conventionally assigned to phases Würm I, II, III and IV. Arctic species such as arctic fox *Alopex lagopus*, lemmings *D. torquatus* and *L. lemmus*, woolly rhino *C. antiquitatis*, mammoth *M. pri-*

migenius, and even rare musk ox *Ovibos moschatus* occur, as in Britain. The southern French faunas, however, also include: red deer *Cervus elaphus*, from all four phases; aurochs *Bos primigenius*; ass *Equus hydruntinus*; rhinos *Dicerorhinus* spp.; fat dormouse *Glis glis*; and other temperate or southern species (Lumley 1976), reflecting milder climatic conditions than in Britain, probably accompanied by the growth of woodland.

Such elements are especially marked in, but by no means confined to, the earliest phase 'Würm I'. The montane ibex *Capra ibex* and chamois *Rupicapra rupicapra* are well represented in French 'Würmian' cave deposits, as in those of the previous cold stage.

European faunas dating from the 'late glacial' (i.e. between about 15 000 and 10 000 years B.P.) all appear to lack *C. antiquitatis*, *M. primigenius* and several other species represented earlier in the Last Cold Stage. There are, however, several isolated finds of *M. primigenius* with radiocarbon dates of about 13 000 years B.P. and even younger, from France, Switzerland, European Russia and Scandinavia (Berglund *et al.* 1976), which, if correct, indicate that mammoth survived until almost the end of the Last Cold stage in some areas.

The best-dated 'late glacial' (Late Weichselian) faunas are from Denmark and north Germany. Vertebrate assemblages mostly obtained from archaeological sites have been dated by pollen analyses to particular zones within the Late Weichselian (Degerbøl 1964). The faunas are generally very similar to those from the British Isles, although Russian desman *Desmana moschata* (zones Ia, III), *Spermophilus major* (Ia, III), and of particular interest European bison *Bison bonasus* (zone III) are recorded from north Germany and Denmark. The more continental situation of the Holstein sites is reflected in the occurrences of *Bos primigenius*, wild boar *Sus scrofa* and elk *Alces alces* in zone III.

9 Faunal history

Chapters 7 and 8 are concerned with the faunal history within interglacial and cold stages respectively. In this chapter the overall changes in the vertebrate faunas through the entire Pleistocene are considered.

Lower Pleistocene

Because most of the deposits are marine and generally contain only sparse fossils of non-marine origin, the vertebrate faunas of the Lower Pleistocene in Britain are much less well known than those of the Middle and Upper Pleistocene. Moreover, there are undoubted hiatuses in the known stratigraphical sequence, which will probably prove more complex with further work.

It is, however, possible to discern some important faunal changes. The Red Crag Nodule Bed fauna, of mixed provenance, includes a number of Lower Villafranchian, i.e. Pliocene taxa which have not been recorded from later horizons (see Ch. 6). The most significant changes within the Lower Pleistocene are probably the disappearance of the gomphothere *Anancus arvernensis* and the deer *Eucladoceros falconeri* prior to the Pre-Pastonian. Both species are widely recorded in the earlier crags and the former in particular is very easily identified and unlikely to be overlooked where present. The complete absence of *A. arvernensis* from the comparatively rich faunas of the Pre-Pastonian and Pastonian stages of the Cromer Forest-bed Formation was pointed out repeatedly during the last century. Similarly, gazelles *Gazella* spp. are absent from the youngest Lower Pleistocene deposits.

Middle and Upper Pleistocene

There are very marked faunal differences between the Pre-Pastonian/Pastonian stages and the Cromerian stage. In particular, the older horizons contain exclusively voles with rooted cheek teeth (*Mimomys pliocaenicus*, *M. newtoni*, etc.) whereas the Cromerian has yielded mainly advanced voles with permanently growing non-rooted cheek teeth (*Microtus* spp., *Pitymys* spp.) and the phylogenetically most advanced species of *Mimomys* – *M. savini*. Similarly, the earlier deer faunas are characterized by several species of *Eucladoceros*, whereas those of the Cromerian are equally characterized by the appearance of *Megaceros*, *Dama*, *Cervus elaphus*, and others. A few taxa, e.g. *Dicerorhinus etruscus* and *Trogontherium cuvieri*, nevertheless do occur in both the Cromerian and the Pre-Pastonian/Pastonian horizons.

These faunal differences are not, however, the result of sudden environmental changes, but are entirely consistent with other evidence for a stratigraphical hiatus within the Cromer Forest-bed Formation, probably representing a considerable period of time (Ch. 2).

The stratigraphical ranges of those Middle and Upper Pleistocene taxa for which adequate fossil records are available, is presented in Fig. 9.1. It is apparent that with the exception of Devensian faunas, the faunas of the interglacials are much better known and more accurately dated than those from the cold stages. A faunal history of the Middle and Upper Pleistocene is therefore largely restricted to an account of the faunal changes in successive interglacials.

When making comparisons between fossil and modern faunas, due allowance has to be made for the inevitable incompleteness of the former. A

Table 9.1. Overall patterns of change in terrestrial mammalian faunas from zones II, III of successive interglacials. In calculating gains and losses, species not recorded from a particular interglacial, but recorded both before and after, are counted as present. The numbers of species *actually* recorded are included to demonstrate the varying completeness of the fossil record.

	Cromerian	Hoxnian	Ipswichian	Flandrian (species with fossil record only)
Numbers of species *actually* recorded from each stage	46	29	32	25
Numbers assumed present for purposes of calculation	46	39	37	25
Gains (cf. previous stages)	—	11	7	1
Losses (cf. previous stages)	—	18	9	13

Table 9.2. Numbers of terrestrial mammalian species, by taxonomic groups, recorded as fossils from zones II, III of successive interglacials, compared with the modern indigenous faunas (including recent extinctions) of Britain and the adjacent Continent. (The latter is given to compensate for the impoverishment of the British fauna due to early Flandrian isolation from the Continent).

	Cromerian	Hoxnian	Ipswichian	Flandrian Britain	Belgium and N.E. France
Insectivora	9	1	4	5	7
Primates (including man)	1	2	1	1	1
Lagomorpha	1	1	1	2	1
Rodentia	12	9	6	9	13
Carnivora	11	6	8	9	10
Proboscidea	1	1	2	0	0
Perissodactyla	2	3	2	0	0
Artiodactyla	9	6	8	4	5
Total	46	29	32	30	37

comparison of the earliest and latest records of particular species in the typical interglacial assemblages dating from pollen zones II and III of each interglacial, indicates that the rate of extinction has generally exceeded the rate of replacement either by immigration of new species from elsewhere or by evolution from earlier European species (Table 9.1).

More detailed analysis by taxonomic groups (Table 9.2) needs careful interpretation because of the uneven coverage of the fossil record. In particular, the low values for the Hoxnian are due to the paucity of known vertebrate assemblages of this age, and the apparent increase in Carnivora in the

Flandrian is because of their relative rarity as fossils. From the Cromerian to the Ipswichian the progressive decrease in overall faunal diversity mainly involved the Insectivora and Rodentia, although there was considerable turnover in species within the other groups. By contrast, the faunal changes from the Ipswichian to the Flandrian are essentially restricted to the extinction of several large mammals with no replacement by other taxa (see below).

The progressive trend of decreasing species diversity, leaving out for the moment the late Pleistocene extinctions, can be seen in the fossil records for Continental Europe, both in mammal faunas

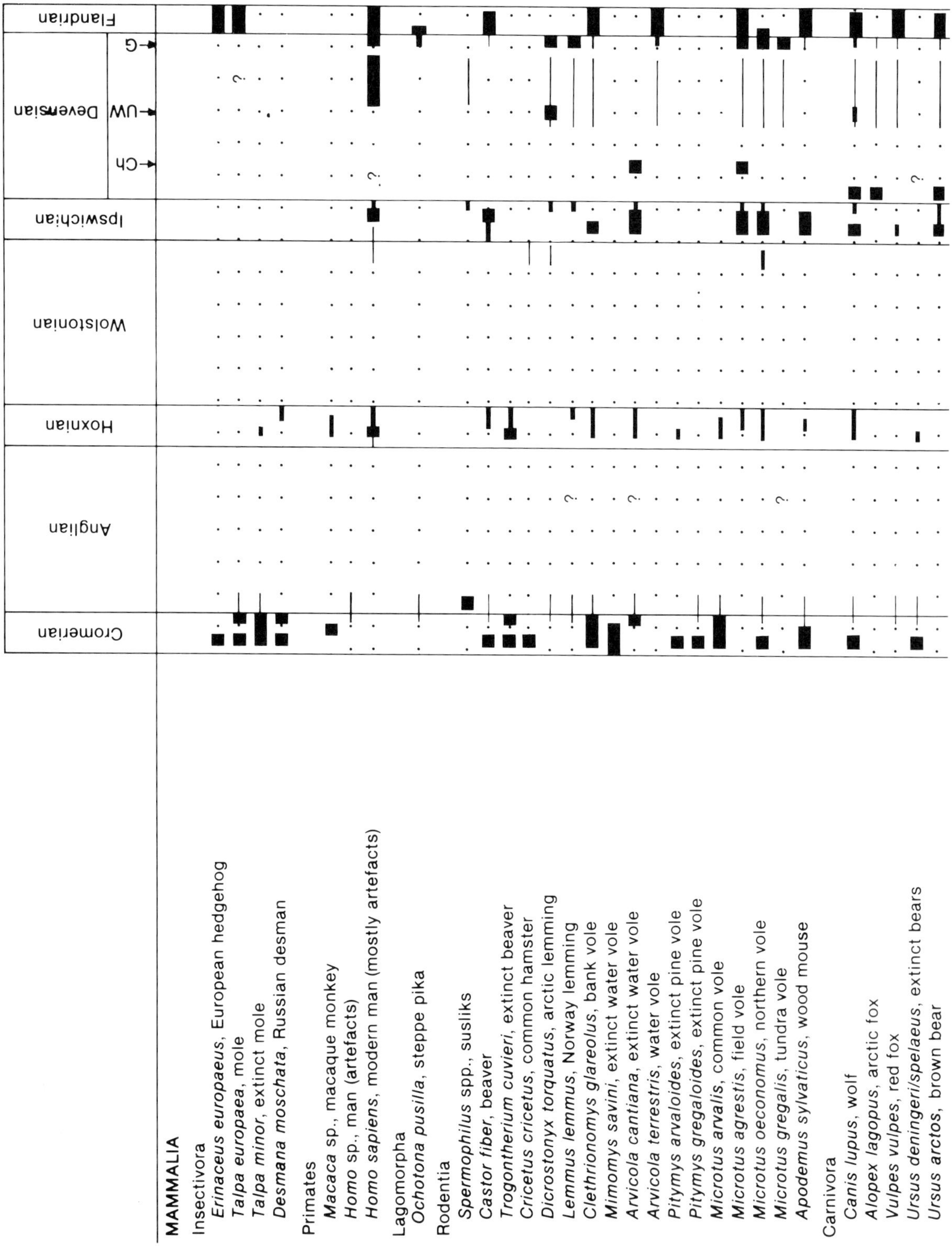

Flandrian

Devensian — G, UW, Ch

Ipswichian

Wolstonian

Hoxnian

Anglian

Cromerian

MAMMALIA

Insectivora
Erinaceus europaeus, European hedgehog
Talpa europaea, mole
Talpa minor, extinct mole
Desmana moschata, Russian desman

Primates
Macaca sp., macaque monkey
Homo sp., man (artefacts)
Homo sapiens, modern man (mostly artefacts)

Lagomorpha
Ochotona pusilla, steppe pika

Rodentia
Spermophilus spp., susliks
Castor fiber, beaver
Trogontherium cuvieri, extinct beaver
Cricetus cricetus, common hamster
Dicrostonyx torquatus, arctic lemming
Lemmus lemmus, Norway lemming
Clethrionomys glareolus, bank vole
Mimomys savini, extinct water vole
Arvicola cantiana, extinct water vole
Arvicola terrestris, water vole
Pitymys arvaloides, extinct pine vole
Pitymys gregaloides, extinct pine vole
Microtus arvalis, common vole
Microtus agrestis, field vole
Microtus oeconomus, northern vole
Microtus gregalis, tundra vole
Apodemus sylvaticus, wood mouse

Carnivora
Canis lupus, wolf
Alopex lagopus, arctic fox
Vulpes vulpes, red fox
Ursus deningeri/spelaeus, extinct bears
Ursus arctos, brown bear

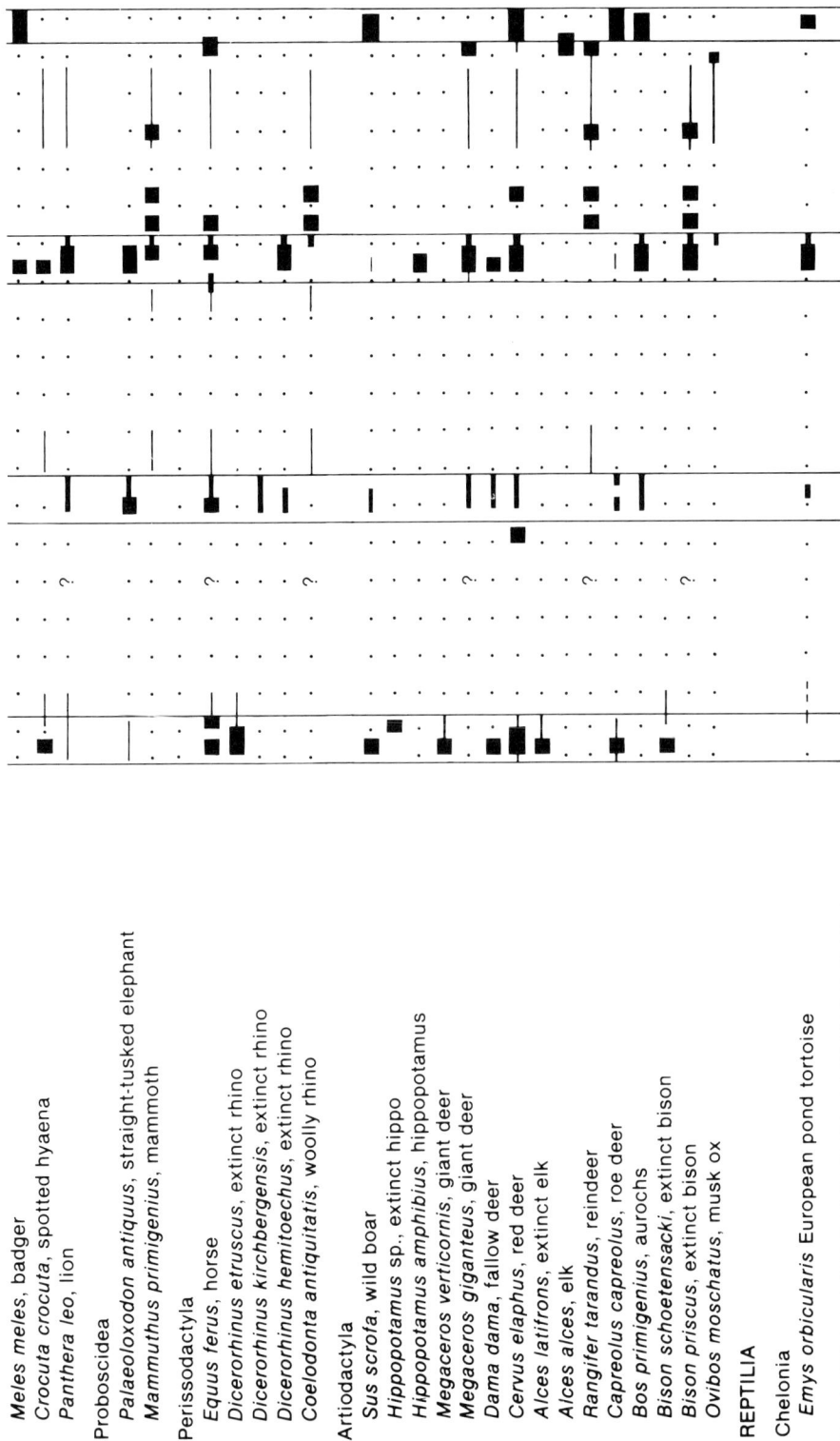

Fig. 9.1. Synthesis of faunal history of the Middle and Upper Pleistocene, for well-represented taxa only. Note that the relative time scale allotted to each stage is schematic.

Meles meles, badger
Crocuta crocuta, spotted hyaena
Panthera leo, lion

Proboscidea
Palaeoloxodon antiquus, straight-tusked elephant
Mammuthus primigenius, mammoth

Perissodactyla
Equus ferus, horse
Dicerorhinus etruscus, extinct rhino
Dicerorhinus kirchbergensis, extinct rhino
Dicerorhinus hemitoechus, extinct rhino
Coelodonta antiquitatis, woolly rhino

Artiodactyla
Sus scrofa, wild boar
Hippopotamus sp., extinct hippo
Hippopotamus amphibius, hippopotamus
Megaceros verticornis, giant deer
Megaceros giganteus, giant deer
Dama dama, fallow deer
Cervus elaphus, red deer
Alces latifrons, extinct elk
Alces alces, elk
Rangifer tarandus, reindeer
Capreolus capreolus, roe deer
Bos primigenius, aurochs
Bison schoetensacki, extinct bison
Bison priscus, extinct bison
Ovibos moschatus, musk ox

REPTILIA
Chelonia
Emys orbicularis European pond tortoise

Key
Ch.   Chelford Interstadial
UW. Peak of Upton Warren Interstadial
G   Main Devensian glaciation

▮ Well-dated records based on pollen, radiocarbon, historical records
│ Probable occurrences based on other evidence for dating
─ Probable uncertainty ranges for poorly-dated records
? Dating even to stage not certain

and plants. The phenomenon is presumably the result of the repeated climatic fluctuations causing continual shifts in the distributions of plants and animals, with attendant intensification of competition. Competition is likely to have been especially heightened during cold stages due to the geography of Europe, i.e. with the east-west Alpine mountains and bounded by the Mediterranean to the south, which would have provided only limited refugia for temperate and southern species. Comparison of the European Middle and Upper Pleistocene faunas with those of the Lower Pleistocene gives an impression of accelerated faunal turnover involving increased rates of evolution, extinction and immigration of new forms.

The two known faunas of probable Anglian age are closely similar to those known from the Devensian. The same can be said of the Wolstonian faunas, with the exception of the Glutton and Bear Strata of Tornewton Cave, Devon, which contain hamsters and the steppe lemming *Lagurus lagurus*, none of which is known from the Devensian. Unfortunately, as discussed in Chapter 7, the exact provenance of the fossils from these horizons is uncertain, although a Wolstonian age for most of the material seems probable. At present, therefore, we have little evidence of faunal change from one cold stage to another in the Middle and Upper Pleistocene of Britain.

Late Pleistocene extinctions

The question of what caused the greatly accelerated rate of extinction of large mammals in many parts of the world in the late Pleistocene is one of the most intriguing unsolved mysteries in palaeontology. Much thorough research needs to be done on this subject, but the extinctions appear to have been especially marked in North and South America, Australia, and to a lesser extent Europe and Asia (Martin & Wright 1967).

Of the mammals present in north-west Europe during the middle of the Eemian/Ipswichian Interglacial, *Ursus spelaeus*, *Palaeoloxodon antiquus*, *Mammuthus primigenius*, *Dicerorhinus hemitoechus*, *D. kirchbergensis* (if correctly identified), *Megaceros giganteus* and *Bison priscus* became completely extinct in the course of the Weichselian/Devensian Cold Stage, as did *Coelodonta antiquitatis*, known from

the end of the Ipswichian as well as from cold-stage faunas. In addition, *Crocuta crocuta* and *Panthera leo*, known from both interglacial and cold-stage faunas, *Hippopotamus amphibius*, present in the Ipswichian interglacial, and *Ovibos moschatus*, recorded from the late Ipswichian and sparsely from cold stages, are now absent from Europe, although the lion *P. leo* was present in the Balkans in historical times (see Ch. 5). The timing of these extinctions is difficult to assess accurately, but *P. antiquus* and *Dicerorhinus* spp. may have survived in the still forested parts of southern Europe into at least the early part of the Last Cold Stage (Freeman 1973). The cave bear *U. spelaeus* appears to have become extinct by the middle of the Last Cold Stage. On the other hand, the spotted hyaena *C. crocuta*, lion *P. leo*, mammoth *M. primigenius*, woolly rhinoceros *C. antiquitatis*, bison *B. priscus* and musk ox *O. moschatus* survived late enough to be depicted by the cave artists of southern Europe, i.e. probably well after about 25 000 years B.P. None of these animals is recorded from faunas from the very end of the Last Cold Stage, i.e. later than about 14 000 radiocarbon years B.P., but radiocarbon dates on individual mammoth finds suggests that this species may perhaps have survived until nearly 10 000 radiocarbon years B.P. in some parts of western Europe (Berglund *et al.* 1976). As with other dates based on isolated finds, however, there is always uncertainty as to their reliability.

The records for *C. antiquitatis* and *M. primigenius* in the Devensian of the British Isles are discussed in Chapter 8.

The giant deer *Megaceros giganteus* is last recorded from pollen zone II of the Late Devensian and Late Weichselian of north-west Europe, i.e. not later than about 11 500 years B.P.

Of the 13 species of large herbivores with body weights exceeding 200 kg, known from the Upper Pleistocene of Europe, 9 were extinct in Europe before the end of the Last Cold Stage. Of the 8 species with body weights over 600 kg (the rhinoceroses, *Bos*, *Bison*, *Hippopotamus* and the elephants), 7 were lost from the European fauna, and the sole survivor *Bos primigenius* was exterminated, in its wild form, by man in historical times. Similarly, of the 4 largest Carnivora exceeding 50 kg body weight, known from the European Upper Pleistocene, 3 became extinct prior to the Flandrian; the exception being the brown bear *Ursus arctos*.

The possibility that these extinctions were partly

or entirely due to human interference is discussed in Chapter 10. In the event, as seems very probable, that the hunting activities of early man would not have had sufficient impact on the fauna, it is extremely difficult to find natural phenomena that will account for the greatly increased rate of extinction in the late Pleistocene of Europe or elsewhere.

The most frequently suggested alternatives to the human 'overkill' hypothesis are: (a) that the fauna of the Last Cold Stage was adapted to the 'steppe-tundra' biome, and many were unable to survive when this disappeared at the end of the stage (e.g. Kowalski, in Martin & Wright 1967); and (b) that many animals were exterminated as the result of severe cold towards the end of the stage. Neither hypothesis takes into account that the fauna adjusted successfully, with few casualties, to the very similar changes of climatic and vegetational conditions during previous cold stage/interglacial cycles, and that in any case conditions did not remain stable for long periods within stages either. There is no evidence as yet for any unprecedented climatic or other event within the Last Cold Stage which could be linked to the extinction phenomenon.

Since these extinctions of large mammals occurred in the late Plcistocene, and fall within the range of radiocarbon dating, the potential for intensive study of the subject is considerable. A precise knowledge of the pattern and timing of extinctions in different areas in relation to climatic, vegetational and other changes and to human populations and technology is essential before we can begin to determine the causes.

Stratigraphical significance of fossil vertebrate records

Lower Pleistocene faunas as a whole in Britain and Continental Europe are characterized by the occurrence of a wide range of voles of the genus *Mimomys*, the comb-antlered deer *Eucladoceros* spp., the gomphothere *Anancus arvernensis*, the horse *Equus stenonis*, gazelles *Gazella* sp. and other taxa. The faunal changes through the Lower Pleistocene outlined above, can be used as a rough guide to the broad age of unknown faunas.

The following taxa recorded from the Middle and Upper Pleistocene of Britain appear to be char-acteristic of interglacial stages only (rare taxa are omitted):

Macaca
Trogontherium cuvieri
Clethrionomys glareolus
Pitymys arvaloides
Apodemus sylvaticus
Palaeoloxodon antiquus

Dicerorhinus
Sus scrofa
Hippopotamus spp.
Dama dama
Capreolus capreolus
Bos primigenius
Emys orbicularis

Similarly, apart from the exceptions noted, the following appear to have been restricted to cold stages:

Spermophilus spp. (?also late Ipswichian)
Dicrostonyx torquatus (?also late Ipswichian)
Microtus gregalis (occurs at Westbury)
Alopex lagopus
Mammuthus primigenius (also Ipswichian)
Coelodonta antiquitatis (?also late Ipswichian)
Rangifer tarandus
Ovibos moschatus (?also late Ipswichian)

It will be apparent from the above that interglacial faunal assemblages are more easily recognizable as such than are those of cold stages. It is quite possible, however, that many taxa regarded as characteristic of interglacials were also present in interstadials, since few interstadial faunas have so far been discovered.

The faunas of two of the three Middle and Upper Pleistocene cold stages are insufficiently well known to attempt to define faunal differences between them.

The occurrences of many taxa in the much better-studied interglacial stages are contrastingly almost certainly of stratigraphical significance, and the vertebrate faunal list from a site may often enable the deposits to be assigned to a particular interglacial. These occurrences (Table 9.3) reflect patterns of immigration, evolution and extinction, and evidence from the Continent suggests that many of these changes were approximately synchronous over much of Europe and beyond.

The Flandrian is marked even from its outset by the lack of many large mammals that were present in earlier interglacials. Flandrian faunal assemblages from after about 6 000 years B.P. are of course also likely to include taxa introduced by man.

Table 9.3. Interglacial occurrences of important mammalian taxa.

	Cr	Ho	Ip	Fl
Sorex araneus, common shrew	−	(+)	+	+
Sorex savini, S. runtonensis, Beremendia cf. *fissidens*, extinct shrews	+	−	−	−
Talpa minor, extinct mole	+	(+)	−	−
Desmana moschata, Russian desman	+	+	−	−
Macaca sp., macaque monkey	+	+	−	−
Trogontherium cuvieri, extinct beaver	+	+	−	−
Mimomys savini, extinct water vole	+[1]	−	−	−
Arvicola cantiana, extinct water vole	+[1]	+	+	−
Arvicola terrestris, water vole	−	−	−	+
Pitymys arvaloides, extinct pine vole	+	+	−	−
Microtus agrestis, short-tailed vole	−	+	+	+
Pliomys episcopalis, extinct vole	+	−	−	−
Ursus deningeri/spelaeus, extinct bears	+	+	−	−
Ursus arctos, brown bear	−	−	+	+
Panthera leo, lion	+[2]	+	+	−
Crocuta crocuta, spotted hyaena	+	−	+	−
Palaeoloxodon antiquus, straight-tusked elephant	+[3]	+	+	−
Mammuthus primigenius, mammoth	−	−	+[4]	−
Dicerorhinus etruscus, extinct rhinoceros	+	−	−	−
Dicerorhinus hemitoechus, extinct rhinoceros	−	+	+	−
Hippopotamus spp., hippopotamuses	+	−	+	−
Megaceros verticornis, M. savini, M. dawkinsi, giant deer	+	−	−	−
Megaceros giganteus, giant deer	−	+	+	−
Dama dama, fallow deer	+	+	+	−
Alces latifrons, extinct elk	+	−	−	−
Alces alces, elk	−	−	−	+
Bos primigenius, aurochs	−	+	+	+
Bison schoetensacki, extinct bison	+	−	−	−
Bison priscus, extinct bison	−	−	+	−

Cr : Cromerian   1. *A. cantiana* is known from zone Cr IV, *M. savini* from Cr II, Cr III.
Ho: Hoxnian   2. Single CF–bF find, probably Cromerian
Ip : Ipswichian   3. Several CF–bF finds, probably Cromerian
Fl : Flandrian   4. Zones Ip III, IV only.

10 Man in the Pleistocene of the British Isles

Introduction

For almost his entire history on earth, man's existence has been intimately interwoven with those of his vertebrate relations. Until about 10 000 years ago the economic basis of human life everywhere was by hunting and food-gathering, but after this date animals and crops were first domesticated in south-west Asia. Farming communities, however, did not penetrate as far as the British Isles until after 6 000 years B.P., and to the far north of Europe very much later.

Record of man in Europe

Homo erectus appears to have been the first species of man to expand beyond his probable origins in Africa; spreading as far as China and southern Asia in the Middle Pleistocene. The earliest European sites with skeletal remains of man, regarded either as an advanced *H. erectus* or early form of *H. sapiens* (Mauer, West Germany, and Vértesszöllös, Hungary), are of approximately Cromerian age, i.e. early Middle Pleistocene. Skulls of Holsteinian/ Hoxnian Interglacial age are referable to an early form of modern man *Homo sapiens*, but material dating from the Eemian Interglacial and the early part of the Last Cold Stage (Weichselian) is of Neanderthal man *Homo sapiens neanderthalis* (Ch. 3). Later finds are all attributed to modern man.

Presumably, from the Middle Pleistocene onwards human populations were continuously present in at least some areas of Europe.

Record of man in the British Isles

The detailed evidence for man's presence in Britain during the Pleistocene is in many ways rather unsatisfactory, since beyond the range of radiocarbon dating, few finds of artefacts or bones can be precisely related to pollen stratigraphy. It is clear, however, from the summary in Fig. 10.1 that the British Isles were not continuously occupied, although there may have been more occupation within the pre-Devensian cold stages than is shown here.

Lower and Middle Palaeolithic finds are virtually confined to southern and eastern England, with sparse evidence from the north and west, including Wales. Upper Palaeolithic populations possibly reached Scotland but not Ireland, and Mesolithic man was the first to spread over the entire British Isles.

Archaeology of man in the British Isles

The following brief account of the British archaeological sequence is based largely on very useful reviews by Mellars (1974) and Wymer (1977).

Lower and Middle Palaeolithic

The vast bulk of the evidence for the prehistory of man in the British Isles comes from artefacts. There is an overall succession of assemblages of

Thousands of years B.P.		Record of Man	Industry	Example Sites

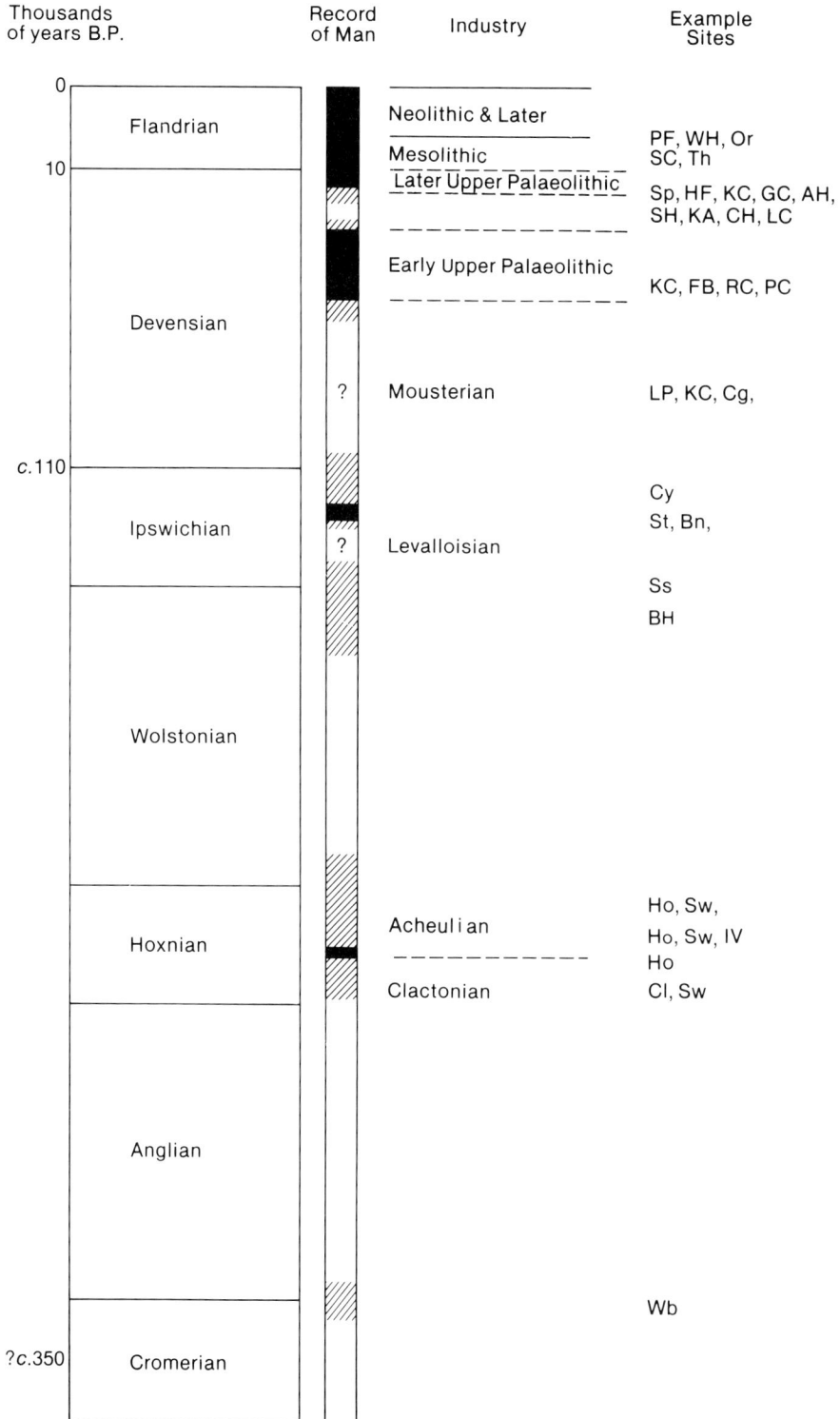

Thousands of years B.P.	Stage	Industry	Example Sites
0	Flandrian	Neolithic & Later	
			PF, WH, Or
10		Mesolithic	SC, Th
		Later Upper Palaeolithic	Sp, HF, KC, GC, AH, SH, KA, CH, LC
	Devensian	Early Upper Palaeolithic	KC, FB, RC, PC
		? Mousterian	LP, KC, Cg,
c.110			Cy
	Ipswichian		St, Bn,
		? Levalloisian	Ss
			BH
	Wolstonian		
	Hoxnian	Acheulian	Ho, Sw,
			Ho, Sw, IV
		-----------	Ho
		Clactonian	Cl, Sw
	Anglian		
			Wb
?c.350	Cromerian		

artefact types (industries) with time, which are named after the sites from which they were first described. The precise uses of many of the tools, e.g. hand-axes, are uncertain, although microwear studies promise to clarify this problem.

None of the many supposed artefacts found in the Lower Pleistocene crags of East Anglia is unequivocally of human manufacture, and it seems very probable that man had not reached the British Isles at this time.

The earliest plausible, although scanty, evidence for human occupation in Britain comes from the cave deposits of Westbury-sub-Mendip in Somerset (Bishop 1975). The artefacts comprise flint flakes and what may be a small broken hand-axe (Wymer 1977). As discussed in Chapter 7, these were found in association with a mammal fauna, probably dating from the end of the Cromerian and certainly pre-dating the Hoxnian. A series of crude hand-axes from Kent's Cavern, Devon, may also date from approximately this time, but the documentation of these old finds in relation to a possible 'Cromerian' fauna in this cave is unsatisfactory.

There is little or no evidence for the presence of man in Britain during the Anglian Cold Stage, in marked contrast to the abundance of artefacts available from the succeeding Hoxnian interglacial. The freshwater deposits of the Clacton Channel, probably dating in the main from subzone Ho IIb of the Hoxnian Interglacial (Ch. 7), have yielded a characteristic Clactonian industry, characterized by pebble and biconical chopper cores, unspecialized flake tools and an absence of hand-axes (Warren 1951; Oakley & Leakey 1937; Wymer 1974, 1977). A spear made of yew (*Taxus*) wood was also found by Warren (1951). This has been recently re-evaluated by Oakley *et al.* (1977).

A similar Clactonian flint industry is also found in the Lower Gravel and Lower Loam at Swanscombe, which may be of approximately zone Ho II age (Ch. 7).

The only securely dated artefacts of Hoxnian age were found in the lake deposits at the type site of Hoxne, Suffolk, and are pollen-dated to subzone Ho IIc (Bed E) (West & McBurney 1955; Wymer 1974). The artefacts comprise flint flakes and a single Acheulian hand-axe found by workmen. The later industries from this site are also of Acheulian type. The 'Hoxne Lower Industry', an assemblage of artefacts resting on lake deposits of zone Ho III age, comprises hand-axes and flake tools (Wymer 1974). Similarly, at Swanscombe the Lower and Upper Middle Gravels, probably dating from the second half of the Hoxnian Interglacial, contain beautiful pointed Acheulian hand-axes. Although there is a clear temporal succession of industries, it is not possible to say whether the two distinct industries reflect different cultural groups, or were simply made by the same group at different times.

The ovate and heart-shaped hand-axes from the Upper Loam at Swanscombe and perhaps the 'Hoxne Upper Industry' may date from the opening phases of the Wolstonian Cold Stage. It is difficult to assess the status of human occupation of Britain during the Wolstonian because of the poor stratigraphical control. Transported and reworked artefacts occur in many river gravels of probable Wolstonian age.

A Wolstonian industry in primary context is available from Baker's Hole, Northfleet, Kent, probably dating from the end of the stage. The artefacts from this site comprise large flakes struck from prepared cores by a characteristic Levallois technique. Acheulian-style hand-axes also occur.

Fig. 10.1 Record of man and succession of industries in the Pleistocene of the British Isles. (Note that the relative time scale is schematic only) Solid black, pollen or radiocarbon-dated finds; cross hatching, stratigraphical position less reliably known). Sites: PF, Peacock's Farm, Cambridgeshire, WH, Westward Ho! Devonshire; Or, Oronsay, Inner Hebrides; SC, Star Carr, Yorkshire; Th, Thatcham, Berkshire; Sp, Sproughton, Ipswich, Suffolk; HF, High Furlong, Blackpool, Lancashire; KC, Kent's Cavern, Torquay, Devonshire; GC, Gough's Cave, Somerset; AH, Aveline's Hole, Somerset; SH, Sun Hole, Somerset; KA, King Arthur's Cave, Herefordshire; CH, Cat Hole, South Wales; LC, Langwith Cave, Derbyshire; FB, Ffynnon Bueno, Flintshire; RC, Robin Hood's Cave and PC, Pin Hole Cave, Creswell Crags, Derbyshire; LP, Little Paxton, Huntingdonshire; Cg, Coygan Cave, Camarthenshire; Cy, Crayford, Kent; St, Stutton, Suffolk; Bn, Brundon, Suffolk; Ss, Selsey, Sussex; BH, Baker's Hole, Northfleet, Kent; Ho, Hoxne, near Diss, Suffolk; SW, Swanscombe, Kent; IV, Ingress Vale, Kent; Cl, Clacton, Essex; Wb, Westbury-sub-Mendip, Somerset.

The artefact assemblages from High Lodge, Mildenhall, Suffolk, which include finely worked ovate hand-axes, have been attributed to an interstadial within the Wolstonian Cold Stage. Unfortunately, the stratigraphical position of these beds remains highly enigmatic.

In contrast to the Hoxnian Interglacial, sites with artefacts of Ipswichian age are very sparse. A few flakes from Selsey, Sussex, can be attributed only to the early part of the interglacial. They could date from as late as the beginning of subzone Ip IIb. Again at Stutton, Suffolk, sandy brickearths, with a mammalian fauna, of zone Ip III age (Ch. 7), have yielded rare flint flakes. Levallois flakes and blades, in association with apparently reworked hand-axes, are known from deposits, thought to be of similar age to Stutton, at Brundon, Suffolk (Moir & Hopwood 1939) (Ch. 7). By far the richest site, however, is Crayford, Kent, where most of the artefacts are elongated flake blades, manufactured by Levallois technique, and once again associated with hand-axes (Kennard 1944). Some of the flakes were found in association with a mandible of woolly rhinoceros *Coelodonta antiquitatis*. The Crayford deposits probably date from towards the end of the Ipswichian Interglacial.

Curiously, with the doubtful exception of Selsey, there is no trace of man during zone II of the Ipswichian Interglacial, although there is an abundance of both open-site and cave deposits of this age. This was first pointed out by Sutcliffe (1960), and has not been refuted by subsequent discoveries.

Evidence of human occupation during the first half of the Devensian in Britain is meagre. 'Bout coupé' axes, known from a few sites in poorly dated contexts, are, however, highly distinctive and occur on the Continent only in Mousterian industries of Early Weichselian age. At Little Paxton, Huntingdonshire, 'bout coupé' hand-axes were found in association with reindeer *Rangifer tarandus*, in the low terrace of the River Ouse, which is consistent with a Devensian date (Patterson & Tebbutt 1947).

Upper Palaeolithic

The problem of determining the stratigraphical position of finds is considerably improved for the Upper Palaeolithic, because associated organic material can be dated by radiocarbon. Unfortunately, however, most British sites were excavated in the last century without adequate documentation of finds. The whole period has now been intensively reviewed and reassessed by Campbell (1977), who abandoned any attempt to correlate it with the much richer and better-known French Upper Palaeolithic, and divided it simply into two periods: Early Upper Palaeolithic (EUP) and Later Upper Palaeolithic (LUP). The EUP is thought to have lasted from about 38 000 to 28 000 radiocarbon years B.P., perhaps as late as 18 000 years B.P. This was followed by an apparent gap of several thousand years in which the climate became very cold and ice sheets advanced over a large part of the British Isles. After this period human occupation resumed, and the LUP dates from about 14 500 to 10 000 radiocarbon years B.P. From the beginning of the LUP man appears to have been continuously present in Britain.

The EUP, rather sparsely represented in a number of cave sites, and hardly at all at open sites, is characterized by leaf points which appear to be missile heads (probably spear heads). The radiocarbon dates for this period are based mainly on assays of bone collagen.

The LUP is much better represented. Open sites are few but include Sproughton, near Ipswich, Suffolk, with long flint blades and uniserial barbed projectile points, made from antler, one pre-dating, and the other post-dating a radiocarbon date of 9 880 years B.P. (Lab. no.: HAR-259), i.e. contemporary with zone L-De III and the beginning of Flandrian subzone Fl-Ia (IV) (Wymer *et al.* 1975). At High Furlong, near Blackpool, Lancashire, two bone barbed points were found in association with a complete skeleton of an elk *Alces alces* (Barnes *et al.* 1971; Hallam *et al.* 1973). The skeleton bore a number of lesions clearly sustained in an attack by hunters armed with flint-tipped weapons, as well as bone projectile points (Ch. 5). The bones and artefacts were found in detritus mud with zone L-De II pollen spectra, and bracketed by radiocarbon dates obtained on the mud of 12 000 ± 160 and 11 665 ± 140 years B.P. (IGS-C14/135, IGS-C14/134). The highly incomplete skeletons of three horses *Equus ferus*, with associated flint flakes, found at Flixton, Yorkshire, probably date from within pollen zone L De III (Clark 1954). The radiocarbon date for the horizon immediately above of 10 413 ± 210 years B.P. (Q-66) is consistent with this date. Flixton evidently represents a 'kill site', with the bones representing the parts discarded by the hunters who used the flints in butchering the carcasses.

Finds from LUP cave sites and other open sites

include the characteristic angle-backed blades (Creswellian Industry) and artefacts of bone and antler, notably biserial bone points ('harpoon heads'), perforated 'batons' and sewing needles. The authenticity of the engraving of a horse's head on antler from Robin Hood's Cave, Derbyshire, described by Dawkins (1877), has been questioned.

Mesolithic

The Mesolithic industries of Britain have been reviewed by Mellars (1974), and of those Ireland by Woodman (1978).

The early Mesolithic industries in England appear to have developed from those of the Later Upper Palaeolithic. The two principal sites are Star Carr, east Yorkshire, with assemblages dated to about 9 5000 years B.P., and Thatcham, Berkshire, with dates ranging from 10 365 years B.P. (i.e. prior to the conventional Devensian–Flandrian boundary) to 9 480 years B.P.

At Star Carr, occupation debris from a hunters' camp accumulated in organic deposits near the edge of a lake, so that wood, bone and antler artefacts are exceptionally well preserved (Clark 1954, 1972). The implements include microliths (some evidently used to tip wooden arrows), 'tranchet' axes and uniserial barbed points manufactured from red-deer antler. The latter were probably fixed to wooden shafts using birch-bark resin. Similar flint artefacts occur at Thatcham, but there are no barbed points, only smooth points manufactured from bone (Wymer 1962).

The oldest Mesolithic artefacts from the southern Pennines and North York Moors, at heights of up to nearly 500 m O.D., are some 500 to 700 years younger than those from Thatcham (Jacobi 1978). These presumably represent summer camps and indicate that different hunting areas were exploited according to the season.

The earliest evidence of man in Ireland is from the Mesolithic site of Mount Sandel, County Derry, with radiocarbon dates between 8 960 and 8 440 years B.P. (Woodman 1978).

Later Mesolithic sites include the shell-midden settlements along the coasts of Scotland. These 'Obanian' occupations have been dated on Oronsay, in the Inner Hebrides, to the range 5 015–5 850 years B.P. Marine shellfish were largely exploited, but remains of red deer *Cervus elaphus* also occur (Mellars 1974; Mellars & Payne 1971). The

youngest dates obtained for any Mesolithic industry are those of 5 620 and 4 200 years B.P. from the Isle of Jura, Inner Hebrides. These are at least 600 to 700 years later than the dates of the earliest Neolithic settlements in southern Britain (Mellars 1974).

Neolithic and later

The earliest dated Neolithic site in the British Isles is Ballynagilly, Tyrone, Northern Ireland, with radiocarbon dates of 5 745 and 5 625 years B.P. (Smith 1974). Landnam horizons, showing local forest clearance for farming, however, occur in pollen diagrams from both England and Ireland only from about 5 350–4 950 years B.P. At the upper limit, the Neolithic grades into the Bronze Age from approximately 4 000 years B.P. and is succeeded by the Iron Age only some 1 000 years later.

The beginning of the Neolithic marks the arrival of farming communities in Britain from the Continent. Neolithic technology was much more sophisticated than that of the Palaeolithic and Mesolithic. Important innovations include the introduction of cereal crops and domestic animals, and the manufacture of pottery and polished-stone implements. The latter were subsequently superseded by metal tools in the Bronze and Iron Ages.

Man and the vertebrate fauna

Palaeolithic and Mesolithic

Palaeolithic man neither grew plants nor domesticated animals but was, like other animals, entirely dependent on what he could catch or collect from his natural environment. Such a hunter-gatherer based economy requires extensive, geographical areas to support small populations (Clark 1971). Comparison with present-day hunter-gatherers cannot be taken too far, since these are restricted to marginal areas of the world, but bearing the figures for recent populations in mind, speculative estimates for the Palaeolithic population of England and Wales, e.g. during the Hoxnian interglacial or LUP, might be an absolute maximum of a few thousands, probably only a few hundreds of individuals. Figures for the rest of the Palaeolithic were probably even lower – dropping to zero for much of the period. Rather heavier population densities probably would have been found further south in Europe.

Again, comparison with modern parallels, plus archaeological evidence, indicates that Palaeolithic man lived in small, widely dispersed groups, moving over extensive areas through the year so as to best exploit natural sources of food as they became seasonally available. Most groups appear to have moved from one to another of a series of seasonal base camps, which were sometimes caves or huts or tents (known from the Upper Palaeolithic) at open sites. They were then sheltered from the weather and predators, and could carry out such essential activities as cooking food, dressing skins, and manufacturing tools.

It is very difficult to assess the relative importance of various items in the diet of Paleolithic man. The mere presence of artefacts and the bones of animals in the same deposit is no proof that they were hunted by man, since accumulations of bones may originate in a number of ways without human intervention (Ch. 4). There is, unfortunately, very little information on the vegetable diet of Palaeolithic man. In Britain he would presumably have exploited nuts, fruits, seeds and rhizomes during the interglacial periods, although during the cold stages fewer plant foods would have been available.

Hunting techniques in use during the Lower and Middle Palaeolithic probably included stampeding animals over cliffs, or into wet ground where they would become mired and could be easily despatched, and possibly the excavation of pitfall traps. At La Cotte de Saint Brelade, Jersey (Channel Islands), groups of mammoth and woolly rhino appear to have been driven to their deaths in a ravine by Neanderthal hunters, during the penultimate (Saalian, Wolstonian) cold stage (Scott 1980). There is no definite evidence of specialized projectile-points for this period, although it is just possible that some of the Levallois and Mousterian points were so used. The Clacton wooden spear, of Hoxnian age, has already been mentioned. Another spear, also of yew, and 2.4 m long, was found among the ribs of a skeleton of straight-tusked elephant *Palaeoloxodon antiquus* at Lehringer, Lower Saxony, West Germany (Movius 1950). The find is thought to date from the Eemian Interglacial. From a detailed reappraisal of the Clacton spear,

Oakley *et al.* (1977) concluded that it was used as a thrusting weapon, and would not have been suitable for throwing.

Fire was certainly used during the Middle Pleistocene, by *Homo erectus* in the cave at Choukoutien near Peking, China, and may have been mastered much earlier. Mellars (1976) has discussed the use of fire by modern primitive cultures to burn off areas with the main object of improving the quantity and nutritional value of the vegetation for herbivorous mammals. Fire also considerably facilitates the mobility of human groups for hunting and food-gathering. It can also be used to drive animals into traps, natural or man-made.

At Hoxne, Suffolk, Marks Tey, Essex, and Barford, near Norwich, Norfolk (the last two sites are about 85 km apart), the pollen diagrams from lacustrine Hoxnian Interglacial deposits show a puzzling decrease in most forest trees and increase in grasses during subzone Ho IIc (see Ch. 2). Evidence from probable annular laminations at Marks Tey indicates that this phase lasted approximately 350 years (Turner 1970). The abundance of charcoal in the sediments at this level at Marks Tey and the pattern of vegetational change led Turner to suggest that a forest fire was responsible. If one speculates that this fire was deliberately started by man, for any of the reasons suggested above, it evidently got out of control and destroyed a large area of forest – an undesirable result. The absence of charcoal at Barford (Phillips 1976), however, does not support the fire hypothesis, and even if a fire was responsible for the destruction of the Hoxnian forest it would seem impossible to demonstrate that it was started by man rather than naturally by lightning. Certainly, evidence of human occupation occurs at Hoxne in association with subzone Ho IIc.

With the possible exception of those of Hoxnian Interglacial, the Lower and Middle Palaeolithic populations in Britain were probably too low to have made much impression on the vertebrate fauna. Even further south on the Continent and elsewhere, the rather low technological level may have restricted man's efficiency as a hunter. In Britain a wide variety of potential game was available during the interglacials and some phases of the cold stages, but it is difficult at present to assess to what extent these were exploited.

The Upper Palaeolithic cultures beginning about 40 000 years ago in Europe, show considerable technological sophistication in comparison with their predecessors. The period is well documented by the French cave sequences and in Spain, Germany and elsewhere.

The flint industries are dominated by punch-struck blades, used as blanks for the manufacture of a wide range of implements. These include burins used for working wood, bone and antler. Projectile points were certainly in use during the Early Upper Palaeolithic (EUP) for tipping spears, and in the Later Upper Palaeolithic (LUP) a wide variety of bone and flint projectile points were used to tip spears and arrows. Upper Paleolithic peoples also indulged in personal adornment, and were motivated to produce cave art.

This considerable advance in technology may have resulted in increased success in hunting – greater exploitation of mammals, in particular, as a source of food. Indeed this was perhaps the main factor that enabled human populations to survive in Britain through much of the Middle and Upper Devensian in Britain, and especially throughout the cold phase of Late Devensian pollen zone III, where the hunters probably specialized in reindeer *Rangifer tarandus* or horse *Equus ferus* as they are known to have done on the Continent.

In Britain the Upper Palaeolithic cultures grade into those of the Mesolithic. The spread of forests in the early Flandrian, replacing the tundra-like vegetation of the end of the Late Devensian, however, forced the human populations to alter drastically their way of life. The evidence from sites at Star Carr, and those of the Maglemosian cultures of the North European Plain, show that the populations were adapted to exploiting a wide variety of food sources. At Star Carr, where the material at the site appears to have been entirely accumulated by man, red deer *Cervus elaphus* was the main prey animal, and elk *Alces alces*, aurochs *Bos primigenius*, roe. *Capreolus capreolus*, pig *Sus scrofa* and water-fowl were also taken. Dogs were probably used in hunting. The tool-kit included tranchet axes used in felling trees, barbed points for killing large mammals, and specialized arrowheads for birds and small mammals. Fishing using hooks and nets is attested from Maglemosian sites, but not from Star Carr. Dug-out canoes propelled by paddles have been preserved. Fruits, nuts, seeds and rhizomes were probably also gathered, but these are unlikely to leave any trace in the archaeological record.

Certain later Mesolithic populations extensively exploited marine molluscs as well as mammals.

'Overkill'

One of the most fascinating problems in the study of Pleistocene vertebrates is presented by the suggestion that Palaeolithic man was responsible for the extinction of many large mammals throughout the world (Ch. 9). The hypothesis of 'overkill' by human hunters has been championed especially by P. S. Martin (Martin & Wright 1967). The largest mammals would have been affected most because of their low population numbers and slow rate of breeding. The extinction of many large mammals in North America between approximately 10 000 and 20 000 years B.P. may be plausibly, although not necessarily correctly, correlated with the arrival of human hunters, since man is unknown in the New World before this time. In the case of Europe, however, man had been present since the Middle Pleistocene, but there is still an unprecedented increased extinction of large mammals, although much less marked than in North America, within the Last Cold Stage. Explanations of changes in climate seem totally inadequate to explain this phenomenon in view of the resilience of the fauna when subjected to previous climatic oscillations (Ch. 9).

Marked changes in the available fauna occurred during the British Upper Palaeolithic. During the EUP important potential prey animals included the mammoth *Mammuthus primigenius*, woolly rhinoceros *Coelodonta antiquitatis*, horse *Equus ferus* and reindeer *Rangifer tarandus* (Ch. 8). Smaller prey animals were few but may have included arctic hare *Lepus timidus* and a number of birds, including ptarmigan *Lagopus mutus*. By the LUP in Britain, and the end of the Upper Palaeolithic elsewhere in Europe (i.e. the late-glacial period) the two largest mammals *M. primigenius* and *C. antiquitatis* were extinct. Upper Palaeolithic man is known to have hunted *M. primigenius* on a large scale in eastern Europe, and in fact to have had a largely mammoth-based economy. It is tempting to conclude, therefore, that the extinction of these two animals at least, can be attributed to the improved hunting technology of the peoples of this time. There is considerable doubt, however, whether such small populations of hunters without firearms could have been responsible for, or even contributed significantly to, the complete destruction of any species.

Neolithic to present day

From Neolithic times onwards, man's influence on the vertebrate fauna of the British Isles has been profound, both in the introduction of exotic species and in the reduction, extermination or redistribution of many natives.

Introduced aliens

The non-indigenous vertebrates introduced by man to the fauna of the British Isles include both domesticated species, some of which have subsequently become feral, and wild species.

Finds from the early Flandrian sites of Star Carr and Thatcham show that the early Mesolithic hunter-gatherers in Britain possessed domestic dog *Canis* (domestic) at least as early as 9 500 radiocarbon years B.P. The wolf *Canis lupus* ancestry of the domestic dog is now generally accepted.

No further domestic animals were introduced to the British Isles for several thousands of years until Neolithic farmers arrived by sea from the Continent, after about 6 000 radiocarbon years B.P.

They brought with them sheep *Ovis* (domestic) and goat *Capra* (domestic), both ultimately derived from non-indigenous wild ancestors in south-west Asia. The domestic pig *Sus* (domestic) and cow *Bos* (domestic) could have been derived from native wild boar *Sus scrofa* and aurochs *Bos primigenius* respectively, both indigenous to Britain. Alternatively, they may have been brought over already domesticated; or perhaps both processes occurred. Domestic horse *Equus* (domestic) derived from wild *Equus ferus* outside Britain probably arrived in the Bronze Age about 4 000 years B.P. Animals arriving within the last 2 000 years include domestic chicken derived from the jungle fowl *Gallus gallus* of southern Asia, and ass from the wild *Equus asinus* of North Africa. The domestic duck derived from the wild mallard *Anas platyrhynchos*, domestic goose from the wild *Anser anser*, domestic cat from the wild cat *Felis sylvestris*, and the ferret from the polecat *Mustela putorius*, could either have been imported from the Continent or have been domesticated from indigenous wild British stock. The domestic cat appears to have originated in ancient Egypt.

Many of the vertebrates now living wild in the British Isles are non-indigenous, having been accidentally or deliberately introduced by man from perhaps as early as Neolithic times onwards. The subject has been extensively reviewed by Lever (1979), mostly on the basis of documentary evidence. Much work, however, needs to be done with accurately dated skeletal material, mostly from archaeological sites. Species introduced prior to A.D. 1800 will be considered first.

Those highly successful cosmopolitan parasites of man, the house mouse *Mus musculus*, originating in south-west Asia, the black rat *Rattus rattus* and the brown rat *Rattus norvegicus*, both from south-east Asia, may have arrived in Britain as stowaways on ships and boats before about 2 500 years B.P. (Corbet 1974), before 1 200–1 600 years B.P. (Rackham 1979) and about A.D. 1728–29 respectively. The fallow deer *Dama dama*, whose natural Flandrian distribution appears to have been confined to the Mediterranean area, was probably introduced in Roman times or perhaps a little earlier for hunting and ornamental purposes. The common pheasant *Phasianus colchicus*, a native of south-west Asia, may also have been introduced by the Romans, and is definitely known from the twelfth century A.D. in Britain. The case of the rabbit *Oryctolagus cuniculus*, is especially intriguing. In Britain it was undoubtedly kept in a semi-domesticated state in managed warrens from the twelfth century onwards; the animals having been derived from Continental stock. The single enigmatic fossil record of this species from the early Flandrian of England suggests the possibility that modern British rabbits are descended mainly from native stock, although this seems very improbable (see Ch. 7).

The carp *Cyprinus carpio*, appears to have been introduced from the Continent in the fifteenth century, and was reared for food in monastic stews.

Ornamental fowl introduced during the seventeenth and eighteenth centuries include Egyptian goose *Alopochen aegyptiacus* and, originating from south-west Europe, the red-legged partridge *Alectoris rufa*.

The following species now found in the British Isles are restricted to offshore islands: lesser white-toothed shrew *Crocidura suaveolens* (Jersey, Sark, Scilly Isles); greater white-toothed shrew *Crocidura russula* (Guernsey, Alderney, Herm); and common vole *Microtus arvalis* (Orkney, Guernsey). Although these occurrences have been supposed to represent relict populations of species formerly present on the British mainland (Barrett-Hamilton & Hinton 1910–

12), the apparently random presence of species on these islands, and the extreme improbability that either the Orkneys or Scillies were over connected to the mainland during the Pleistocene, strongly suggests accidental introduction by man, probably in prehistoric times (Corbet 1961). A study of non-metrical skull characters shows that the Orkney *M. arvalis* most closely resembles Yugoslav populations of this species (Berry & Rose, 1975).

The nineteenth and twentieth centuries have seen an enormous increase in the number of alien species introduced by man (Lever 1979). Mammals include the North American grey squirrel *Sciurus carolinensis* and mink *Mustela vison*, the edible dormouse *Glis glis* from southern and central Europe, the coypu *Myocastor coypus* from South America, sika deer *Cervus nippon* from Japan, and most remarkable of all, the marsupial red-necked wallaby *Macropus rufogrisseus* from Australia. Birds include mandarin duck *Aix galericulata* from China, while amphibians are represented by edible frog *Rana esculenta* from the Continent, and fishes by the North American rainbow trout *Salmo gairdneri* and pumpkinseed *Lepomis gibbosus*.

It is difficult to say if any of these recent introductions is likely to survive in the long term. One species, the highly destructive North American musk rat *Ondatra zibethica*, was systematically exterminated by man within ten years of its introduction in 1927. Even without direct human intervention, many will probably succumb to such factors as habitat destruction, pollution, summer droughts or a run of bad winters, while others may establish themselves as more permanent members of the British fauna.

Effect on the native fauna

There is no doubt that from Neolithic times onwards the composition and distribution of the indigenous vertebrates of the British Isles has been greatly altered by man. Although predominantly farming-based economies replaced those based on hunting and food-gathering, hunting continued as a means of supplementing the diet, and especially later for prestige and sporting purposes. As a result of the greatly increased human population densities that this change in the economic basis made possible, the hunting pressure on the wild vertebrate fauna was maintained, or even increased, in comparison with the situation in the Palaeolithic and Mesolithic. From the fifteenth century this pressure was accentuated by the use of firearms. Other important factors potentially affecting the survival of the indigenous vertebrate fauna are the destruction of habitats, especially forests and wetlands, and competition from introduced aliens.

The pattern of extinction in mammals, and pond tortoise *Emys orbicularis*, during the Flandrian can be seen from Fig. 7.16. As has been discussed in Chapters 7 and 9, the extinctions within the early part of the Flandrian, involving both large and small species, can be plausibly connected with known climatic and vegetational changes, although it is possible that the demise of elk *Alces alces* in the British Isles was at least partly due to hunting by Mesolithic man. The later wave of extinctions, largely confined to within the last 1 000 years or so and in many cases to within the last few hundred years, however, can be directly ascribed to human activities. Mammals extinct within this period, with probable extinction dates based on documentary evidence, comprise: beaver *Castor fiber* (twelfth century or later); wolf *Canis lupus* (eighteenth century in Scotland and Ireland, earlier in England); brown bear *Ursus arctos* (probably about tenth century); wild boar *Sus scrofa* (about seventeenth century). Aurochs *Bos primigenius* was probably extinct by the Iron Age. The wolf was deliberately exterminated because of its depredations on domestic livestock, and the brown bear may have met a similar fate. On the other hand, aurochs and wild boar were probably unintentionally over-hunted. Bird species lost within this period, due mainly to persecution in the case of predatory birds, and destruction of wetlands, include white-tailed eagle *Haliaetus albicilla* (early twentieth century), great bustard, *Otis tarda* (early nineteenth century) and great auk *Pinguinus impennis* (early nineteenth century) (Sharrock 1974). Others such as the osprey *Pandion haliaetus* died out and subsequently reestablished themselves, sometimes aided by the efforts of ornithologists. A few species such as Dalmatian pelican *Pelecanus crispus*, common crane *Grus grus* and white stork *Ciconia ciconia*, all wetland species, have become extinct in Britain since the Iron age.

Of the mammal species which have survived until the present day in the British Isles, many have been considerably reduced in distribution. These include pine marten *Martes martes* (restricted to the Scottish Highlands, part of North Wales, several areas in Ireland, and scattered small populations in northern England), polecat *Mustela putorius* (found over most of Wales and into the Welsh border counties) and wild cat *Felis sylvestris* (widespread throughout the Scottish Highlands). All three species have expanded their ranges within the last few decades, following the nadir of their fortunes at the beginning of the present century, after a century of persecution in the interests of game preservation (Corbet 1974). The red deer *Cervus elaphus* and roe *Capreolus capreolus* had disappeared from most of the lowland Britain prior to A.D. 1800, because of extensive deforestation coupled with hunting pressures. Similarly, the red squirrel *Sciurus vulgaris* had become virtually extinct in Scotland and scarce in England. The fortunes of all three species revived during the nineteenth century because of reafforestation, although the red squirrel has, from about 1890 onwards, vacated large areas of lowland England, apparently in the face of competition from the introduced grey squirrel *Sciurus carolinensis*. The harvest mouse *Micromys minutus* is now restricted mainly to the south-eastern half of England, and may have been formerly more widespread. The dormouse *Muscardinus avellanarius* appears to have declined since the beginning of the century due to destruction of deciduous woodland, and is probably now extinct in the northern half of Britain.

The status of many British birds has been similarly reduced during historical times by persecution, especially of predatory birds, drainage of wetlands, or other factors. For example, the golden eagle *Aquila chrysaetus*, formerly widespread over most of the British Isles, is now found only in the Scottish Highlands.

Within the past few decades the commoner British amphibians and reptiles have declined locally, while the rarer species already confined to scattered isolated areas due to a combination of climatic and human factors, viz. the natterjack *Bufo calamita*, sand lizard *Lacerta agilis* and smooth snake *Coronella austriaca*, are unfortunately declining seriously because of afforestation, urbanization and disturbance by man (Prestt, Cooke & Corbet 1974). Some freshwater fish species have been reduced or exterminated locally by such factors as pollution, changes in river flow and eutrophication. Those most affected have been the salmonid fishes, genera *Salmo*, *Salvelinus*, *Thymallus*, whitefishes genus *Coregonus*, the shads *Alosa* and the sturgeon *Acipenser* (Wheeler 1974).

When one reflects on how profoundly man has altered the landscape and vegetation of the British Isles from its natural state, it is perhaps surprising that so many native vertebrate species have managed to survive at all. To some species, however, human activities have been beneficial, for example in introducing many vertebrates to Ireland, and a number of fishes to many parts of Britain, where they would not otherwise occur. Animals such as the short-tailed vole *Microtus agrestis* have benefited from deforestation, because they require open grassland habitats. Others, such as the feral pigeon, which roosts on buildings and is derived from the wild rock dove *Columba livia* whose natural habitat is sea cliffs, and the red fox *Vulpes vulpes*, have been very successful in adapting to urban environments.

11 Evolution

The rich fossil record for Pleistocene mammals provides in many ways ideal material for the study of evolutionary changes both within a temporal species, and between species and sometimes even genera, on a time scale of hundreds of thousands of years down to a thousand years and finer (Joysey 1972). The abundance of fossil mammal material from closely spaced time-stratigraphical horizons is but rarely matched by material from earlier geological periods. By far the most detailed studies on pre-Pleistocene mammalian evolution have been made on Palaeocene and Eocene primates and other groups from the western United States (Gingerich 1980). An advantage of working with Pleistocene material is that many species are still living, and all have surviving close relatives, so that fossil assemblages are directly comparable with modern populations. Moreover, environmental changes can be followed with much greater precision than for earlier periods.

The main difficulty of the Pleistocene period for the study of evolution in the fossil record, although it applies to a varying extent further back in geological time, is that the many fluctuations in climate resulted in the repeated shifting of geographical distributions. On the other hand, there are indications that the overall rates of evolution may have been faster than average during the Middle and Upper Pleistocene, due to the stresses caused by these changes.

Analyses of fossil samples from closely spaced time-stratigraphic horizons can reveal much about the patterns and rates of evolutionary change. The process of evolution involves changes in the genetic composition (genotype) of a population with time, which are expressed as changes in morphology (phenotype). Non-inheritable phenotypic changes can occur, however, in response to environmental factors, and it is difficult to distinguish these from genuine evolutionary character changes. A further difficulty arises in attempting to distinguish between the effects of evolution more or less *in situ*, and the origination of new forms elsewhere followed by immigration to the area under study (Joysey 1972). Since a new form could conceivably originate anywhere within the range of a species, and exist at the same time as the older forms as a geographical variety or subspecies, it follows that the fossil record in any one locality or area may not faithfully reflect the timing of the evolutionary changes within the species. Moreover, if climatic changes cause shifts in the geographical range, apparent reversals may result.

To understand fully the patterns of evolutionary change, therefore, it will be necessary to analyse series of samples from successive stratigraphical horizons throughout the geographical range of each species. Such studies would require an enormous amount of work, and are at present hampered by the uncertainties in the correlation of Pleistocene deposits, even within such a relatively small area as western Europe.

The importance of using a stratigraphical framework based on independent evidence, e.g. pollen biostratigraphy or radiocarbon dating, cannot be overemphasized. The method, widely used on the Continent, of relatively dating Pleistocene deposits and faunas by the evolutionary grade of particular taxa, notably rodents, in a conjectural progressive evolutionary lineage, is useful only in a very general way. On a finer scale it can be highly misleading because at any one locality apparent reversals may occur (see above). A further criticism of this approach is that it is based not on standard well-stratified sequences, but largely on assemblages from caves and fissures, which cannot be related stratigraphically on independent evidence.

Any evolutionary study on British material relies on the validity of the stratigraphical framework for the Middle and Upper Pleistocene (Ch. 2.). A few of the most fossiliferous deposits, however, can as yet only be dated approximately within this sequence, and there is also the possibility that certain sites represent hitherto unrecognized stages. In such cases, dating within a broader age-range may still contribute usefully to reconstructing the evolutionary history of many species.

Examples

Following on from the pioneer work of Kurtén (1953, 1958, 1963, 1964, 1965) interest has recently increased in the study of evolution in Pleistocene mammals, utilizing the comparatively firm stratigraphical framework which now exists for the Pleistocene of the British Isles. In many cases, fossil samples are available from successive interglacial periods and/or cold stages, and can be pinpointed stratigraphically within each stage with some precision. Only a few such studies, however, have been published to date.

In most of the examples of evolution in Pleistocene mammals quoted in the literature, the evidence is of a rather general nature, as much of the material on which it is based is inadequately stratified, and sample sizes are commonly too small to represent the range of variation within a population. A notable example is the evolution of two lineages of elephants from *Archidiskodon meridionalis* (Lower to early Middle Pleistocene) (e.g. Kurtén, 1968):

(a) *Archidiskodon meridionalis* → *Palaeoloxodon antiquus* (Middle and Upper Pleistocene)

(b) *Archidiskodon meridionalis* → *Mammuthus trogontherii* (Middle Pleistocene)

→ *Mammuthus primigenius* (Middle and Upper Pleistocene).

Evolutionary changes occur in skull morphology and in the tusks and molars (see Fig. 3.40). In both lineages there is a thinning of the enamel, accompanied by closer packing and increased number of enamel ridges on the molars, but this is much more marked in the line leading to *M. primigenius* (see Fig. 3.43).

The elks, genus *Alces*, of the European Pleistocene show a marked size increase from *A. gallicus* (late Lower Pleistocene) to *A. latifrons* (early Middle Pleistocene) – some populations of which were the largest of any known deer, followed by a decrease in size to *A. alces* (Upper Pleistocene and extant). The antlers increase in proportion to body

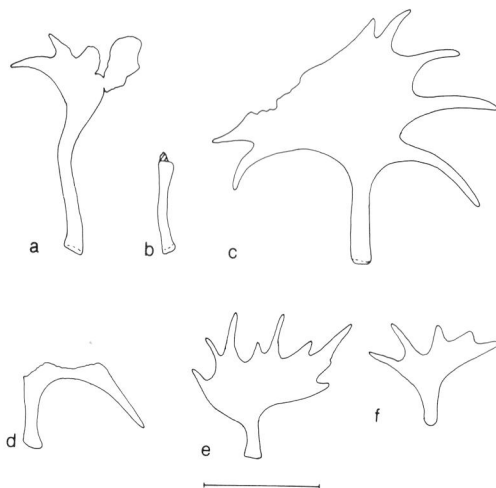

Fig. 11.1. Changes in absolute size and relative proportions of beam and palmation in European elks during the Pleistocene (after Lister 1981). (a, b), *Alces (Libracles) gallicus*: (a) Senèze, France; (b) East Runton, Norfolk (both late Lower Pleistocene). (c, d), *Alces (Libralces) latifrons*: (c) Mosbach, West Germany; (d) Happisburgh, Norfolk (both of approximately Cromerian age). (e, f), *Alces alces*: (e) Neasham, Co. Durham (Late Devensian); (f) Sweden (modern).

size from *A. gallicus* to *A. latifrons* but there is a reduction of the length of the beam relative to the palmation (Fig. 11.1). In *A. alces* there is a decrease in antler size both relatively and absolutely, together with marked further reduction in the relative length of the beam.

Mayhew (1978) in a detailed study of the extinct beaver *Trogontherium* in Europe, was able to demonstrate an overall increase in size within a single lineage from *T. minutum* to *T. minus* (Pliocene) through to *T. cuvieri* (Lower Pleistocene to early Middle Pleistocene. The lineage reached its peak size in the Cromerian with *T. cuvieri*, declined again in the Hoxnian/Holsteinian, and subsequently became extinct.

The history of *Trogontherium* contrasts with that of the living genus *Castor* which merely shows fluctuations in size with no overall trend (Mayhew 1975, 1978). Mayhew suggests that the increase in size in the *Trogontherium* lineage may have brought it into more direct competition with *Castor*, since later populations of the two species were of similar body size. This competition could have contributed to the extinction of *Trogontherium*.

Corbet (1975) described an apparent evolutionary change in a dental character over the relatively short-term period of a few thousand years. He found a progressive decrease in the development of a postero-medial angle on M^1 in the short-tailed role *Microtus agrestis* in successive levels within a cave on Jura, Inner Hebrides, from the Bronze Age to the present day.

One of the best examples of evolutionary change in Pleistocene mammals, studied so far, is seen in the water-vole lineage, which includes the genera *Mimomys* and *Arvicola*.

The general evolutionary trends from *Mimomys pliocaenicus* through to the modern water vole *Arvicola terrestris* were pointed out by Hinton (1926). Later workers have traced the lineage through from the origin of *Mimomys*, from brachyodont cricetid ancestors in the Upper Pliocene. Progressive changes during the Pliocene and Lower Pleistocene include: increasing hypsodonty, accompanied by an increase of crown-cementum to strengthen the tooth; increased height of enamel-free areas on the external angles, allowing improved attachment in the jaw; and simplification of the anterior loop of M_1 (Chaline, 1974; Chaline & Mein, 1979). During this period several species of *Mimomys*, all with rooted cheek teeth – one of the characters of the genus – co-existed at any one time (Ch. 3).

In Britain the Lower Pleistocene sequence is incomplete and fossil voles, including *Mimomys pliocaenicus*, are available only from the Antian onwards. The fossil record from the Middle and Upper Pleistocene, however, is sufficiently good to allow evolutionary changes to be followed in some detail.

Figure 11.2 illustrates the various character changes in water voles from the Cromerian to the present day. The most important change is the attainment of permanently growing cheek teeth (the incisors of all rodents are permanently growing). This change, of great advantage for dealing with a high proportion of abrasive grasses in the diet, is the culmination of the trend towards increased hyposonty throughout the Lower Pleistocene. The formation of roots was retarded until progressively later in life, until a point was reached where the cheek teeth ceased to root altogether, and had become permanently growing. This step is generally accepted as marking the boundary between the genera *Mimomys* and *Arvicola*. The last species of *Mimomys*, *M. savini*, is known in Britain from Cromerian subzone Cr IIIb and the first *Arvi-*

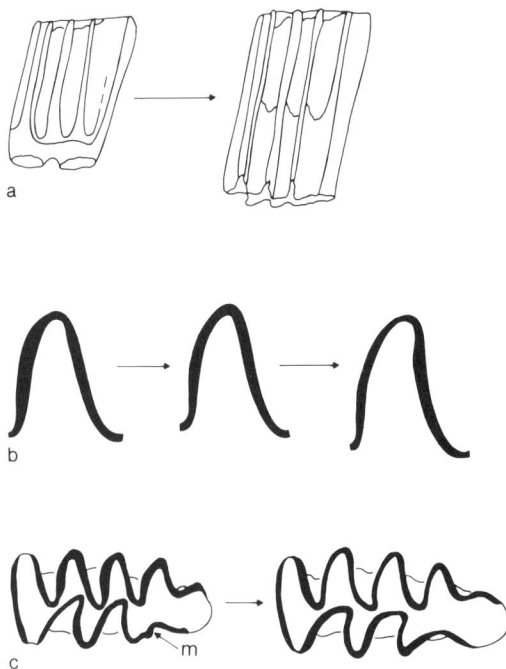

Fig. 11.2. Character changes in M_1, in the lineage of water voles *Mimomys savini – Arvicola cantiana – A. terrestris* in the British Middle and Upper Pleistocene. For the relative timing of these changes see Fig. 11.3 and text. (a) loss of roots, thereby achieving permanently growing molars; (b) progressive reduction of convex-side enamel on the angles of the molars; (c) loss of '*Mimomys* fold' (m).

cola, A. cantiana, is recorded from zone CrIV.

A small fold on the anterior loop of M_1 ('*Mimomys* fold') is present in most of the young (unrooted) teeth of *M. savini*. The character is retained in about 30 per cent of Cromerian *A. cantiana*, but is rarer in later samples, and virtually absent from the Ipswichian onwards. The third main morphological character to change is the thickness of enamel on the convex angles of the cheek teeth. In all species of *Mimomys* it is considerably thicker than on the concave side – an adaptation that reduces the rate at which the teeth wear down. The character is retained in Cromerian and Hoxnian *A. cantiana*, possibly because the teeth did not grow as fast as in later *Arvicola*. It is also present, to a variable extent, in Ipswichian and early Devensian samples, but subsequently disappears. For convenience the species boundary between *A. cantiana* and the living *A. terrestris* can be drawn after the last appearance of this character. Of particular interest

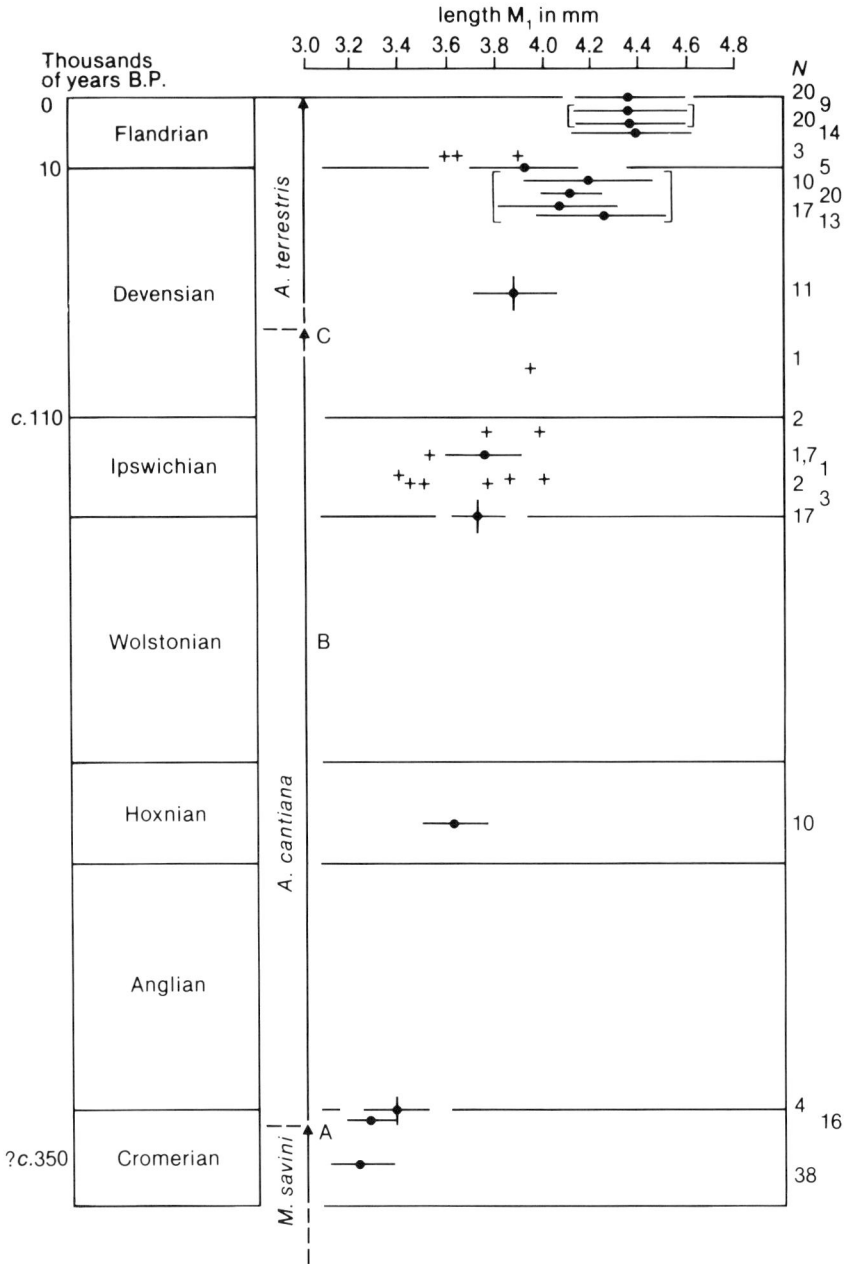

Fig. 11.3. Preliminary diagram of size changes in the *Mimomys savini* to *Arvicola terrestris* lineage, relative timing of morphological changes and suggested taxonomic divisions. Means of samples are indicated by dots, standard deviations by horizontal bars. Single measurements are indicated by crosses. Vertical bars denote some uncertainty in stratigraphical position. (a) loss of roots and achievement of permanently growing molars; (b) last occurrence of '*Mimomys* fold'; (c) last occurrence of convex-thickened enamel. Note that the relative time scale is schematic only.

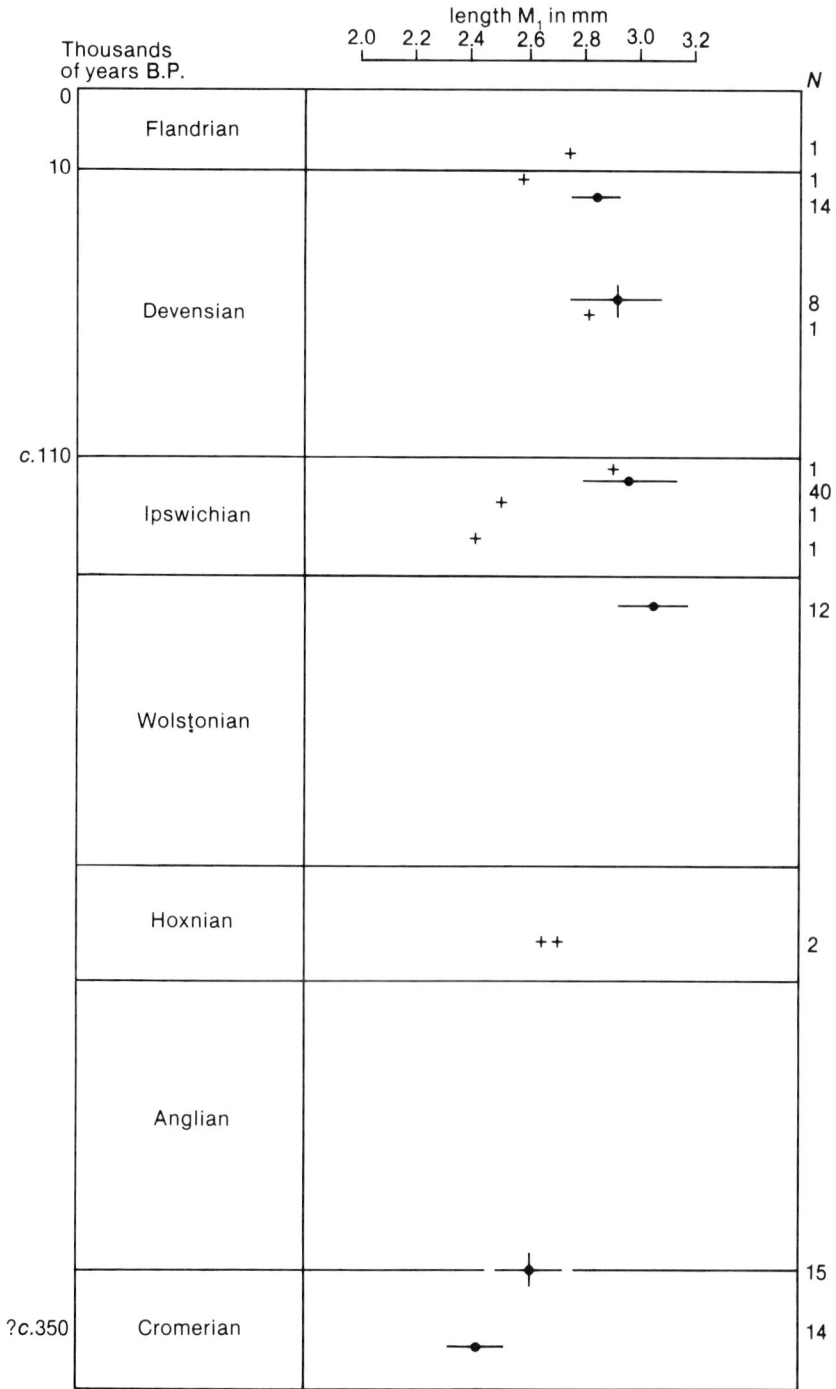

Fig. 11.4. Fluctuations in size in northern vole *Microtus oeconomus* during the British Middle and Upper Pleistocene. Symbols as in Fig. 11.3. Note that the relative time scale is schematic only.

is the fact that the later Ipswichian populations of zones IpIII–IV have a higher proportion of specimens with concave thicker enamel, than have most samples from earlier in the stage and from the Late Wolstonian (Stuart & Joysey, in preparation).

In addition to the character changes described above, there is a trend towards increased size, so that modern *A. terrestris* molars from England are some 30% per cent larger than those of Cromerian *M. savini* (Fig. 11.3). Most of this size increase occurs, however, between the Ipswichian and later Flandrian and even within this period there is by no means a uniform progression, as shown especially by the anomolously small form from the early Flandrian.

The deviations from a temporal progressive sequence of changes within an evolutionary lineage probably result from the fact that our samples are taken from a small geographical area. On any one time plane, variation in the characters discussed above may have existed between populations in different geographical areas. Changes in climatic or other factors could then have resulted in the geographical shifting of these populations, resulting at a given location in apparent minor evolutionary reversals, superimposed on the overall trend.

Changes in overall size correlated with climatic fluctuations between cold and temperate stages are known to have occurred in several species of Pleistocene mammals in Europe (Kurtén 1968). Such changes are probably not genotypic but nevertheless can be conveniently considered here.

This phenomenon is seen in the northern vole *Microtus oeconomus*, where samples from the cold stages are considerably larger than those from interglacials, although specimens from the end of the Ipswichian interglacial are also large (Fig. 11.4). Samples from successive levels, probably covering much of the Ipswichian, at Bacon Hole Cave, Glamorganshire (Fig. 11.5) record such changes at a single site.

This pattern can be interpreted in terms of the shifting of geographical size clines, caused by climatic changes (Fig. 11.6). The absence of *M. oeconomus* both from the mid-Ipswichian, from

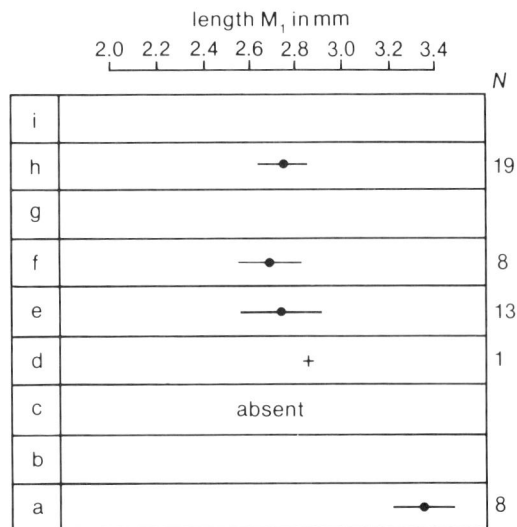

Fig. 11.5. Size changes in northern vole *Microtus oeconomus* at a single locality, Bacon Hole Cave, Glamorganshire. a to i are successive beds. Vertebrate remains have not been found in b, g and i; but in the rich faunas of c and d, *M. oeconomus* is virtually absent (the single record from d may be intrusive).

which rich faunas are known, and from most of the Flandrian, is consistent with this interpretation, although it is not clear to what extent such clines exist across the range of this species at the present day.

During the Flandrian, several species of European mammals showed progressive size changes; generally a decrease in size – 'Postglacial dwarfing' (Kurtén 1968). In the British Isles this phenomenon is seen in a sequence of fossil and modern red deer *Cervus elaphus* populations (Fig. 11.7). Similar sequences are recorded from Sweden, Denmark and Norway (Ahlén 1964). The observation that within a few generations the descendants of European red deer introduced to New Zealand show dramatic size increases, indicates that the Flandrian trend of size reduction is purely phenotypic, probably in response to forest destruction and hunting by man.

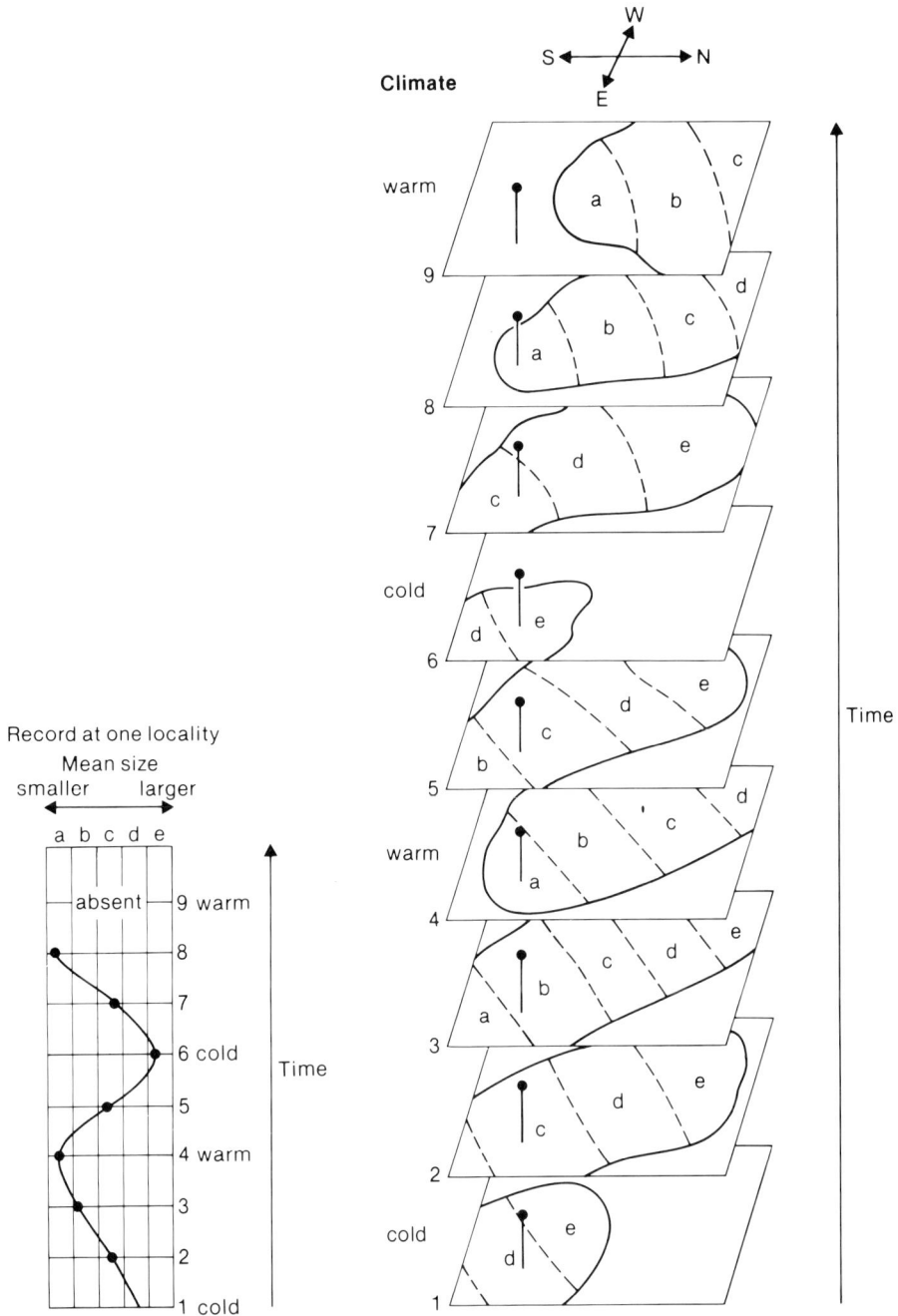

Fig. 11.6. A suggested schematic model showing possible effects of climatic change on geographical distribution. a to e are arbitrary subdivisions of a single continuous cline, where the northern populations are larger. The progressive southward shifting of the cline in response to cooling of the climate, and northward shift as the climate ameliorates, results in oscillations in size of fossils from any one locality (e.g. at *x*, marked by 'pin' in the map). Note that at time 9, *x* is outside the range of the species.

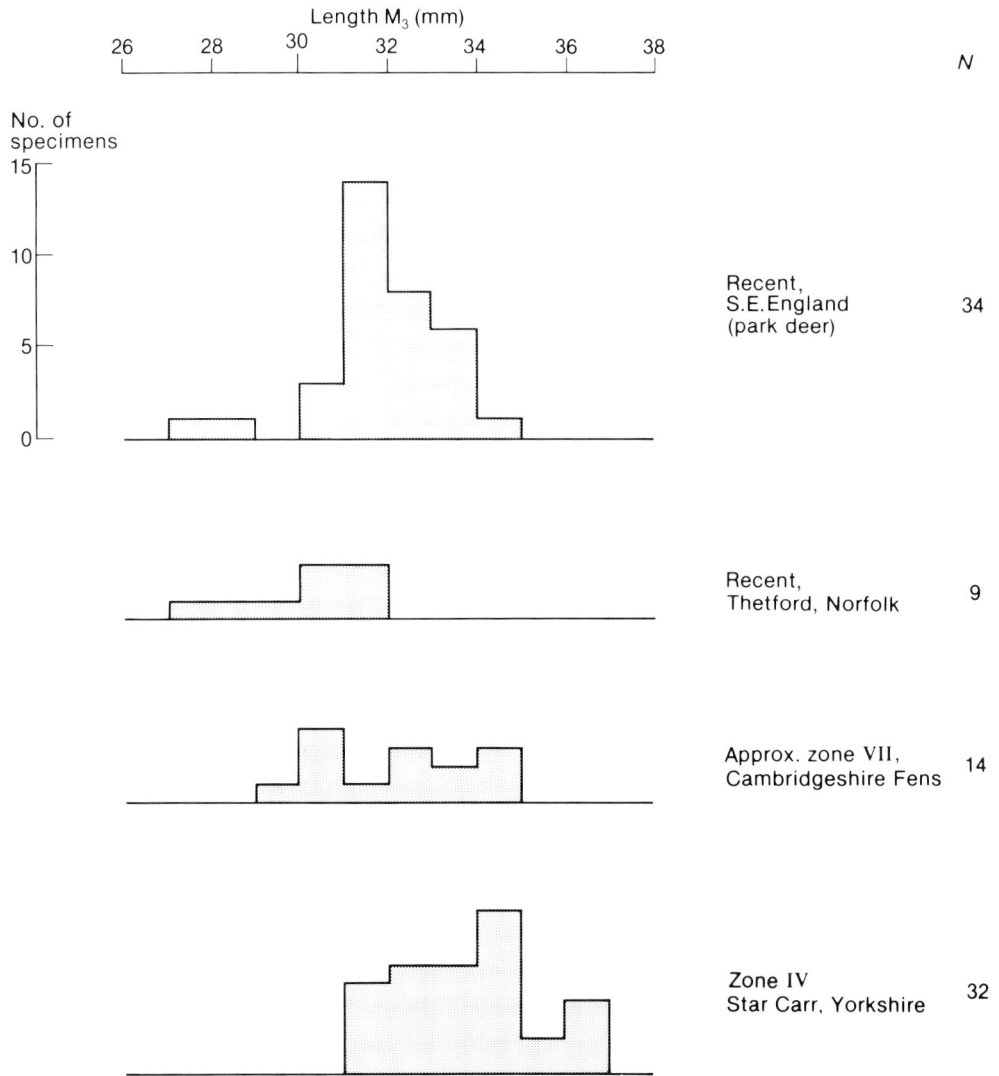

Fig. 11.7. Size changes in red deer *Cervus elaphus* during the Flandrian (after Lister 1981).

Appendix
Collection and conservation of Pleistocene vertebrate fossils

Palaeontological techniques applicable to Pleistocene vertebrate fossils are described by Rixon (1976) and Kummel and Raup (1965).

Large mammals

Large-mammal bones and teeth discovered in the field can usually be extracted simply by careful excavation with trowel and knife, and after wrapping can be transported to the laboratory for any necessary cleaning and conservation. The precise stratigraphical position of material found *in situ* should of course be carefully recorded, with sketches, drawn sections, and also, if possible, photographs. Samples of sediment adjacent to the find should be taken where appropriate for subsequent pollen analyses and study of invertebrates (see West 1977a, Appendix 1). In the case of Devensian and Flandrian finds, the possibilities of taking samples of plant material or charcoal for radiocarbon dating should be investigated.

Cracked, fragmented and soft, partly decalcified bones may need conservation in the field if they are to survive excavation and transport. Field conservation techniques for large-vertebrate remains, involving supporting the specimen with plaster bandages, or polyurethane foam, and splints, are described in detail by Rixon (1976).

Bones and teeth of large mammals generally require conservation treatment in the laboratory. Unless highly mineralized, the bones can be impregnated with PVA which adds considerable strength, retains the shape, and prevents, or at least minimizes, cracking. The bones can be soaked in a water-based PVA emulsion for several hours or days as necessary, and subsequently left to dry. Best results are obtained by vacuum impregnation. Care must be taken that the emulsion does not leak out and form a lump of plastic on one side. Small amounts of PVA can, however, be picked or peeled from the bone surface. The technique is especially useful since it is unnecessary to dry out a damp bone before treatment. For very large specimens the emulsion can be liberally brushed on to the surface of the bone. It is advisable always to leave some material untreated for possible radiocarbon or other chemical assay.

PVA emulsion is sold commercially as an adhesive and for consolidating cracked concrete, etc. In this form it requires dilution with water.

Large specimens should be labelled by writing on the bone itself in some indelible medium. The label should include above all the locality and horizon, since, unlike the identification of the specimen, this information is irreplaceable. Methods of storing large-vertebrate material are discussed by Gentry (1979).

Small vertebrates

Small-vertebrate material can occur in abundance in Pleistocene sediments containing calcium carbonate. In lacustrine and fluviatile deposits, horizons containing molluscan shells may be worth sieving to look for small-vertebrate remains, since elsewhere the sediments may have been leached, destroying both shells and vertebrate fossils. Remains of terrestrial vertebrates in fluviatile deposits seem to be invariably associated with shells of terrestrial molluscs and relatively coarse sediments, indicating erosion and transport of bank material.

For sieving, a mesh of stainless steel or brass wire, retaining everything exceeding 1 mm, has been found to be practicable. Some very small shrew and mouse teeth may be lost, but this is not serious, and a smaller mesh size produces considerable problems in the much larger amounts of concentrate retained and clogging during use. It is usually desirable to have above a second sieve with larger holes, say 1 cm square, to retain large stones, shells, etc., and to hold lumps of sediment while they are breaking down. A pair of sieves each about 60 cm square, used in conjunction, have been found adequate for work in the field and for many purposes also in the laboratory. Large models are useful for processing large quantities from one site in the laboratory.

Sieving is usually only possible in water, and is best done on site, in the sea, in a stream, or in pools in gravel pits. If water is not available on site, or if the sediment does not break down readily, it may be worth transporting it in sacks and subsequently sieving it using a hose.

Intractable clay-rich sediments are best disaggregated by thorough drying and then immersing in water. Other methods include boiling, and treatment with hydrogen peroxide or 'Calgon'.

The wet concentrate can be sun- or oven-dried. The author uses a specially constructed drying cabinet containing a stack of fitted drying trays with fine nylon mesh. A through draught of hot air is provided by a 1 kW electric fan heater and a pipe at the top of the cabinet connected to the outside.

The dried concentrate is spread in small quantities on paper under a desk lamp and systematically sorted for small-vertebrate material, all of which is retained. Conservation treatment is usually unnecessary and the fossils can be stored in labelled glass tubes in boxes, or embedded in strips of soft wax in transparent plastic containers.

References

Abbott, W. J. L. (1890). Notes on some Pleistocene sections in and near London, *Proc. geol. Ass. Lond.* **11**, 473–80.

Adam, K. D. (1954). Die mittelpleistozänen Faunen von Steinheim an der Murr (Würtemburg), *Quaternaria* **1**, 131–44.

Adam, K. D. (1975). Die mittelpleistozäne Säugetier-Fauna aus dem Heppenloch bei Gutenberg (Württemberg), *Stuttgarter Beitr. Naturk. Ser. B.* **3**, 1–247.

Adams, L. (1877–81). *British Fossil Elephants.* Mon. palaeontogr. Soc.

Ahlén, I. (1964). Studies on the red deer, *Cervus elaphus* L., in Scandinavia, *Viltrevy* **3**, 1–376.

Allison, J., Godwin, H. & **Warren, S. H.** (1952). Late-glacial deposits at Nazeing in the Lea Valley, North London, *Phil. Trans. R. Soc. Lond. B.* **236**, 169–240.

Anderson, S. C. (1979). Synopsis of the turtles, crocodiles and amphisbaenids of Iran, *Proc. Calif. Acad. Sci.* **41**, 501–28.

Andrews, C. W. (1928). *On a Specimen of* Elephas antiquus *from Upnor.* London: British Museum (Natural History).

Apsimon, A. M., Donovan, D. T. & **Taylor, H.** (1961). The stratigraphy and archaeology of the late-glacial and post-glacial deposits at Brean Down, Somerset, *Proc. Speleol. Soc.* **9**, 67–136.

Arnold, H. R. (ed.) (1973). *Provisional Atlas of the Amphibians and Reptiles of the British Isles.* Abbots Ripton, Huntingdon: Biological Records Centre, Monks Wood Experimental Station.

Arnold, E. N. & **Burton, J. A.** (1978). *A Field Guide to the Reptiles and Amphibians of Britain and Europe.* London: Collins.

Azzaroli, A. (1953). The deer of the Weybourne Crag and Forest Bed of Norfolk, *Bull. Br. Mus. Nat. Hist.* (A. Geology) **2**, 3–96.

Azzaroli, A. (1965). The two Villafranchian horses of the Upper Valdarno, *Palaeontogr. ital.* **59**, 1–12.

Azzaroli, A. (1966). La valeur des caractères crâniens dans la classification des éléphants, *Eclog. Geol. Helv.* **59**, 541–64.

Azzaroli, A. (1970). Villafranchian correlations based on large mammals, *Giorn. Geol.* **35**, 111–31.

Azzaroli, A. (1977a). Evolutionary patterns of Villafranchian elephants in central Italy, *Atti. del. Accad. Naz. dei Lincei* **14**, 149–68.

Azzaroli, A. (1977b). The Villafranchian Stage in Italy and the Plio-Pleistocene boundary, *Giorn. Geol.* **41**, 61–79.

Azzaroli, A. & **Vialli, V.** (1971). Villafranchian, *Giorn. Geol.* **37**, 221–32.

Backhouse, J. (1886). On a mandible of *Machaerodus* from the Forest-Bed. Appendix by Lydekker, R., *Quart. Jl. Geol. Soc. Lond.* **42**, 309–12.

Banfield, A. W. F. (1974). *The Mammals of Canada.* Toronto: University of Toronto Press.

Bang, P. & **Dahlstrøm, P.** (1974). *Animal Tracks and Signs.* London: Collins.

Bannikov, A. G., Derevskii, I. S. & **Ischenko, V. G.** (1977). *Guide to the Amphibians and Reptiles of the USSR* (In Russian). Moskva 'Prosveshenie' 592(083).

Barnes, B., Edwards, B. J. N., Hallam, J. S. & **Stuart, A. J.** (1971). Skeleton of a Late Glacial elk associated with barbed points from Poulton-le-Fylde, Lancashire, *Nature Lond.* **232**, 488–9.

Barrett-Hamilton, G. E. H. & **Hinton, M. A. C.** (1910–12). *A History of British Mammals.* London: Gurney & Jackson.

Beck, R. B., Funnell, B. M. & **Lord, A. R.** (1972). Correlation of Lower Pleistocene Crag at depth in Suffolk, *Geol. Mag.* **109**, 137–9.

Behrensmeyer, A. K. & **Hill, A. P.** (eds) (1980). *Fossils in the Making: Vertebrate Taphonomy and Paleoecology.* Chicago and London: University of Chicago Press.

Bell, F. G. & **Dickson, C. A.** (1971). The Barnwell Station arctic flora: a reappraisal of some plant identifications, *New Phytol.* **70**, 627–38.

Bemrose, H. H. A. & **Newton, E. T.** (1905). On an ossiferous cavern of Pleistocene age at Hoe Grange Quarry, Longcliffe, near Brassington (Derbyshire), *Quart. Jl. Geol. Soc. Lond.* **61**, 43–63.

Berglund, B. E., Hakansson, S. & **Lagerlund, E.** (1976). Radiocarbon-dated mammoth (*Mammuthus primigenius* Blumenbach) finds in South Sweden, *Boreas* **5**, 177–91.

Berry, R. J. & **Rose, F. E. N.** (1975). Islands and the evolution of *Microtus arvalis* (Microtinae), *J. Zool. Lond.* **177**, 395–409.

Birks, H. J. (1977). The Flandrian forest history of Scotland: a preliminary synthesis. Chapter 10 in: Shotton (1977a), pp. 119–35.

Bishop, M. J. (1974). A preliminary report on the Middle Pleistocene mammal-bearing deposits of Westbury-sub-Mendip, Somerset, *Proc. Speleol. Soc.* **13**, 301–18.

Bishop, M. J. (1975). Earliest record of man's presence in Britain, *Nature, Lond.* **253**, 95–7.

Bishop, M. J. (1982). The early Middle Pleistocene Mammal Fauna of Westbury-sub-Mendip, Somerset, *Palaeontology, Special paper*, (in press).

Blackburn, K. B. (1952). The dating of a deposit containing an elk skeleton at Neasham near Darlington, County Durham, *New Phytol.* **51**, 364–77.

Blandamura, F. & Azzaroli, A. (1977). L' 'Ippopotamo Maggiore' die Fillipo Nesti, *Atti del. Accad. Naz. Linc.* **14**, 169–88.

Böhme, G. (1977). Zur Bestimmung quartärer Anuren Europas an Hand von Skelettelementen, *Wiss. Zeitschrift der Humboldt-Universität zu Berlin. Math.-Nat. R.* **26**, 283–300.

Borsuk-Bialynicka, M. (1973). Studies on the Pleistocene rhinoceros *Coelodonta antiquitatis* (Blumenbach), *Acadamie Polonaise des Sciences Institute de Paleozoologie* **29**, 1–94.

Bouchud, J. (1966). *Essai sur le Renne et la climatologie du Paleolithique moyen et superieur.* Perigueux: Imprimerie Magne.

Bowen, D. Q. (ed.) (1977). *X INQUA Congress Excursion Guides.* Norwich: Geo. Abstracts.

Boylan, P. J. (1967a). The Pleistocene mammalia of the Sewerby-Hessle buried cliff East Yorkshire, *Proc. Yorks. Geol. Soc.* **38**, 175–200.

Boylan, P. J. (1967b). Dean William Buckland 1784–1856 – a pioneer in cave science, *Stud. Spel.* **1**, 237–53.

Boylan, P. J. (1972). The scientific significance of the Kirkdale Cave hyaenas, *Yorkshire Philosophical Society. Annual Report for 1971*, 38–47.

Bramwell, D. (1960). Some research into bird distribution in Britain during the late-glacial and post glacial periods, *Bird Rep. Merseyside Nat. Ass.* 1959–60, 51–8.

Bramwell, D. (1964). The excavations at Elderbush Cave, Wetton, Staffs, *N. Staffs. J. Field Stud.* **4**, 46–50.

Bramwell, D. (1976). The vertebrate Fauna at Wetton Mill rock shelter, Ch. 3 in Kelly, J. H., (ed.), (1976). *The excavation of Wetton Mill Rock Shelter, Manifold valley*, Staffs, Stoke-on-Trent; City Museums and Art Gallery.

Bramwell, D. (1977). Archaeology and palaeontology. Chapter 14 in: Ford, T. D., 1977, *Limestone and Caves of the Peak District.* Norwich: Geo Abstracts Ltd.

Brenan, E. (1860). Notice of the discovery of extinct elephant and other animal remains, occurring in a fossil state under limestone, at Shandon, near Dungarvan, County of Waterford, *J. R. Dublin Soc.* **2**, 344–50.

Briggs, D. J., Coope, G. R. & Gilbertson, D. D. (1975). Late Pleistocene terrace deposits at Beckford, Worcestershire, England, *Geol. J.* **10**, 1–16.

Briggs, D. J., Gilbertson, D. D., Goudie, A. S., Osborne, P. J., Osmaston, H. A., Pettit, M. E., Shotton, F. W. & Stuart, A. J. (1975). New interglacial site at Sugworth, *Nature, Lond.* **257**, 477–9.

Brink, F. H. van den (1967). *A Field Guide to the Mammals of Britain and Europe.* London: Collins.

Bryant, I. D. & Holyoak, D. T. (1980). Devensian deposits at Brimpton, Berkshire, *Quaternary Newsletter* No. 30, p. 17.

Buckland, W. (1822). An account of an assemblage of fossil teeth and bones discovered in a cave at Kirkdale, *Phil. Trans. R. Soc. Lond.* **122**, 171–236.

Brüning, H. (1978). Zur Untergliederung der Mosbacher Terrassenabfolge und zume klimatischen Stellenwert der mosbacher Tierwelt im Rahmen des Cromer-Komplexes, *Mz. Naturw. Arch.* **16**, 143–90.

Butzer, K. W. & Isaac, G. L. (eds) (1975). *After the Australopithecines.* The Hague: Mouton.

Campbell, J. B. (1977). *The Upper Palaeolithic of Britain. A Study of Man and Nature in the Late Ice Age* (2 vols). Oxford: Clarendon Press.

Carreck, J. N. (1966). Microtine remains from the Norwich Crag (Lower Pleistocene) of Easton Bavents, Suffolk, *Proc. Geol. Ass.* **77**, 491–6.

Carreck, J. N. (1976). Pleistocene mammalian and molluscan remains from 'Taplow' Terrace deposits at West Thurrock, near Grays, Essex, *Proc. Geol. Ass. Lond.* **87**, 83–92.

Carte, A. (1860). Description of the fossil discovery by Mr Brenan at Shandon near Dungarvan, *J. R. Dublin Soc.* **2**, 351–7.

Catt, J. A. (1977). Yorkshire and Lincolnshire, *X Inqua Congress Excursion Guides.* Norwich: Geo Abstracts.

Chaline, J. (1974). Equisse de l'évolution morphologique, biométrique et chromosomique du genre *Microtus* (Arvicolidae, Rodentia) dans le Pléistocène de l'hémisphère nord. *Bull. Soc. Géol. France* **16**, 440–450.

Chaline, J. & Mein, P. (1979). *Les Rongeurs et l'Evolution.* Paris: Doin Editeurs.

Chapman, D. I. (1975). Antlers-bones of contention, *Mammal Review* **5**, 121–72.

Churchill, D. M. (1962). The stratigraphy of the Mesolithic sites III and IV at Thatcham, Berkshire, England, *Proc. Prehist. Soc.* **28**, 362–70.

Clark, J. G. D. (1954). *Excavations at Star Carr.* Cambridge: Cambridge University Press.

Clark, J. G. D. (1971). *World Prehistory. A New Outline.* Cambridge: Cambridge University Press.

Clark, J. G. D. (1972). Star Carr; a case study in Bioarchaeology. *Addison Wesley Modular Publication* **10**, 1–42.

Coope, G. R. (1962). A Pleistocene coleopterous fauna with arctic affinities from Fladbury, Worcestershire, *Quart. Jl. Geol. Soc. Lond.* **118**, 103–23.

Coope, G. R. (1959). A late Pleistocene insect fauna from Chelford, Cheshire. *Proc. R. Soc. Lond. B.* **151**, 70–86.

Coope, G. R. (1968a). An insect fauna from Mid-Weichselian deposits at Brandon, Warwickshire. *Phil. Trans. R. Soc. Lond. B.* **254**, 425–56.

Coope, G. R. (1968b). Coleoptera from the 'Arctic Bed' at Barnwell Station, Cambridge, *Geol. Mag.* **105**, 482–6.

Coope, G. R. (1973). The ancient world of '*Megaceros*', *Deer* **2**, 10 Feb. 1973.

Coope, G. R. (1974). Interglacial Coleoptera from Bobbitshole, Ipswich, Suffolk, *Jl. Geol. Soc. Lond.* **130**, 333–40.

Coope, G. R. (1977). Fossil coleopteran assemblages as sensitive indicators of climatic changes during the Devensian (Last) cold stage. *Phil. Trans. R. Soc. Lond. B.* **280**, 313–40.

Coope, G. R. & Angus, R. B. (1975). An ecological study of a temperate interlude in the middle of the Last Glaciaton, based on fossil Coleoptera from Isleworth, Middlesex, *J. Anim. Ecol.* **44**, 365–91.

Coope, G. R., Morgan, A. & Osborne, P. J. (1971). Fossil Coleoptera as indicators of climatic fluctuations during the last glaciation in Britain, *Palaeogeogr., Palaeoclimatol., Palaeoecol.* **10**, 87–101.

Coope, G. R. & Pennington, W. (1977). The Windermere Interstadial of the Late Devensian, *Phil. Trans. R. Soc. Lond. B.* **280**, 337–9.

Coope, G. R., Shotton, F. W. & Strachan, I. (1961). A late Pleistocene fauna and flora from Upton Warren, Worcestershire, *Phil. Trans. R. Soc. Lond. B.* **244**, 379–421.

Corbet, G. B. (1961). Origin of the British insular races of small mammals and of the 'Lusitanian' fauna, *Nature, Lond.* **191**, 1037–40.

Corbet, G. B. (1966). *The Terrestrial Mammals of Western Europe.* London: Foulis.

Corbet, G. B. (1974). The distribution of mammals in historic times. Chapter 11 in Hawksworth (1974), pp. 179–202.

Corbet, G. B. (1975). Examples of short- and long-term changes of dental pattern in Scottish voles (Rodentia; Microtinae), *Mammal Rev.* **5**, 17–21.

Corbet, G. B. (1978). *The Mammals of the Palaearctic Region: a taxonomic review.* London and Ithaca: British Museum (Natural History), Cornell University Press.

Corbet, G. B. & Southern, H. N. (eds) (1977). *The Handbook of British Mammals* (2nd edn). Oxford: Blackwell.

Cotton, R. P. (1847). On the Pliocene deposits of the Valley of the Thames at Ilford, *Ann. Mag. Nat. Hist.* **20**, 164–9.

Coxon, P. (1979). Pleistocene Environmental History in Central East Anglia. Ph.D. Thesis, University of Cambridge.

Coxon, P., Hall, A. R., Lister, A. & Stuart, A. J. (1980). New evidence on the vertebrate fauna, stratigraphy and palaeobotany of the interglacial deposits at Swanton Morley, Norfolk, *Geol. Mag.* **117**, 525–546.

Davies, J. A. (1922). Aveline's Hole, Burrington Combe, *Proc. Speleol. Soc.* **1**, 61–8.

Dawkins, W. B. (1866). On the dentition of *Rhinoceros leptorhinus* Owen, *Proc. R. Soc. Lond.* **15**, 106–7.

Dawkins, W. B. (1867). On the dentition of *Rhinoceros leptorhinus* Owen, *Q. Jl. Geol. Soc. Lond.* **23**, 213–27.

Dawkins, W. B. (1868). On the dentition of *Rhinoceros etruscus* Falconer, *Q. Jl. Geol. Soc. Lond.* **24**, 207–18.

Dawkins, W. B. (1871). On the discovery of the glutton (*Gulo luscus*) in Britain, *Q. Jl. Geol. Soc. Lond.* **27**, 406–10.

Dawkins, W. B. (1877). On the mammal-fauna of the caves of Creswell Crags, *Quart. Jl. Geol. Soc. Lond.* **33**, 589–612.

Dawkins, W. B. (1903). On the discovery of an ossiferous cavern of Pleistocene age at Dove Holes, Buxton (Derbyshire), *Quart. Jl. Geol. Soc. Lond.* **59**, 105–33.

Dawkins, W. B. & Reynolds, S. H. (1872–1939). The British Pleistocene Mammalia. 3. The British Pleistocene Artiodactyla, *Palaeontogr. Soc.* (Monogr.).

Dawkins, W. B. & Sanford, W. A. (1866–72). The British Pleistocene Mammalia. I. The British Pleistocene Felidae, *Palaeontogr. Soc.* (Monogr.).

Deckert, K. & Karrer, C. (1965). Die Fischreste des Frühpleistozäns von Voigtstedt in Thüringen, *Paläont. Abh. AII 2/3*, 299–322.

Degerbøl, M. (1961). On a find of a Preboreal domestic dog from Star Carr, Yorkshire, *Proc. Prehist. Soc.* **27**, 35–55.

Degerbøl, M. (1964). Some remarks on late and post-glacial vertebrate fauna and its ecological relations in northern Europe, *J. Anim. Ecol.* **33** (Supplement), 71–85.

Degerbøl, M. & Krog, H. (1951). Den europaieske Sumpskilpadde (*Emys orbicularis* L.) i Danmark (with English summary), *Dan. Geol. Unders. II Raekke* **78**, 1–130.

Delair, J. B. (1969). North of the hippopotamus belt: a brief review of Scottish fossil mammals, *Bull. Mammal Soc. Br. Isl.* **31**, 16–21.

Dorst, J. & Dandelot, P. (1970). *A Field Guide to the Larger Mammals of Africa.* London: Collins.

Duigan, S. L. (1955). Plant remains from the gravels of the Summertown-Radley Terrace near Dorchester, Oxfordshire, *Quart. Jl. Geol. Soc. Lond.* **3**, 225–38.

Erd, K. (1965). Pollenanalytische Untersuchungen im Altpleistozän von Voigtstedt in Thüringen, *Paläontol. Abh. A.* **2**, 261–72.

Felten, H., Helfricht, A. & Storch, G. (1973). Die Bestimmung der europäischen Fledermäuse nach der distalen Epiphyse des Humerus, *Senckenbergiana biol.* **54**, 291–7.

Fisher, O. (1879). On a mammaliferous deposit at Barrington near Cambridge, *Q. Jl. Geol. Soc. Lond.* **35**, 670–7.

Flerov, K. K. (1952). *Fauna of the USSR. Mammals Vol. I. Musk deer and deer.* Moscow and Leningrad (English translation: Jerusalem, 1960).

Forbes, C. L., Joysey, K. A. & West, R. G. (1958). Post-glacial pelicans in Britain, *Geol. Mag.* **95**, 153–60.

Franks, J. W. (1960). Interglacial deposits at Trafalgar Square, London, *New Phytol.* **59**, 145–50.

Franks, J. W., Sutcliffe, A. J., Kerney, M. P. & Coope, G. R. (1958). Haunt of elephant and rhinoceros: the Trafalgar Square of 100 000 years ago – new discoveries, *Illustrated London News*, 14 June 1958, 1011–13.

Fraser, F. C. & King, J. E. (1954). Faunal remains. Chapter 3 in Clark (1954).

Freeman, L. G. (1973). The significance of mammalian faunas from Palaeolithic occupation sites in Cantabrian Spain, *Am. Antiq.* **38**, 3–44.

Freshwater Biological Association (1960). 28th Annual Report, *Freshwater Biol. Ass.*, 35–6.

Freudenthal, M., Meijer, T. & Meulen, A. J. van der. (1976). Preliminary report on a field campaign in the continental Pleistocene of Tegelen (Netherlands), *Scripta. Geol.* **34**, 1–27.

Funnell, B. M. (1961). The Palaeogene and early Pleistocene of Norfolk, *Trans. Norfolk Norwich Nat. Soc.* **19**, 340–64.

Funnell, B. M., Norton, P. E. P. & West, R. G. (1979). The crag at Bramerton, near Norwich, Norfolk, *Phil. Trans. R. Soc. B.* **287**, 489–534.

Funnell, B. M. & West, R. G. (1962). The early Pleistocene of Easton Bavents, *Quart Jl. Geol. Soc. Lond.* **118**, 125–41.

Funnell, B. M. & West, R. G. (1977). Preglacial Pleistocene deposits in East Anglia. Chapter 19 in Shotton (1977a), pp. 247–65.

Gascoyne, M. (1981). Chronology and climate of the middle and late Pleistocene from speleothems in caves in north-west England, *Quaternary Newsletter.* **34**, 36–7.

Gaunt, G. D., Coope, G. R. & Franks, J. W. (1970). Quaternary deposits at Oxbow opencast coal site in the Aire Valley, Yorkshire, *Proc. Yorks. Geol. Soc.* **38**, 175–200.

Gentry, A. W. (1979). Curation of fossil vertebrates, *Special Papers in Palaeontology* **22**, 87–95.

Gibbard, P. L. & Pettit, M. (1978). The palaeobotany of interglacial deposits at Sugworth, Berkshire, *New Phytol.* **81**, 465–77.

Gibbard, P. L. & Stuart, A. J. (1975). Flora and vertebrate fauna of the Barrington Beds, *Geol. Mag.* **112**, 493–501.

Gingerich, P. D. (1980). Evolutionary patterns in early Cenozoic mammals, *Ann. Rev. Earth Planet. Sci.* **8**, 407–24.

Girling, M. (1974). Evidence from Lincolnshire of the age and intensity of the mid-Devensian temperate episode, *Nature, Lond.* **250**, 270.

Gladfelter, B. G. & Singer, R. (1975). Implications of East Anglian glacial stratigraphy for the British Lower Palaeolithic. In Suggate, R. P. & Cresswell, M. M. (eds). *Quaternary Studies.* The Royal Society of New Zealand, pp. 139–45.

Godwin, H. (1943). Coastal peat beds of the British Isles and North Sea, *J. Ecol.* **31**, 199.

Godwin, H. (1975). (2nd edn). *The History of the British Flora.* Cambridge: Cambridge University Press.

Godwin, H. (1977). Quaternary history of the British flora. Chapter 9 in Shotton (1977a), pp. 107–18.

Godwin, H. (1978). *Fenland: its Ancient Past and Uncertain Future.* Cambridge: Cambridge University Press.

Godwin, H. & Tallantire, P. A. (1951). Studies in the post-glacial history of British vegetation. XII. Hockham Mere, Norfolk. *Jl. Ecol.* **39**, 285–307.

Gould, S. J. (1974). The origin and function of 'bizarre' structures: antler size and skull size in the 'Irish elk' *Megaloceros giganteus*, *Evolution* **28**, 191–220.

Gregory, J. W. & Currie, E. D. (1928). The vertebrate fossils from the glacial and associated postglacial beds of Scotland in the Hunterian Museum, University of Glasgow, *Monographs of the Geol. Dept. of the Hunterian Museum, Glasg. Univ.* **2**, 1–21.

Groves, C. P. (1974). *Horses, Asses and Zebras in the Wild.* Newton Abbot, London: David & Charles.

Hall, A. R. (1980). Late Pleistocene deposits at Wing, Rutland, *Phil. Trans. R. Soc. Lond. B.* **289**, 135–64.

Hall, J. & Yalden, D. W. (1978). A plea for caution over the identification of late Pleistocene *Microtus* in Britain, *J. Zool. Lond.* **186**, 556–60.

Hallam, J. S., Edwards, B. J. N., Barnes, B. & Stuart, A. J. (1973). The remains of a Late Glacial elk with associated barbed points from High Furlong, near Blackpool, Lancashire, *Proc. Prehist. Soc.* **39**, 100–28.

Haltenorth, T. and Diller, H. (1980). *A Field guide to the mammals of Africa including Madagascar*, London: Collins.

Harmer, S. F. (1899). On a specimen of *Cervus belgrandi* Lart. (*C. verticornis* Dawk.) from the Forest Bed of East Anglia, *Trans. Zool. Soc. Lond.* **15**, 97–108.

Harrison, C. J. O. (1978). A new jungle fowl from the Pleistocene of Europe, *J. Arch. Sci.* **5**, 373–6.

Harrison, C. J. O. (1979a). Birds of the Cromer Forest Bed. Series of the East Anglian Pleistocene, *Trans. Nflk & Norwich Nat. Soc.* **24**, 277–86.

Harrison, C. J. O. (1979b). Pleistocene birds from Swanscombe, Kent, *London Nat.* **58**, 6–8.

Harrison, C. J. O. (1980). Pleistocene bird remains from Tornewton Cave and the Brixham Windmill Hill Cave in south Devon, *Bull. Br. Mus. Nat. Hist. (Geol.)* **33**(2), 91–100.

Harrison, C. J. O. & Cowles, G. S. (1977). The extinct large cranes of the north-west Palaearctic, *J. Arch. Sci.* **4**, 25–7.

Harrison, C. J. O. & Walker, C. A. (1977). A re-examination of the fossil birds from the Upper Pleistocene of the London Basin, *London Nat.* **56**, 6–9.

Hawksworth, D. L. (ed.) (1974). *The Changing Flora and Fauna of Britain.* London & New York: Academic Press (for the Systematics Association, Special Vol. No. 6).

Heintz, A. (1958). On the pollen analysis of the stomach contents of the Beresorvka mammoth (In Norwegian with an English summary), *Blyttia, Oslo* **16**, 122–42.

Heintz, A. & Garutt, V. E. (1965). Determination of the absolute age of the fossil remains of mammoth and woolly rhinoceros from the permafrost in Siberia by the help of radiocarbon (C_{14}), *Norsk. Geol. Tidsskr.* **45**, 73–9.

Heintz, E. (1970). Les Cervidés Villafranchiens de France et d'Espagne, *Mémoires du Museum National d'Histoire Naturelle Ser. C.* **22**, 1–303.

Heinzel, H., Fitter, R. S. R. & Parslow, J. L. F. (1972). *The Birds of Britain and Europe.* London: Collins.

Hill, W. C. O. (1974). *Primates, Comparative Anatomy and Taxonomy. VII Cynopithecinae.* Edinburgh: The University Press.

Hinton, M. A. C. (1908). Note on the discovery of the bone of a monkey in the Norfolk Forest Bed, *Geol. Mag.* **5**, 440–4.

Hinton, M. A. C. (1911). The British fossil shrews, *Geol. Mag.* **8**, 529–39.

Hinton, M. A. C. (1912). Note on the lemming remains from the Arctic Bed at Angel Road, *Q. Jl. Geol. Soc. Lond.* **68**, 249.

Hinton, M. A. C. (1914). On some remains of rodents from the Red Crag of Suffolk and from the Norfolk Forest Bed, *Ann. Mag. Nat. Hist.* **13**, 186–195.

Hinton, M. A. C. (1915). British fossil specimens of *Apodemus, Ann. Mag. Nat. Hist.* **15**, 580–4.

Hinton, M. A. C. (1926). *Monograph of the Voles and Lemmings (Microtinae), living and extinct.* Vol. I (Vol. II not published). London: British Museum (Natural History).

Hooijer, D. A. (1959). *Trogontherium cuvieri* Fischer from the Neede Clay (Mindel-Riss Interglacial) of the Netherlands, *Zool. Meded., Leiden* **36**, 275–80.

Hughes, T. M. (1911). Excursions to Cambridge and Barrington, *Proc. Geol Ass.* **22**, 268–78.

Jacobi, R. M. (1978). Northern England in the eighth millenium BC: an essay. Chapter 12 in Mellars (1978).

Jánossy, D. (1965). Vogelreste aus den altpleistozänen Ablagerungen von Voigtstedt in Thüringen, *Paläont. Abh. AII* **2/3** 335–61.

Jánossy, D. (1975). Mid-Pleistocene microfaunas of Continental Europe and adjoining areas. In Butzer & Isaac (1975).

Jessen, K. & Farrington, A. (1938). The bogs at Ballybetagh, near Dublin, with remarks on late-glacial conditions in Ireland, *Proc. R. Irish Acad.* **44** (B), 205–60.

Joysey, K. A. (1972). The fossil species in space and time: some problems of evolutionary interpretation among Pleistocene mammals. In Joysey, K. A. & Kemp, T. S. (1972), *Studies in Vertebrate Evolution.* Edinburgh: Oliver & Boyd.

Kahlke, H. D. (ed.) (1965). Das Pleistozän von Voigtstedt, *Paläont. Abh. AII* **2/3**, 227–692.

Kahlke, H. D. (ed.) (1969). Das Pleistozän von Süssenborn, *Paläont. Abh. AIII,* **3/4**, 367–788.

Kahlke, H. D. (ed.) (1974). Das Pleistozän von Weimar-Ehringsdorf. Teil 1, *Paläont. Abh.* **21**, 1–351.

Kahlke, H. D. (1975a). The macro-faunas of Continental Europe during the Middle Pleistocene: stratigraphic sequence and problems of intercorrelation. In Butzer & Isaac (1975), pp. 309–74.

Kahlke, H. D. (1975b). Der Saiga-Fund von Bottrop/Westfalen, *Quartär* **26**, 135–46.

Kahlke, H. D. (ed.) (1975c). Das Pleistozän von Weimar-Ehringsdorf. Teil 2. *Paläont. Abh.* **23**, 1–594.

Kahlke, H. D. (ed.) (1977). Das Pleistozän von Taubach bei Weimar, *Quartärpaläontologie. Berlin* **2**, 1–509.

Kahlke, H. D. (ed.) (1979). Das Pleistozän von Burgtonna in Thüringen, *Quartärpaläontologie Berlin* **3**, 1–359.

Kelly, M. R. (1964). The Middle Pleistocene of north Birmingham, *Phil. Trans. R. Soc. Lond. B.* **247**, 533–92.

Kelly, M. R. (1968). Floras of Middle and Upper Pleistocene age from Brandon, Warwickshire, *Phil. Trans. R. Lond. Soc. B.* **254**, 401–15.

Kennard, A. S. (1944). The Crayford brickearths, *Proc. Geol. Ass.* **55**, 121–69.

Kerney, M. P. (1971). Interglacial deposits in Barnfield Pit, Swanscombe, and their molluscan fauna, *Jl. Geol. Soc. Lond.* **127**, 69–93.

King, C. A. M. (1977). The early Quaternary landscape with consideration of neotectonic matters. Chapter 11 in Shotton (1977a), pp. 137–52.

Klein, R. G. (1971). The Pleistocene prehistory of Siberia, *Quaternary Research* **1**, 133–61.

Koenigswald, W. R. von (1973). Veranderungen in der Kleinsäugerfauna von Mitteleuropa zwischen Cromer und Eem (Pleistocän), *Eiszeitalter Gegenw.,* **23–24**, 159–167.

Koenigswald, W. von & Golenishev, F. N. (1979). A method for determining growth rates in continuously growing molars, *Jl. Mammalogy* **60**, 397–400.

Kortenbout van der Sluijs, G. & Zagwijn, W. H. (1962). An introduction to the stratigraphy and geology of the Tegelen clay-pits, *Meded. Geol. Stichting. N.S.* **15**, 31–7.

Kowalski, K. (1967). *Lagurus lagurus* (Pallas 1773) and *Cricetus cricetus* (L. 1758) (Rodentia, Mammalia) in the Pleistocene of England, *Acta Zool. Cracov.* **12**, 111–22.

Kretzoi, M. (1965). Die Nager und Lagomorphen von Voigtstedt in Thüringen und ihre chronologische Aussage, *Palaontol. Abh. AII* 2/3, 585–661.

Kummel, B. & Raup, D. (eds.) (1965). *Handbook of Paleontological Techniques.* San Francisco and London: W. H. Freeman and Company.

Kurtén, B. (1953). On the variation and population dynamics of fossil and recent mammal populations, *Acta Zool. Fenn.* **76**, 1–122.

Kurtén, B. (1958). The bears and hyaenas of the interglacials, *Quaternaria* 4, 69–81.

Kurtén, B. (1963). Villafranchian faunal evolution, *Soc. Sci. Fenn. Comment. Biol.* **26**, 3.

Kurtén, B. (1964). The evolution of the polar bear *Ursus maritimus* Phipps, *Acta Zool. Fenn.* **108**, 1–26.

Kurtén, B. (1965). On the evolution of the European wild cat *Felis sylvestris* Schreber, *Acta Zool. Fenn.* **111**, 1–26.

Kurtén, B. (1968). *Pleistocene Mammals of Europe.* London: Weidenfeld and Nicolson.

Kurtén, B. (1969). Sexual dimorphism in fossil mammals. In Westermann, G. E. G. (ed.) (1969). *Sexual Dimorphism in Fossil Metazoa and Taxonomic Implications.* Stuttgart: Schweizerbart.

Kurtén, B. (1973). Fossil glutton (*Gulo gulo* (L.)) from Tornewton Cave, South Devon, *Commentat. Biol.* **66**, 1–8.

Lambert, C. A., Pearson, R. G. & Sparks, B. W. (1962). Pleistocene deposits from Sidgwick Avenue, Cambridge, *Proc. Linn. Soc. Lond.* **174**, 13–29.

Layard, N. F. (1920). The Stoke Bone Bed, Ipswich, *Proc. Prehist. Soc. E. Anglia*, 210–19.

Leonardi, G. & Petronio, C. (1976). The fallow deer of European Pleistocene, *Geologica Romana* 25, 1–67.

Lever, C. (1979). The Naturalised Animals of the British Isles. London, Toronto, Sydney, New York: Granada Publishing.

Lister, A. (1981). Evolutionary Studies on Pleistocene Deer. Ph.D. Thesis, University of Cambridge.

Lock, J. M. (1972). The effects of hippopotamus grazing on grasslands, *J. Ecol.* **60**, 445–67.

Lumley, H. de (ed.) (1976). *La Prehistoire Française* (2 vols). Paris: C.N.R.S.

McWilliams, B. (1967). *Fossil vertebrates of the Cromer Forest Bed in Norwich Castle Museum.* Norwich: City of Norwich Museums.

Maglio, V. J. (1973). Origin and evolution of the Elephantidae, *Trans. Am. Phil. Soc.* **62**, 1–149.

Martin, P. S. & Wright, H. E. (eds.) (1967). *Pleistocene Extinctions, the Search for a Cause.* Yale: University Press.

Marr, J. E. & Gardner, E. W. (1916). On some deposits containing an arctic flora in the Pleistocene beds of Barnwell, Cambridge, *Geol. Mag.* **3**, 339–43.

Mayhew, D. F. (1975). The Quaternary History of some British Rodents and Lagomorphs. Ph.D. Thesis, University of Cambridge.

Mayhew, D. F. (1977). Avian predators as accumulators of fossil mammal material, *Boreas* **6**, 25–31.

Mayhew, D. F. (1978). Reinterpretation of the extinct beaver *Trogontherium* (Mammalia, Rodentia), *Phil. Trans. R. Soc. Lond. B.* **281**, 407–38.

Mayhew, D. F. (1979). The vertebrate fauna of Bramerton. Appendix III in Funnell, Norton & West (1979).

Mellars, P. A. (1974). The Palaeolithic and Mesolithic. Chapter 2 in Renfrew C. (1974), pp. 41–99.

Mellars, P. (1976). Fire ecology, animal populations and man: a study of some ecological relationships in prehistory, *Proc. Prehist. Soc.* **42**, 15–45.

Mellars, P. (ed.) (1978) *The early postglacial settlement of northern Europe. An ecological perspective*, London: Duckworth.

Mellars, P. & Payne, S. (1971). Excavation of two Mesolithic shell middens on the Island of Oronsay (Inner Hebrides). *Nature, Lond.* **231**, 397–8.

Mellet, J. S. (1974). Scatological origin of microvertebrate fossil accumulations, *Science N.Y.* **185**, 349–50.

Miller, G. S. (1912). *Catalogue of the Mammals of Western Europe.* London: British Museum.

Mitchell, G. F. (1941). Studies in Irish Quaternary deposits. 3. The Reindeer in Ireland, *Proc. R. Ir. Acad.* **46**(B), 183–8.

Mitchell, G. F. (1958). A late-glacial deposit near Ballaugh, Isle of Man, *New Phytol.* **57**, 256–63.

Mitchell, G. F. (1960). The Pleistocene history of the Irish Sea, *Advmt. Sci. Lond.* **17**, 313–25.

Mitchell, G. F. (1976). *The Irish Landscape.* London: Collins.

Mitchell, G. F. & Parkes, H. M. (1949). The giant deer in Ireland, *Proc. R. Ir. Acad.* **52**(B), 291–314.

Mitchell, G. F., Penny, L. F., Shotton, F. W. & West, R. G. (1973). A correlation of Quaternary deposits in the British Isles, *Geol. Soc. Lond. Spec. Rep.* **4**.

Młynarski, M. & Ullrich, H. (1975). Amphibien-und Reptilienreste aus dem Travertin von Weimar-Ehringsdorf, *Pal. Abh.* **23**, 137–45.

Moir, J. R. & Hopwood, A. T. (1939). Excavations at Brundon, Suffolk (1935–37), *Proc. Prehist. Soc.* **5**, 1–32.

Mollison, T. (1977). Skeletal remains of man in the British Quaternary. Chapter 7 in Shotton (1977a), pp. 83–92.

Montfrans, H. M. van (1971). *Palaeomagnetic dating in the North Sea Basin.* Rotterdam: Prince N.V.

Morgan, A. V. (1973). The Pleistocene geology of the area north and west of Wolverhampton, Staffordshire, England, *Phil. Trans. R. Soc. Lond. B.* **265**, 233–97.

Morris, P. (1972). A review of mammalian age determination methods, *Mammal Review* **2**, 69–104.

Mourer-Chauviré, C. (1975a). *Les Oiseaux du Pléistocène Moyen et Supérieur de France* (Thesis, Université Claude Bernard, Lyon). Documents des Laboratoires de Géologie de la Faculté des Sciences de Lyon, No. 64.

Mourer-Chauviré, C. (1975b). Faunes d'oiseaux du Pléistocène de France: systematique, evolution et adaptation, interpretation paleoclimatique, *Géobios* **8** (fasc. 5), 333–52.

Movius, H. L. (1950). A wooden spear of third interglacial age from Lower Saxony, *Southwestern Journal of Anthropology* **6**, 139–42.

Muus, B. J. & **Dahlstrøm, P.** (1971). *The Freshwater Fishes of Britain and Europe.* London: Collins.

Murchison, C. (ed.) (1868). *Palaeontological memoirs and notes of the late Hugh Falconer, A.M., M.D.*, 2 vols. London: Hardwiche.

Newton, E. T. (1882a). The vertebrata of the Forest Bed Series of Norfolk and Suffolk, *Mem. Geol. Surv. U.K.*

Newton, E. T. (1882b). On the occurrence of *Spermophilus* beneath the glacial till of Norfolk, *Geol. Mag.* **9**, 51–4.

Newton, E. T. (1883). On the remains of a red-throated diver, *Colymbus septentrionalis* Linn., from the Mundesley River Bed, *Geol. Mag.* **10**, 97–100.

Newton, E. T. (1891) The vertebrata of the Pliocene deposits of Britain, *Mem. Geol. Surv. U.K.*

Newton, E. T. (1894). The vertebrate fauna collected by Mr Lewis Abbott from the fissure near Ightham, Kent, *Quart. Jl. Geol. Soc. Lond.* **50**, 188–210.

Newton, E. T. (1909). Hamster from the Norfolk Forest Bed, *Geol. Mag.* **6**, 110–13.

Noe-Nygaard, N. (1975). Two shoulder blades with healed lesions from Star Carr, *Proc. Prehist. Soc.* **41**, 10–16.

Northcote, E. M. (1980a). Sexual dimorphism of the long bones of whooper swans *Cygnus cygnus cygnus, Ibis* **122**, 369–72.

Northcote, E. M. (1980b). Some Cambridgeshire Neolithic to Bronze Age birds and their presence or absence in England in the Late Glacial and early Flandrian, *J. Arch. Sci.* **7**, 379–80.

Northcote, E. M. (1981). Size differences between limb bones of recent and subfossil mute swans *Cygnus olor, J. Arch. Sci.* **8**, 89–98.

Norton, P. E. P. (1967). Marine mollusca in the early Pleistocene of Sidestrand and the Royal Society borehole at Ludham, Norfolk, *Phil. Trans. R. Soc., Lond. B.* **253**, 161–200.

Norton, P. E. P. (1977). Marine mollusca in the East Anglian preglacial Pleistocene. In Shotton (1977a), pp. 43–53.

Norton, P. E. P. & **Beck, R. B.** (1972). Lower Pleistocene molluscan assemblages and pollen from the Crag of Aldeby (Norfolk) and Easton Bavents (Suffolk), *Bull. Geol. Soc. Norfolk* **22**, 11–31.

Oakley, K. P., Andrews, P., Lawrence, H. K. & **Clark, J. D.** (1977). A reappraisal of the Clacton spearpoint, *Proc. Prehist. Soc.* **43**, 13–30.

Oakley, K. P. & **Leakey, M.** (1937). Report on excavations at Jaywick Sands, Essex (1934) with some observations on the Clactonian industry, and on the fauna and geological significance of the Clacton Channel, *Proc. Prehist. Soc.* **3**, 217–60.

Ognev, S. I. (1928). *Mammals of Eastern Europe and Northern Asia. I. Insectivora and Chiroptera.* (English translation: Israel programme for scientific translations, 1962, Jerusalem).

Osborn, H. F. (1936). *Proboscidea.* Vol. I. *Moeritheroidea, Deinotheroidea, Mastodontoidea.* New York: American Museum Press.

Osborn, H. F. (1942). *Proboscidea.* Vol. II. *Stegodontoidea, Elephantoidea.* New York: American Museum Press.

Osborne, P. J. & **Shotton, F. W.** (1968). The fauna of the channel deposit of early Saalian age at Brandon, Warwickshire, *Phil. Trans. R. Soc. Lond. B.* **254**, 417–24.

Ovey, C. D. (ed.) (1964). The Swanscombe skull. A survey of research on a Pleistocene site, *Roy. Anthrop. Inst. of G. B. & Ireland*, Occasional Paper No. 20.

Owen, R. (1846). *A History of British Fossil Mammals, and Birds.* London: Van Voorst.

Owen, R. (1856). Description of a fossil cranium of the musk-buffalo from the lower level drift at Maidenhead, Berkshire, *Quart. Jl. Geol. Soc. Lond.* **12**, 124–31.

Patterson, T. T. & **Tebbutt, C. F.** (1947). Studies on the Palaeolithic succession in England. No. 3: Palaeoliths from St Neots, Huntingdonshire, *Proc. Prehist. Soc.* **13**, 37–46.

Pennington. W. (1977). The Late Devensian flora and vegetation of Britain, *Phil. Trans. R. Soc. Lond. B.* **280**, 247–71.

Pernetta, J. C. & **Handford, P. T.** (1970). Mammalian and avian remains from possible Bronze Age deposits on Nornour, Isles of Scilly, *J. Zool. Lond.* **162**, 534–40.

Peterson, R. L. (1955). *North American Moose.* Toronto: University of Toronto Press.

Phillips, L. (1974). Vegetational history of the Ipswichian/Eemian interglacial in Britain and Continental Europe, *New Phytol.* **73**, 589–604.

Phillips, L. (1976). Pleistocene vegetational history and geology in Norfolk, *Phil. Trans. R. Soc. Lond. B.* **275**, 215–86.

Pike, K. & **Godwin, H.** (1952). The interglacial at Clacton-on-Sea, *Q. Jl. Geol. Soc. Lond.* **108**, 261–72.

Prater, S. H. (1965) (2nd edn.) *The Book of Indian Animals.* Bombay: Bombay Natural History Society and Prince of Wales Museum of Western India.

Prestt, I., Cooke, A. S. & **Corbet, K. F.** (1974). British amphibians and reptiles. Chapter 14 in Hawksworth (1974), pp. 229–54.

Rackham, D. J. (1978). Evidence for changing vertebrate communities in the Middle Devensian, *Quaternary Newsletter* **25**, 1–3.

Rackham, D. J. (1979). *Rattus rattus*: the introduction of the black rat into Britain, *Antiquity* **53**, 112–20.

Reid, C. (1882). The geology of the country around Cromer, *Mem. Geol. Surv. U.K.*

Renfrew, C. (ed.) (1974). *British Prehistory. A New Outline.* London: Duckworth.

Reynolds, S. H. (1902–12). The British Pleistocene Mammalia. 2. The British Pleistocene Hyaenidae, Ursidae, Canidae and Mustelidae, *Palaeontogr. Soc.* (Monogr.).

Reynolds, S. H. (1922). Hippopotamus. In Dawkins & Reynolds (1872–1939).

Rixon, A. E. (1976). *Fossil Animal Remains: their Preparation and Conservation.* London: Athlone Press, University of London.

Rollinat, R. (1946). *La Vie des Reptiles de la France Centrale* (3rd edn). Paris: Libraire Delagrave.

Ruddiman, W. F., Sancetta, C. D. & McIntyre, A. (1977). Glacial/interglacial response rate of subpolar North Atlantic waters to climatic change: the record in ocean sediments, *Phil. Trans. R. Soc. Lond. B.* **280**, 119–42.

Rzebik, B. (1968). *Crocidura* Wagler and other Insectivora (Mammalia) from the Quaternary deposits at Tornewton Cave in England, *Acta Zool. Cracov.* **13**, 251–63.

Savage, R. J. G. (1964). Post glacial wild boar from Belfast Lough, *Ir. Nat. J.* **14**, 303–4.

Savage, R. J. G. (1966). Irish Pleistocene mammals, *Ir. Nat. J.* **15**, 117–30.

Scharff, R. F., Seymour, H. J. & Newton, E. T. (1918). The exploration of Castlepook Cave, County Cork, *Proc. R. Ir. Acad.* **34**(B), 33–72.

Schmid, E. (1972). *Atlas of Animal Bones.* Amsterdam, London, New York: Elsevier.

Schreuder, A. (1935). A note on the Carnivora of the Tegelen Clay with some remarks on the Grisoninae, *Arch. Neerl. Zool.* **2**, 73–94.

Schreuder, A. (1940). A revision of the fossil water moles (Desmaninae), *Arch. Neerl. Zool.* **4**, 201–333.

Scott, K. (1980). Two hunting episodes of Middle Palaeolithic age at La Cotte de Saint-Brelade, Jersey (Channel Islands), *World Archaeology* **12**, 137–52.

Segre, A. G. (1948). Sulla stratigrafia dell' antica cava di Saccopastore pressa Roma, *Atti Accad. Naz. Lincei Rc.* **4**, 743–51.

Shackleton, N. J. (1977a). The oxygen isotope stratigraphic record of the Late Pleistocene, *Phil. Trans. R. Soc. Lond. B.* **280**, 169–82.

Shackleton, N. J. (1977b). Oxygen isotope stratigraphy of the Middle Pleistocene. In Shotton (1977a), pp. 1–16.

Shackleton, N. J. & Opdyke, N. D. (1973). Oxygen isotope and palaeomagnetic stratigraphy of Equatorial Pacific core V28–238: oxygen isotope temperatures and ice volumes on a 10^5 year and 10^6 year scale, *Quaternary Res.* **3**, 39–55.

Sharrock, J. T. R. (1974). The changing status of breeding birds in Britain and Ireland. Chapter 12 in Hawksworth (1974), pp. 203–20.

Sharrock, J. T. R. (1976). *The Atlas of Breeding Birds in Britain and Ireland.* Tring: British Trust for Ornithology.

Shephard-Thorn, E. R. & Wymer, J. J. (1977). South-east England and the Thames Valley. *X Inqua Congress Excursion Guides.* Norwich: Geo. Abstracts.

Shotton, F. W. (1953). Pleistocene deposits of the area between Coventry, Rugby and Leamington and their bearing on the topographic development of the Midlands, *Phil. Trans. R. Soc. Lond. B.* **237**, 209–60.

Shotton, F. W. (1968). The Pleistocene succession around Brandon, Warwickshire, *Phil. Trans. R. Soc. Lond. B.* **254**, 387–400.

Shotton, F. W. (ed.) (1977a). *British Quaternary Studies: Recent Advances.* Oxford: Clarendon Press.

Shotton, F. W. (1977b). Chronology, climate and marine record. The Devensian stage: its development, limits and substages, *Phil. Trans. R. Soc. Lond. B.* **280**, 107–18.

Shotton, F. W. (1977c). The English Midlands. *X Inqua Congress Excursion Guides.* Norwich: Geo. Abstracts.

Shotton, F. W., Banham, P. H. & Bishop, W. W. (1977). Glacial-interglacial stratigraphy of the Quaternary in Midland and eastern England. Chapter 19 in Shotton (1977a), pp. 267–82.

Shotton, F. W., Goudie, A. S., Briggs, D. J. & Osmaston, H. A. (1980). Cromerian interglacial deposits at Sugworth, near Oxford, England, and their relation to the Plateau Drift of the Cotswolds and the terrace sequence of the Upper and Middle Thames, *Phil. Trans. R. Soc. Lond. B.* **289**, 55–86.

Shotton, F. W. & Osborne, P. J. (1965). The fauna of the Hoxnian interglacial deposits of Nechells, Birmingham, *Phil. Trans. R. Soc. B.* **248**, 353–78.

Shotton, F. W., Sutcliffe, A. J. & West, R. G. (1962). The fauna and flora from the brick pit at Lexden, Essex, *Essex Naturalist* **31**, 15–22.

Simons, J. W. (1962). New records of musk ox from Plumstead, Kent and Cosgrove, Northants, *Lond. Nat.* **41**, 42–53.

Simpson, I. M. & West, R. G. (1958). On the stratigraphy and palaeobotany of a late Pleistocene organic deposit at Chelford, Cheshire, *New Phytol.* **57**, 239–50.

Singer, R., Wymer, J. J., Gladfelter, B. G. & Wolff, R. G. (1973). Excavation of the Clactonian industry at the Golf Course, Clacton-on-Sea, Essex, *Proc. Prehist. Soc.* **39**, 100–28.

Sissons, S. & Grossman, J. D. (1968). *The Anatomy of the Domestic Animals.* Philadelphia, London: W. B. Saunders.

Smith, A. G. & Pilcher, J. R. (1973). Radiocarbon dates and the vegetational history of the British Isles, *New Phytol.* **72**, 903–14.

Smith, I. F. (1974). The Neolithic. Chapter 3 in Renfrew (1974), pp. 100–36.

Smith, M. (1969). *The British Amphibians and Reptiles* (4th edn). London: Collins.

Smith, R. A. (1911). A Palaeolithic industry at Northfleet, Kent, *Archaeologia* **62**, 515–32.

Sparks, B. W. (1964). The distribution of non-marine Mollusca in the Last Interglacial in the south-east of England, *Proc. Malac. Soc. Lond.* **36**, 7–25.

Sparks, B. W. & West, R. G. (1959). The palaeoecology of the interglacial deposits at Histon Road, Cambridge, *Eiszeitalter Gegenw.* **10**, 123–43.

Sparks, B. W. & West, R. G. (1963). The interglacial deposits at Stutton, Suffolk, *Proc. Geol. Ass.* **74**, 419–32.

Sparks, B. W. & West, R. G. (1968). Interglacial deposits at Wortwell, Norfolk, *Geol. Mag.* **105**, 471–81.

Sparks, B. W. & West, R. G. (1970). Late Pleistocene deposits at Wretton, Norfolk. I. Ipswichian Interglacial deposits, *Phil. Trans. R. Soc. Lond. B.* **258**, 1–30.

Spencer, H. E. P. (1964). The contemporary mammalian fossils of the Crags, *Trans. Suffolk Nat. Soc.* **12**, 333–44.

Spencer, H. E. P. (1966). New mammalian fossils from the Red Crag, *Trans. Suffolk Nat. Soc.*, **13**, 154–6.

Spencer, H. E. P. & Melville, R. V. (1974). The Pleistocene mammalian fauna of Dove Holes, Derbyshire, *Bull. Geol. Surv. Gt. Britain* **48**, 43–53.

Spiess, A. (1976). Determining season of death of archaeological fauna by analysis of teeth, *Arctic* **29**, 53.

Spillman, C. J. (1961). *Faune de France*, 65. *Poissons d'Eau Douce*. Paris: Lechavalier.

Stach, J. (1930). The second woolly rhinoceros from the diluvial strata of Starunia. In Nowak, J. *et al.* The second woolly rhinoceros (*Coelodonta antiquitatis* Blum.) from Starunia, Poland, *Bull. Acad. Polonaise Sci.* suppl., 1–47.

Stringer, C. B. (1974). Population relationships of later Pleistocene hominids: a multivariate study of available crania, *Jl. Archaeol. Sci.* **1**, 317–42.

Stringer, C. B. (1975). A preliminary report on new excavations at Bacon Hole Cave, *Gower*, Swansea, **26**, 32–7.

Stringer, C. B. (1977). Evidence of climatic change and human occupation during the Last Interglacial at Bacon Hole Cave, Gower. *Gower* **28**, 36–44.

Stuart, A. J. (1974). Pleistocene history of the British vertebrate fauna, *Biol. Rev.* **49**, 225–66.

Stuart, A. J. (1975). The vertebrate fauna of the type Cromerian, *Boreas* **4**, 63–76.

Stuart, A. J. (1976a). The history of the mammal fauna during the Ipswichian/Last interglacial in England, *Phil. Trans. R. Soc. Lond. B.* **276**, 221–50.

Stuart, A. J. (1976b). The nature of the lesions on the elk skeleton from High Furlong near Blackpool,

Lancashire, *Proc. Prehist. Soc.* **42**, 323–4.

Stuart, A. J. (1977a). The vertebrates of the Last Cold Stage in Britain and Ireland, *Phil. Trans. R. Soc. Lond. B.* **280**, 295–312.

Stuart, A. J. (1977b). British Quaternary vertebrates. Chapter 6 in Shotton (1977a).

Stuart, A. J. (1979). Pleistocene occurrences of the European pond tortoise (*Emys orbicularis* L.) in Britain, *Boreas* **8**, 359–71.

Stuart, A. J. (1980). The vertebrate fauna from the interglacial deposits at Sugworth, near Oxford, *Phil. Trans. R. Soc. Lond. B.* **289**, 87–97.

Stuart, A. J. (1981). A comparison of the Middle Pleistocene mammal faunas of Voigtstedt (Thüringia, German Democratic Republic) and West Runton, Norfolk, England). *Quartärpaläontologie*, Berlin **4**, 155–63.

Stuart, A. J. (1982). Pleistocene occurrences of *Hippopotamus* in Britain. *Quartärpaläontologie*, Berlin. (in press).

Stuart, A. J. & West, R. G. (1976). Late Cromerian fauna and flora at Ostend, Norfolk. *Geol. Mag.* **113**, 469–73.

Sutcliffe, A. J. (1960). Joint Mitnor Cave, Buckfastleigh, *Trans. Proc. Torquay Nat. Hist. Soc.* **13**, 1–26.

Sutcliffe, A. J. (1964). The mammalian fauna. In Ovey (1964).

Sutcliffe, A. J. (1969). Adaptations of spotted hyaenas to living in the British Isles, *Bull. Mam. Soc. Br. Isl.* **31**, 4 pages.

Sutcliffe, A. J. (1970). Spotted hyaena: crusher, gnawer, digester and collector of bones, *Nature, Lond.* **227**, 1110–13.

Sutcliffe, A. J. (1973). Similarity of bones and antlers gnawed by deer to human artefacts, *Nature, Lond.* **246**, 428–30.

Sutcliffe, A. J. (1977). Further notes on bones and antlers chewed by deer and other ungulates, *Deer* **4** (2), Feb. 1977, 73–82.

Sutcliffe, A. J. & Kowalski, K. (1976). Pleistocene rodents of the British Isles, *Bull. Br. Mus. Nat. Hist.* (*Geol.*) **27**(2), 33–147.

Sutcliffe, A. J. & Zeuner, F. E. (1962). Excavations in the Torbryan Caves, Devonshire. 1. Tornewton Cave, *Proc. Devon Archaeol. Exploration Soc.* **5**, 127–45.

Szabo, B. J. & Collins, D. (1975). Ages of fossil bones from British interglacial sites, *Nature, Lond.* **254**, 680–2.

Tratman, E. K. (1964). Picken's Hole, Crook Peak, Somerset. A Pleistocene site, *Proc. Speleol. Soc.* **10**, 1–4.

Trechmann, C. T. (1939). A skeleton of elk (*Cervus alces*) from Neasham, near Darlington, *Proc. Yorks. Geol. Soc.* **24**, 100–2.

Turner, C. (1970). The Middle Pleistocene deposits at Marks Tey, Essex, *Phil. Trans. R. Soc. B.* **257**, 373–440.

Turner, C. (1975a). The correlation and duration of Middle Pleistocene Interglacial periods in North-west Europe. In Butzer & Isaac (1975), pp. 259–306.

Turner, C. (1975b). Der Einfluss grosser Mammalier auf die interglaziale Vegetation, *Quartärpaläontologie*, Berlin **1**, 13–19.

Turner, C. & Kerney, M. P. (1971). A Note on the age of the freshwater beds of the Clacton channel. Appendix in Kerney (1971).

Turner, C. & West, R. G. (1968). The subdivision and zonation of interglacial periods, *Eiszeitalter Gegenw.* **19**, 93–101.

Voous, K. H. (1960). *Atlas of European Birds*. London: Nelson.

Warren, S. H. (1912). On a late glacial stage in the valley of the River Lea subsequent to the epoch of river-drift Man., *Q. Jl. Geol. Soc. Lond.* **68**, 213–29.

Warren, S. H. (1951). The Clacton flint industry: a new interpretation, *Proc. Geol. Ass.* **62**, 107–35.

Warren, S. H. (1955). The Clacton (Essex) Channel deposits, *Q. Jl. Geol. Soc. Lond.* **111**, 283–307.

Watts, W. A. (1977). The Late Devensian vegetation of Ireland, *Phil. Trans. R. Soc. Lond. B.* **280**, 273–93.

Wells, C. & Lawrence, P. (1976). A pathological cannon bone of a giant deer cf. *Praemegaceros verticornis* (Dawkins), *Ossa* **3/4**, 3–9.

West, R. G. (1956). The Quaternary deposits at Hoxne, Suffolk, *Phil. Trans. R. Soc. Lond. B.* **239**, 265–356.

West, R. G. (1957). Interglacial deposits at Bobbitshole, Ipswich, *Phil. Trans. R. Soc. Lond. B.* **241**, 1–31.

West, R. G. (1961). Vegetational history of the early Pleistocene of the Royal Society borehole at Ludham, Norfolk, *Proc. R. Soc. Lond. B.* **155**, 437–53.

West, R. G. (1969). Pollen analyses from interglacial deposits at Aveley and Grays, Essex, *Proc. Geol. Ass.* **80**, 271–82.

West, R. G. (1970). Pleistocene history of the British Flora. In Walker, D. & West, R. G. (eds), *Studies in the Vegetational History of the British Isles*. Cambridge: University Press.

West, R. G. (1970). Pollen zones in the Pleistocene of Great Britain and their correlation, *New Phytol.* **69**, 1179–83.

West, R. G. (1972). Relative land-sea-level changes in south eastern England during the Pleistocene, *Phil. Trans. R. Soc. Lond. A* **272**, 87–98.

West, R. G. (1977a). *Pleistocene Geology and Biology – with especial reference to the British Isles* (2nd edn). London: Longman.

West, R. G. (1977b). Early and Middle Devensian flora and vegetation, *Phil. Trans. R. Soc. Lond. B.* **280**, 229–46.

West, R. G. (1977c). East Anglia. *X Inqua Congress Excursion Guides*. Norwich: Geo. Abstracts.

West, R. G. (1980a). *The Pre-glacial Pleistocene of the Norfolk and Suffolk Coasts*, Cambridge: Cambridge University Press.

West, R. G. (1980b). Pleistocene forest history in East Anglia, *New Phytol.* **85**, 571–622.

West, R. G., Dickson, C. A., Catt, J. A., Weir, A. H. & Sparks, B. W. (1974). Late Pleistocene deposits at Wretton, Norfolk. II. Devensian deposits, *Phil. Trans. R. Soc. Lond. B.* **267**, 337–420.

West, R. G., Lambert, C. A. & Sparks, B. W. (1964). Interglacial deposits at Ilford, Essex, *Phil. Trans. R. Soc. Lond. B.* **247**, 185–212.

West, R. G. & McBurney, C. M. P. (1955). The Quaternary deposits at Hoxne, Suffolk, and their archaeology, *Proc. Prehist. Soc.* **20**, 131–54.

West, R. G. & Sparks, B. W. (1960). Coastal interglacial deposits of the English Channel, *Phil. Trans. R. Soc. Lond. B.* **243**, 95–133.

West, R. G. & Wilson, D. G. (1968). Plant remains from the Corton Beds at Lowestoft, Suffolk, *Geol. Mag.* **105**, 116–23.

Wheeler, A. (1969). *The Fishes of the British Isles and North West Europe*. London: Macmillan.

Wheeler, A. (1974). Changes in the freshwater fish fauna of Britain. Chapter 10 in Hawksworth (1974), pp. 157–78.

Wheeler, A. (1977). The origin and distribution of the freshwater fishes of the British Isles, *J. Biogeog.* **4**, 1–24.

Wheeler, A. (1978). Why were there no fish remains at Star Carr? *J. Arch. Sci.* **5**, 85–9.

Wijmstra, T. A. (1969). Palynology of the first 30 metres of a 120 m deep section in Northern Greece, *Acta Bot. Neerl.* **18**, 511–27.

Woillard, G. M. (1978). Grande Pile Peat Bog, a continuous pollen record for the last 140 000 years, *Quaternary Research* **9**, 1–21.

Woillard, G. M. (1979). The Last Interglacial–Glacial cycle at Grande Pile in northeastern France, *Bull. Soc. belge de Geologie* **88**, 51–69.

Woodman, P. C. (1978). The chronology and economy of the Irish, Mesolithic: some working hypotheses. Chapter 13 in Mellars (1978).

Woodward, H. (1874). On the remains of *Rhinoceros leptorhinus* (= *R. hemitoechus* Falconer) in the collection of Antonio Brady F. G. S. from the Pleistocene deposits of the Thames at Ilford, Essex, *Geol. Mag.* **1**, 398–403.

Woodward, H. & Davies, W. (1874). Note on the Pleistocene deposits yielding mammalian remains in the vicinity of Ilford, Essex, *Geol. Mag.* **1**, 390–8.

Wymer, J. (1962). Excavations at the Maglemosian sites at Thatcham, Berkshire, England, *Proc. Prehist. Soc.* **28**, 329–61.

Wymer, J. J. (1974). Clactonian and Acheulean industries in Britain – their chronology and significance, *Proc. Geol. Ass., Lond.* **85**, 391–421.

Wymer, J. J. (1977). The archaeology of man in the British Quaternary. Chapter 8 in Shotton (1977a), pp. 93–106.

Wymer, J. J., Jacobi, R. M. & **Rose, J.** (1975). Late Devensian and early Flandrian barbed points from Sproughton, Suffolk, *Proc. Prehist. Soc.* **41**, 235–41.

Yalden, D. W. (1980). An alternative explanation of the rare herptiles in Britain, *British Journal of Herpetology* **6**, 37–40.

Zagwijn, W. H. (1974). The Pliocene – Pleistocene boundary in western and southern Europe, *Boreas* **3**, 75–97.

Zagwijn, W. H. (1975). Variations in climate as shown by pollen analysis, especially in the Lower Pleistocene of Europe. In Wright, A. E. & Mosely, F. (eds) 1975. *Ice Ages Ancient and Modern Geol. Jl. Special Issue* No. 6, pp. 137–152.

Zeuner, F. E. (1932). Die Beziehung zwischen Schadelform und Lebenweise bei den rezenten und fossilen Nashörnen, *Ber. Naturf. Geo. Freiburg i. Br.* **34**, 21–80.

Zeuner, F. E. (1946). *Cervus elaphus jerseyensis* and other fauna in the 25-ft. beach of Belle Hougue Cave, Jersey, C. I., *Bull. Soc. Jers.* **14**, 238–50.

Zeuner, F. E. (1959). *The Pleistocene Period* (2nd ed). London: Hutchinson.

Index

Page nos. in bold type refer to figs; italics refer to tables.
Page nos. followed by ^{d} signify description/taxonomy; ^{e} signifies ecology/distribution.